SUBJECT GUIDE TO COMMUNICATION, INFORMATICS AND LIBRARIANSHIP IN INDIA

CONCEPTS IN COMMUNICATION INFORMATICS & LIBRARIANSHIP (CICIL)

For a list of titles in this series,
see pp. 259-262 at the end of the book.

ABOUT THE AUTHORS

S.P. AGRAWAL (*b.* 1929) was Director, National Social Science Documentation Centre, ICSSR, and Member Secretary, Indian Association of Social Science Institutions. He was also the Vice-Chairman of the Asia and Pacific Information Network in Social Sciences (APINESS). In 1988, he was awarded the degree of Doctor of Philosophy in Education (honoris causa) by International University Foundation. Presently, he is Member, Round Table on Research in Reading, IFLA, and Member, International Committee for Social Science Information and Documentation. He is also Member of Board of Archival Studies, National Archives of India, and Member, Hindi Advisory Committee, Ministry of Coal, Government of India. He has written extensively on various aspects of education, Indian polity, and library and information science.

PUSHPA RANI SHARMA (*b.* 1960) holds Master's Degree in Sociology and in Hindi literature, as also a degree in Library and Information Science from University of Delhi. She has been associated with Indian Council of Social Science Research Projects of Retrospective Indexing of Indian Social Science Periodicals, Union Catalogue of Reference Books, Bibliographies, Social Science Periodicals and Serials, etc. Her forthcoming publication in collaboration with S.P. Agrawal is *Government of India Publications*. She is presently working in National Social Science Documentation Centre of ICSSR, New Delhi.

Concepts in Communication Informatics & Librarianship-53

General Editor : **S.P. Agrawal**

SUBJECT GUIDE TO COMMUNICATION, INFORMATICS AND LIBRARIANSHIP IN INDIA

Based on A Survey of Library Holdings in Capital City of India

S.P. AGRAWAL
former Director
National Social Science Documentation Centre, ICSSR, New Delhi

PUSHPA RANI SHARMA
National Social Science Documentation Centre, ICSSR, New Delhi

Assisted by
Pratima Rani Sharma

CONCEPT PUBLISHING COMPANY, NEW DELHI 110059

ISBN 81-7022-495-0

First Published 1994

Published and Printed by
Ashok Kumar Mittal
Concept Publishing Company
A/15-16, Commercial Block, Mohan Garden
NEW DELHI-110059 (India)

Lasertypeset by
Printing Express
H-13, Bali Nagar
NEW DELHI-110015

GENERAL EDITOR'S INTRODUCTION

It is truism to say that we are living in an age of rapid technological advances. Every day we have been witnessing increasing progress in every field of human knowledge. It is *Information Explosion* they say. We do not however exactly know whether it is so – or else whether it is *Mis-Information Explosion* or *Dis-Information Explosion* – be that as it may; for proper growth of any profession it is utmost desirable for its members to keep themselves face to face with the new-and-latest-thereto developments in the field of their activity. Only with the acquisition of new knowledge and new techniques, one can do one's jobs effectively and competently. Moreover, the professionals have also to play an essential part in creative process by engaging themselves in research activities and by making every endeavour to widen the frontiers of knowledge in the subjects of their interest.

Of all the major cities in India, the Capital-City DELHI with a network of well-developed and well-equipped educational (Universities and Institutions) as well government departmental and public libraries on diverse subjects has by far the richest library and information resources. Quite naturally, one shares the feeling that what is available in India as a whole, is available by and large in Delhi. Notwithstanding this primary matter-of-fact feeling, the effort should motivate others to repeat the exercise in other metropolitan cities. The present publication, which has attempted to enlist in one single sequence the national information resources in Communication, Information and Librarianship, of 44 important libraries of the city, is intended to serve three purposes among others. Firstly (and to begin with it is felt), it will help the practising Librarians and working Information Scientists to update their knowledge and skill, to broaden their horizons and to meet the challenges of the changing times. Undoubtedly, continuing education is also one of the measures to reduce the professional obsolescence and to keep the professionals abreast of the new trends and the latest techniques in their profession. But it has its own limitations. Continuing education fails to satisfy adequately those Librarians and Information Scientists who would like to deepen their understanding in their area of specialisation. The present guide, which lists items on almost every aspect of library and information science, can certainly accomplish this task; it can very well cater to the needs of this type of professionals. Secondly, it is a handy tool for the Teaching Faculty who will find it (with listing of rare and out-of-print editions) of immense value in their teaching work. Thirdly, this publication is particularly valuable for Researchers and Scholars who will not only find in it listing of most of their required material in their area of study, but will also be able to locate the place where the material is available. Additionally, to Acquisition Librarian it will help indicate the gaps and to Reference Librarian a pointer for referral service.

In the Subject Guide entries, within alphabetically recorded subject-descriptors, are arranged by tittle, in an alphabetical order with the name of the author, editor or compiler, etc., if any, mentioned in general entry form on the pattern of UNESCO Catalogue, which, when first brought out, was found to be very much user friendly. The year of publication precedes the title entry.

Thereafter, series in round brackets – (CICIL series) – and the issuing authority, if any, in square brackets – [American Library Association] followed by Library Symbols in brackets – {JNU} – are given. Library Index with Library symbol used in this publication has also been provided. Efforts have been made to restrict the number of locations – but in some cases it has been passed off to indicate the acquisition-popularity of the publication.

Basic guide arranged alphabetically by title, etc., is issued as a separate volume. It also includes Author Approach.

One word of caution, nevertheless. There are variations in some entries, since these have been recorded from secondary sources, i.e., the catalogues or listing in the process files of the library concerned.

The behaviour-pattern of individuals (cataloguers and typists) must have been on play in rendering Author entries (including names and surnames of Personal Author, and preferential treatment of corporate Authors). The ideocyncracies of survey team also perhaps did not lag behind in confounding the confusion. The blunders (or howlers, one could say) have crept in, therefore, automatically and these were found unsurmountable. Efforts to cross-check, from the publication itself, these confusing and contradictory entries yielded scanty results if only because several publications were reported 'not on self' or even 'not in this library' at the time of verification.

S.P. AGRAWAL

CONTENTS

1

DESCRIPTORS

AACR
ALA
ABBREVIATIONS
ABSTRACTS AND ABSTRACTING SERVICES
ABSTRACTS AND ABSTRACTING SERVICES : GEOGRAPHICAL AREA : GREAT BRITAIN
ABSTRACTS AND ABSTRACTING : GEOGRAPHICAL AREA : INDIA
ACADEMIC LIBRARIES
ACADEMIC LIBRARIES : GEOGRAPHICAL AREA : AFRICA : EAST
ACADEMIC LIBRARIES : GEOGRAPHICAL AREA : CANADA
ACADEMIC LIBRARIES : GEOGRAPHICAL AREA : DEVELOPING COUNTRIES
ACADEMIC LIBRARIES : GEOGRAPHICAL AREA : EUROPE : WESTERN
ACADEMIC LIBRARIES : GEOGRAPHICAL AREA : GREAT BRITAIN
ACADEMIC LIBRARIES : GEOGRAPHICAL AREA : INDIA
ACADEMIC LIBRARIES : GEOGRAPHICAL AREA : INDIA : DELHI
ACADEMIC LIBRARIES : GEOGRAPHICAL AREA : INDIA : GUJARAT
ACADEMIC LIBRARIES : GEOGRAPHICAL AREA : INDIA : KERALA
ACADEMIC LIBRARIES : GEOGRAPHICAL AREA : INDIA : MADHYA PRADESH
ACADEMIC LIBRARIES : GEOGRAPHICAL AREA : INDIA : RAJASTHAN
ACADEMIC LIBRARIES : GEOGRAPHICAL AREA : INDIA : UTTAR PRADESH
ACADEMIC LIBRARIES : GEOGRAPHICAL AREA : PACIFIC : NORTH WEST
ACADEMIC LIBRARIES : GEOGRAPHICAL AREA : PACIFIC : SOUTH
ACADEMIC LIBRARIES : GEOGRAPHICAL AREA : PUERTO RICO
ACADEMIC LIBRARIES : GEOGRAPHICAL AREA : USA
ACQUISITION IN LIBRARIES
ACQUISITION IN LIBRARIES : GEOGRAPHICAL AREA : GREAT BRITAIN
ACQUISITION IN LIBRARIES : GEOGRAPHICAL AREA : INDIA : DELHI
ACQUISITION IN LIBRARIES : GEOGRAPHICAL AREA : LATIN AMERICA
ACRONYMS
ADMINISTRATION AND ORGANISATION
ADMINISTRATION AND ORGANISATION : GEOGRAPHICAL AREA : INDIA
ADMINISTRATION AND ORGANISATION : GEOGRAPHICAL AREA : USA
ADULT EDUCATION AND LIBRARIES

Italics indicate cross reference entries.

ADVERTISING : LIBRARIES

AFRICA

AFRICA : BIBLIOGRAPHY

AFRICA : WEST

AGLIS

AGRICULTURAL LIBRARIES

AGRICULTURE

AGRICULTURE : DOCUMENTATION

ALLAHABAD UNIVERSITY LIBRARY, ALLAHABAD

ALPHABETIZATION

AMERICAN LIBRARY ASSOCIATION

ANALYSIS OF CONTENTS : COMMUNICATION

ANDHRA PRADESH

ANDHRA PRADESH PUBLIC LIBRARIES ACT, 1960

ANGLO-AMERICAN CATALOGUING RULES

ANONYMS AND PSEUDONYMS

ARABIC CHARACTERS : TRANSLITERATION

ARCHIVES

ARCHIVES : GEOGRAPHICAL AREA : AFRICA

ARCHIVES : GEOGRAPHICAL AREA : INDIA

ARCHIVES : GEOGRAPHICAL AREA : USA

ART LIBRARIES

ARTIFICIAL INTELLIGENCE

ASIA

ASIA : SOUTH

ASIA : SOUTH EAST

ASSOCIATION OF GOVERNMENT LIBRARIANS AND INFORMATION SCIENTISTS

ASSOCIATION OF METROPOLITAN CHIEF LIBRARIANS

ASSOCIATION OF NEW YORK LIBRARIES FOR TECHNICAL SERVICES

AUDIO-VISUALS

AUDIO-VISUALS : CATALOGUING

AUSTRALIA

AUSTRALIA : GOVERNMENT PUBLICATIONS

AUTHORS

AUTHORS : GEOGRAPHICAL AREA : INDIA

AUTOMATIC INDEXING

AUTOMATIC TRANSLATING

AUTOMATION

BANKS AND BANKING : BIBLIOGRAPHY

BARODA

BIBLIOGRAPHIC CLASSIFICATION

BIBLIOGRAPHY : NATIONAL

BIBLIOGRAPHY : STUDY AND TEACHING

BIBLIOGRAPHY AND BIBLIOGRAPHICAL CONTROL

BIBLIOGRAPHY AND BIBLIOGRAPHICAL CONTROL : EARLY PRINTED BOOKS

BIBLIOGRAPHY AND BIBLIOGRAPHICAL CONTROL : GEOGRAPHICAL AREA : AFRICA

BIBLIOGRAPHY AND BIBLIOGRAPHICAL CONTROL : GEOGRAPHICAL AREA : ASIA

BIBLIOGRAPHY AND BIBLIOGRAPHICAL CONTROL : GEOGRAPHICAL AREA : CANADA

BIBLIOGRAPHY AND BIBLIOGRAPHICAL CONTROL : GEOGRAPHICAL AREA : FRANCE

BIBLIOGRAPHY AND BIBLIOGRAPHICAL CONTROL : GEOGRAPHICAL AREA : GREAT BRITAIN

BIBLIOGRAPHY AND BIBLIOGRAPHICAL CONTROL : GEOGRAPHICAL AREA : INDIA

BIBLIOGRAPHY AND BIBLIOGRAPHICAL CONTROL : GEOGRAPHICAL AREA : RUSSIA

BIBLIOGRAPHY AND BIBLIOGRAPHICAL CONTROL : GEOGRAPHICAL AREA : THAILAND

BIBLIOGRAPHY AND BIBLIOGRAPHICAL CONTROL : UN

BIBLIOGRAPHY AND BIBLIOGRAPHICAL CONTROL : UNESCO

BIBLIOGRAPHY AND BIBLIOGRAPHICAL CONTROL : GEOGRAPHICAL AREA : USA

BIBLIOGRAPHY AND BIBLIOGRAPHICAL SERVICES
BIBLIOGRAPHY AND BIBLIOGRAPHICAL SERVICES : GEOGRAPHICAL AREA : INDIA
BIBLIOGRAPHY AND BIBLIOGRAPHICAL SERVICES GEOGRAPHICAL AREA : PAKISTAN
BIBLIOGRAPHY OF BIBLIOGRAPHIES : GEOGRAPHICAL AREA : INDIA
BIBLIOMETRICS
BLISS BIBLIOGRAPHIC CLASSIFICATION
BOMBAY
BOOK BINDING
BOOK CATALOGUES
BOOK CENSORSHIP
BOOK COLLECTION
BOOK DESIGN
BOOK INDUSTRY AND TRADE
BOOK JACKET
BOOK LENDING
BOOK MOBILES
BOOK NUMBERS
BOOK REPAIRING
BOOK REVIEWS AND BOOK REVIEWING
BOOK SELECTION
BOOK THEFT
BOOK SELLERS AND BOOK SELLING
BOOKS
BOOKS : CONSERVATION AND PRESERVATION
BOOKS : REFERENCE
BOOKS AND READING
BOOKS AND READING : GEOGRAPHICAL AREA : ASIA
BOOKS AND READING : GEOGRAPHICAL AREA : PAKISTAN
BOOKS AND READING : GEOGRAPHICAL AREA : USA
BRANCH LIBRARIES
BRITISH PERIODICALS
BUILDINGS : LIBRARY
BUREAU OF INDIAN STANDARDS
BURMA
BUSINESS : BIBLIOGRAPHY
BUSINESS INFORMATION SERVICES
BUSINESS LIBRARIES
CALDECOTT MEDAL BOOKS
CANADA
CATALOGUE CARDS
CATALOGUE CARDS : REPRODUCTION
CATALOGUES
CATALOGUES : BOOKS
CATALOGUES : CLASSIFIED
CATALOGUES : COLLEGE
CATALOGUES : DICTIONARY
CATALOGUES : SUBJECT
CATALOGUES : UNION
CATALOGUES : UNIVERSITIES AND COLLEGES
CATALOGUES AND CATALOGUING
CATALOGUING : COOPERATIVE
CATALOGUING : DICTIONARIES
CATALOGUING OF FILMSTRIPS
CATALOGUING OF MUSIC AND MUSICAL INSTRUMENTS
CATALOGUING OF NON BOOK MATERIALS
CATALOGUING OF PERSIAN LITERATURE
CATALOGUING OF PHONORECORDS
CATALOGUING OF RARE BOOKS
CENSORSHIP
CENTRALIZED PROCESSING : LIBRARIES
CEYLON
CHAIN INDEXING
CHARGING SYSTEMS : LIBRARIES
CHEMICAL LITERATURE SEARCH
CHEMISTRY : INFORMATION SERVICES
CHICAGO PUBLIC LIBRARY
CHILDREN'S LIBRARIES
CHILDREN'S LITERATURE
CHILDREN'S LITERATURE : HINDI
CHILDREN'S LITERATURE : INFORMATION SOURCES
CIRCULATION
CITATION INDEXES AND INDEXING
CLASSIFICATION
CLASSIFICATION : BIBLIOGRAPHY
CLASSIFICATION : DICTIONARIES
CLASSIFICATION : TERMINOLOGY
CLASSIFICATION SCHEMES : BIBLIOGRAPHIC

LIBRARIANS AND LIBRARIANSHIP : GEOGRAPHICAL AREA : ASIA : SOUTH EAST
LIBRARIANS AND LIBRARIANSHIP : GEOGRAPHICAL AREA : AUSTRALIA
LIBRARIANS AND LIBRARIANSHIP : GEOGRAPHICAL AREA : GREAT BRITAIN
LIBRARIANS AND LIBRARIANSHIP : GEOGRAPHICAL AREA : INDIA
LIBRARIANS AND LIBRARIANSHIP : GEOGRAPHICAL AREA : INDIA : DELHI
LIBRARIANS AND LIBRARIANSHIP : GEOGRAPHICAL AREA : THAILAND
LIBRARIANS AND LIBRARIANSHIP : GEOGRAPHICAL AREA : THIRD WORLD
LIBRARIES
LIBRARIES : ADMINISTRATION AND ORGANISATION
LIBRARIES : AUTOMATION
LIBRARIES : BIBLIOGRAPHY : GEOGRAPHICAL AREA : THAILAND
LIBRARIES : BRANCHES, DELIVERY STATIONS, ETC.
LIBRARIES : CENTRALISATION
LIBRARIES : CIRCULATION/LOANS
LIBRARIES : COMMERCIAL
LIBRARIES : COMMUNICATION SYSTEMS
LIBRARIES : COUNTY
LIBRARIES : DEPOSITORY
LIBRARIES : DIRECTORIES
LIBRARIES : GEOGRAPHICAL AREA : AFRICA
LIBRARIES : GEOGRAPHICAL AREA : ASIA : SOUTH EAST
LIBRARIES : GEOGRAPHICAL AREA : AUSTRALIA
LIBRARIES : GEOGRAPHICAL AREA : BURMA
LIBRARIES : GEOGRAPHICAL AREA : CANADA
LIBRARIES : GEOGRAPHICAL AREA : CEYLON
LIBRARIES : GEOGRAPHICAL AREA : DENMARK
LIBRARIES : GEOGRAPHICAL AREA : FINLAND
LIBRARIES : GEOGRAPHICAL AREA : FRANCE
LIBRARIES : GEOGRAPHICAL AREA : GERMANY : WEST
LIBRARIES : GEOGRAPHICAL AREA : GREAT BRITAIN
LIBRARIES : GEOGRAPHICAL AREA : GREAT BRITAIN : OXFORD
LIBRARIES : GEOGRAPHICAL AREA : HONGKONG
LIBRARIES : GEOGRAPHICAL AREA : HUNGARY
LIBRARIES : GEOGRAPHICAL AREA : INDIA
LIBRARIES : GEOGRAPHICAL AREA : INDIA : BARODA
LIBRARIES : GEOGRAPHICAL AREA : INDIA : BOMBAY
LIBRARIES : GEOGRAPHICAL AREA : INDIA : CALCUTTA
LIBRARIES : GEOGRAPHICAL AREA : INDIA : DELHI
LIBRARIES : GEOGRAPHICAL AREA : INDIA : DIRECTORIES
LIBRARIES : GEOGRAPHICAL AREA : INDIA : GUJARAT : BARODA
LIBRARIES : GEOGRAPHICAL AREA : INDIA : JAMMU AND KASHMIR
LIBRARIES : GEOGRAPHICAL AREA : INDIA : KERALA
LIBRARIES : GEOGRAPHICAL AREA : INDIA : MAHARASHTRA : BOMBAY
LIBRARIES : GEOGRAPHICAL AREA : INDIA : UTTAR PRADESH : ALIGARH
LIBRARIES : GEOGRAPHICAL AREA : INDIA : UTTAR PRADESH : ALLAHABAD
LIBRARIES : GEOGRAPHICAL AREA : INDIA : WEST BENGAL
LIBRARIES : GEOGRAPHICAL AREA : INDIA : WEST BENGAL : CALCUTTA
LIBRARIES : GEOGRAPHICAL AREA : MALAYSIA
LIBRARIES : GEOGRAPHICAL AREA : MYANMAR
LIBRARIES : GEOGRAPHICAL AREA : NEPAL

PUBLIC LIBRARIES : GEOGRAPHICAL AREA : INDIA : DELHI
PUBLIC LIBRARIES : GEOGRAPHICAL AREA : INDIA : KARNATAKA
PUBLIC LIBRARIES : GEOGRAPHICAL AREA : INDIA : MAHARASHTRA
PUBLIC LIBRARIES : GEOGRAPHICAL AREA : LATIN AMERICA
PUBLIC LIBRARIES : GEOGRAPHICAL AREA : SRI LANKA
PUBLIC LIBRARIES : GEOGRAPHICAL AREA : SWEDEN
PUBLIC LIBRARIES : GEOGRAPHICAL AREA : USA
PUBLIC LIBRARIES : GEOGRAPHICAL AREA : USA : NEW YORK
PUBLIC RELATIONS IN LIBRARIES
PUBLISHERS AND PUBLISHING

RAMESES, THE GREAT
RAMPUR RAZA LIBRARY BILL
RANGANATHAN, S.R.
RANGOON
RATTAN TATA LIBRARY, NEW DELHI
RAZA LIBRARY, RAMPUR : BILL
READING
REFERENCE BOOKS
REFERENCE BOOKS : ACADEMIC LIBRARY
REFERENCE BOOKS : ARCHITECTURE
REFERENCE BOOKS : BIBLIOGRAPHY
REFERENCE BOOKS : ENGINEERING
REFERENCE BOOKS : GEOGRAPHICAL AREA : ASIA : SOUTH
REFERENCE SERVICES : LIBRARIES
REFERENCE SERVICES : LIBRARIES : GEOGRAPHICAL AREA : JAPAN
REGIONAL LIBRARIES
REPRODUCTION OF CATALOGUE CARDS
REPROGRAPHY
RESEARCH
RESEARCH : STATISTICAL METHODS
RESEARCH LIBRARIES
RESEARCH LIBRARIES : GEOGRAPHICAL AREA : DEVELOPING COUNTRIES
RESEARCH LIBRARIES : GEOGRAPHICAL AREA : GREAT BRITAIN
RESTORATION OF MANUSCRIPTS
RIGHT TO READING PROGRAM
ROCHESTER PUBLIC LIBRARY
RURAL LIBRARIES

SDI
SMART (INFORMATION RETRIEVAL SYSTEM)
SPINES
SYNTOL (INFORMATION RETRIEVAL SYSTEM)
SANSKRIT MANUSCRIPTS
SAYERS, WILLIAM CHARLES BERWICK
SCHOOL LIBRARIES
SCHOOL LIBRARIES : GEOGRAPHICAL AREA : AFRICA : WEST
SCHOOL LIBRARIES : GEOGRAPHICAL AREA : AUSTRALIA
SCHOOL LIBRARIES : GEOGRAPHICAL AREA : INDIA : UTTAR PRADESH
SCHOOL LIBRARIES : GEOGRAPHICAL AREA : NEW ZEALAND
SCHOOL LIBRARIES : GEOGRAPHICAL AREA : PACIFIC : NORTH WEST
SCHOOL LIBRARIES : GEOGRAPHICAL AREA : PUERTO RICO
SCHOOL LIBRARIES : GEOGRAPHICAL AREA : USA
SCIENCE : ACRONYMS
SCIENCE : DOCUMENTATION
SCIENCE : INFORMATION SERVICES

SCIENCE : INFORMATION SERVICES : GEOGRAPHICAL AREA : INDIA
SCIENCE : METHODOLOGY
SCIENCE AND TECHNOLOGY POLICIES INFORMATION EXCHANGE SYSTEM
SCIENCE INFORMATION SERVICES
SCIENTIFIC AND TECHNICAL INFORMATION
SCIENTIFIC LIBRARIES
SCIENTIFIC METHODS
SELECTIVE DISSEMINATION OF INFORMATION
SERIALS
SERIALS : BIBLIOGRAPHY
SERIALS : GEOGRAPHICAL AREA : GREAT BRITAIN
SERIALS : GEOGRAPHICAL AREA : INDIA
SHELVING
SHERA, JESSE H.
SIMULATION : COMPUTER
SIMULATION METHODS
SLAVIC CHARACTERS : TRANSLITERATION
SOCIAL SCIENCE LIBRARIES
SOCIAL SCIENCES
SOCIAL SCIENCES : ABSTRACTING AND INDEXING
SOCIAL SCIENCES : BIBLIOGRAPHY
SOCIAL SCIENCES : DOCUMENTATION
SOCIAL SCIENCES : INFORMATION SERVICES
SOCIAL SCIENCES : LIBRARIES
SOCIAL SCIENCES : SERIALS
SOCIETIES : PROFESSIONAL
SOCIOLOGY OF KNOWLEDGE
SOFTWARE : COMPUTER
SOUTHEASTERN STATES COOPERATIVE LIBRARY SURVEY, 1972-74
SOUTH WEST MISSION LIBRARY SERVICE
SPECIAL COLLECTIONS IN LIBRARIES
SPECIAL LIBRARIES
SPECIAL LIBRARIES : ADMINISTRATION
SPECIAL LIBRARIES : DIRECTORIES
SPECIAL LIBRARIES : GEOGRAPHICAL AREA : GREAT BRITAIN
SPECIAL LIBRARIES : GEOGRAPHICAL AREA : INDIA
SPECIAL LIBRARIES : GEOGRAPHICAL AREA : NETHERLANDS
SPECIAL LIBRARIES : GEOGRAPHICAL AREA : SRI LANKA
SPECIAL LIBRARIES : GEOGRAPHICAL AREA : USA
SRI LANKA
STANDARDS
STATISTICAL DESIGN
STATISTICAL METHODS
STATISTICS
STOCK VERIFICATION IN LIBRARIES
STORAGE
SUBJECT ANALYSIS
SUBJECT CATALOGUES
SUBJECT CATALOGUING
SUBJECT HEADINGS
SURVEYS
SURVEYS : BIBLIOGRAPHY
SWEDEN
SYSTEMS ANALYSIS
SYSTEMS THEORY

TECHNICAL INFORMATION : COMMUNICATION
TECHNICAL LIBRARIES
TECHNICAL LIBRARIES : GEOGRAPHICAL AREA : INDIA
TECHNICAL LITERATURE SEARCH
TECHNICAL PROCESSING
TECHNOLOGY : INFORMATION SERVICES
THAILAND
THESAURI
TRANSLATION
TRANSLITERATION
TRINIDAD AND TOBAGO

UN
UNESCO
US LIBRARY OF CONGRESS
US NATIONAL ARCHIVES

2

SUBJECT GUIDE

AACR
=Anglo American Cataloging Rules

ALA
=American Library Association

ABBREVIATIONS

Kimey, 1967, **Abbreviated citation.** {DEPT}

Mary, R. Kenney, 1967, **Abbreviated citation** : A bibliographical problem. {DUL}

Anon, n.d., **Abbreviations for titles of periodicals.** [Indian Standards Institution]. {AIU}

Anon, 1968, **Abbreviations of generic names in titles of periodicals.** [International Organisation for Standardisation, Geneva]. (ISO/R 833-1968) (E/F). {NASSDOC}

Anon, 1968, **Abbreviations of typical words in bibliographical references.** [International Organisation for Standardisation, Geneva]. (ISO/R 832-1968) (E/F). {NASSDOC}.

See also Acronyms

ABSTRACTS AND ABSTRACTING SERVICES

Collison, Robert, 1971, **Abstract and abstracting services.** {JNU NASSDOC USIS}

Rowley, Jennifer E., 1982, **Abstracting and indexing.** {ISI JNU}

Rowley, Jennifer E., 1988, **Abstracting and indexing**, 2nd edn. {NASSDOC}

Borko, Harold and Bernier, Charles L., 1975, **Abstracting concepts and methods.** {DEPT JNU}

Kesarwani, S.K. and Bhat, S.G. eds., n.d., **Abstracting, indexing and current awareness services in environmental science.** {INSA}

Maizell, Robert E., et al, 1971, **Abstracting scientific and technical literature.** {BIS CRRI IIMC ISI JNU USIS}

Anon, n.d., **Abstracting services in science, technology, medicine agriculture, social science, humanity.** [International Federation for Documentation and Information]. {DEPT JNU}

Muhammad, Riaz, 1989, **Advanced indexing and abstracting practices.** {NASSDOC}

Note: Entries under Descriptors are arranged alphabetically by **TITLE** given in bold letters.

{NASSDOC}

Edwards, Tom, ed., 1982, **A comparative analysis of the major abstracting and indexing services for library and information science** : With notes on their coverage of archive material. [UNESCO]. {NASSDOC}

Shypla, Bana Bihari, 1984, **Fundamental theories in abstracting and fundamental laws in library science.** {JNU}

Anon, 1973, **Introduction to indexing and abstracting for technical information systems.** {TDA}

Jain, Nem Chand, 1975, **National abstracting services** : Need, purpose and scope. {JNU}

Anon, 1976, **The planning of indexing and abstracting services in the social sciences** : Coverage overlap and content. [Bath University Library]. {BCL}scope. {JNU}

Costello, John C., n.d., **Training manual and work book for use in abstracting and coordinate indexing.** [Battelle Memorial Institute, Ohio]. {BIS}

See also Social Sciences : Abstracting and Indexing

ABSTRACTS AND ABSTRACTING SERVICES : GEOGRAPHICAL AREA : GREAT BRITAIN

East, H., 1979, **Some statistical indicators of UK abstracting and indexing services.** {BCL}

ABSTRACTS AND ABSTRACTING SERVICES: GEOGRAPHICAL AREA : INDIA

Anon, 1967, **Indian library science abstracts.** [Indian Association of Special Libraries and Information Centres]. {NASSDOC}

ACADEMIC LIBRARIES

Poole, Herbert, ed., 1977, **Academic libraries by the year 2000.** {DEPT DUL ISI JNU USIS}

Farber, Evan Ira and Walling, Ruth, 1974, **Academic library** : Essays in honour of Guy R. Lyle. {JNU}.

Osburn, Charles B., ed., 1979, **Academic research and library resources :** Changing patterns in America. {DEPT IIT JNU NIPCCD}

Lyle, Guy R., 1961, **Administration of the college library.** {DUL NERC}

Lyle, Guy R., 1974, **The administration of the college library,** 4th edn. {DUL NIEPA USIS}

Avery, Louis and Hulthciss, S.C., 1962, **Advanced data processing in university library.** {JNU}

Leimkuhler, F.F. and Cooper, M.D., n.d., **Analytical planning for university libraries.** [University of California]. {IIT}

McCullough, Kathleen, et al, 1977, **Approval plans and academic libraries** : An interpretive survey. {IIT}

Mohanrajan, P.A., 1983, **Ascent of a university library.** {NMML}

Martin, Murray, S., 1978, **Budgetary control in academic libraries.** {AIU DUL}

Anon, 1976, **Capital provision for university libraries** : Report of a working party. [University Grants Commission, London]. {IIT JNU NIEPA ZHL}

Morrison, Perry, D., 1969, **Career of the academic librarian** : A study of the social origins. {JNU}

Comb, Lewis C. Brans, n.d., **Case for faculty status for academic librarians.**

{JNU}

Burkhalter, Barten R., 1968, **Case studies in systems analysis in a university library**. {JNU}

Weber, David C., 1976, **Century of cooperative programme among academic libraries**. {BIS}

Fry, George, et al, 1961, **Circulation systems selection manual for college and university libraries.** {JNU}

Martell, Charles R., 1983, **Client-centred academic library** : An organisational model. {JNU}

Hanley, E.R., 1939, **College and university library building**. [American Library Association]. {IIT}

Erickson, E. Walfred, 1961, **College and university library surveys**, 1938-52. {JNU}

Burlingame, Dwight F., 1978, **College learning resource centre**. {NIEPA}

Anon, 1971, **College libraries** : Recommended standards of library provision in colleges of technology and other establishment of further education. [Library Association, London]. {DUL ICA}

Jefferson, George and Burnett, C.C.K. Smith, 1978, **College library** : A collection of essays. {DUL NIEPA}

Gunjal, S.R. and Sangam, S.L., 1987, **College library** : Problems and prospects. [Gulbarga University, Gulbarga]. {NASSDOC}

Smith, D.L. and Baxter, E.G., 1965, **College library administration**. {DUL IIT SPA}

Gerould, James Thayer, n.d., **College library building** : Its planning and equipment. {DUL}

Trehan, G.L., 1985, **College library management** : Academic library system, services and use. {JNU}

Lyle, Guy R., 1935, **College library publicity**. {USIS}

Lyle, Guy R., 1986, **College library publicity**. {DUL}

Line, Maurice, B., 1986, **College students and the library** : Report of a survey in May 1964 of the use of libraries and books, by students in five teacher training colleges. {JNU}

Knapp, Particia B., n.d., **College teaching and the college library**. {AIU JNU}

Anon, 1968, **Development of library facilities in universities and colleges.** [University Grants Commission, New Delhi]. {AIU IIT MHA}

Baumel, W.J. and Marcus, M., n.d., **Economics of academic libraries.** [American Council of Education]. {AIU NIEPA USIS}

Elisworth, Ralph E., 1969, **Economics of book storage in college and university libraries**. {NASSDOC}

Dupuy, Trevor N., 1968, **Ferment in college libraries** : The impact of information technology. {JNU}

Anon, 1969, **Final report** : Project for evaluating the benefits from university libraries. [University of Durham]. {NIEPA}

Morehouse, Ward, ed., 1965, **Foreign area studies and the college library** : Bibliographies, reference service, acquisitions programmes and other activities and services for undergraduate librarians in African, Asian, Latin American and Russian studies. [Foreign Area Materials Center, University of the State of New York]. {NASSDOC}

Fussler, Herman, ed., 1954, **Functions of the library in the modern college** : Conference of the Graduate Library School, 19th, 1954, Chicago. {IIT SPA}

Oboler, Eli M., 1977, **Ideas and the university library** : Essays of an unorthodox academic librarian. {DUL}

McClure, Charles R., 1980, **Information for academic library decision making** : The case for organisational information management. {JNU}

Sharma, C.D. and Boonlia, Naresh, n.d., **Information services for college librarians.** {JNU}

Thompson, James, 1980, **Introduction to university library administration,** 3rd edn. {DUL IIT NIH ZHL}

Schatz, Birdie B., 1968, **Joint university libraries** : Staff handbook. {JNU}

Moore, Everett Leroy, 1968, **Junior college libraries development needs and prospective.** {JNU}

Lyle, Guy R., 1970, **Librarian speaking** : Interview with university librarians. {JNU USIS}

Bergen, Dan and Duryea, E.D., 1964, **Libraries and college climate of learning.** {JNU}

Buck, Paul, 1964, **Libraries and universities** : Addresses and reports, ed. by E.E. Williams {JNU}

Wild, Friedemann, 1972, **Libraries for schools and universities.** {CRRI}

Cowley, John, ed., 1975, **Libraries in higher education** : The user approach to service. {INSA NIEPA}

Shores, Louis, et al, ed., 1966, **The library college** : Contributions for American higher education at the Jamestown college workshop. {USIS}

Wilson, Louis Round, et al, 1951, **Library in college instruction.** {ZHL}

Wright, Gordon H., ed., 1966, **Library in colleges of commerce and technology.** {DUL IIT}

Gujarati, Balwant Singh, 1961, **Library in education** : With special reference to school libraries. {JNU}

Anon, 1967, **The library in the university** : The University of Tennessee library lectures, 1949-1967. {USIS}

Taylor, Robert S., 1972, **Making of a library** : Academic library in transition. {CRRI DUL JNU}

Sharma, H.D. and Singh, B.N., 1990, **Manual for college libraries.** {UGC}

Ingraham, Mark H., 1968, **Mirror of brass** : Compensation and working condition of college and university administrators. {JNU}

Dupuy, Trevor N., 1968 **Modern libraries for modern colleges.** {JNU}

McInnis, Raymond G., 1978, **New perspectives for reference service in academic libraries.** {CRRI IIT NIPCCD}

Grove, Pearce S., ed., 1975, **Non-print media in academic libraries.** [American Library Association]. {USIS}

Sharma, Hari Krishan, 1977, **Organisation and administration of college libraries.** {DUL ICA}

Johnson, Edward R. and Mann, Stuart H., **Organisation development for academic libraries.** {JNU}

Marchant, Maurice P., 1976, **Participative management in academic libraries.** {DUL NIEPA}

Freeman, Patricia, 1975, **Pathfinder** : An operational guide for the school librarian. {JNU}

Ireland, Norma Olin, 1952, **Picture file in school, college and public libraries,** rev edn. {ZHL}

Brown, Harry Faulkner, 1971, **Planning the academic library.** {JNU}

Ellsworth, Ralph Eugene, 1960, **Planning college and university library** : A book for campus planners and architects. {USIS}

Burke, J.E., 1961, **Planning functional college library**. {IIT}

Ellsworth, Ralph E., 1973, **Planning manual for academic library buildings.** {JNU}

Burchard, John E., et al, eds., 1949, **Planning the university library building** : A summary of discussions by librarians, architects and engineers. {NASSDOC ZHL}

Schad, J.G. and Tanis, N.E., 1974, **Problems in developing academic library collections**. {DUL IIT ISI}

Sharma, B.N., 1977, **Pustakalaya siddhant avam vyavahar** : College pustakalaya ke sandarbh mein. {NMML}

Reynolds, Michael M., ed., 1970, **Reader in the academic library**. {USIS}

Mews, Hazel, 1942, **Reader instruction in colleges and universities** : An introduction handbook. {AIU JNU NIEPA}

Stevens, Rolland E. and Smith, Linda C., 1986, **Reference work in the university library**. {JNU}

Ranganathan, S.R., 1942, **School and college libraries**. {JNU}

Durey, Peter, 1976, **Staff management in university and college libraries**, ed. by G. Chandler. {ISI}

Steele, Colin, ed., 1978, **Steady-state, zerogrowth and the academic library** : A collection of essays. {DUL NASSDOC NIEPA}

Anon, 1964, **Student use of libraries** : An inquiry into the needs of students, libraries and the educational process. [American Library Association]. {USIS}

Branscomb, Harvie, 1940, **Teaching with books** : A study of college libraries. [American Library Association]. {ZHL}

Neal, K.W., 1965, **Technical college libraries** : Finchfield. {DUL IIT}

Thompson, G.A., 1969, **Technical college library** : A primer for its development. {AIU DUL IIT}

Anon, 1965, **University and college libraries.** [University Grants Commission, New Delhi]. {BIS DUL IEG IIMC IIT JNU NIEPA}

Anon, 1959, **University and college libraries** : Containing the report and the proceedings of the Seminar on 'from publisher to reader' held on March 4-7, 1966. [University Grants Commission, New Delhi]. {DUL NASSDOC}

Saunders, W.L., ed., 1968, **University and research library studies**. {AIU DUL IIC IIT ISI JNU SPA}

Stirling, John K., 1987, **Univesity librarianship**. {JNU}

Lincoln, Cynthia Mary, ed., 1976, **University libraries as information centres** : Proceedings of IATUL sixth meeting, 1975. {DCL}

Sharma, Chandra Kant, 1977, **University library** : Its management and organisation. {DUL JNU}

Wilson, Louis Round and Tauber, Maurice F., 1945, **University library** : Its organisation, administration and functions, 2nd edn. {JNU}

Rogers, Rutherford D. and Weber, David C., 1971, **University library administration**. {DUL NASSDOC USIS}

Mount, Ellis, 1975, **University science and engineering libraries** : Their operations, collections and facilities. {CRRI IIT}

See also Community College Libraries; School Libraries

ACADEMIC LIBRARIES : GEOGRAPHICAL AREA : AFRICA : EAST

Saith, S.S., 1968, **East African School of Librarianship.** [UNESCO].

{NASSDOC*}

ACADEMIC LIBRARIES : GEOGRAPHICAL AREA : CANADA

Anon, 1964, **Forecast of the cost of academic library services in Canada, 1965-1975**. [Association of College and University Libraries, Canada]. {JNU}

Downs, Robert B., n.d., **Resources of Canadian academic and research libraries**. {AIU}

Williams, Edwin E., 1962, **Resources of Canadian university libraries for research in the humanities and social sciences** : Report of a survey. [National Conference of Canadian Universities and Colleges, Ottawa]. {DUL NASSDOC}

ACADEMIC LIBRARIES : GEOGRAPHICAL AREA : DEVELOPING COUNTRIES

Gelfand, M.A., 1971, **University libraries for developing countries**. [UNESCO]. {AIU DUL ICA IIMC IIT JNU NIEPA NMML USIS}

ACADEMIC LIBRARIES : GEOGRAPHICAL AREA : EUROPE : WESTERN

Koops, William R.H. and Stellingwerff, Johannes, eds., 1977, **Developments in collection building in university libraries in Western Europe**: Symposium on . . ., March 31-April 2, 1976, Amsterdam. {IIT}

ACADEMIC LIBRARIES : GEOGRAPHICAL AREA : GREAT BRITAIN

Neal, K.W., 1973, **British academic libraries**. {JNU}

Munby, A., 1960, **Cambridge college libraries** : Aid for research studies. {JNU}

Bryan, Harrison, 1976, **University libraries in Britain** : A network. {JNU NIEPA}

ACADEMIC LIBRARIES : GEOGRAPHICAL AREA : INDIA

Narayana Rao, B., 1982, **Academic libraries in India** : An enquiry into their organisation and professional aspect. {JNU}

Datta, N., 1985, **Academic status for university and college librarians in India**. {JNU}

Trehan, G.L., 1969, **Administration and organisation of college libraries in India**. {AIU DUL JNU SPA ZHL}

Anon, 1967, **Centres of advanced study in Indian universities**. [University Grants Commission, New Delhi]. {NASSDOC}

Bavakutty, M., 1986, **College libraries in India** : A case study: Photocopy from: *Library management* 7(1) 1986. {NASSDOC}

Goil, N.K., n.d., **College libraries in India** : Needed a policy for development. {AIU IEG}

Anon, n.d., **Final report on the ICAR institutions and Agricultural University libraries**. [ICAR]. {IEG}

Anon, n.d., **First seminar of university librarians in India, Jaipur.** {NMML}

Sharma, Ravindra Nath, 1986, **Indian academic libraries and Dr. S.R. Ranganathan** : A critical study. {JNU NMML}

Hingwe, K.S., 1982, **Management of university libraries in India** : Principles and practices. {AIU IIT}

Anon, 1971, **National catalogue of university level books**. {DSSW NASSDOC}

Inamdar, N.B. and Ramaiah, L.S., eds., 1990, **National policy for university libraries on India** : Problems and perspectives. {NASSDOC}

Ranganathan, S.R., 1973, **New education and school library** : Experience of half a century. {DUL ICA JNU NIEPA}

Anon, 1986, **New Education Policy** : Libraries and information system : Papers and proceedings. [NCERT; Raja Rammohan Roy Library Foundation, Calcutta].

{NMML}

Vashishth, C.P., ed., 1986, **New education policy vis-a-vis library development** : Papers presented in the seminar held at New Delhi on February 13, 1986. [Indian Library Association]. {NASSDOC}

Sewa Singh, 1986, **Reference service in academic libraries in India**. {JNU NASSDOC NMML}

Anon, 1974, **Report** : University Grants Commission committee on scales of pay and qualification, etc., for library staff in universities and colleges. [University Grants Commission, New Delhi]. {NIEPA}

Anon, 1958, **Report** : University Grants Commission library committee. [University Grants Commission, New Delhi]. {SPA}

Kesavan, B.S., 1967, **University libraries and education for librarianship in India**. {JNU}

Srivastava, Shyam Nath, 1980, **University libraries in India** : Their organisation and administration. {DUL IIT ISI JNU NERC NIEPA NIPCCD}

Viswanathan, C.G., 1972, **University libraries of India** : Principles and policy. {AIU DUL IIC JNU NIEPA NMML}

Rajwant Singh, 1984, **University library bulidings in India**. {AIU BIS DUL IIT JNU MMTC NASSDOC NIEPA}

Deshpande, K.S., 1985, **University library system in India**. {JNU NASSDOC NMML}

ACADEMIC LIBRARIES : GEOGRAPHICAL AREA : INDIA : DELHI

Anon, n.d., **Delhi University Library** : The opening of the new library by S. Radhakrishnan. {JNU}

Sircar, Pankti, 1970, **Evaluation of the acquisition policy and procedure of periodicals in the Indian Institute of Foreign Trade Library and Rattan Tata Library**. {DUL}

Gupta, S.R., 1978, **Evaluation of collection of Jawaharlal Nehru University Library from the point of view of Indian reference sources**. [University of Delhi, Department of Library and Information Science Sessional Project]. {DUL}

Gupta, Shamsher, 1973, **Evaluation of Indian reference sources published during last ten years available in Delhi University Library**. (University of Delhi, Department of Library and Information Science, Sessional Project). {DUL}

Majumdar, S., 1980, **Evaluation of reference service in JNU library**. {JNU}

Sachdev, Surinder Mohan, 1976, **Evaluation of the reference sources in the field of Hindi language and literature serving the needs of post-graduates and faculty of Delhi University campus college libraries**. (University of Delhi, Department of Library and Information Science, Sessional Project). {DUL}

Kaul, B.K., 1962, **Examination of current practices in Delhi college libraries and suggestion for improvement.** {JNU}

Anon, 1976, **Management services** : Report on the library system of the Jawaharlal Nehru University. [Institute of Secretariat Training and Management, New Delhi]. {JNU ZHL}

Humphrey, K.W., 1966, **Report on the library of the Indian Institute of Technology, New Delhi**. [Indian Institute of Technology]. {IIT}

White, Carl M., 1965, **Survey of the University of Delhi library**. {AIU DSSW DUL IEG IIC NASSDOC NERC SPA}

ACADEMIC LIBRARIES : GEOGRAPHICAL AREA : INDIA : GUJARAT

Sudame, G.R., 1972, **Study of the effect of library use on academic achievement of post-graduate students in the M.S. University of Baroda.** {NASSDOC}

ACADEMIC LIBRARIES : GEOGRAPHICAL AREA : INDIA : KERALA

Bavakutty, M., 1984, **A critical study of the organisation and utilisation of libraries in higher educational institutions in Kerala**. [University of Calicut]. {NASSDOC}

ACADEMIC LIBRARIES : GEOGRAPHICAL AREA : INDIA : MADHYA PRADESH

Tejomurty, A., 1981, **University library finances in Madhya Pradesh** : A comparative study. {NASSDOC}

ACADEMIC LIBRARIES : GEOGRAPHICAL AREA : INDIA : RAJASTHAN

Anon, 1967, **Seminar of college librarians in Rajasthan, Jaipur, 1966**. {JNU NMML}

ACADEMIC LIBRARIES : GEOGRAPHICAL AREA : INDIA : UTTAR PRADESH

Razvi, M.H., 1973, **Aligarh Muslim University library** : An approach paper on Fifth Five Year Plan including statistical analysis. {JNU}

Anon, n.d., **Secondary school libraries in Uttar Pradesh**. [Department of Education, Allahabad University]. {IEG}

Anon, 1957, **Survey of secondary school libraries in U.P.** : Report. [Ministry of Education, New Delhi]. {MHA}

ACADEMIC LIBRARIES : GEOGRAPHICAL AREA : PACIFIC : NORTH WEST

Kroll, Morton, 1961, **College, university and special libraries of the Pacific North West.** {JNU}

Kroll, Morton, 1960, **Elementary and secondary school libraries of the Pacific North West.** {JNU}

ACADEMIC LIBRARIES : GEOGRAPHICAL AREA : PACIFIC : SOUTH

Tast, Margret, 1984, **South Pacific region pilot project on school library development** : Training programmes for teachers. {JNU}

ACADEMIC LIBRARIES : GEOGRAPHICAL AREA : PUERTO RICO

Gaver, Mary Virginia and Velazquer, Gonzal, 1963, **School libraries in Puerto Rico** : A survey and plan for development. {NASSDOC}

ACADEMIC LIBRARIES : GEOGRAPHICAL AREA : USA

Anon, 1976, **Community college libraries in the United States**. {USIS}

Anon, 1971, **Directory of college and university libraries in New York State.** [University of the State of New York; State Education Department]. {JNU}

Anon, 1963, **Introduction to the University of Chicago library** : A brief guide to the location and use of the library's service and resources. {NMML}

Shiflett, Orvin Lee, 1981, **Origins of American academic librarianship**. {JNU}

Anon, 1966, **Origins of the America's college library, 1838-1900**. {JNU}

Cecil, Henry L. and Heap, Willard A., 1940, **School library service in the United States**. {ZHL}

Maheu, Mary Helen, 1960, **State Department of Education responsibilities for**

school libraries. {JNU}

Gardin, J.C., 1965, **SYNTOL**, ed. by Susan Artandi, 2 vols. [New Jersey Graduate School of Library Science]. {IIT MFL}

Kent, Allen, et al, 1979, **Use of library materials** : The University of Pittsburg study. {CRRI USIS}

ACQUISITION IN LIBRARIES

Grieder, T.E.D., 1978, **Acquisition** : Where, what and how. {CRRI DUL NIEPA}

Randall, William, ed., 1944, **Acquisition and cataloguing of books** : Papers presented before the library institute at the University of Chicago, July 29 to August 9, 1940. {JNU NAI ZHL}

Kohl, David F., 1985, **Acquisition, collection development and collection use.** {JNU}

Ford, Stephen, 1973, **The acquisition of library materials.** [American Library Association]. {DUL ICA USIS}

Anon, 1964, **Acquisition, organisation and use of books and related materials.** [Trustees of New South Wales Public Library]. {JNU}

Wulfekoelter, G., ed., 1961, **Acquisition work** : Process involved in building library collections. {DUL IEG SPA}

Lee, Sul H., ed., 1988, **Acquisitions budgets and material costs** : Issues and approaches. {NASSDOC}

Clarke, D.A., ed., 1975, **Acquisitions from the Third World.** {DUL NASSDOC}

Boss, Richard W., 1982, **Automating library acquisitions** : Issues and outlook. {JNU}

Wynar, Bohdan S., 1968, **Library acquisition** : A classified bibliographic guide to the literature and reference tools. {JNU}

Futas, Elizabeth, 1977, **Library acquisition policies and procedures.** {IIT}

Saual, Margaret and Melcher, Daniel, 1971, **Melcher on acquisition.** [American Library Association]. {AIU NASSDOC}

Wildman, Panline G., 1980, **Order procedure.** {JNU}

Sfrigai, Frances and Jacor, Marry, 1968, **PILOT** : An on-line library acquisition system. {JNU}

Falk, Leslie K., n.d., **Procurement of library materials in the federal government** : An orientation prepared for Federal Library Committee. {JNU}

See also Book Collection ; Book Selection

ACQUISITION IN LIBRARIES : GEOGRAPHICAL AREA : GREAT BRITAIN

Bloomfield, B.C., 1972, **Acquisition and provision of foreign books by national and university libraries in the United Kingdom :** Papers of the Morecamb conference, April 16, 1972. {NMML}

ACQUISITION IN LIBRARIES : GEOGRAPHICAL AREA : INDIA : DELHI

Sircar, Pankti, 1970, **Evaluation of the acquisition policy and procedure of periodicals in the Indian Institute of Foreign Trade Library and Rattan Tata Library.** {DUL}

ACQUISITION IN LIBRARIES : GEOGRAPHICAL AREA : LATIN AMERICA

Savary, M.J., 1968, **Latin American cooperative acquisitions programme.** {IIFT}

ACRONYMS

Montgomery, A.C., ed. 1982, **Acronyms and abbreviations in library and information work** : A reference handbook of British usage, 2nd. edn. {JNU}

Montgomery, A.C., 1986, **Acronyms and abbreviations in library and information work**, 3rd edn. [Library Association, London]. {NASSDOC}

Chakrabarti, Bhubaneswar and Chakraborty, A.R. 1983, **Acronyms, initialisms and abbreviations in library and information science** : An annotated guide. {NASSDOC}

See also Abbriviations; Subdivision 'Acronym' under subjects, e.g., Library Science : Acronyms

ADMINISTRATION AND ORGANISATION

Gardiner, Jewel, 1954, **Administering library service in the elementary school**, 2nd edn. [American Library Association]. {DUL NIEPA ZHL}

Gillespie, John T. and Spirt, Diana L., 1983, **Administering the school library media centre.** {JNU}

Neal, Harcon, et al, 1969, **Administration and change** : Continuing education in library administration. {JNU}

Trehan, G.L., 1965, **Administration and organisation of school libraries.** {NASSDOC}

Hodson, J.H., 1972, **Administration of archives.** {JNU ZHL}

Lyle, Guy R., 1961, **Administration of the college library**. {DUL NERC}

Lyle, Guy R., 1974, **The administration of the college library**, 4th edn. {DUL NIEPA USIS}

Harleston, Robekah M. and Stoffle, Carla J., 1974, **Administration of government documents collections.** {USIS}

Sinclair, Dorothy, 1965, **Administration of the small public library**. [American Library Association]. {NASSDOC}

Sarkar, P.K., 1977, **Administration of technical libraries**. {BIS CRRI ICHR NCAER ZHL}

Kohl, D.F., 1985, **Administration, personnel, buildings and equipment** : A handbook for library management. {NASSDOC}

Cassata, Mary B. and Totten, Herman L., ed., 1975, **The administrative aspects of education for librarianship** : A symposium. {NIEPA USIS}

McCabe, Gerard B. and Kreissman, Bernard, eds., 1983, **Advances in library administration and organisation.** {IIT}

Thomas, P.A. and Ward, V.A., 1974, **Analysis of managerial activities in libraries**. [Association of Special Libraries and Information Bureaux]. {DUL IIT}

Weiner, Margery, 1974, **Answering any questions** : How to set up an information office. {BCL DUL}

Kapoor, S.K., ed., 1979, **Applications of management techniques to library and information system**. {JNU NIPCCD}

Anon, 1973, **Aspects of public library management** : The application of new management processes to the library services. [Library Advisory Council for England]. {NIPCCD ZHL}

Jones, Ken, 1984, **Conflict and change in library organisation** : People, power and service. {DUL JNU}

Anon, 1976, **A course in administration for managers of information services** :

Design, implementation and topical outline. [UNESCO; UNISIST]. {NASSDOC}

Boaz, Martha, ed., 1979, **Current concepts in library management.** {USIS}

Hakam Singh and Narang, S.P., 1973, **Current trends in library organisation.** {JNU}

Shaffer, Kenneth, R., 1971, **Decision making** : A seminar in public library management. {USIS}

Bommer, Michael R.W. and Chorba, Ronald W., 1982, **Decision-making for library management**. {JNU NIEPA}

Hastings, N.A. and Mello, J.M., 1978, **Decision networks.** {JNU}

Keen, Peter F. and Scott-Morten, Michael S., 1978, **Decision support systems** : An organisational perspective. {JNU}

Anon, 1979, **Decision tables in data processing** : A report. [National Computer Centre, Manchester]. {NASSDOC}

Georgi, C. and Bellanti, Robert, eds., 1985, **Excellence in library management.** {NASSDOC*}

Wallace, Sarah Leslie, ed., 1962, **Friends of the library** : Organisation and activities. [American Library Association]. {NASSDOC USIS}

Schutz, H., 1975, **Function and organisation of a national documentation centre in developing country**. [FID/DC Working Group]. {ICA JNU NASSDOC}

Ram Shobhit Prasad Singh, 1990, **Fundamentals of library administration and management**. {NMML}

Khanna, J.K., 1984, **Fundamentals of library organisation.** {DSSW IIMC}

Corbett, Edmund V., 1978, **Fundamentals of library organisation and administration** : A practical guide. {NCDC NERC NIEPA ZHL}

Agarwal, Shyam Sunder, 1978, **Granthalaya sangathan.** {BIS}

Anon, 1960, **Guidelines for library planners.** [American Library Association]. {IIT}

Neal, K.W., 1975, **Introduction to library administration.** {JNU}

Rice, James, 1984, **Introduction to library automation.** {NASSDOC NMML}

Anon, 1972, **Issues in library administration** : Papers presented at the U.S.-Japan conference on libraries and information science in higher education, 2nd, 1972. {JNU}

Jain, H.C., 1972, **Law library administration and reference.** {CRRI MMTC}

Savage, Ernest A., 1942, **The librarian and his committee.** {CRRI}

Ganguly, N., 1933, **Librarian and library administration.** {NAI}

Wasserman, Paul, 1965, **Librarian and the machine** : Observations on the applications of machines in administration of college and university libraries. {JNU}

Gujarati, B.S., 1966, **Library administration**, 2nd edn. {DUL NASSDOC ZHL}

Lock, Reginald Northwood, 1961, **Library administration.** {CRRI IIT}

Lock, Reginald Northwood, 1973, **Library administration**, 3rd edn. {DUL ICA}

Ranganathan, S.R., 1959, **Library administration,** 2nd edn. {AIU BIS CRRI DSSW DUL IEG IIC IIT JNU MMTC NAI NASSDOC NIH NMML SPA ZHL}

Mittal, R.L., 1964, **Library administration** : Theory and practice. {DUL ICA NAI NCAER NIH NMML SPA ZHL}

Mittal, R.L., 1969, **Library administration** : Theory and practice, 2nd edn. {DUL JNU NASSDOC NIEPA SPA}

Mittal, R.L., 1973, **Library administration** : Theory and practice, 3rd edn. {CRRI DUL JNU NIH TDA}

Mittal, R.L., 1978, **Library administration** : Theory and practice, 4th edn. {BIS DUL JNU NIEPA ZHL}

Mittal, R.L., **Library administration** : Theory and practice, 5th edn. {ZHL}

Krishan Kumar, 1987, **Library administration and management.** {JNU NASSDOC}

Panwar, B.S. and Vyas, S.D., 1986, **Library management.** {JNU}

Stueart, Robert D. and Eastlick, John Taylor, 1977, **Library management.** {DUL USIS}

Stueart, Robert D. and Eastlick, John Taylor, 1981, **Library management**, 2nd edn. {BIS DUL USIS}

Anon, 1985, **Library management** : Units 1-10. [Andhra Pradesh Open University, Hyderabad]. {NASSDOC*}

Sharma, C.K., 1983, **Library management and organisation**, Vol. I. {DUL ICHR IIFT IIT}

Hewitt, Roy, 1969, **Library management case studies.** {JNU}

Boss, Richard W., 1983, **The library manager's guide to automation**, 2nd edn. {NASSDOC USIS}

Krishan Kumar, 1982, **Library manual.** {BIS DSSW ICA IIC IIFT IIMC IIT ISI JNU NCDC NERC NIH ZHL}

Ranganathan, S.R. and Sivaraman, K.M., 1951, **Library manual.** [Indian Library Association]. {BIS DSSW INSA NERC ZHL}

Ranganathan, S.R., 1966, **Library manual**, 2nd edn. {BIS CRRI DSSW ICHR IIT INSA MMTC NASSDOC NERC NIPCCD}

Toser, Marie A., 1964, **Library manual** : A study work manual of lessons on the use of books and libraries, 6th edn. {USIS}

Ranganathan, S.R., 1960, **Library manual for library authorities, librarians and honorary library workers.** {ICA}

Ranganathan, S.R., 1966, **Library manual for library authorities, librarians and honorary library workers**, 2nd edn. {BIS ISI JNU NIEPA NMML ZHL}

Gujarati, B.S., 1963, **Library organisation.** {SPA}

Krishan Kumar, 1987, **Library organisation.** {JNU NASSDOC}

Sharma, J.S., 1981, **Library organisation.** {CRRI ISI MMTC NIEPA}

Mookerjee, S.K. and Sengupta, B., 1972, **Library organisation and library administration.** {NIEPA NIH}

Mookerjee, S.K. and Sengupta, B., 1977, **Library organisation and library administration**, 2nd edn. {DUL ICA IIT ISI NIEPA NMML}

Saini, B.S., 1976, **Library organisation for higher education** : The status and role of university librarian. {AIU JNU NIEPA}

Shaffer, Kenneth Raymond, 1963, **Library personnel administration and supervision**, 2nd edn. {DUL}

Hamburg, Morris, et al, 1974, **Library planning and decision-making systems.** {DUL NIEPA}

Bowler, Reberta, ed., 1964, **Local public library administration.** [International Managers Association, Illinois]. {SPA USIS}

Tauber, Maurice Falcolm, 1967, **Louis Round Wilson** : Librarian and administrator. {USIS}

Beckett, John A., 1975, **Management dynamics** : The new synthesis. {JNU}

Cloke, J., ed., 1986, **Management for librarians** : Based on a course of lectures at the Library Association in 1967. {JNU}

Rizzo, John R., 1980, **Management for librarians** : Fundamentals and issues. {NIEPA USIS}

Ponder, John, 1971, **Management in libraries.** {NASSDOC}

Blagden, John Frederick, 1969, **Management information retrieval** : A new indexing language. {BCL NASSDOC}
Goldberg, Walter, n.d., **Management information systems** : Selected papers from MIS conferences. {JNU}
Schellenberg, T.R., 1965, **The management of archives.** {NASSDOC USIS}
Arnold, Denis Victor, 1976, **The management of the information department.** {BCL}
Cook, Michael, 1986, **Management of information from archives.** {NMML}
Howerton, Paul W., ed., 1974, **Management of information handling systems.** {NIEPA}
Anon, 1978, **Management of information resources at the national level.** [UNESCO]. {NASSDOC*}
Lowell, Milred Hawksworth, n.d., **The management of libraries and information centres**, 4 vols. {DUL NIPCCD USIS}
Rouse, William B., 1980, **Management of library networks** : Policy analysis, implementation and control. {IIT}
Cowley, J., ed., 1985, **The management of polytechnic libraries.** {NASSDOC}
Vyas, S.D., 1990, **Management of technical services in libraries.** {JNU}
Hingwe, K.S., 1982, **Management of university libraries in India** : Principles and practices. {AIU IIT}
Anon, 1976, **Management services** : Report on the library system of the Jawaharlal Nehru University. [Institute of Secretariat Training and Management, New Delhi]. {JNU ZHL}
Evans, G. Edward, 1976, **Management techniques for librarians.** {AIU IIT JNU NIEPA USIS}
Evans, G. Edward, 1983, **Management techniques for librarians**, 2nd edn. {BCL DUL IIT JNU NMML USIS}
Anderson, Ursula, 1977, **Management training for libraries.** [Library Association, London]. {NIEPA NIPCCD}
Cortz, Edwin M. and Kazlaushas, Edwin John, 1986, **Managing informations systems and technologies** : A basic guide for design, selection, evaluation and use. {NASSDOC}
Hicks, Warren B. and Tillin, Alma M., 1977, **Managing multimedia libraries.** {DUL USIS}
Taylor, David C., 1982, **Managing the serials explosion** : 1982 {JNU NMML}
White, Herbert S., 1984, **Managing the special library** : Strategies for success within the larger organisation. {NASSDOC}
Dutta, D.N., 1978, **Manual of library management.** {DUL IIT}
Headicar, B.M., 1935, **Manual of library organisation.** {NAI}
Ranganathan, S.R., 1963, **Organisation of libraries**, 3rd edn. {JNU NIH}
Chaplin, H., ed., 1976, **Organisation of the library profession.** {CRRI}
Allen, Joan, 1961, **Organisation of small libraries** : A manual of educational institutions in tropical countries. {JNU NIEPA}
Heintze, Ingeborg, 1963, **The organisation of the small public library.** [UNESCO]. {ICA IEG NASSDOC NERC NIEPA}
Anon, 1983, **Organisation of social science information and documentation:** Reports on 11 Asian countries. [UNESCO Regional Adviser for Social Science in Asia and the Pacific, Bangkok]. {NASSDOC}
Anon, 1982, **Personnel administration for libraries** : A bibliographic essay. [American Library Association]. {BIS DUL}

Martin, Lowell, 1946, **Personnel administration in libraries.** {JNU}

Stebbins, K.B., 1966, **Personnel administration in libraries**, 2nd edn. rev. by P.G. Mohrhardt. {JNU NIH USIS}

Herbert, Clara W., 1939, **Personnel administration in public libraries.** [American Library Association]. {CRRI}

Maloney, R. Kay, ed., 1977, **Personnel development in libraries.** [Bureau of Library and Information Science Research, Rutgers University Graduate School of Library Science]. {NIPCCD USIS}

Savage, A.W., 1977, **Personnel management.** {JNU}

Khanna, J.K., 1981, **Personnel management in libraries.** {BIS IIFT IIMC ISI JNU NIEPA ZHL}

Juggal Kishore, 1981, **Personnel management in libraries.** {JNU}

Cowley, John, 1982, **Personnel management in library.** {DUL IIT}

Goswami, Badri Prasad, 1972, **Personnel motivation and work efficiency in libraries.** {NASSDOC}

Anon, 1966, **Personnel organisation and procedure** : A manual suggested for use in public libraries, 2nd edn. [American Library Association]. {DUL USIS}

Umapathy, K.S., 1984, **Problems in library management.** {DUL ICA ICHR ISI JNU NIEPA NIH NIPCCD}

Gupta, Chandra Prakash, n.d., **Pustakalaya prashasan** : Sidhant evam vyavahar. {BIS}

Singh, R.S.P., 1973, **Pustakalaya sanghatan evam prashasan.** {DUL}

Srivastava, Shyam Nath and Verma, Subhash Chandra, n.d., **Pustakalaya sangathan evam sanchalan.** {DUL IIMC}

Wasserman, Paul and Bundy, Mary Lee, eds., 1970, **Reader in library administration.** {DUL USIS}

Simmon, Ross, 1976, **Reader in library management.** {JNU}

Jones, Noragh and Jordon, Peter, 1982, **Staff management in library and information work.** {IIT NASSDOC NIH}

Durey, Peter, 1976, **Staff management in university and college libraries**, ed. by G. Chandler. {ISI}

Metcalf, Keyes D., ed., 1960, **Studies in library administrative problems** : Eight reports from a seminar on library administration. {DUL USIS}

Holroyd, Gileon, ed., 1974, **Studies in library management**, vol. 2. {DUL ICA NIPCCD}

Stene, Elizabeth, 1967, **Training for the improvement of library administration.** {JNU}

ADMINISTRATION AND ORGANISATION : GEOGRAPHICAL AREA : INDIA

Trehan, G.L., 1969, **Administration and organisation of college libraries in India.** {AIU DUL JNU SPA ZHL}

Girja Kumar, 1990, **Crisis management of libraries in India.** {NASSDOC}

Gujarati, B.S., 1970, **Library organisation and its development in India**, 2nd edn. {NIH}

ADMINISTRATION AND ORGANISATION : GEOGRAPHICAL AREA : USA

McDiarmid, W.W., et al, 1942, **Administration of the American public library.** [American Library Association]. {NAI}

Wheeler, Joseph L. and Githens, Alfred Morton, 1941, **The American public library building** : Its planning and design with special reference to its administration and service. [American Library Association]. {USIS}

ADULT EDUCATION AND LIBRARIES
See Libraries and Adult Education

ADVERTISING : LIBRARY
See Library Programmes; Library Publicity

AFRICA
See Geographical Area subdivision under main Descriptor, e.g., Archives : Geographical Area : Africa

AFRICA : BIBLIOGRAPHY
Zell, Hans M., 1975, **African books in print** : An Index by author, title and subject, Pt. 1: English language and African language. {NASSDOC}

AFRICA : WEST
See Geographical Area subdivision under main Descriptor, e.g., School Libraries : Geographical Area : Africa : West

AGLIS
=Association of Government Librarians and Information Scientists (formarly Government of India Librarians Association)

AGRICULTURAL LIBRARIES
Anon, 1981, **Papers** : All India seminar on agricultural library and information services, December 29-January 16, 1980. [Andhra Pradesh Agricultural University, Hyderabad; Indian Council of Agricultural Research, New Delhi]. {IIMC}

AGRICULTURE
Grounds, Roger, 1971, **Agriculture** : Library of knowledge. {ICA}

AGRICULTURE : DOCUMENTATION
Anon, n.d., **Agricultural documentation** : Responsibilities of libraries and information services. {IIMC}

ALLAHABAD UNIVERSITY LIBRARY, ALLAHABAD
Ranganathan, S.R., 1947, **Library development plan for Allahabad University**. {AIU NASSDOC}

ALPHABETIZATION
Anon; 1969, **Aligned list of descriptors** : Alphabetical order. [Organisation for Economic Co-operation and Development, Paris]. {NASSDOC}

Anon, 1951, **Alphabetical arrangement**. (BS 1749 : 1951). [British Standards Institution]. {CRRI}

Metcalfe, John, ed., 1965, **Alphabetical subject indication of information**. {IIT USIS}

See also Filing

AMERICAN LIBRARY ASSOCIATION
Anon, 1979, **ALA handbook of organisation, 1979-80.** [American Library

Association]. {NASSDOC USIS}

Anon, 1979, **ALA membership directory, 1979-80.** [American Library Association]. {NASSDOC USIS}

Anon, 1980, **ALA year book**: A review of library events, 1979. [American Library Association] {IIT JNU USIS}

ANALYSIS OF CONTENTS : COMMUNICATION

See Content Analysis : Communication

ANDHRA PRADESH

See Geographical Area Subdivision under main Descriptor, e.g., Library Legislation : Geographical Area : India : Andhra Pradesh

ANDHRA PRADESH PUBLIC LIBRARIES ACT, 1960

Narasimhan, P.V.A. and Majeed Khan, M.A., 1980, **Andhra Pradesh Public Libraries Act, 1960 with latest amendments and commentaries.** [Andhra Pradesh Public Library Association]. {NASSDOC*}

ANGLO-AMERICAN CATALOGUING RULES

Varma, A.K., 1986, **AACR2** : Entries and procedure. {NASSDOC}

Uppal, O.P., 1987, **AACR2** : Practice and theory. {JNU NASSDOC}

Cook, C. Donald, comp., 1982, **AACR2 decisions and rule interpretations :** A consolidation of the decision and rule interpretations for the Anglo-American Cataloguing Rules, 2nd. edn. assisted by Glenna E. Stevens. [Canadian Library Association]. {USIS}

Anon, 1980, **AACR2 institute handbook** : The Library of Congress interpretation and application of the Anglo-American Cataloguing Rules, 2nd. edn. [U.S. Library of Congress; American Library Association]. {USIS}

Anon, 1967, **Anglo-American Cataloguing Rules**. [American Library Association]. {NASSDOC}

Anon, 1978, **Anglo-American Cataloguing Rules**, 2nd edn. [American Library Association]. {CRRI IIC ISI JNU MHA NCAER NERC NIH NIPCCD USIS ZHL}

Anon, 1975, **Anglo-American Cataloguing Rules** : Amendment bulletin. [Library Association, London] {ZHL}

Anon, 1974, **Anglo-American Cataloguing Rules** : British text. [Library Association, London]. {AIU IIT ISI JNU ZHL}

Anon, 1976, **Anglo-American Cataloguing Rules** : North American text. [Library Association, London]. {NASSDOC NMML USIS}

Anon, 1976, **Anglo-American Cataloguing Rules** : North American text : Chapter 6 : Separately published monographs. [American Library Association]. {JNU}

Anon, 1975, **Anglo-American Cataloguing Rules** : North American text : Chapter 12 : Audiovisual media and special instructional materials, rev. [American Library Association]. {USIS}

Anon, 1971, **Anglo-American Cataloguing Rules :** North American Text, with supplement of additions and changes. [American Library Association]. {JNU}

Hunter, Eric J., 1972, **Anglo-American Cataloguing Rules, 1967** : An introduction. {JNU NERC}

Anon, 1981, **The concise AACR2** : Being a rewritten and simplified version of Anglo-American Cataloguing Rules, 2nd edn. [American Library Association]. {NASSDOC USIS}

Hunter, Eric J. and Fox, Nicholas J., 1980, **Examples illustrating AACR2** : Anglo-American Cataloguing Rules, 2nd ed. [Library Association, London]. {NASSDOC}

Anon, 1972, **Examples illustrating Anglo-American Cataloguing Rules** : British text. [Library Association, London]. {ZHL}

Hoffmann, Christa F., 1980, **Getting ready for AACR2** : The cataloguer's guide. {JNU USIS}

Maxwell, Margaret F., 1980, **Handbook for AACR2** : Explaining and illustrating Anglo-American Cataloguing Rules, 2nd ed. [American Library Association]. {USIS}

Lehnus, Donal J., 1971, **How to determine author and title entries according to AACR** : An interpretive guide with card examples. {AIU USIS}

Escreet, P.K., 1971, **Introduction to the Anglo-American cataloguing rules.** {MFL NASSDOC ZHL}

Winkler, Paul Walter, 1980, **Introduction to the Anglo-American cataloguing rules** : History and development. [American Library Association]. {USIS}

Clack, Doris Hargrett, 1979, **The making of a code** : The issues underlying AACR2 : Papers : International conference on AACR2, March 11-14, 1979, Florida. [American Library Association]. {USIS}

Gorman, Michael, 1968, **Study of the rules for entry and heading in the Anglo-American Cataloguing Rules, 1967** : British text. [Library Association, London]. {ZHL}

ANONYMS AND PSEUDONYMS

Goil, N.K., ed., 1973, **Dictionary of pseudonyms in Indian literature**. [Delhi Library Association]. {NASSDOC}

ARABIC CHARACTERS : TRANSLITERATION

Anon, 1961, **International system for the transliteration of Arabic characters.** (ISO/R 233-1961) (E). [International Organisation for Standardisation]. {NASSDOC}

ARCHIVES

Hodson, J.H., 1972, **Administration of archives**. {JNU ZHL}

Duchein, Michel, 1977, **Archive buildings and equipment**. {DUL}

Clark, Robert L., ed., 1976, **Archive-library relations.** {ISI}

Taylor, Hugh, 1980, **Arrangement and description of archival materials.** {IIT}

Anon, 1964, **Code of practice relating to primary elements in the design of buildings for archives.** (IS : 2663-1964). [Indian Standards Institution]. {NASSDOC}

Kathpalia, Yash Pal, 1973, **Conservation and restoration of archive materials.** {NASSDOC}

Anon, 1982, **Guidelines for curriculum development in records management and administration of modern archives.** [UNESCO]. {NASSDOC}

Hildesheimer, Francoise, 1983, **Guidelines for the preparation of general guides to national archives.** [UNESCO]. {NASSDOC}

Evans, Frank B., comp., 1979, **The history of archives administration** : A select bibliography. [UNESCO] {NASSDOC}

Fang, Josephine Riss and Songe, Alice H., 1976, **International guide to library, archival and information science associations.** {USIS}

Stephen, Parker J., 1984, **Library and information science and archive administration** : A guide to building a basic collection for library schools. {JNU}

Anon, 1968, **Library, information and archive work**. [Ministry of Labour, Great Britain]. {JNU}

Cook, Michael, 1986, **Management of information from archives**. {NMML}

Strassberg, Richard, 1974, **Manual of archival and manuscript processing procedures**. {DUL}

Jenkinson, Hilary, 1973, **Manual of archive administration**. {NAI}

Mc Coy, Donald R., comp., 1978, **The National Archives** : America's Ministry of Documents, 1934-1968. {USIS}

Choudhary, Anil Roy, 1959, **National standards for cataloguing and indexing art museum objects and documents**. {ZHL}

D'Olier, J.H. and Delmas, B., 1975, **Planning national infrastructures for documentation, libraries and archives** : Outline of a general policy. {DUL IIMC JNU NASSDOC NIEPA}

Mukherjee, B.B., 1973, **Preservation of library materials, archives and documents**. {DUL ICHR NASSDOC NERC NIH NIPCCD NMML ZHL}

See also Manuscripts ; Museum

ARCHIVES : GEOGRAPHICAL AREA : AFRICA

Zidoemba, Dominique, 1977, **Directory of documentation, libraries and archives services in Africa**, 2nd edn. [UNESCO]. {JNU NASSDOC}

ARCHIVES : GEOGRAPHICAL AREA : INDIA

Gupta, B.M., et al, eds., 1984-89, **Handbook of libraries, archives and information centres in India**, 8 vols. : Vol. 1 : Libraries and archives; Vol. 2 : Libraries and archives; Vol. 3 : Information policy system and network; Vol. 4 : Asia-Pacific co-operative information systems and networks and programmes; Vol. 5 : Information technology industry and networks; Vol. 6 : International co-operative information systems, network and programmes; Vol. 7 : Science and technology information systems and centres; Vol. 8 : Social sciences information systems and centres. {DSIW IDSA JNU NASSDOC NCAER NMML}

Gupta, R.D., 1970, **Preserving manuscripts and other research material in the Braj area of India**, (reprinted from the Bulletin of the British Association of Orientalists). [Vrindaban Research Institute]. {NMML}

See also National Archives of India

ARCHIVES : GEOGRAPHICAL AREA : USA

Hamer, Philip M., ed., 1961, **A guide to archives and manuscripts in the United States**. [U.S. National Historical Publications Commission]. {USIS}

See also US National Archives

ART LIBRARIES

Pacay, Philip, 1977, **ED art library manual** : A guide to resources and practice. {IIT}

ARTIFICIAL INTELLIGENCE

Elithorn, Alick and Jones, David, eds., 1973, **Artificial and human thinking**.

{NASSDOC}

Stagle, James R., 1971, **Artificial intelligence** : The heuristic programming approach. {NASSDOC}

ASIA

See Geographical Area Subdivision under main Descriptor, e.g., Books and Reading : Geographical Area : Asia

ASIA : SOUTH

See Geographical Area subdivision under main Descriptor, e.g., Reference Books : Geographical Area : Asia : South

ASIA : SOUTH EAST

See Geographical Area subdivision under main Descriptor, e.g., Library Education : Geographical Area : Asia : South East

ASSOCIATION OF GOVERNMENT LIBRARIANS AND INFORMATION SCIENTISTS

Anon, 1983, **Fifty years of Government of India Librarians Association.** [Government of India Librarians Association]. {NASSDOC NMML}

ASSOCIATION OF METROPOLITAN CHIEF LIBRARIANS

Hunt, K.G., 1967, **Association of metropolitan chief librarians.** {JNU}

ASSOCIATION OF NEW YORK LIBRARIES FOR TECHNICAL SERVICES

Anon, 1970, **Library automation at the New York Public Library and the Association of New York Libraries for Technical Services.** [LARC]. {USIS}

AUDIO-VISUALS

Rice, Margaretta G., 1966, **Audio-visual aids for teaching the use of school library**. {JNU}

Anon, n.d., **Audio-visual materials** : Development of a national cataloguing and information service : Report of joint feasibility study for the British Library and the Council for Educational Technology. {IIMC}

Rufsvold, Margaret I., 1949, **Audio-visual school library service** : A handbook for librarians. [American Library Association]. {ZHL}

Auduson, Herschel V., 1969, **Audio-visual services in the small public library.** {JNU}

Anon, 1988, **Convention and exposition** : Micrographic Congress (India), 2nd, January 20-22, 1988, New Delhi. {NASSDOC}

Thompson, Anthony H., 1983, **Guide to production and use of audio-visual aids in library and information science teaching.** [UNESCO]. {NASSDOC*}

See also Microfilms/ Microfiche ; Microforms

AUDIO-VISUALS : CATALOGUING

See Cataloguing of Non-Book Materials

AUSTRALIA

See Geographical Area subdivision under main Descriptor, e.g.,

Libraries : Geographical Area : Australia

AUSTRALIA : GOVERNMENT PUBLICATIONS

See Government Publications : Geographical Area : Australia

AUTHORS

Collins, F. Howard, 1956, **Author's and printer's dictionary**. {IIC}

Collins, F. Howard, 1973, **Author's and printer's dictionary**. {DUL}

Anon, 1971 **Authors and writer's who's who**, 6th. edn. {NMML RTL}

Anon, n.d., **A guide for authors in the preparation of manuscripts and illustrations.** {IIPA}

AUTHORS : GEOGRAPHICAL AREA : INDIA

Kaul, H.K., ed., 1975, **Handbook of Indian writers**. {ICCR MMTC NASSDOC UGC}

AUTOMATIC INDEXING

See Indexes and Indexing : Automatic

AUTOMATIC TRANSLATING

See Machine Translating

See also Automation

AUTOMATION

Mossberg, Thomas, et al, 1976, **ADDLIB** : A packaged computer programme for processing, etc. {JNU NIH}

Keren, Carl and Perlmutter Linda, 1985, **Applications of mini and micro computers in information, documentation and libraries**. {JNU NASSDOC}

Elithorn, Alick and Jones, David, eds., 1973, **Artificial and human thinking**. {NASSDOC}

Stagle, James R., 1971, **Artificial intelligence** : The heuristic programming approach. {NASSDOC}

Nicolaus, John J., 1964, **Automated approach to technical information retrieval** : Library application. {JNU}

Anon, 1978, **Automated centre for scientific and technical information.** [UNESCO]. {ISI}

Belongov, G. and Kotov, R., 1971, **Automated information** : Retrieval system. {JNU}

Anon, 1973, **Automated information management in public administration** : Present development and impacts. [Organisation of Economic Co-operation and Development, Paris]. {TDA}

Borko, Harold, 1967, **Automated language processing**. {NASSDOC}

Dranov, Paula, 1977, **Automated library circulation systems**. {IIT}

Evans, Lynn, 1976, **Automatic aids to profile construction** : Expansion of search terms by thesaurus. [Institute of Electrical Engineers]. {BCL}

Steven, Mary Elizabeth, 1965, **Automatic indexing** : A state of the art report. [U.S. National Bureau of Standards]. {USIS}

Jones, Karen Spark, 1971, **Automatic keyword classification for information retrieval**. {BCL BIS NASSDOC}

Melton, Jessica S., 1963, **Automatic processing of metallurgical abstracts for purpose of information retrieval.** {JNU}

Boss, Richard W., 1982, **Automating library acquisitions** : Issues and outlook.

{JNU}

Ian, Lovecy, 1984, **Automating library procedures** : A survivor's handbook. {NMML}

Hattery, Lowell H. and Bush, George P. eds., n.d., **Automation and electronics in publishing**. {DUL}

Anon, 1963, **Automation and the Library of Congress**. [U.S. Library of Congress]. {BIS}

Luhn, H.P., 1963, **Automation and scientific communication** : Short papers contributed to the theme sessions of the 26th annual meeting of the American Documentation Institute at Chicago. {JNU}

Rigby, Malcolm, 1981, **Automation and the UDC**, 1948-1980, 2nd edn. [International Federation for Documentation and Information]. {CRRI}

Kimber, Richard T., 1968, **Automation in libraries**. {AIU BIS IIT ISI JNU NASSDOC NCAER NIH SPA}

Kimber, Richard T., 1974, **Automation in libraries**, 2nd edn. {USIS}

Singh, S.P., 1975, **Automation in libraries.** {ICHR NASSDOC NIPCCD SPA}

Anon, n.d., **Automation in union catalogue of periodicals** : India and abroad, typed short bibliography. {NASSDOC}

Cohen, Aaron and Cohen, Elaine, 1982, **Automation, space management and productivity** : A guide for libraries. {IIT USIS}

Tedd, L.A., 1979, **Case studies in computer-based bibliographic information services**. {BCL}

Palmer, Richard Phillips, 1973, **Case studies in library computer systems**. {ISI USIS}

Matthews, Joseph, R., 1980, **Choosing an automated library system** : A planning guide. [American Library Association]. {USIS}

Anon, 1974, **Clinic on library applications of data processing**, 24th, 1974, Illinois. [University of Illinois at Urbana-Champaign]. {USIS}

Anderson, R.G., 1984, **Concise dictionary of data processing and computer terms,** 2nd edn. {NCERT}

Anon, 1967, **Conference on mechanised information storage, retrieval and dissemination**. {NMML}

Anon, 1976, **DEVSIS** : The preliminary design of an international information system for the development sciences. [International Development Research Centre, DEVSIS Study Team, Ottawa]. {NASSDOC}

Anon, 1975, **Development of resource sharing networks in the framework of UNISIST World Science Information System**. [National Library of Australia]. {JNU}

Trollhani, Lilian and Wittmann, Alfred, 1964, **Dictionary of information processing**, including fields of application. {RTL}

Foulkes, John, ed., 1986, **Down loading bibliographic records.** {NASSDOC*}

Kent, Allen, et al, eds., 1967, **Electronic handling of information** : Testing and evaluation. {DUL INSA}

Christien, Roger, 1978, **The electronic library** : Bibliographic databases, 1978-79, 2nd rev. edn. {USIS}

Yadubaities, E.A., ed., 1981, **English-Russian glossary of computer systems and networks terminology**. {NASSDOC}

Stone, Phillip, J., et al, 1966, **General inquirer** : A computer approach to content analysis. {NASSDOC}

Campey, Lucille H., 1972, **Generating and printing indexes by computer.**

[Association of Special Libraries and Information Bureaux]. {CRRI}

Negus, Ron, 1972, **Guide to Computer Bureau Services**. {NASSDOC}

Conning, Arthur M., 1983, **Guide to the computerisation of population documentation storage and retrieval systems**. [United Nations]. {NASSDOC}

Anon, 1972, **Guide to selected computer-based information services.** [Association of Special Libraries and Information Bureaux]. {CRRI}

Johnson, Edwin G. and Corliss, William R., 1971, **Human factors applications in tele-operator design and operation**. {INSA}

Kapur, Gopal K., 1970, **IBM 360 assembler language programming**. {NASSDOC}

Anon, 1973, **ISIS** : A general description of an approach to computerised bibliographical control. [International Labour Office]. {NASSDOC}

Singer, T.E.R., ed., n.d., **Information and communication practice in industry**. {IEG}

Anon, 1977, **Information networks for on-line bibliography retrieval.** [UNESCO]. {BIS}

Clark, F.J., 1970, **Information processing.** {NASSDOC NIH}

Anon, n.d., **Information processing** : Proceedings : International conference on information processing. {JNU}

Anon, 1960, **Information processing** : Proceedings : International conference on information processing. {JNU}

Hill, H.C., 1973, **Information processing and computer programming** : An introduction. {NIH}

Doss, Milburn Price, 1955, **Information processing equipment.** {JNU}

Mc Maron, et al, 1969, **Information processing laboratory for education and research in library science** : Phase-I. {IIT}

Szweda, Ralph A., 1981, **Information processing systems.** {JNU}

Davis, William S., 1981, **Information processing systems**, 2nd edn. {JNU}

Wood, D.N. and Hamilton, D.R.L., 1967, **Information requirements of mechanical engineers** : Report of a recent survey. {DUL}

Doednikoff, Basic, 1973, **Information retrieval.** {JNU}

Paice, D.B., 1977, **Information retrieval and the computer**. {BCL}

Kent, Allen, ed., 1960, **Information retrieval and machine translation.** {CRRI DUL}

Doyle, Lauren B., 1975, **Information retrieval and processing.** {BIS CRRI DUL IIMC ISI NASSDOC NIH USIS}

Jones, Karen Spark, ed., 1981, **Information retrieval experiment.** {BIS IIMC IIT}

Haltery, Loweld H. and McCormik, Edmaral M., 1962, **Information retrieval management**. {JNU}

Lancaster, F.W. and Fayen, E.G., 1973, **Information retrieval on-line.** {DUL INSA ISI NASSDOC USIS}

Oddy, R.N., et al, eds., 1981, **Information retrieval research.** {IIMC JNU NASSDOC}

Lancaster, F.W., 1968, **Information retrieval systems** : Characteristics, testing and evaluation. {TDA}

Lancaster, F.W., 1979, **Information retrieval systems** : Characteristics, testing and evaluation, 2nd edn. {CRRI DUL IIT USIS}

Anon, 1970, **Information retrieval systems** : Subject authority list, 7th edn. [American Petroleum Institute]. {IIT}

Barhydt, Gordon, C. and Schmidt, Charles T., n.d., **Information retrieval thesaurus of education terms.** {AIU}

Lamberton, Donald M., ed., 1974, **The information revolution**: Annals. [American Academy of Political and Social Science]. {USIS}
Balmforth, C.L. and Cox, N.S., eds., 1971, **Interface** : Library automation with special reference to computing activity. {JNU NASSDOC}
Anon, n.d., **International standards for computers and information processing**. [International Organisation for Standardisation]. {BIS}
Saffady, William,1983, **Introduction to automation for librarians.** [American Library Association]. {USIS}
Colin, A.J.T., 1971, **Introduction to operating systems.** {NASSDOC}
Atherton, Pauline and Chiristian, Roger W., 1977, **Librarians and online services.** {BCL IIT}
Woods, Lawrence A. and Pope, Nolan F., 1983, **Librarians' guide to microcomputer technology and applications.** {JNU NIEPA USIS}
Markuson, B.E., 1964, **Libraries and automation.** {IIT}
Edelman, H., ed., 1986, **Libraries and information science in the electronic age.** {NASSDOC}
Lancaster, F.W., 1982, **Libraries and librarians in an age of electronics.** {USIS}
Hoover, Ryan E., ed., 1980, **The library and information manager's guide to online services.** {USIS}
Heiliger, Edward M. and Henderson, Paul B., 1971, **Library automation** : Experience, methodology and technology of the library as an information system. {AIU INSA JNU NASSDOC NIPCCD NMML}
Reynolds, Dennis, 1985, **Library automation** : Issues and applications. {JNU NASSDOC NMML}
Salmon, Stephen R., ed., 1969, **Library automation** : A state of art review : Papers : Pre-conference institute on library automation, 1967, San Francisco. [American Library Association]. {USIS}
Butler, Brett and Martin, Susan K. eds., 1975, **Library automation-II** : The state of art : Papers : Pre-conference institute on library automation, June 22-23, 1973, Las Vegas. [American Library Association, Information Science and Automation Division]. {USIS}
Lucy, Te-Chu Lee, 1985, **Library automation and information science** : A collection of essays. {NASSDOC}
Anon, 1970, **Library automation at the New York Public Library and the Association of New York Libraries for Technical Services**. [LARC]. {USIS}
Salmon, Stephen R., 1975, **Library automation systems**, 2nd edn. {CRRI JNU NIH}
Devarajan, G. and Rahelamma, A.V., 1990, **Library computerisation in India** : Isaac festschrift. {JNU}
Boss, Richard W., 1983, **The library manager's guide to automation**, 2nd edn. {NASSDOC USIS}
Perry, James W., et al, 1956, **Machine literature searching.** {CRRI}
Sackman, Harold, 1970, **Man-computer problem solving** : Experimental evaluation of time-sharing and batch processing. {NASSDOC}
Meadow, Charles T., 1970, **Man-machine communication**. {INSA NASSDOC}
Shericlam, Thomas B. and Farrell, William R., 1974, **Man-machine systems** : Information control and decision models of human performance. {JNU}
Jacker, Corinne, 1964, **Man, memory and machines** : An introduction to cybernetics. {INSA}
Kutuzona, N.P., et al, 1979, **Mechanisation information retrieval and**

processing : Application of punched. {NASSDOC}

Flannery, Anne and Mack, James D., 1966, **Mechanised circulation system, Leh University Library**. {JNU}

Rowley, J.E., 1979, **Mechanised in-house information systems**. {BCL CRRI NIPCCD}

Samuelson, Kjell, 1968, **Mechanised information storage, retrieval and dissemination** : Proceedings. {JNU}

Verry, H.R., 1967, **Microcopying methods**, ed., by Gordon H. Wright. {DUL}

Vashishth, C.P., ed., 1987, **Modernisation in libraries** : Seminar Papers : All India Library Conference, 33rd, December 28-31, 1987, Tiruchirapalli. [Indian Library Association]. {NASSDOC}

Hall, James L. and Brown, Marjorie J., 1981, **On-line bibliographic databases** : An international directory, 2nd edn. [Association of Special Libraries and Information Bureaux]. {USIS}

Mildreth, C.R., ed., 1989, **On line catalogue**. [Library Association, London. {NASSDOC}

Fayen, Emily Gallup, 1973, **The online catalogue** : Improving public access to library materials. {USIS}

Harter, Stephen P., 1986, **On-line information retrieval** : Concepts, principles and techniques. {JNU}

Holmes, P.L., 1978, **On-line information retrieval** : An introduction and guide to British library's short term experimental information network project, Vol. 1 : Experimental use of non-medical information services; Vol. 2 : Experimental use of medical information services. [British Library]. {BCL}

Hall, J.L., comp., 1977, **On-line information retrieval, 1965-76** : A bibliography with a guide to on-line data bases and systems. [Association of Special Libraries and Information Bureaux]. {BCL CRRI NASSDOC}

Houghton, Bernard and Convey, John, 1977, **On-line information retrieval systems** : An introductory manual to principles and practices. {BCL CRRI DUL NIH}

Kent, Allen and Galvin, Thomas J., eds., 1978, **The on-line revolution in libraries** : Proceedings of the 1977 conference in Pittsburgh. {JNU}

Sieburth, J.F., 1988, **Online search services in the academic library** : Planning, management and operation. [American Library Association]. {NASSDOC}

Hoover, Ryan, E., ed., 1982, **On-line search strategies**. {USIS}

Henry, W.M., 1980, **Online searching**. {IIT}

Byerly, Greg, 1983, **Online searching** : A dictionary and bibliographic guide. {NASSDOC USIS}

Maloney, James J., ed., 1983, **Online searching technique and management**. [American Library Association]. {USIS}

Garvin, Paul L., 1972, **On machine translation** : Selected papers. {USIS}

Valls, J., 1974, **Pilot project on the mechanisation of documentation services in Asia** : Thailand. [UNESCO]. {NASSDOC*}

Barnes, R.C.M., 1964, **Present state of information retrieval by computer**. {JNU}

Williams, William F., 1966, **Principles of automated information retrieval**. {JNU}

Kochen, Manfred, 1974, **Principles of information retrieval**. {CRRI DUL ISI MHA USIS}

Jelinek, Frederick, 1968, **Probabilistic information theory** : Discrete and memoryless models. {INSA}

Anon, 1979, **Problems and failures in library automation** : Clinic on library applications of data processing, 1978, Illinois. [University of Illinois at Urbana-Champaign]. {USIS}

Anon, 1980, **The professional librarian's reader in library automation and technology**. {JNU USIS}

Sherman, Philip M., 1970, **Programming and coding digital computers.** {NASSDOC}

Lancaster, G.T., n.d., **Programming in COBOL**. {NASSDOC}

Weinberg, Gerald M., 1971, **Psychology of computer programming.** {NASSDOC}

Lancaster, F.W., 1980, **The role of the library in an electronic society** : Proceedings : Library applications of data processing clinic, 1979, Illinois. [University of Illinois at Urbana-Champaign]. {USIS}

Salton, Gerald, ed., 1971, **The SMART retrieval system** : Experiments in automatic document processing. {MHA NASSDOC}

Farr, M.A.L., et al, 1973, **Security for computer systems.** {NIPCCD}

Wilson, Vivian, 1970, **Strategies for problem solving** : Programmed instruction. {NASSDOC}

Dahl, O.J., et al, 1972, **Structured programming**. {NASSDOC}

Taylor, James C. and Bowers, David G., 1967, **Survey of organisations : A machine standardised questionnaire instruments.** [Institute of Social Research, Michigan]. {NASSDOC}

Stabley, Don H., 1967, **System/360 Assembler language.** {NASSDOC}

Anon, 1970, **System scope for library automation and generalised information storage and retrieval at Stanford University**. {IIT}

Charen, Thelma, 1975, **Technical notes** : MEDLARS indexing instructions. [National Library of Medicine, Maryland]. {CRRI}

Anon, 1975, **UK MARC manual**. {Bibliographic Services Division, British Library, London]. {JNU}

Anon, 1980, **UK MARC manual**, 2nd edn. [Bibliographic Services Division, British Library, London]. {BIS}

Jeffreys, A.E. and Wison, T.D., 1970, **UK MARC project** : Proceedings of seminar organised by the cataloguing and indexing group of the Library Association at the University of Southampton, March 28-30, 1976. {NASSDOC}

Coblans, Herbert, 1966, **Use of mechanized methods in documentation work.** {JNU}

Anon, 1985, **Use of microprocessors in information analysis and library applications**. [Society for Information Science]. {NASSDOC}

Nagarajan, S., ed., 1988, **Use of microprocessor in information analysis and library applications.** {NASSDOC}

Katz, Bill and Fraley, Ruth A., 1983, **Video to online** : Reference services and the new technology. {JNU}

Cooper, M.J., 1969, **What computers can do** : A guide to the plain man. {DUL}

Anon, 1986, **Workshop on computer application to library and information activities.** [ILA NISSAT]. {JNU}

See also Computers; Electronic Data Processing; Machine Translating

BANKS AND BANKING : BIBLIOGRAPHY

See under Bibliography and Bibliographical Services : Geographical Area : India

BARODA

See Geographical Area subdivision under main Descriptor, e.g., Libraries :

Geographical Area : India : Gujarat : Baroda

BIBLIOGRAPHIC CLASSIFICATION

See Bliss Bibliographic Classification; Classification Schemes : Bibliographic

BIBLIOGRAPHY : NATIONAL

See National Bibliography

BIBLIOGRAPHY : STUDY AND TEACHING

Horne, Thomas Hartwell, 1981, **Introduction to the study of bibliography, to which is prefixed a memoir on the public libraries of America,** 2 vols. {DUL}

Esdaile, Arundell, 1964, **Student's manual of bibliography,** 3rd edn. {CRRI}

Boswell, David, B., 1952, **Text-book on bibliography.** {DUL}

Oberman, Cerise and Strauch, Katina, eds., 1982, **Theories of bibliographic education** : Designs for teachings. {JNU}

BIBLIOGRAPHY AND BIBLIOGRAPHICAL CONTROL

Stueart, Robert D., 1972, **Area specialist bibliographer** : An inquiry into his role. {NASSDOC}

Bliss, Henry Evelyn, 1977, **Bibliographic Classification,** 2nd edn., ed. by J. Mills {IIT JNU}

Bliss, Henry Evelyn, 1953, **Bibliographic Classification** : Classes L-Z, 3 vols, {CRRI}

Davinson, Donald Edward, 1975, **Bibliographic control.** {AIU DUL NASSDOC}

Reichmann, Felix and Tharpe, Josephine M., 1972, **Bibliographic control of microforms.** {ISI JNU}

Grove, Pearce S. and Clement, Evelyn G., eds., 1972, **Bibliographic control of nonprint media.** [American Library Association]. {NASSDOC}

Pemberton, John E., 1982, **Bibliographic control of official publications.** {IIT}

Cowley, J.D., 1939, **Bibliographic description and cataloguing.** {DUL}

Thomas, P.A., 1973, **Bibliographic information in library systems.** [Association of Special Libraries and Information Bureaux]. {CRRI JNU}.

Renford, Beverly and Hendrickson, Linnea, 1980, **Bibliographic instruction** : A handbook. {IIT}

Sahai, S.N. 1976, **Bibliographic methods and reading behaviour.** {ICHR NASSDOC NERC NIPCCD}

Hagler, Ronald, and Simmons, Peter, 1982, **Bibliographic record and information technology.** {DUL JNU}

Stockes, Roy, 1965, **Bibliographical control and service.** {DUL IIT MFL NASSDOC}

Cameron, William J., 1978, **Bibliographical control of early books.** {JNU}

Awad, Atef Kamel, 1975, **Bibliographical control of patent literature.** [University of Delhi, Department of Library Science, Sessional Project]. {DUL}

Cowley, J.D., 1970, **Bibliographical description and cataloguing.** {NASSDOC}.

Anon, 1950, **Bibliographical references.** (BS 1629 : 1950). [British Standards Institution]. {CRRI NASSDOC}

Anon, 1968, **Bibliographical references** : Essential elements. (ISO/R 690-1968) (E). [International Organisation for Standardisation, Geneva]. {NASSDOC}

Patil, P.K., 1972, **Bibliographical services for Indian studies** : A guide to printed sources of information. [Mysore Institute of Development Studies]. {NASSDOC}

Anon, 1950-1974, **Bibliographical services throughout the world,** 1950-54; 1955-59; 1960-64; 1965-69; 1970-74. [UNESCO]. {DSSW DUL IIMC JNU

NASSDOC NIEPA ZHL}

Collison, R.L., 1951, **Bibliographies** : Subject and national : A guide to their contents, arrangement and use. {MFL}

Collison, R.L., 1962, **Bibliographics** : Subject and national : A guide to their contents and use, 2nd ed. {MFL}

Anon, 1968, **Bibliographies and reference works including abstract journals, library journals, books about books and standard works,** 2 parts, pt 1: A-J. {NASSDOC}

Sharma, Ram Saroop, ed., 1974, **Bibliography and documentation.** {ICHR IIT JNU NIPCCD}

Hurt, Peyton, 1968, **Bibliography and footnotes** : A style manual for students and writers. 3rd edn. [University of California]. {NASSDOC}

Gore, Daniel, 1973, **Bibliography for beginners**, 2nd edn. {NASSDOC}.

Chakraborti, M.L. 1971, **Bibliography in theory and practice.** {MFL NASSDOC}

Chakraborti, M.L. 1975, **Bibliography in theory and practice,** 2nd rev edn. {ICA ICHR IIMC INSA JNU NIPCCD}

Kalia, D.R. and Jain, M.K., 1975, **A bibliography of bibliographies on India.** {ICA}

Anon, 1964, **Bibliography of dictionaries and encyclopaedias in Indian languages**. [National Library, Calcutta]. {ZHL}

Aitchison, Jean and Allen, C.G., eds., 1982, **Bibliography of mono and multilingual vocabularies, thesauri, subject headings and classification schemes in the social sciences** : Prepared by the ASLIB Library. [UNESCO]. {NASSDOC}

Davis, Richard A. and Bailey, Catherine A., 1964, **Bibliography of use studies.** {JNU}

Anon, 1970, **Bibliography on documentation**. {JNU}

Neeland, Frances, 1967, **Bibliography on information science and technology for 1966**. {JNU}

Havelock, Ronald G., 1968, **Bibliography on knowledge utilisation and dissemination**. [University of Michigan]. {NASSDOC}

Anon, 1966, **Bibliography on work-flow in libraries.** [Council of Scientific and Industrial Research, New Delhi]. {INSDOC NASSDOC}.

Patil, G.M., 1967, **Bibliography technical** : An illuminating exposition. {NASSDOC}

Sharma, C.K., n.d., **Book selection and bibliography**. {ICHR}

Sharma, C.D., 1976, **Book selection and physical bibliography.** {CRRI}

Mukherjee, A.K., 1960, **Book selection and systematic bibliography** {IIT MFL NMML SPA}

Anon, 1963, **A comprehensive bibliography on operations research, 1957-58.** [Operations Research Society of America]. {INSA}

Murty, A.T., 1979, **Document bibliography**. {NIPCCD NASSDOC}

Foulkes, John, ed., 1986, **Down loading bibliographic records.** {NASSDOC*}

Bry, Ilse, 1977, **Emerging field of socio-bibliography** : The collected essays of Ilse Bry, comp. and ed. by Lois Afflerback and Marga Franck {BCL IIT}

Esdaile, A., 1967, **Esdaile's manual of bibliography**, rev edn., by Roy Stockes. {MFL}

Dasgupta, A.K., 1967, **Essays in personnel bibliography** : A bibliography of the writings on and by S.R. Ranganathan. {DUL NASSDOC NMML}

Brenni, Vito J., comp. and ed., 1975, **Essays on bibliography.** {NASSDOC}

Hants, Roy Stokes, 1982, **The function of bibliography**. {AIU NASSDOC}

Sharma, Jagdish Saran, 1977, **Fundamentals of bibliography with special**

reference to India. {JNU NASSDOC}

Anon, 1971, **A general description of an approach to computerised bibliographical control.** [International Labour Office, Intergrated Scientific Information System]. {TDA}

Kennedy, James R., ed., 1972, **Guide to reference sources on Africa, Asia, Latin America and the Caribbean, Middle East and North Africa and Russia and East Europe** : Selected and annotated. {NASSDOC}

Hewitt, A.R., 1957, **Guide to resources for Commonwealth studies in London, Oxford and Cambridge with bibliographical and other information.** {IEG JNU NIEPA}

Anon, 1982, **Guidelines for the preparation of bibliography.** [U.S. National Agricultural Library]. {NASSDOC}

Rolland, E. Stevens, ed., n.d., **Historical and bibliographical methods in library research.** {ICHR}

Peereault, Jean M., 1978, **Idea of order in bibliography.** {JNU}

Curran, Ann T. and Auram, Henriette D., n.d., **Identification of data elements in bibliographic records.** {BIS}

Coward, R.E. and Yelland, H., eds., 1975, **Interchange of bibliographic information in machine readable form** : Papers given at the Western European seminar, May 12-16, 1974, England. [Library Association, London]. {BCL}

Anon, 1978, **International bibliography of directories**, 6th edn. {NASSDOC}

Jell, Hans and Machesney, Robert, 1965, **International bibliography of non-periodical literature on documentation and information.** {JNU}

Anon, 1968-71, **International computer bibliography**, 1968; 1971. {NASSDOC}

Wynar, Bohdan S., 1967, **Introduction to bibliography and reference work** : A guide to materials and sources. {JNU}

Mc Kerrow, Ronald B., 1965, **Introduction to bibliography for literary students.** {DUL}

Binns, Norman, E., 1962, **Introduction to historical bibliography**, rev. edn. {DUL}

Anon, n.d., **Library and information science journals in India**, typed short bibliography. {NASSDOC}

Agrawal, S.P., ch. ed., 1985, **Library and information science literature** : SSDC resources. {NASSDOC}

Anon, 1949-83, **Library literature** : An index to library and information science, 1949-51 to 1982-83. {NASSDOC USIS}

Cohen, Nathan M., et al, 1963, **Library science dissertations, 1925-1960** : An annotated bibliography of doctoral studies. {USIS}

Shaw, Charles B., comp., 1940, **List of books for college libraries, 1931-38.** [American Library Association]. {ZHL}

Welch, Helen, M., 1963, **Literature of technical services.** {DUL}

Anon, n.d., **Literature recommendation** : Basic reference list for establishing an industrial library. [U.S. International Cooperation Administration]. {BIS}

Anon, 1975, **Literature survey and trends in library cataloguing, 1970-1975.** (Mimeo; short bibliography). {NASSDOC}

Anon, 1983, **Manual of bibliographic control.** [UNESCO]. {NASSDOC*}

Gaskell, Philip, 1972, **New introduction to bibliography.** {INSA}

Staveley, Ronald, 1962, **Notes on subject bibliography.** {DUL IEG MFL}

Hall, James L. and Brown, Marjorie J., 1981, **On-line bibliographic databases** : An international directory, 2nd edn. [Association of Special Libraries and Information Bureaux]. {USIS}

Ranganathan, S.R. and Neelameghan, A., 1974, **Physical bibliography for librarians**, 2nd ed. {AIU ICA INSA}

Fredson, Bowers, 1949, **Principles of bibliographical description.** {DUL}

Thomas, P.A., 1970, **Procedural model for the use of bibliographic records in libraries.** [Association of Special Libraries and Information Bureaux]. {DUL NASSDOC}

Sharma, Chandra Kant, 1975, **Pustak chayan evam rachna** : Book selection and physical bibliography. {BIS NMML}

Anon, 1973, **Recommendations for bibliographical catalogue reference.** [Indian Standards Institution]. {NAI}

Anon, 1978, **Recommendations for bibliographical references.** Essential and supplementary elements, rev. edn., (IS : 2381-1978). [Indian Standards Institution]. {NASSDOC}

Ranganathan, S.R., 1940, **Reference service and bibliography**, Vol. 1, Pts. 1-4. {DSSW DUL}

Judge, Peter and Gerrie, Brenda, 1987, **Small scale bibliographic database.** {JNU}

Ranganathan, S.R., 1952, **Social bibliography or physical bibliography for libraries.** {BIS CRRI DSSW}

Anon, n.d., **Specification for bibliographic information interchange format for magnet tape.** (BS 4748 : 1971). [British Standards Institution]. {CRRI}

Needham, Christopher D. and Herman, Esther, eds., 1970, **Study of subject bibliography with special reference to the social sciences.** [School of Library and Information Services, Maryland]. {NASSDOC}

Hale, Barbara M., 1970, **Subject bibliography of the social sciences and humanities.** {IEG NASSDOC}

Bliss, H.E., 1936, **System of bibliographic classification**, 2nd edn. {NAI}

Roy, R. Paul Mohan, 1984, **Systematic bibliography** : An introduction. {NASSDOC}

Robinson, A.M. Lewin, 1966, **Systematic bibliography** : A practical guide to the work of compilation. {ICHR NASSDOC SPA}

Ohdedar, A.K., 1975, **Systematic bibliography and documentation.** {ICA ICHR NASSDOC NIH}

Manzoor, Suhail, 1982, **Systems bibliography** : A thirty years' literature survey. {NASSDOC}

Boswell, David, B., 1952, **Text-book on bibliography.** {DUL}

Schneider, George, 1961, **Theory and history of bibliography**, tr. by Ralph Robert Shaw. {NASSDOC}

Anderson, Dorothy, 1974, **Universal bibliographic control** : A long term policy, a plan for action. {JNU}

Thempson, Anthony, comp., n.d., **Vocabularium bibliothecari** {IEG}

BIBLIOGRAPHY AND BIBLIOGRAPHICAL CONTROL : EARLY PRINTED BOOKS

Cameron, William J., 1978, **Bibliographical control of early books.** {JNU}

BIBLIOGRAPHY AND BIBLIOGRAPHICAL CONTROL : GEOGRAPHICAL AREA : AFRICA

Zell, Hans M., 1975, **African books in print** : An Index by author, title and subject, Pt. 1: English language and African language. {NASSDOC}

BIBLIOGRAPHY AND BIBLIOGRAPHICAL CONTROL : GEOGRAPHICAL AREA : ASIA

Anon, 1965, **Papers** : Seminar on library science in Southeast Asia, December 18-20, 1964, Bangkok. [Association of Southeast Asian Institutions of Higher Learning]. {NASSDOC NIEPA}

BIBLIOGRAPHY AND BIBLIOGRAPHICAL CONTROL : GEOGRAPHICAL AREA : CANADA

Anon, 1977, **Development index Canada** : Index to 1976 Canadian literature on economic and social development. [International Development Research Centre]. {IIFT}

BIBLIOGRAPHY AND BIBLIOGRAPHICAL CONTROL : GEOGRAPHICAL AREA : FRANCE

Gournay, Bernard, 1963, **French bibliographical digest** : Public administration. {MFL}

BIBLIOGRAPHY AND BIBLIOGRAPHICAL CONTROL : GEOGRAPHICAL AREA : GREAT BRITAIN

Anon, 1970-1984, **British books in print** {NASSDOC}

Anon, 1976, **Inventory of bibliographic data bases produced in the UK** : Report. [British Library, Department of Research and Development]. {JNU}

Rayward, W. Boyd, 1967, **Systematic bibliography in England, 1850-95.** {DUL}

BIBLIOGRAPHY AND BIBLIOGRAPHICAL CONTROL : GEOGRAPHICAL AREA : INDIA

Ahmad, Syed Reyaz, 1979, **Annotated and classified bibliography of project reports submitted to the Department of Library Science, University of Delhi since 1968.** {DUL}

Pathak, Vijay, and Ramaiah, L.S. 1986, **Bibliography of research in library and information in India**. {NMML}

Anon, 1976, **Bibliography of selected Indian books, 1970-71**. {NASSDOC}

Vaswani, H.P., comp., 1964, **Books of India, 1963** : A reference catalogue of Indian book published in English in 1963. {NASSDOC}

Sandhu, S.N., 1969, **Critical evaluation of the bibliographical sources for manuscript in modern Indian languages**. (University of Delhi, Department of Library Science. Sessional Project). {DUL}

Sharma, Jagdish Saran, 1977, **Fundamentals of bibliography with special reference to India**. {JNU NASSDOC}

Prasher, Ram Gopal, et al, 1971-72, **Indian books** : An annual bibliography. {NASSDOC}

Anon, 1955-1983, **Indian books in print** : A bibliography of Indian books in English language, 3 vols, Vol 1 : Author; Vol 2 : Title; Vol 3 : Subject guide. {ICA INSA NASSDOC}

Sharma, H.D., et al, n.d., **Indian reference sources** : An annotated guide to Indian reference books. {ICHR IIC NASSDOC ZHL}

Anon, 1960, **Indian scientific and technical publications** : Exhibition. (National Library, Calcutta). {DUL}

Jain, M.K., 1989, **Indiana** : A bibliography of bibliographical sources. {NASSDOC}

Kaul, R.K., 1980, **Indic names** : Documentation list. {BIS NASSDOC ZHL}
Anon, n.d., **Reference catalogue of Indian books in print,** 3 vols. {NASSDOC}

BIBLIOGRAPHY AND BIBLIOGRAPHICAL CONTROL : GEOGRAPHICAL AREA : RUSSIA

Horecky, Paul L., **Libraries and bibliographic centres in the Soviet Union.** {IEG}
Chandler, George, 1972, **Libraries, documentation and bibliography in the USSR, 1917-1971** : Survey and critical analysis of Soviet studies. {JNU NASSDOC}

BIBLIOGRAPHY AND BIBLIOGRAPHICAL CONTROL : GEOGRAPHICAL AREA : THAILAND

Minaikit, Nonglak, 1968, **Annotated bibliography on librarianship in Thailand.** {JNU}

BIBLIOGRAPHY AND BIBLIOGRAPHICAL CONTROL : UN

Anon, n.d., **Bibliography of United Nations thesauri, classification nomenclatures.** [Inter-Organisation Board for Information Systems, Geneva]. {BIS}

BIBLIOGRAPHY AND BIBLIOGRAPHICAL CONTROL : UNESCO

Anon, 1973, **Bibliography of publications issued by UNESCO or under its auspices, 1946-1971**. [UNESCO]. {NASSDOC}
Anon, 1977-81, **List of documents and publications of General Information Programme and UNISIST, 1977-81**. [UNESCO]. {JNU}

BIBLIOGRAPHY AND BIBLIOGRAPHICAL CONTROL : GEOGRAPHICAL AREA : USA

Anon, 1969-1983, **Books in print 1969-71; 1973-74 to 1982-83**. {NASSDOC NIH}

BIBLIOGRAPHY AND BIBLIOGRAPHICAL SERVICES

Anon, 1950-1974, **Bibliographical services throughout the world,** 1950-54; 1955-59; 1960-64; 1965-69; 1970-74. [UNESCO]. {DSSW DUL IIMC JNU NASSDOC NIEPA ZHL}

BIBLIOGRAPHY AND BIBLIOGRAPHICAL SERVICES : GEOGRAPHICAL AREA : INDIA

Patil, P.K., 1972, **Bibliographical services for Indian studies** : A guide to printed sources of information. [Mysore Institute of Development Studies]. {NASSDOC}

BIBLIOGRAPHY AND BIBLIOGRAPHICAL SERVICES GEOGRAPHICAL AREA : PAKISTAN

Usmani, M. Adil, 1978, **Bibliographical services throughout Pakistan.** {ZHL}

BIBLIOGRAPHY OF BIBLIOGRAPHIES : GEOGRAPHICAL AREA : INDIA

Kalia, D.R. and Jain, M.K., 1975, **A bibliography of bibliographies on India**. {ICA}
Gidwani, N.N. and Navalani, K., 1974, **A guide to reference materials on India**, 2 vols. {INSA NAI NASSDOC NCAER NERC ZHL}

BIBLIOMETRICS

Nicholas, David and Ritchies, Maureen, 1978, **Literature and bibliometrics**. {BCL

IIT NASSDOC}

BLISS BIBLIOGRAPHIC CLASSIFICATION

Anon, 1969, **Abridged Bliss Classification** : The bibliographic classification of Henry Evelyn Bliss revised for school libraries. [Bliss Classification Working Party]. {DUL}

See also Classification Schemes : Bibliographic

BOMBAY

See Geographical Area subdivision under main Descriptor, e.g., Libraries : Geographical Area : India : Maharashtra : Bombay

BOOK BINDING

Clements, Jaff, n.d., **Bookbinding.** {ISI}

Hewitt-Bates, F. S.A.M., 1954, **Bookbinding.** {NASSDOC}

Diehl, Edith, 1965, **Bookbinding** : Its background and technique, 2 vols. {DUL}

Cockerell, Douglas, 1925, **Bookbinding and the care of the books,** 5th edn. {CRRI ZHL}

Town, Laurence, 1973, **Bookbinding by hand for students and craftsmen,** 2nd edn. {BIS}

Clugh, Eric A., 1967, **Bookbinding for librarians.** [Association of Assistant Librarians, London]. {NASSDOC}

Lehmann-Haupt, Helimut, et al, 1967, **Bookbinding in America** : Three essays. {DUL}

Agrawal, O.P., 1977, **Care and preservation of museum objects.** {NASSDOC}

Lydenberg, Harry Miller and Archer, John, 1980, **Care and repair of books,** 4th rev edn. {DUL ISI}

Anon, 1972, **Care of books and documents.** [Library Association, London] {ZHL}

Horton, Carolyn, 1967, **Cleaning and preserving bindings and related materials.** [American Library Association]. {DUL IIT}

Horton, Carolyn, 1969, **Cleaning and preserving bindings and related materials,** 2nd edn. [American Library Association]. {USIS}

Anon, 1965, **Code of practice for reinforced binding of library books and periodicals.** (IS : 3050-1965). [Indian Standards Institution]. {CRRI NASSDOC}

Anon, 1966, **Development of performance standards for library binding,** Phase 1 : Report of the survey, April, 1961; Phase 2: Report on a study conducted by library technology project. [American Library Association]. {BIS IIT}

Darley, Lionel S., 1965, **Introduction to bookbinding.** {CRRI}

Anon, n.d., **Library binding handbook.** [Library Building Institute]. {ISI}

Anon, 1951, **Library binding manual.** [American Library Association]. {IIT}

Johnson, Arthur W., 1978, **Manual of book binding.** {ZHL}

Edgar, Mansfield, 1966, **Modern design in book binding.** {DUL}

Whetton, Harry, ed., 1963, **Practical printing binding.** {INSA}

Anon, n.d., **Specification for book binding leather.** (IS : 2960-1964). [Indian Standards Institution]. {CRRI}

See also Preservation, Restoration and Storage

BOOK CATALOGUES

See Catalogues : Books

BOOK CENSORSHIP
See Censorship

BOOK COLLECTION

Van Orden, Phyllis and Phillips, Edith B., eds., 1979, **Background readings in building library collections**, 2nd edn. {USIS}

Wheeler, Helen R., 1968, **Basic book collection for the community college library.** {JNU}

Anon, 1960, **Basic book collection for elementary grades**. [American Library Association]. {NIEPA USIS}

Chapman, R.W., 1950, **Book collecting** : Four broadcast talks. {DUL}

Collison, Robert Lewis, 1957, **Book collection** : An introduction to modern methods of literary and bibliographical detection. {DUL}

Shaffer, Kenneth R., 1961, **Book collection** : Policy case studies in public and academic libraries. {DUL}

Carter, Mary Duncan and Bonk, Wallace John, 1969, **Building library collections,** 3rd edn. {USIS}

Carter, Marry Duncan, et al, 1974, **Building library collections,** 4th edn. {USIS}

Bonk, Wallace John and Marymagril, Rose, 1979, **Building library collections**, 5th edn. {USIS}

Mangla, P.B., ed., 1985, **Building library collections and national policy for library** : Seminar papers : All India library conference, 30th, January 28-31, 1985, Jaipur. [Indian Library Association]. {NASSDOC}

Anon, 1976, **Collection building in special purpose libraries.** {USIS}

Evans, G. Edward, 1979, **Developing library collections**. {USIS}

Harmon, Robert B., 1976, **Developing the library collection in political science.** {JNU}

Koops, William R.H. and Stellingwerff, Johannes, eds., 1977, **Developments in collection building in university libraries in Western Europe**: Symposium on . . ., March 31-April 2, 1976, Amsterdam. {IIT}

Gupta, S.R., 1978, **Evaluation of collection of Jawaharlal Nehru University Library from the point of view of Indian reference sources.** [University of Delhi, Department of Library and Information Science Sessional Project]. {DUL}

Perkins, David, ed., 1979, **Guidelines for collection development.** [American Library Association]. {USIS}

Lynes, Alice, 1974, **How to organise a local collection.** {NASSDOC}

Fisher, Margery, 1962, **Intent upon reading** : A critical appraisal of modern fiction for children. {DUL}

Gardner, Richard K., 1981, **Library collections** : Their origin, selection and development. {DUL}

Lee, C.P., 1971, **Library resources** : How to research and write a paper. {IIMC IIT NASSDOC NCAER}

Smith, C. and Walker, R., n.d., **Library resources in Scotland**. {JNU}

Siddiqui, Akhtar H., n.d., **Library resources of Pakistan**. {JNU}

Anon, 1967, **Library resources on East Asia** : Reports and working papers for the 10th meeting of the committee on American library resources. [Association for Asian Studies]. {JNU}

Meckler, Alan M. and Mc Mullin, Ruth, 1975, **Oral history collections.** {USIS}

Vakata, Yuri, et al, 1979, **Organising local government documents collection.**

[American Library Association]. {USIS}

Beswick, Norman, 1975, **Organising resources** : Six case studies : Final report of the Schools Council Resources Centre project. {NIPCCD}

Winterich, John Tracy and Randall, David A., 1966, **Primer of book collecting.** {DUL}

Hickec, Doralyn J., 1972, **Problems in organising library collections.** {JNU NERC}

Archer, H. Richard, ed., 1965, **Rare book collections** : Some theoretical and practical suggestions for use by librarians and students. [American Library Association]. {NAI}

Downs, Robert B., n.d., **Resources of Canadian academic and research libraries**. {AIU}

Williams, Edwin E., 1962, **Resources of Canadian university libraries for research in the humanities and social sciences** : Report of a survey. [National Conference of Canadian Universities and Colleges, Ottawa]. {DUL NASSDOC}

Patterson, Maureen L.P., ed., 1975, **South Asian library resources in North America** : A survey prepared for the Boston conference, 1974. {NASSDOC}

Melville, Annette, comp., 1980, **Special collection in the Library of Congress** : A selective guide. [U.S. Library of Congress]. {USIS}

Lane, Margaret T., 1981, **State publications and depository libraries** : A reference handbook. {USIS}

Vernon, Jackson William, 1988, **Studies in library resources.** {JNU}

Ash, Lee, comp., 1978, **Subject collections** : A guide to special book collections and subject emphasis as reported by university, college, public and special libraries and museums in the United States and Canada, 5th edn. {USIS}

Lewanski, Richard C., ed. and comp., 1978, **Subject collections in European libraries**, 2nd edn. {IIT}

Moir, P.H., ed., 1952, **Talks on book collecting**. {DUL}

Goodrum, Charles A., 1980, **Treasures of the Library of Congress.** {USIS}

Stefferud, Alfred, ed., 1972, **Wonderful world of books.** {ZHL}

See also Acquisition in Libraries; Book Selection

BOOK DESIGN

Williamson, Hugh, 1966, **Methods of book design** : The practices of an industrial craft, 2nd edn. {INSA}

BOOK INDUSTRY AND TRADE

Dikshit, S.R. and Dikshit, S.D., comps., 1970-72, **All India booksellers and publishers directory, 1970, 1971, 1972.** {ICCR JNU NASSDOC}

Gupta, K.R., 1980-82, **All India directory of book trade**, vol. 1: Libraries; vol. 2; Booksellers and publishers {NASSDOC NCAER NCERT}

Anon, 1981, **Bombay Booksellers and Publishers Association Members' Directory**. [Bombay Booksellers and Publishers Association]. {NASSDOC}

Punnoose, Kunnuparampil P., 1977, **Book dealers in India, Pakistan, Sri Lanka** : A directory of dealers in second hand and antiquarian books in the sub-continent of South Western Asia. {NMML}

Sankaranarayanan, N., 1964, **Book distribution and promotion problems in South Asia**. {DUL}

Miller, William, 1950, **The book industry** : A report of the public library enquiry.

{CRRI}

Turner, Mary C., 1961, **Bookman's glossary**, 4th edn. {DUL}

Peters, Jean, ed., 1961, **The bookmen's glossary**. 5th edn. {NCERT}

Peters, Jean, ed., 1983, **The bookmen's glossary**. 61th edn. {NASSDOC}

Liebaers, Herman, 1975, **Book promotion through libraries**. {DUL}

Madison, Charles A., 1966, **Book publishing in America**. {DUL}

Thomas, Joy, 1952, **Book selling**. {DUL}

Kenneth, Day, ed., 1966, **Book typography, 1815-1965, in Europe and the United States of America**. {DUL}

Hill, Henry H., et al, eds., 1956, **Books and publishing**, vol. 3. {DUL}

Sharma, Jai Kishore, 1973, **Directory of book trade in India**. JNU RTL}

Trivedi, Dinkar, ed., 1973, **Directory of Indian publishers**. [Federation of Publishers and Booksellers Association in India]. {IIPA NASSDOC RTL UGC}.

Khandwala, Vidyut K. and Naidu, M.K.R., eds., 1965, **Directory of libraries, publishers, booksellers in the city of Bombay**. [SNDT Women University Library]. {NASSDOC}

Smith, Datus C., 1977, **Economics of book publishing in developing countries.** {DUL}

Eric, Bailey, 1965, **Economics of book selling**. {DUL}

Smith, Datus C., 1966, **Guide to book publishing**. {DUL}

Rhodes, Dennis E., 1969, **History of printing in the India, Pakistan, Ceylon, Burma and Thailand.** {DUL}

Anon; n.d., **Indian publishers directory**, {NASSDOC}

Clarke, Tom, 1975, **International academic and specialist publishers directory**. {NASSDOC}

Goyal, S.P., 1973, **International directory of dealers of back-sets of periodicals.** {NASSDOC}

Dewe, Michael, 1968, **Library supply agencies in Europe**. {JNU}

Wallick, Clair H., 1970, **Looking for ideas** : A display manual for libraries and bookstores. {USIS}

Anderson, Charles B., et al, 1969, **Manual of book selling**. {DUL}

Dorothy, Harrop, n.d., **Modern book production**. {DUL}

Kim, Ung C., 1976, **Policies of publishers** : A handbook for order librarians. {JNU}

Heys, H., 1965, **Preparation and production of technical books.** {DUL}

George, Mann, 1951, **Print** : A manual for librarians and students describing in detail the history, methods and applications of printing and paper making. {DUL}

Mac Robert, T.M., 1957, **Printed books** : A short introduction to fine typography. {DUL}

Priolker, Anant Kakba, 1958, **Printing presses in India** : Its beginning and early development. {DUL}

Anon, 1958, **Proof corrections for printers and authors**. (IS : 1250-1958). [Indian Standards Institution]. {NASSDOC}

Gorkhoff, Boris I., n.d., **Publishing in the USSR**. {DUL}

Veaner, Allen B., ed., 1977, **Studies in micropublishing**, 1853-1976. {USIS}

Plant, Marjorie, n.d., **Supply of foreign books and periodicals to the libraries of the United Kingdom**. {DUL}

Hattery, Lowell H. and Bush, George P., 1973, **Technological change in printing and publishing**. {INSA}

Anon, 1968, **USA standard for compiling book publishing statistics**. (USAS Z 39.8-1968). [American National Standards Institute]. {NASSDOC}

BOOK JACKET

Charles, Rosner, n.d., **Growth of the book-jacket.** {DUL}

BOOK LENDING

See Libraries : Circulation/Loans

BOOK MOBILES

Brown, Eleanor Frances, 1967, **Bookmobiles and bookmobile service.** {USIS}

BOOK NUMBERS

Barden, Bertha R., 1937, **Book numbers** : A manual for students with a basic code of rules. {DUL}

Satija, M.P. and Agrawal, S.P., 1990, **Book numbers** : Some Indian methods. {NASSDOC}

Cutter, C.A., n.d., **Cutter's three figure author table.** {IIT ISI}

Zubair, Mohamad and Agrawal, S.P., 1954, **Pustak sankhya praveshika** : Introduction to book numbers in Hindi. {NASSDOC}

BOOK REPAIRING

See Book Binding; Preservation, Restoration and Storage

BOOK REVIEWS AND BOOK REVIEWING

McCanse, Ralph Alan, 1963, **Art of the book review** : A comprehensive working outline. {DUL}

Chen, Ching-Chih, 1976, **Biomedical, scientific and technical book reviewing**. {DUL}

Anon, 1948-1981, **Book review digest 1948-73; 1976-77; 1979-80; 1980-81.** {NASSDOC}

Drewry, John E., n.d., **Book reviewing.** {DUL}

Merritt, LeRoy C., 1958, **Reviews in library book selection**. {DUL}

Drewry, John Eldridge, 1966, **Writing book reviews**. {DUL}

BOOK SELECTION

Spiller, David, 1971, **Book selection** : An introduction to principles and practice, 2nd ed. {BIS}

Spiller, David, 1986, **Book selection** : An introduction to principles and practice. {NASSDOC}

Wellard, J.H., 1937, **Book selection** : Its principles and practice. {NAI}

Lunati, Rinaldo, 1975, **Book selection** : Principles and procedures. {DUL}

Mukherjee, A.K., 1974, **Book selection** : Principles, practices and tools. {ICHR IEG}

Kee, S. Janice and Smith, Dorothy K., eds., 1955, **Book selection** : Proceedings of a work conference. {DUL}

Sharma, C.K., n.d., **Book selection and bibliography**. {ICHR}

Marjorie, Fiske, 1959, **Book selection and censorship** : A study of school and public libraries in California. {JNU}

Moon, Eric, ed., 1969, **Book selection and censorship in the sixties**. {DUL IIT USIS}.

Danton, J. Periam, 1963, **Book selection and collections** : A comparison of

German and American university libraries. {JNU}
Merritt, Le Roy Charles, 1970, **Book selection and intellectual freedom**. {USIS}
Sharma, C.D., 1976, **Book selection and physical bibliography.** {CRRI}
Mukherjee, A.K., 1960, **Book selection and systematic bibliography** {IIT MFL NMML SPA}
Wofford, Azile, 1967, **Book selection for school libraries** {JNU}
Danton, J. Periam, 1959, **Climate of book selection** : Social influences on school and public libraries. {DUL}
Mosher, Frederic J., ed., 1954, **Freedom of book selection** : Proceedings : Conference on intellectual freedom, 2nd, June 20-21, 1953. [American Library Association]. {AIU USIS}
Kujoth, Jean Spealman, 1969, **Libraries, readers and book selection**. {USIS}
Ranganathan, S.R., 1952, **Library book selection**. [Indian Library Association]. {BIS DSSW INSA}
Ranganathan, S.R., 1966, **Library book selection**, 2nd rev edn. {BIS CRRI IIT ISI NMML SPA}
Haines, Helen E., 1965, **Living with books** : Art of book selection, 2nd edn. {DUL IIC IIT USIS}
Bonny, Harold V., 1939, **A manual of practical book selection for public libraries**. {CRRI DUL}
Sharma, Chandra Kant, 1975, **Pustak chayan evam rachna** : Book selection and physical bibliography. {BIS NMML}
Merritt, LeRoy C., 1958, **Reviews in library book selection**. {DUL}
Broadus, Robert N., 1973, **Selecting materials for libraries**. {USIS}
Job, M.M., 1978, **Theory of book selection**. {NERC NIPCCD}
Chakrabarti, A.K., 1983, **A treatise on book selection**. {NERC NIH ZHL}

See also Acquisition in Libraries; Book Collection

BOOK THEFT
see Damage/Loss/Theft of Books

BOOK-SELLERS AND BOOK SELLING
See Book Industry and Trade

BOOKS
Broyard, Anatole, 1974, **Aroused by books.** {USIS}
Mc Mustrie, Douglas C., 1943, **Book** : The story of printing and bookmaking, 3rd rev ed. {DUL}
Morpurgo, J.E., 1969, **Book and journal services for doctors and nurses** : An interim report on a National Book League investigation. {DUL}
Buckland, Michael K., 1975, **Book availability and the library user**. {JNU NASSDOC USIS}
Walker, Elinor, comp., 1969, **Book bait** : Detailed notes on adult books popular with young people. 2nd edn. [American Library Association]. {USIS}
Anon, 1967, **Book development in Asia** : A report on the production and distribution of books. [UNESCO]. {DUL}
Escarpit, Robert, 1966, **Book revolution**. {DUL}
Kenyon, Frederic G., 1951, **Books and readers in ancient Greece and Rome**, 2nd edn. {DUL}

Jones, Mander, 1962, **Books and related materials.** {JNU}

Marshall, Lee, ed., 1951, **Books are for our time.** {DUL}

Dearden, James, 1969, **Books are for people** : Librarian's life educational explorers. {IIT}

Mews, Hazel, 1951, **Books are tools** : The organisation of small technical libraries for South African industry. {JNU}

David, Kaser, ed., 1966, **Books in America's past** : Essays honouring Rudolph H. Gjelsness. {DUL}

Powell, Lawrence Clark, 1960, **Books in my baggage** : Adventures in reading and collecting. {JNU}

Anon, 1969-1983, **Books in print 1969-71; 1973-74 to 1982-83.** {NASSDOC NIH}

Yefimova, A.N. et al, eds., 1974, **Books in the service of society** : Collection of articles of Soviet authors. [Ministry of Culture of the USSR, Main Library Inspectorate]. {NASSDOC}

Conlon, Eileen, 1964, **Books lead the way** : Library and reading skill-text. {JNU}

Sigel, Efrem, et al, 1982, **Books, libraries and electronics** : Essays on the future of written communication. {USIS}

Boyd, Jessie, et al, 1941, **Books, libraries and you,** {ZHL}

Boyd, Jessie, et al, 1965, **Books, libraries and you** : A handbook on the use of reference books and the reference resources of the library, 3rd edn. {USIS}

Vaswani, H.P., comp., 1964, **Books of India, 1963** : A reference catalogue of Indian book published in English in 1963. {NASSDOC}

Downs, Robert B., 1977, **Books that changed America.** {USIS}

Downs, Robert B., 1956, **Books that changed the world**, 2nd ed. [American Library Association]. {USIS}

Downs, Robert B., 1978, **Books that changed the world**, 2nd edn., [American Library Association]. {USIS}

Sabine, Gordon and Sabine, Patricia, 1983, **Books that made the difference** : What people told us. {USIS}

Langwell, W.H., 1974, **Conservation of books and documents.** {NERC}

Chuna, George M. and Chuna, Dorothy G., 1972, **Conservation of library materials** : Manual of bibliography on the care, repair and restoration of library materials, 2 vols. {DUL IIT NMML USIS}

Mann, Peter, 1982, **From author to reader** : A social study of books. {AIU}

Hutchins, Robert M., 1954, **Great books** : The foundation of liberal education. {USIS}

Thomas, Alan G., 1975, **Great books and book collectors.** {NASSDOC*}

Daedalus, 1976, **In praise of books**. [Academy of Arts and Sciences, Cambridge]. {USIS}

Fussler, Herman H. and Simon, Julian L., 1969, **Patterns in the use of books in large research libraries.** {NMML}

See also Reference Books

BOOKS : CONSERVATION AND PRESERVATION
See Perservation, Restoration and Storage

BOOKS : REFERENCE
See Reference Books

BOOKS AND READING

Pocock, Guy, 1942, **Brush up your reading**. {ZHL}

Adler, Mortimer J. and Van Doren, Charles, 1972, **How to read a book**, rev. edn. {USIS}

Marjarum, E. Warne, 1947, **How to use a book.** {JNU}

Gates, Arthur I., 1947, **Improvement of reading**. 3rd edn. {ZHL}

West, Roland, 1965, **Individualised reading instructions** : Its implication for teacher and librarian. {JNU}

Anon, 1964, **Let's read together** : Books for family enjoyment, 2nd edn. [American Library Association; Association for Library Service to Children]. {USIS}

Narasimharao, K.V.V.L. and Oommen, Chinna, 1972, **Read faster and understand better,** 2 pts. [Central Institute of Indian Languages, Mysore]. {MHA}

Webster, O., 1965, **Read well and remember**. {IIT}

Karetzkey, Stephen, 1982, **Reading research and librarianship** : A history and analysis. {CRRI IIT JNU}

Chambers, A., 1969, **Reluctant reader**. {DUL}

Khurshid, Anis, 1976, **What children read** : A survey. [National Book Council of Pakistan, Karachi]. {ZHL}

Waples, Douglas, et al, 1940, **What reading does to people**. {NAI}

Stefferud, Alfred, ed., 1972, **Wonderful world of books**. {ZHL}

BOOKS AND READING : GEOGRAPHICAL AREA : ASIA

Insha, Ibne, 1967, **Developing reading habits in Asian conditions.** {ZHL}

BOOKS AND READING : GEOGRAPHICAL AREA : PAKISTAN

Anon, 1981, **Promotion of reading habits in Pakistan** : A study on methods and measures to promote reading habits in Pakistan. [Pakistan National Book Council]. {ZHL}

Earuqui, Jalees A., ed., 1974, **Reading habits in Pakistan** : A report. {ZHL}

BOOKS AND READING : GEOGRAPHICAL AREA : USA

Smith, Roger H., 1963, **The American reading public** : What it reads, why it reads. {USIS}

Anon, 1974, **The right to read and the nation's libraries**. [American Association of School Libraries, Children's Services Division; Public Library Association; American Library Association]. {USIS}

BRANCH LIBRARIES

See Libraries : Branches, Delivery Stations, etc.

BRITISH PERIODICALS

See Serials : Geographical Area : Great Britain

BUILDINGS : LIBRARY

See Library Architecture

BUREAU OF INDIAN STANDARDS

Surinder Kumari, 1975-76, **Indian Standards Institution and its role in the development of library and documentation standards**. (University of Delhi,

Department of Library and Information Science, Sessional project 1975-76). {BIS}

BURMA
See Myanmar

BUSINESS : BIBLIOGRAPHY
Schlessinger, Bernard S., ed., 1983, **The basic business library** : Core resources. {USIS}

BUSINESS INFORMATION SERVICES
Spencer, J., 1976, **Business information in London** : A study of the demand and supply of business information in 13 London business libraries. [Association of Special Libraries and Information Bureaux]. {NASSDOC}
Campbell, Malcolm James, 1974, **Business information services** : Some aspects of structure organisation and problems. {BCL}

BUSINESS LIBRARIES
Johnson, Herbert Weber, et al, 1972, **How to use the business library** : With sources of business information, 4th edn. {USIS}

CALDECOTT MEDAL BOOKS
Miller, Bertha Mahony and Field, Elinor Whitney, eds., 1957, **Caldecott medal books**, with the artists' acceptance: Papers and related material chiefly from the Horn Book Magazine 1938-1957. {USIS}

CANADA
See Geographical Area subdivision under main Descriptor, e.g., Information Services : Geographical Area : Canada

CATALOGUE CARDS
Anon, 1942, **ALA rules for filing catalogue cards**. [American Library Association]. {CRRI IIT}
Giljarevskij, R.S., 1968-74, **International distribution of catalogue cards** : Present situation and future prospects 1968; 1969; 1974. [UNESCO]. {CRRI IIMC IIT JNU NERC NIEPA NIPCCD}
Slocum, R.B., 1962, **Sample catalog cards**. {IIT}
Anon, 1951, **Sample catalog cards**, 2nd edn. [School of Library Science, Columbia University]. {ZHL}

CATALOGUE CARDS : REPRODUCTION
Anon, 1965, **Catalogue card reproduction.** [American Library Association]. {IIT}

CATALOGUES
Haughney, John D., 1968, **Effective catalogues.** {NIPCCD}

CATALOGUES : BOOKS
Kingery, Robert E. and Tauber, Maurice F., eds., 1963, **Book catalogs.** {USIS}
Tauber, Maurice F. and Feinberg, Hilda, 1971, **Book catalogs**. {NASSDOC}

CATALOGUES : CLASSIFIED
Shera, Jesse H. and Egan, M.E., 1956, **Classified catalogue** : Basic principles and

practices. [American Library Association]. {CRRI NASSDOC}

Ranganathan, S.R., 1945, **Classified catalogue code**, 2nd edn. [Madras Library Association]. {CRRI DSSW NAI}

Ranganathan, S.R., 1951, **Classified catalogue code**, 3rd edn. {DSSW}

Ranganathan, S.R., 1958, **Classified catalogue code**, with additional rules for dictionary catalogue code, 4th edn. [Madras Library Association]. {DSSW IEG NERC}

Ranganathan, S.R., 1965, **Classified catalogue code**, with additional rules for dictionary catalogue code, 5th edn. {AIU BIS CRRI DSSW ICHR IIT ISI MHA NAI NASSDOC NMML SPA ZHL}

Varma, A.K., 1988, **Classified catalogue code** : Entries and procedure. {JNU}

Sharma, C.D., 1973, **Classified catalogue code in theory and practice.** {CRRI}

Sharma, C.D. and Dave, Meenakshi, 1990, **Classified catalogue code in theory and practice** {DUL}

CATALOGUES : COLLEGE

See Catalogues : Universities and Colleges

CATALOGUES : DICTIONARY

Mittal, R.L. and Gupta, Shamsher, 1966, **Dictionary catalogue** : A practical manual. {ICHR IIT IIMC NERC NIPCCD}

Ranganathan, S.R., 1952, **Dictionary Catalogue Code**, 2nd edn. [Madras Library Association]. {CRRI}

Cutter, C.A., 1891, **Rules for a dictionary catalog.** {IIT}

Cutter, C.A., 1953, **Rules for dictionary catalog**, 4th edn. [Library Association, London]. {BIS CRRI JNU MFL NAI NIEPA NMML}

CATALOGUES : SUBJECT

Clarke, Archibald Leycester, 1933, **Manual of practical indexing including arrangement of subject catalogues.** {NAI}

Lewin, Evan, 1967, **Subject catalogue of the library of the Royal Empire Society**. {NASSDOC}

Coates, E.J., 1960, **Subject catalogues** : Headings and structure. [Library Association, London]. {IIT NASSDOC}

CATALOGUES : UNION

See Union Catalogues

CATALOGUES : UNIVERSITIES AND COLLEGES

Anon, 1971, **National catalogue of university level books.** {DSSW NASSDOC}

CATALOGUES AND CATALOGUING

Varma, A.K., 1986, **AACR2** : Entries and procedure. {NASSDOC}

Uppal, O.P., 1987, **AACR2** : Practice and theory. {JNU NASSDOC}

Cook, C. Donald, comp., 1982, **AACR2 decisions and rule interpretations :** A consolidation of the decision and rule interpretations for the Anglo-American Cataloguing Rules, 2nd. edn. assisted by Glenna E. Stevens. [Canadian Library Association]. {USIS}

Anon, 1980, **AACR2 institute handbook** : The Library of Congress interpretation and application of the Anglo-American Cataloguing Rules, 2nd. edn. [U.S. Library of Congress; American Library Association]. {USIS}

Beetle, Clara, 1970, **ALA cataloguing rules for author and title entries**. {BIS CRRI DSSW ICA IIFT IIT MFL NIEPA SPA TDA USIS ZHL}

Anon, 1942, **ALA rules for filing catalogue cards**. [American Library Association]. {CRRI IIT}

Seely, Pauline A., ed., 1968, **ALA rules for filing catalogue cards**, 2nd. edn. [American Library Association]. {BIS IIT JNU NIEPA NMML USIS}

Kimey, 1967, **Abbreviated citation**. {DEPT}

Randall, William, ed., 1944, **Acquisition and cataloguing of books** : Papers presented before the library institute at the University of Chicago, July 29 to August 9, 1940. {JNU NAI ZHL}

Anon, 1967, **Anglo-American Cataloguing Rules**. [American Library Association]. {NASSDOC}

Anon, 1978, **Anglo-American Cataloguing Rules**, 2nd edn. [American Library Association]. {CRRI IIC ISI JNU MHA NCAER NERC NIH NIPCCD USIS ZHL}

Anon, 1975, **Anglo-American Cataloguing Rules** : Amendment bulletin. [Library Association, London] {ZHL}

Anon, 1974, **Anglo-American Cataloguing Rules** : British text. [Library Association, London]. {AIU IIT ISI JNU ZHL}

Anon, 1976, **Anglo-American Cataloguing Rules** : North American text. [Library Association, London]. {NASSDOC NMML USIS}

Anon, 1976, **Anglo-American Cataloguing Rules** : North American text : Chapter 6 : Separately published monographs. [American Library Association]. {JNU}

Anon, 1975, **Anglo-American Cataloguing Rules** : North American text : Chapter 12 : Audiovisual media and special instructional materials, rev. [American Library Association]. {USIS}

Anon, 1971, **Anglo-American Cataloguing Rules :** North American Text, with supplement of additions and changes. [American Library Association]. {JNU}

Hunter, Eric J., 1972, **Anglo-American Cataloguing Rules, 1967** : An introduction. {JNU NERC}

Anon, n.d., **Author catalogue of printed books in European languages,** 8 vols. [National Library, Calcutta]. {NASSDOC}

Anon, 1941, **Author entry for government publications**. [U.S. Library of Congress]. {NAI}

Tait, James A., 1969, **Authors and titles** : An analytical study of the author concept in codes of cataloguing rules in the English language from that of the British Museum. {NMML}

Anon, n.d., **Automation in union catalogue of periodicals** : India and abroad, typed short bibliography. {NASSDOC}

Anon, 1976, **BIB DATA network** : A draft proposal for an Australian national shared cataloguing system. [National Library of Australia]. {JNU}

Cowley, J.D., 1939, **Bibliographic description and cataloguing.** {DUL}

Rowland, Arthur Ray, 1969, **Catalogue and cataloguing**. {IIFT IIT NMML SPA}

Anon, 1965, **Catalogue card reproduction.** [American Library Association]. {IIT}

Agrawal, S.S., 1972, **Catalogue entries and procedure** : A guide to cataloguing work according to ALA and AACR and CCC. {IEG IIT ISI}

Anon, 1985, **Catalogue of back volumes of periodicals in Punjabrao Krishi Vidyapeeth Library, Akola, 1985**. [Punjabrao Krishi Vidyapeeth, Akola]. {NASSDOC}

Anon, 1959, **Catalogue of Government of India civil publications** : Subject-wise arranged corrected up to 31st December, 1959. [Controller of Publications, Delhi].

{NASSDOC NIPCCD}

Anon, n.d., **Catalogue of Government of India civil publications** : Subject-wise arranged corrected up to 31st December, 1959 : Supplement for the years 1968-70. [Controller of Publications, Delhi]. {IIFT ISI NASSDOC TDA}

Anon, 1977, **Catalogue of Government of India civil publications** : Subject-wise arranged, corrected up to 31st December, 1977, 8th supplement for the year 1977. {MMTC}

Anon, 1970-1971, **Catalogue of government publications.** [HMSO, Great Britain]. {NASSDOC}

Momoh, O.A., 1975, **Catalogue of new accessions in the headquarter's library, National Archives of India, April 1966 to March 1974**. {NAI}

Anon, 1967, **Catalogue of publications issued by Government of Uttar Pradesh and obtainable from the book depot, Government Press, Allahabad, for the year ending, 1965-66** : Corrected up to September, 1966. {NASSDOC}

Gaur, Ganesh, comp., 1975, **Catalogue of Punjabi printed books added to the India Office Library, 1902-1964**. [India Office Library, London]. {NASSDOC}

Shah, Ambalal P., ed., n.d. **Catalogue of Sanskrit and Prakrit manuscripts**, 4 parts. [Lalbhai Dalpatbhai Institute of Indology]. {INSA}

Anon, n.d., **Catalogue of serials** : Indian Institute of Science Library, Bangalore. [INSDOC Union Catalogue Series, 2]. {DUL}

Anon, 1980, **Catalogue of special collections in National Library, Baghdad**. [National Library, Baghdad]. {NASSDOC}.

Anon, n.d., **Catalogue of type specimens**. {DUL}

Vishva Bandhu, n.d., **Catalogue of Vishvesharananda Vedic Research Institute manuscript collection**, 2 vols. {INSA}

Dunkin, Paul S., 1969, **Cataloguing**. [American Library Association]. {USIS}

Hunter, Eric J., 1974, **Cataloguing**. {NASSDOC}

Hunter, Eric J., 1979, **Cataloguing**, 2nd rev. edn. {IIT}

Sharma, C.K., 1984, **Cataloguing**. {NASSDOC}

Sengupta, B., 1964, **Cataloguing** : Its theory and practice. {CRRI ICHR MHA NMML SPA ZHL}

Sengupta, B., 1970, **Cataloguing** : Its theory and practice, 2nd edn. {JNU NERC}

Sengupta, B., 1974, **Cataloguing** : Its theory and practice, 3rd rev. edn. {IIT ISIL}

Sharp, H.A., 1950, **Cataloguing** : A textbook for the use in libraries, 4th edn. {IIT ZHL}

Sharp, H.A., 1964, **Cataloguing** : A textbook for use in libraries. {ICA MFL NAI NIPCCD ZHL}

Vishwanathan, C.G., 1959, **Cataloguing** : Theory and practice, 2nd edn. {CRRI NAI}

Vishwanathan, C.G., 1965, **Cataloguing** : Theory and practice, 3rd edn. {ISI MMTC NASSDOC SPA ZHL}

Vishwanathan, C.G., 1970. **Cataloguing** : Theory and practice, 4th edn. {AIU ICA IIFT ISI MMTC NASSDOC NERC NIEPA SPA ZHL}

Vishwanathan, C.G., 1983, **Cataloguing** : Theory and practice, 5th edn. {ICHR IEG IIT MHA MMTC NCAER NCDC ZHL}

Kohl, D.F., 1986, **Cataloguing and catalogue** : A handbook for library management. {NASSDOC}

Chan, Lois Mai, 1985, **Cataloguing and classification** : An introduction. {JNU}

Eaton, Thelma, 1963, **Cataloguing and classification** : An introductory manual, 3rd edn. {DUL}

Manhieimer, Martha L., 1980, **Cataloguing and classification** : A workshop, 2nd edn. {NASSDOC NIPCCD}

Friedman, Joan and Jeffreys, Alan, 1967, **Cataloguing and classification in British university libraries** : A survey of practices and procedures. [Sheffield University Post Graduate School of Librarianship]. {DUL IIT}

Aman, Mohammad M., ed., 1980, **Cataloguing and classification of non-Western materials** : Concerns, issues and practices. {IIT}

Collison, Robert L., 1950, **Cataloguing arrangement and filing of special material in special libraries**. {NAL}

Fleischer, Eugene and Goodman, Helen, 1980, **Cataloguing audio-visual materials** : A manual based on the Anglo-American Cataloguing Rules-2. {IIT}

Titchler, Therea, 1926, **Cataloguing for small libraries**, 3rd edn. {ZHL}

Bennett, Frederick, 1972, **Cataloguing in practice** : Organisation of book acquisition in libraries. {CRRI ICHR NASSDOC NIPCCD}

Thornton, J.L., 1930, **Cataloguing in special libraries** : A survey of methods. {CRRI MFL NAL}

Rescoe, A., 1962, **Cataloguing made easy**. {DUL}

Singh, S.N. and Prasad, H.N., 1985, **Cataloguing manual** : AACR-2, {JNU}

Haroon, Mohammed, 1984, **Cataloguing of Indian Muslim names**. {NASSDOC NMML}

Anon, 1953, **Cataloguing of musical instruments.** [Government Museum, Madras]. {NAL}

Sharify, Nasser, 1959, **Cataloguing of Persian works including rules for transliteration, entry and description.** [American Library Association]. {JNU NASSDOC}

Daily, Jay, E., 1975, **Cataloguing phonorecordings** : Problems and possibilities. {BIS}

Ranganathan, S.R., 1974, **Cataloguing practice**, 2nd edn. {ICA ICHR IEG JNU NERC NMML ZHL}

Khan, Noorul Hassan, Kamleshwar Nath and Sardana, J.L., 1984, **Cataloguing practice** : Classified catalogue code and Anglo- American cataloguing rules. {IIMC JNU NASSDOC NIH}

Anon, 1961, **Cataloguing rules** : Author and title entries. [American Library Association; Library Association, London]. {IIT MFL}

Beetle, Clara, 1970, **Cataloguing rules for author and title entries,** 2nd edn. [American Library Association]. {NAI}

Anon, n.d., **Cataloguing rules of the American Library Association and the Library of Congress, 1949-1958**. [American Library Association; U.S. Library of Congress]. {BIS IEG ZHL}

Fellows, Doracas, 1926, **Cataloguing rules with explanations and illustrations,** 2nd edn. {NAI}

Colvin, Laura C., 1973, **Cataloguing sampler** : Comparative and interpretive guide. {IIT}

Pandey, S.K., 1986, **Cataloguing theory**. {JNU}

Viswanathan, C.G., 1965, **Cataloguing theory and practice.** {NMML}

Anon, 1969, **Children's catalogue,** 12th edn. {USIS}

Shera, Jesse H. and Egan, M.E., 1956, **Classified catalogue** : Basic principles and practices. [American Library Association]. {CRRI NASSDOC}

Ranganathan, S.R., 1945, **Classified catalogue code**, 2nd edn. [Madras Library Association]. {CRRI DSSW NAI}

Ranganathan, S.R., 1951, **Classified catalogue code**, 3rd edn. {DSSW}

Ranganathan, S.R., 1958, **Classified catalogue code**, with additional rules for dictionary catalogue code, 4th edn. [Madras Library Association]. {DSSW IEG NERC}

Ranganathan, S.R., 1965, **Classified catalogue code**, with additional rules for dictionary catalogue code, 5th edn. {AIU BIS CRRI DSSW ICHR IIT ISI MHA NAI NASSDOC NMML SPA ZHL}

Varma, A.K., 1988, **Classified catalogue code** : Entries and procedure. {JNU}

Sharma, C.D., 1973, **Classified catalogue code in theory and practice.** {CRRI}

Sharma, C.D. and Dave, Meenakshi, 1990, **Classified catalogue code in theory and practice** {DUL}

Packer, Katherine H. and Phillips, Delores, eds., 1969, **Code and the cataloguer** : Proceedings of the colloquium on the Anglo-American Cataloguing Rules held at the School of Library Science, University of Toronto on March 31 and April 1, 1967. {NASSDOC}

Piercy, Esther J., 1974, **Commonsense cataloguing** : A manual for the organization of books and other materials in school and small public libraries, 2nd rev ed., by Marian Sannar. {USIS}

Hanson, J.C.M., 1939, **A Comparative study of cataloguing rules** : Based on Anglo-American code of 1908. {NASSDOC*}

Dolby, J.L., et al, 1969, **Computerised library catalogues** : Their growth, costs and utility. {IIT JNU NMML USIS}

Anon, 1981, **The concise AACR2** : Being a rewritten and simplified version of Anglo-American Cataloguing Rules, 2nd edn. [American Library Association]. {NASSDOC USIS}

Ranganathan, S.R. and Bhattacharya, G., 1970, **Conflict of authorship.** [Sarada Ranganathan Endowment for Library Science]. {ZHL}

Anon, n.d., **Cooperative cataloguing manual for the use of contributing libraries.** [U.S. Library of Congress]. {DUL}

Verona, Eva, 1975, **Corporate headings** : Their use in library catalogues and national bibliographies : A comparative and critical study. [International Federation of Library Associations and Institutions]. {JNU NASSDOC ZHL}

Cutter, C.A., n.d., **Cutter's three figure author table.** {IIT ISI}

Anon, 1955, **Descriptive catalogue of documentary films.** [Films Division, Government of India]. {NAL}

Tait, James A. and Anderson, F. Douglas, 1968, **Descriptive cataloguing** : A students introduction to the Anglo-American Cataloguing Rules, 1967. {NASSDOC}

Tait, James A. and Anderson, F. Douglas, 1971. **Descriptive cataloguing** : A students introduction to the Anglo-American Cataloguing Rules, 1967, 2nd edn. {IIC IIT}

Delbigio, G. and Ruckenbaver, E. Inis, 1978, **Descriptive cataloguing rules**. [International Atomic Energy Agency, Vienna]. {BIS}

Mittal, R.L. and Gupta, Shamsher, 1966, **Dictionary catalogue** : A practical manuai. {ICHR IIT IIMC NERC NIPCCD}

Ranganathan, S.R., 1952, **Dictionary Catalogue Code**, 2nd edn. [Madras Library Association]. {CRRI}

Haughney, John D., 1968, **Effective catalogues**. {NIPCCD}

Hunter, Eric J. and Fox, Nicholas J., 1980, **Examples illustrating AACR2** : Anglo-American Cataloguing Rules, 2nd ed. [Library Association, London].

{NASSDOC}

Anon, 1972, **Examples illustrating Anglo-American Cataloguing Rules** : British text. [Library Association, London]. {ZHL}

Anon, 1963, **Film cataloguing rules**. [Association of Special Libraries and Information Bureaux]. {SPA}

Sayers, W.C., Berwick, 1955, **First steps in annotation in catalogues,** 2nd rev ed. {DUL}

Carpenter, Michael and Svenonius, E., eds., 1985, **Foundations of cataloguing** : A source book. {NASSDOC}

Seal, Alan and Bryant, Philip, 1982, **Full and short entry catalogues** : Library needs and uses. [Centre for Catalogue Research]. {NASSDOC}

Domanovszky, A., 1975, **Functions and objects of author and title cataloguing** : A contribution to cataloguing theory. {NMML}

Taylor, Margaret S., 1948, **Fundamentals of practical cataloguing**. {BIS CRRI ICA IIFT MHA NAI NASSDOC ZHL}

Malinconico, Michael and Fasana, Paul J., 1979, **The future of the catalog** : The library's choices. {USIS}

Anon, 1975, **The future of cataloguing**. {USIS}

Anon, 1946-67, **General catalogue of UNESCO publications and UNESCO sponsored publications**. Supplements : 1946/59-1964/67. [UNESCO]. {NASSDOC}

Hoffmann, Christa F., 1980, **Getting ready for AACR2** : The cataloguer's guide. {JNU USIS}

Anon, 1967, **Glossary of cataloguing terms**. (IS : 796-1966). [Indian Standards Institution]. {NAI NASSDOC}

Anon, 1964, **Glossary of cataloguing terms in Indian regional languages**. [Indian Association of Special Libraries and Information Centres]. {NASSDOC SPA}

Maxwell, Margaret F., 1980, **Handbook for AACR2** : Explaining and illustrating Anglo-American Cataloguing Rules, 2nd ed. [American Library Association]. {USIS}

Norris, Dorothy May, 1939, **History of cataloguing and cataloguing methods, 1100-1880, with an introductory survey of ancient times.** {CRRI}

Dunkin, Paul Shaner, 1973, **How to catalogue a rare book?**, 2nd edn. {JNU}

Lehnus, Donal J., 1971, **How to determine author and title entries according to AACR?** : An interpretive guide with card examples. {AIU USIS}

Kaul, R.K., 1980, **Indic names** : Documentation list. {BIS NASSDOC ZHL}

Giljarevskij, R.S., 1968-74, **International distribution of catalogue cards** : Present situation and future prospects 1968; 1969; 1974. [UNESCO]. {CRRI IIMC IIT JNU NERC NIEPA NIPCCD}

Escreet, P.K., 1971, **Introduction to the Anglo-American cataloguing rules.** {MFL NASSDOC ZHL}

Winkler, Paul Walter, 1980, **Introduction to the Anglo-American cataloguing rules** : History and development. [American Library Association]. {USIS}

Boll, John J., 1970, **Introduction to cataloguing**, 2 vols, Vol. 1: Descriptive cataloguing and an overview of catalogues and cataloguing; Vol 2: Entry headings. {IIT JNU NERC NASSDOC NMML ZHL}

Krishan Kumar, 1983, **Introduction to cataloguing,** 2nd edn. {ZHL}

Wynar, Bohdan S. 1967, **Introduction to cataloguing and classification**, 3rd edn. {IIT}

Wynar, Bohdan S., et al, 1980, **Introduction to cataloguing and classification**, 6th edn. {USIS}

Wynar, Bohdan S., et al, 1985, **Introduction to cataloguing and classification.** (Library Science Text Series). {NASSDOC}

Mann, Margaret, 1943, **Introduction to cataloguing and classification of books.** [American Library Association]. {BIS CRRI ICA NAI NMML SPA USIS ZHL}

Anon, 1965, **Introduction to cataloguing and classification of books**, 2nd edn. [American Library Association]. {IIFT}

Krishan Kumar, 1981, **Introduction to cataloguing practice**. {ISI JNU NASSDOC NERC NMML}

Dutta, D., 1958-1969, **Introduction to library cataloguing**, 1958; 1959; 1969. {CRRI IIT NERC NIPCCD NMML}

Dewey, Harry, 1957, **Introduction to library cataloguing and classification**, 4th rev. edn. {DUL}

Anon, 1970, **Junior high school library catalog**, 2nd edn. {USIS}

Hutchins, W.J., 1975, **Languages of indexing and classification** : A linguistic study of structures and function. {DUL}

Strout, Ruth French, ed., 1964, **Library catalogs** : Changing damnations. {IIT}

Ranganathan, S.R., n.d., **Library catalogue** : Fundamentals and procedure. [Madras Library Association]. {BIS}

Henderson, James W. and Rosenthal, Joseph A., eds., 1968, **Library catalogues** : Their preservation and maintenance by photographic and automated techniques. {AIU IIT SPA}

Jayne, Sears, et al, 1956, **Library catalogues of the English renaissance.** {DUL}

Olney, John C., 1963, **Library cataloguing and classification.** {DUL}

Anon, 1985, **Library cataloguing practice** : Solutions to assignments 1-26. [Andhra Pradesh Open University, Hyderabad]. {NASSDOC*}

Anon, 1985, **Library cataloguing practice** : Unit 1 : Lessons 1-14. [Andhra Pradesh Open University, Hyderabad]. {NASSDOC}

Anon, 1975, **Literature survey and trends in library cataloguing, 1970-1975.** (Mimeo; short bibliography). {NASSDOC}

Annette, Mary, 1955, **Manual for cataloguing school libraries.** {JNU}

Quinn, J.H. and Aconib, H.M., 1937, **Manual of cataloguing and indexing.** {NAI}

Bakewell, K.G.B., 1972, **Manual of cataloguing practice.** {IIT JNU NASSDOC NIPCCD NMML ZHL}

McGaw, Howard F., 1952, **Marginal punched cards in college and research libraries.** {JNU}

Lehnus, Donald J., 1974, **Milestones in cataloguing** : Famous cataloguers and their writings, 1835-1969. {USIS}

Tripathi, S.M., 1969, **Modern cataloguing theory and practice.** {AIU IIC IIT JNU}

Chaplin, A.H., comp., 1967, **Names of person** : National usages for entry in catalogues. [International Federation of Library Association and Institutions]. {NASSDOC}

Anon, 1971, **National catalogue of university level books.** {DSSW NASSDOC}

Choudhary, Anil Roy, 1959, **National standards for cataloguing and indexing art museum objects and documents.** {ZHL}

Anon, 1973, **Non-book materials cataloguing rules** : Integrated code of practice and draft revision of the Anglo-American Cataloguing Rules. [Library Association Media Cataloguing Rules Committee; National Council for Educational Technology, London]. {NASSDOC}

Thomas, Nancy G. and O'Neil, Rosanna, comp., 1986, **Notes for serials cataloguing**. {NASSDOC*}

Needham, C.D., 1966, **Organising knowledge in libraries** : An introduction to classification and cataloguing. {IIC MFL SPA ZHL}

Barrow, W.J., 1961, **Permanence and durability of library catalogue cards.** {DUL}

Dent, Flu W., 1966, **Practical cataloguing.** {ICHR IIC IIT ZHL}

Johnson, A.F., 1962, **Practical cataloguing.** [Association of Assistant Librarians, London]. {IIT}

Zubair, Mohamad, 1951, **Practical cataloguing**. {ZHL}

Sharma, C.D., 1972, **Practical cataloguing** : Classified catalogue. {INSA JNU NCAER}

Sharma, C.D., 1972, **Practical cataloguing** : Classified catalogue, 2nd edn. [ICA ICHR IEC JNU NIPCCD}

Rajjan Lal, 1980, **Practical cataloguing procedure.** {IIT NIPCCD}

Uppal, O.P., n.d., **Practical procedure of cataloguing.** {ICHR}

Anon, n.d., **Practice for layout of library catalogue code.** (IS : 1358-1950). [Indian Standards Institution]. {NAI}

Jolley, L., 1961, **Principles of cataloguing.** {IEG IIT NAI SPA}

Hickec, Doralyn J., 1972, **Problems in organising library collections.** {JNU NERC}

Dowing, J.C. and Sharp, N.F., 1969, **Proceedings** : Seminar on the Anglo-American Cataloguing Rules, 1967. [Library Association, London]. {ZHL}

Herald, Alther Canley, 1963, **Processing manual** : A pictorial work book of catalogue cards, rev. edn. {DUL}

Johnson, A.F., 1968, **Programmed course in cataloguing and classification.** {CRRI IIC IIFT IIT INSA NCAER}

Collison, Robert, 1973, **Published library catalogues** : An introduction to their contents and use. {IIT}

Olding, R.K., ed., 1967, **Readings in library cataloguing.** {NASSDOC NMML SPA ZHL}

Gore, Daniel, et al, eds., 1979, **Requiem for the card catalogue** : Management issues in automated cataloguing. [Associated College of the Midwest]. {IIT NIPCCD USIS}

Anon, 1948, **Rules for the catalog of printed book** : Vatican Library. [American Library Association]. {NAI}

Anon, 1951, **Rules for compiling the catalogues of printed books, maps and music in the British Museum.** [British Museum, London]. {NAI}

Anon, 1913, **Rules for compiling the catalogues of printed books, maps, etc., in the Imperial Library, Calcutta.** [National Library, Calcutta]. {NAI}

Anon, n.d., **Rules for descriptive cataloguing in the Library of Congress.** [U.S. Library of Congress]. {BIS NAI SPA}

Anon, 1954, **Rules for descriptive cataloguing in the Library of Congress** : Phonorecords. [U.S. Library of Congress]. {IEG ZHL}

Anon, n.d., **Rules for descriptive cataloguing in the Library of Congress** : Supplement 1949-1951. [U.S. Library of Congress]. {ISI}

Cutter, C.A., 1891, **Rules for a dictionary catalog.** {IIT}

Cutter, C.A., 1953, **Rules for dictionary catalog.** 4th edn., [Library Association, London]. {BIS CRRI JNU MFL NAI NIEPA NMML}

Leong, C.L.H., 1989, **Serial cataloguing handbook** : An illustrative guide to the use of AACR2 and LC rule interpretations. [American Library Association]. {DUL}

Akers, Susan Grey, 1944, **Simple library cataloguing**, 3rd edn. [American Library Association]. {BIS}

Akers, Susan Grey, 1954, **Simple library cataloguing**, 4th edn. [American Library Association]. {CRRI DSSW MHA SPA ZHL}

Akers, Susan Grey, 1969, **Simple library cataloguing**, 5th edn. {JNU NASSDOC NMML USIS ZHL}

Akers, Susan Grey, 1977, **Simple library cataloguing**, 6th rev and rewritten edn., ed. by Arthur Curlly and Jana Varlejs. {MHA NIEPA}

Mac Pherson, H.D., 1936, **Some practical problems in cataloguing**. {DUL}

Horner, John, 1973, **Special cataloguing with particular reference to music, films, maps, serials and the multi-media computerised catalogue**. {CRRI ICHR IIC IIT JNU NASSDOC NMML ZHL}

Markley, Arme Ethelyn, and Fruge, Grete W., 1963, **Special problems in classification and cataloguing.** {DUL}

Verona, Eva, 1971, **Statement of principles adopted at the international conference on cataloguing principles,** October 1961, Paris. [IFLA Committee on Cataloguing, London]. {NASSDOC}

Gorman, Michael, 1968, **Study of the rules for entry and heading in the Anglo-American Cataloguing Rules, 1967** : British text. [Library Association, London]. {ZHL}

Anon, 1981, **Subject authorities** : A guide to subject cataloguing. {USIS}

Lewin, Evan, 1967, **Subject catalogue of the library of the Royal Empire Society**. {NASSDOC}

Coates, E.J., 1960, **Subject catalogues** : Headings and structure. [Library Association, London]. {IIT NASSDOC}

Berman, Sanford, 1984, **Subject cataloguing** : Critique and innovation. {JNU}

Anon, 1914, **Supplementary cataloguing rules for the guidance of assistants.** [Imperial Record Department]. {NAI}

Ravilious, C.P., 1975, **Survey of existing systems and current proposals for the cataloguing and description of non-book materials collected by libraries with preliminary suggestions for their international co-ordination.** [UNESCO]. {BIS}

Tauber, Maurice F., et al, 1953, **Technical services in libraries** : Acquisitions, cataloguing, classification, binding, photographic. {IEG NAI ZHL}

Willemin, Silvere, 1966, **Technique of union catalogue** : A practical guide. [UNESCO]. {IIMC NASSDOC NERC}

Girja Kumar and Krishan Kumar, 1977, **Theory of cataloguing**, 2nd edn. {ICHR IIT ISIL JNU MMTC NASSDOC NCAER NCDC NERC NIPCCD ZHL}

Girja Kumar and Krishan Kumar, 1982, **Theory of cataloguing**, 4th edn. {ZHL}

Olligg, P.J., 1966, **Theory of cataloguing** : An examination guide book. {NASSDOC SPA}

French, Ruth, ed., n.d., **Toward a better cataloguing code**. {IEG}

Anon, 1969, **USA standard for permanent and durable library catalogue cards**. (USAS Z 35.1-1969). [American National Standards Institute]. {NASSDOC}

Anon, 1970, **Working papers and proceedings** : DRTC seminar on cataloguing, 1970, Bangalore. [Documentation Research and Training Centre, Bangalore]. {NASSDOC}

See also Subject Headings; Union Catalogues

CATALOGUING : COOPERATIVE

Anon, 1976, **BIBDATA network** : A draft proposal for an Australian national shared cataloguing system. [National Library of Australia]. {JNU}

CATALOGUING : DICTIONARIES

Anon, 1967, **Glossary of cataloguing terms.** (IS : 796-1966). [Indian Standards Institution]. {NAI NASSDOC}

Anon, 1964, **Glossary of cataloguing terms in Indian regional languages.** [Indian Association of Special Libraries and Information Centres]. {NASSDOC SPA}

CATALOGUING OF FILMSTRIPS

Anon, 1963, **Film cataloguing rules**. [Association of Special Libraries and Information Bureaux]. {SPA}

Harrison, Helen P., 1973, **Film library techniques** : Principles of administration. {NMML USIS}

Rehrauer, George, 1975, **The film user's handbook** : A basic manual for managing library film services. {USIS}

CATALOGUING OF MUSIC AND MUSICAL INSTRUMENTS

Anon, 1953, **Cataloguing of musical instruments.** [Government Museum, Madras]. {NAL}

CATALOGUING OF NON-BOOK MATERIALS

Grove, Pearce S. and Clement, Evelyn G., eds., 1972, **Bibliographic control of nonprint media.** [American Library Association]. {NASSDOC}

Aman, Mohammad M., ed., 1980, **Cataloguing and classification of non-Western materials** : Concerns, issues and practices. {IIT}

Anon, 1973, **Non-book materials cataloguing rules** : Integrated code of practice and draft revision of the Anglo-American Cataloguing Rules. [Library Association Media Cataloguing Rules Committee; National Council for Educational Technology, London]. {NASSDOC}

Raviliòus, C.P., 1975, **Survey of existing systems and current proposals for the cataloguing and description of non-book materials collected by libraries with preliminary suggestions for their international co-ordination.** [UNESCO]. {BIS}

CATALOGUING OF PERSIAN LITERATURE

Sharify, Nasser, 1959, **Cataloguing of Persian works including rules for transliteration, entry and description.** [American Library Association]. {JNU NASSDOC}

CATALOGUING OF PHONORECORDS

Anon, 1954, **Rules for descriptive cataloguing in the Library of Congress** : Phonorecords. [U.S. Library of Congress]. {IEG ZHL}

CATALOGUING OF RARE BOOKS

Dunkin, Paul Shaner, 1973, **How to catalogue a rare book**, 2nd edn. {JNU}

CENSORSHIP

Marjorie, Fiske, 1959, **Book selection and censorship** : A study of school and public libraries in California. {JNU}

Misra, Jogesh, 1965, **Censorship** : A literature survey. (University of Delhi, Department of Library Science. Sessional Project). {DUL}

Jones, Frances M., 1983, **Defusing censorship** : The librarian's guide to handling censorship conflicts. {JNU}

CENTRALIZED PROCESSING : LIBRARIES

Leonard, Lawrence E., et al, 1969, **Centralised book processing** : A feasibility study based on Colorado academic libraries. {USIS}

CEYLON

See Sri Lanka

CHAIN INDEXING

Narang, Rita, 1974, **Chain procedure** : An annotated bibliography. {JNU}

Wilson, T.D., 1971, **Introduction to chain indexing.** {BCL ICHR IIT JNU NASSDOC}

CHARGING SYSTEMS : LIBRARIES

Geer, H.T., 1955, **Charging system.** [American Library Association]. {DUL IIFT IIT ZHL}

CHEMICAL LITERATURE SEARCH

See Information Storage and Retrieval Systems : Chemistry

See also Chemistry : Information Services

CHEMISTRY : INFORMATION SERVICES

Wolman, Yecheskel, 1983, **Chemical information** : A practical guide to utilisation. {CRRI}

See also Information Storage and Retrieval Systems : Chemistry

CHICAGO PUBLIC LIBRARY

Martin, Lowell A., et al, 1969, **Library response to urban change** : A study of the Chicago Public Library. [American Library Association]. {USIS}

CHILDREN'S LIBRARIES

Fenwick, Sara Innis, 1975, **Library services for children in New Zealand schools and public libraries** : A report. [New Zealand Library Association]. {JNU}

Ray, Colin, 1979, **Library service to schools and children.** {JNU NIPCCD}

Fenwick, Sara Innis, 1966, **School and children's libraries in Australia**. {JNU}

See also School Libraries

CHILDREN'S LITERATURE

Anon, 1969, **Children's catalogue,** 12th edn. {USIS}

Anon, 1966, **Children's literature** : A guide to reference sources. [U.S. Library of

Congress]. {USIS}

Agrawal, Suren, et al, 1972, **Hindi mein bal sahitya** : Children literature in Hindi since independence, Pratham khand 1947-1960. {NASSDOC}

Rue, Eloise and Laplanie, Effie, 1952, **Subject heading for children's materials.** [American Library Association]. {ZHL}

Khurshid, Anis, 1976, **What children read** : A survey. [National Book Council of Pakistan, Karachi]. {ZHL}

See also Newbery Medal Books

CHILDREN'S LITERATURE : HINDI

Agrawal, Suren, et al, 1972, **Hindi mein bal sahitya** : Children literature in Hindi since independence, Pratham khand 1947-1960. {NASSDOC}

CHILDREN'S LITERATURE : INFORMATION SOURCES

Meachan, Mary, 1978, **Information sources in children's literature** : A practical reference guide. {NIPCCD}

CIRCULATION

See Libraries : Circulation/Loans

See also Charging Systems : Libraries

CITATION INDEXES AND INDEXING

Garfield, E., 1979, **Citation indexing** : Its theory and application in science, technology and humanities. {NASSDOC NIH}

CLASSIFICATION

Anon, n.d., **ABC : Abridged building classification for architects, builders, civil engineers**. [International Council for Building Research Studies and Documentation, Rotterdam]. {BIS}

Tripathi, S.M., 1976, **Adhunik granthalaya vargikaran** : Sidhantik vivechan. (Modern library classification : Theoretical analysis). {BIS}

Lynn, Jeannete Murphy, 1965, **Alternative classification for catholic books.** {DUL}

La Montagne, Leo E., 1961, **American library classification with special reference to the Library of Congress**. {DUL}

Anon, 1967, **Application of international classification of diseases and neurology**. [World Health Organisation]. {JNU}

Langridge, Derek, 1973, **Approach to classification for students of librarianship.** {IIC JNU NASSDOC}

Anon, 1951, **Army medical library classification** : Medicine. {DUL}

Richmond, Phyllis A., 1965, **Aspects of recent research in the art and science of classification**. {DUL}

Jones, Karen Spark, 1971, **Automatic keyword classification for information retrieval**. {BCL BIS NASSDOC}

Ranganathan, S.R. and Neelameghan, A., n.d., **Book science** : Depth classification. {DUL}

Bavakutty, M., 1981, **Canons of library classification**. {JNU NIH ZHL}

Chan, Lois Mai, 1985, **Cataloguing and classification** : An introduction. {JNU}

Eaton, Thelma, 1963, **Cataloguing and classification** : An introductory manual,

3rd edn. {DUL}

Manhieimer, Martha L., 1980, **Cataloguing and classification :** A workshop, 2nd edn. {NASSDOC NIPCCD}

Friedman, Joan and Jeffreys, Alan, 1967, **Cataloguing and classification in British university libraries** : A survey of practices and procedures. [Sheffield University Post Graduate School of Librarianship]. {DUL IIT}

Aman, Mohammad M., ed., 1980, **Cataloguing and classification of non-Western materials** : Concerns, issues and practices. {IIT}

Anon, n.d., **Classification** : Class A : General works, polygraphy, 3rd edn. [U.S. Library of Congress] {CRRI}.

Anon, n.d., **Classification** : class B, 2nd edn. [U.S. Library of Congress]. {ISI}

Anon, n.d., **Classification** : Class H : Social sciences, 3rd edn. [U.S. Library of Congress]. {CRRI}

Anon, 1924, **Classification** : Class J : Political science with supplementary pages, 2nd edn. [U.S. Library of Congress]. {DUL}

Anon, 1922, **Classification** : Class N : Fine Arts, 3rd edn., [U.S. Libray of Congress]. {ISI}

Anon, 1948, **Classification** : Class P : Subclass PG : Russian literature. [U.S. Library of Congress]. {DUL}

Anon, 1915, **Classification** : Class P : Subclasses PNPR, PS and PZ, Literature, [U.S. Library of Congress]. {DUL}

Anon, 1937, **Classification** : Class P : Subclass PQ : Italian, Spanish and Portuguese literature with supplementary pages, part 2. [U.S. Library of Congress]. {DUL}

Anon, 1950, **Classification** : Class Q : Science, 5th edn. [U.S. Library of Congress]. {CRRI}

Anon, n.d., **Classification** : Class R : Medicine : 3rd edn. [U.S. Library of Congress]. {ISI}

Anon, 1948, **Classification** : Class S : Agriculture, plant and animal industry, fish culture and fisheries, hunting, sports, 3rd edn. [U.S. Library of Congress]. {DUL}

Anon, 1952, **Classification** : Class U : Military science, 3rd edn. [U.S. Library of Congress]. {JNU}

Anon, 1927, **Classification** : Class Z : Bibliography and library science, 3rd edn. [U.S. Library of Congress]. {CRRI}

Herdman, Margaret M., 1947, **Classification** : An introductory manual, 2nd edn. {DUL NASSDOC}

Richardson, Ernest Cushing, 1964, **Classification** : Theoretical and practical, 3rd edn. {DUL}

Ranganathan, S.R., 1951, **Classification and communication**. {ISI NERC}

Voegelin, C.F. and Voegelin, F.M., 1977, **Classification and index of the world's languages**. {JNU}

Langridge, D.W., 1976, **Classification and indexing in the humanities**. {DUL JNU NASSDOC ZHL}

Vickery, B.C., 1959, **Classification and indexing in science**. {CRRI DUL IIT NAI}

Foskett, D.J., 1963, **Classification and indexing in the social sciences**. {DSSW IEG IIMC IIT NAI NASSDOC NIEPA SPA USIS}

Foskett, D.J., 1971, **Classification and indexing in the social sciences**, 2nd edn. {BIS ICA JNU NASSDOC}

Ranganathan, S.R., 1950, **Classification, coding and machinery for search**. {DUL}

Bakewell, K.G.B., ed., 1968, **Classification for information retrieval** : Papers presented at an intensive course held in September 1967 at the School of Librarianship. [Liverpool College of Commerce]. {NIH}

Schwerin, Kurt, n.d., **Classification for international law and relations,** 2nd edn. {IEG}

Biligiri, B.S. and Sulochna, C.R., 1973, **Classification for linguistics and languages** : A modified approach based on Decimal Classification. [Central Institute of Indian Languages, Mysore]. {ICHR ZHL}

Cunninghan, Eileen R., 1967, **Classification for medical literature**. 5th edn. {DUL}

Maltby, Arthur, ed., 1972, **Classification in the 1970s** : A discussion of the development and prospects for the major schemes. {AIU IIC JNU NASSDOC NIPCCD ZHL}.

Kelley, Grace O., 1938, **Classification of books** : An inquiry into its usefulness to the reader. {DUL}

Anon, 1960, **Classification of business literature**. [Graduate School of Business Administration Library, Harvard University]. {ISI}

Daniel, Ruth and Mills, J., 1975, **Classification of library and information science**. {DUL}

Anon, 1958, **Classification of type design**. {DUL}

Davison, Keith, 1966, **Classification practice in Britain** : Report on a survey of classification opinion, etc. {DUL}

Anon, 1973, **Classification research** : India, 1968-1973. [Documentation Research and Training Centre, Bangalore]. {BIS}

Kalia, D.R., 1988, **Classification schedule for area studies.** {NASSDOC*}

Anon, 1955, **Classification schedules for printed, microcopy and phonorecord materials in the Reference Department**, 2nd edn. [New York Public Library]. {DUL}

Sigmund, Frauendorter Wein, 1960, **Classification scheme of agricultural science**, 3rd rev edn. {DUL}

Dhyani, Pushpa, 1983, **Classification schemes and Indian libraries.** {DUL IIFT IIT ISI NERC NMML}.

Merril, W.S., 1939, **Code for classifiers**. 2nd edn. [American Library Association]. {BIS CRRI IIT NAI USIS ZHL}

Sachdeva, Mohinder Singh, 1975, **Colon Classification** : Theory and practice. {ICA MHA MMTC NIPCCD}

Ranganathan, S.R., 1970, **Colon Classification for library science.** {DU

Gopinath, M.A., **Colon Classification for macro documents in history.** {DUL}

Neelameghan, A., and Seetharam, S., n.d., **Colon Classification for macro documents in mathematics.** {DUL}

Anon, 1966, **DDC descriptor frequencies**. [Defence Documentation Centre]. {IIT}

Parkhi, R.S., 1945, **The Decimal and Colon Classifications** : A summary and a comparison. {NASSDOC}

Pollard, A.F.C., 1926, **Decimal Bibliographical Classification of the Institut International de Bibliographies**. {BIS}

Parkhi, R.S., 1964, **Decimal Classification and Colon Classification in perspective.** {CRRI IEG IIT ISI NAL NERC NMML}

Raju, A.A.N., 1984, **Decimal, Universal Decimal and Colon Classification** : A study in comparison. {ICA NASSDOC NERC NIEPA SPA}

Ranganathan, S.R., 1953, **Depth classification and reference service and reference material**. [Indian Library Association]. {INSA ISI}

Prasad, K.N., 1983, **Development of terminology in the field of library classification with special reference to Indian school of thought**: A case study in terminology development : Thesis. (Karnatak University). {NASSDOC}

Asundi, A.Y., 1983, **Development of an unified scheme of common subdivisions in general classification systems**. Thesis. [Gulbarga University]. {NASSDOC}

Anon, 1967, **Developments in classification** : DRTC annual seminar, 2 vols. [Documentation Research and Training Centre]. {NASSDOC}

Dewey, Melvil, 1989, **Dewey Decimal Classification**, 20th edn. 4 vols, V. 1. : Introduction tables; V. 2. : Schedules 000-599; V. 3. : Schedules 600-990; V. 4. : Index manual, 20th edn. {NASSDOC}

Baba, Abdul Majid, 1988, **Dewey Decimal Classification, Universal Decimal Classification and Colon Classification** : Development structure, comparison. {NASSDOC}

Ranganathan, S.R., 1945, **Elements of library classification**. {ZHL}

Ranganathan, S.R., 1960, **Elements of library classification**, 2nd ed. {INSA NERC SPA}

Ranganathan, S.R., 1962, **Elements of library classification**, 3rd edn. {BIS CRRI IIT ISI NASSDOC}

Palmer, B.I., 1951, **Fundamentals of library classification**. {BIS CRRI NAI SPA}

Bhattacharya, G., n.d., **A general theory of SIL, POPSI and CLASSAURUS** : Results of current classification research in India. {NASSDOC*}

Anon, 1963, **Glossary of classification terms**. (IS : 2550-1963). [Indian Standards Institutions]. {ISI NASSDOC}

Bardeh, Bertha R. and Denison, Barbara, n.d., **Guide to the SLA loan collection, classification schemes and subject heading lists.** [Special Libraries Association] {DUL}

Anon, 1963, **Guide to the Universal Decimal Classification**. (BS 1000 C : 1963). [British Standards Institution]. {AIU IIT JNU NASSDOC}

Anon, 1977, **Indian trade classification**, 2nd rev edn. [Directorate General of Commercial Intelligence and Statistics, New Delhi]. {TDA}

Anon, 1972, **International standard classification of education** (ISCED) : Three stage classification system, 2pts. [UNESCO]. {AIU}

Wynar, Bohdan S. 1967, **Introduction to cataloguing and classification**, 3rd edn. {IIT}

Wynar, Bohdan S., et al, 1980, **Introduction to cataloguing and classification**, 6th edn. {USIS}

Wynar, Bohdan S., et al, 1985, **Introduction to cataloguing and classification**. (Library Science Text Series). {NASSDOC}

Mann, Margaret, 1943, **Introduction to cataloguing and classification of books**. [American Library Association]. {BIS CRRI ICA NAI NMML SPA USIS ZHL}

Anon, 1965, **Introduction to cataloguing and classification of books**, 2nd edn. [American Library Association]. {IIFT}

Bloomberg, Marty and Weber, Hans, 1976, **Introduction to classification and number building in Dewey**. {IIFT}

Dewey, Harry, 1957, **Introduction to library cataloguing and classification**, 4th rev. edn. {DUL}

Sayers, W.C. Berwick, 1938, **Introduction to library classification**. {NAI}

Sayers, W.C. Berwick, 1950, **An introduction to library classification**. {CRRI}

Sayers, W.C. Berwick, 1958, **Introduction to library classification**, 9th edn. {BIS}

Sardar, Ziauddin, 1979, **Islam** : Outline of a classification scheme. {ZHL}
Qaisar, Mahmood Hasan, 1965, **Islamic sciences** : Expansion of Dewey Decimal Classification (16th edn.) for oriental libraries, {ZHL}
Palmer, B.I., 1971, **Itself an education** : Six lectures on classification, 2nd edn. [Library Association, London]. {NASSDOC NMML}
Shera, Jesse H., 1965, **Libraries and the organisation of knowledge**. {IIT USIS}
Olney, John C., 1963, **Library cataloguing and classification.** {DUL}
Sengupta, B. and Ohdedar, A.K., 1977, **Library classification**. {CRRI IIT NMML}
Parkhi, R.S., 1972, **Library classification** : Evolution of a dynamic theory. {AIU BIS IIT ISI JNU MHA NMML}
Ranganathan, S.R., 1964, **Library classification** : Fundamentals and procedure, with graded examples and exercises. [Madras Library Association]. {BIS}
Dutta, D.N., 1962, **Library classification** : Theory and practice. {IIT}
Gliden, Sophia Hall, 1942, **Library classification for public administration materials.** [American Library Association]. {NAI}
Dutta, D.N., 1978, **Library classification manual.** {IIT ZHL}
Anon, 1985, **Library classification practice** : Unit 2 : Lessons 1-16. [Andhra Pradesh Open University, Hyderabad]. {NASSDOC*}
Anon, 1985, **Library classification practice** : Units 1-13. [Andhra Pradesh Open University, Hyderabad]. {NASSDOC*}
Anon, 1985, **Library classification theory** : Units 1-10. [Andhra Pradesh Open University, Hyderabad]. {NASSDOC*}
Foskett, D.J., 1963, **London education classification.** {University of London]. {IIT}
Savage, E.A., 1949, **Manual of book classification and display for public libraries**. {BIS MMTC NAI NIH SPA ZHL}
Sayers, W.C. Berwick, 1955, **Manual of classification**. {NMML}
Sayers, W.C. Berwick, 1962, **Manual of classification**, 3rd edn. {BIS CRRI IIT JNU NAI SPA ZHL}
Sayers, W.C. Berwick, 1975, **Manual of classification**. 5th edn., ed. by Arthur Maltby {BIS ICA ICHR MMTC NERC NIPCCO NMML ZHL}
Doubleday, W.E., 1933, **Manual of library classification.** {NAI}
Anon, 1955, **Medical classification**, 3rd edn. [Boston Medical Library]. {DUL}
Stevenson, Gordon and Kramer-Greene, Judith, eds., 1983, **Melvil Dewey** : The man and the classification. {NASSDOC}
Stevenson, Gordon and Kramer-Greene, Judith, eds., n.d., **Melvil Dewey** : The man and the classification. {DUL}
Mills, J., 1960, **Modern outline of library classification,** 2nd edn. {BIS CRRI IIT MFL NAI NMML}
Anon, 1969, **National Library of Medicine classification** : A scheme for the shelf arrangement of books in the field of medicine and its related sciences, 3rd edn. [U.S. National Library of Medicine]. {USIS}
Dohlbery, Ingetraut, 1978, **Optical structures and Universal Classification**. {DUL JNU}
Bliss, Henry Evelyn, 1939, **Organisation of knowledge in libraries and the subject-approach to books,** 2nd edn. {BIS IEG USIS}
Needham, C.D., 1966, **Organising knowledge in libraries** : An introduction to classification and cataloguing. {IIC MFL SPA ZHL}
Mohinder Singh, 1969, **Outline of library classification.** {NERC}
Broadffield, A., 1946, **Philosophy of classification.** {IEG IIT}
Anon, 1969, **Physics and astronomy classification scheme**. [American Institute

of Physics]. {IIT}

Girja Kumar, 1965, **Politics, international relations and law** : Scope, methodology and classification. {BIS ICHR IEG IIT JNU MFL MHA NASSDOC NMML ZHL}

Kumar, P.S.G., n.d., **Practical classification**, V.I : Colon Classification. {NIH NIPCCD ZHL}

Uppal, O.P., n.d., **Practical procedure of classification.** {IIMC}

Phillips, W. Howard, 1951, **Primer of book classification,** rev. edn. [Association of Assistant Librarians, London]. {INSA ZHL}

Hulme, E. Wyndham, 1950, **Principles of book classification.** {DUL}

Parkhi, R.S., 1950, **Principles of library classification with special reference to Colon and Decimal Classification**, Pt. 1 : General theory of classification. {CRRI}

Samore, Theodore, ed., 1968, **Problems in library classification** : Dewey 17 and conversion. {ISI}

Hickec, Doralyn J., 1972, **Problems in organising library collections.** {JNU NERC}

Johnson, A.F., 1968, **Programmed course in cataloguing and classification.** {CRRI IIC IIFT IIT INSA NCAER}

Ranganathan, S.R., 1937, **Prolegomena to library classification**. [Madras Library Association]. {CRRI NMML}

Ranganathan, S.R., 1957, **Prolegomena to library classification**, 2nd edn. [Madras Library Association]. {IEG IIMC ISI MFL NAI}

Ranganathan, S.R., 1967, **Prolegomena to library classification**, 3rd edn. assisted by M.H. Gopinath, [Madras Library Association]. {AIU ICA IIC INSA JNU NASSDOC NCAER}

Eaton, F. Thelma and Strout, Donald Everett, eds., 1959, **Role of classification in the modern American library** : Papers presented at an institute conducted by the University of Illinois, Graduate School of Library Science, 1959. {DUL}

Leitch, L. and Billewicz, W.Z., 1963, **Scheme for classification of information on nutrition coded for machine retrieval**. {DUL}

Denison, Barbara, comp., 1968, **Selected material in classification** : A bibliography. {JNU}

Markley, Arme Ethelyn, and Fruge, Grete W., 1963, **Special problems in classification and cataloguing.** {DUL}

Brown, James Duff, 1939, **Subject classification for the arrangement of libraries and the organisation of information**, 3rd edn. {DUL}

Ellinger, Werner B., n.d., **Subject classification of law**. {DUL}

Metcalfe, J., 1959, **Subject classifying and indexing of libraries and literature.** {IEG IIT MFL}

Bliss, H.E., 1936, **System of bibliographic classification**, 2nd edn. {NAI}

Tauber, Maurice F., et al, 1953, **Technical services in libraries** : Acquisitions, cataloguing, classification, binding, photographic. {IEG NAI ZHL}

Davison, Fla Keith, 1966, **Theory of classification**. {ICHR IIT MFL NERC ZHL}

Krishan Kumar, 1979, **Theory of classification**. {BIS ICA ISI JNU ZHL}

Krishan Kumar, 1981, **Theory of classification**, 2nd rev. edn. {NASSDOC NMML}

Krishan Kumar, 1983, **Theory of classification**, 3rd edn. {ZHL}

Srivastava, A.P., 1973, **Theory of knowledge classification in libraries**. {CRRI ICA ICHR IIT JNU NASSDOC NERC SPA ZHL}

Kaula, P.N., 1985, **A treatise on Colon Classification appended with a select bibliography on the scheme.** {NASSDOC NMML}

Dhyani, Pushpa, 1979, **Use of library classification schemes in Indian libraries with special reference to Delhi**. {NASSDOC}

Sehgal, R.L., 1985, **Vargikaran siddhant evam vyavhar**. {NASSDOC}

CLASSIFICATION : BIBLIOGRAPHY

Denison, Barbara, comp., 1968, **Selected material in classification** : A bibliography. {JNU}

CLASSIFICATION : DICTIONARIES

Anon, 1963, **Glossary of classification terms**. (IS : 2550-1963). [Indian Standards Institutions]. {ISI NASSDOC}

See also Classification : Terminology

CLASSIFICATION : TERMINOLOGY

Prasad, K.N., 1983, **Development of terminology in the field of library classification with special reference to Indian school of thought**: A case study in terminology development : Thesis. (Karnatak University). {NASSDOC}

See also Classification : Dictionaries

CLASSIFICATION SCHEMES : BIBLIOGRAPHIC

Bliss, Henry Evelyn, 1977, **Bibliographic Classification**, 2nd edn., ed. by J. Mills {IIT JNU}

Bliss, Henry Evelyn, 1953, **Bibliographic Classification** : Classes L-Z, 3 vols, {CRRI}

Bliss, H.E., 1936, **System of bibliographic classification**, 2nd edn. {NAI}

See also Bliss Bibliographic Classification

CLASSIFICATION SCHEMES : BLISS BIBLIOGRAPHIC

See Bliss Bibliographic Classification

CLASSIFICATION SCHEMES : COLON

Khanna, J.K. and Kapil, D.D., 1982, **Colon Classification**. {CRRI ICHR IIFT IIT}

Ranganathan, S.R., 1939, **Colon Classification**, 2nd edn. {DSSW}

Ranganathan, S.R., 1950, **Colon Classification**, 3rd edn. [Madras Library Association]. {CRRI}

Ranganathan, S.R., 1952, **Colon Classification**, 4th edn. [Madras Library Association]. {ISI}

Ranganathan, S.R., 1957, **Colon Classification**, 5th edn. {DSSW IEG NCAER}

Ranganathan, S.R., 1969, **Colon Classification**, 6th edn., reprinted 1960; 1963; 1964; 1969. {AIU BIS CRRI DSSW GPF ICHR IDSA IIFT IIMC IIT INSA ISI JNU MHA NAL NASSDOC NERC NIPCCD NMML SPA UGC ZHL}

Ranganathan, S.R., 1987, **Colon Classification**, 7th edn. {JNU}

Khanna, J.K. and Bhagal, S.R., 1986, **Colon Classification** : Enumerated and expanded schedules alongwith theoretical formulations. {NASSDOC}

Mohinder Pratap Chand, 1978, **Colon Classification** : Its structure and working. {ISI NERC NMML}

Ranganathan, S.R., 1969, **Colon Classification** : A perview, 7th edn. {JNU}

Neelameghan, A., et al, n.d., **Colon Classification** : Schedule of basic subjects, 7th edn. {DUL}

Bhargava, G.D. and Sood, S.P., 1975, **Colon Classification** : Theory and practice. {CRRI ICA ICHR NIPCCD}

Sachdeva, Mohinder Singh, 1975, **Colon Classification** : Theory and practice. {ICA MHA MMTC NIPCCD}

Ranganathan, S.R., 1970, **Colon Classification for library science.** {DUL}

Gopinath, M.A., **Colon Classification for macro documents in history**. {DUL}

Neelameghan, A., and Seetharam, S., n.d., **Colon Classification for macro documents in mathematics**. {DUL}

Parkhi, R.S., 1945, **The Decimal and Colon Classifications** : A summary and a comparison. {NASSDOC}

Parkhi, R.S., 1964, **Decimal Classification and Colon Classification in perspective**. {CRRI IEG IIT ISI NAL NERC NMML}

Raju, A.A.N., 1984, **Decimal, Universal Decimal and Colon Classification** : A study in comparison. {ICA NASSDOC NERC NIEPA SPA}

Ranganathan, S.R., 1967, **A descriptive account of Colon Classification.** {BIS DSSW DUL ISI JNU NAL NASSDOC NERC NMML SPA ZHL}

Baba, Abdul Majid, 1988, **Dewey Decimal Classification, Universal Decimal Classification and Colon Classification** : Development structure, comparison. {NASSDOC}

Satija, M.P., 1979, **An epostle to dean Shera on the gravity of notation in colon classification**. {NASSDOC}

Mukhopadhyay, Ajoy, 1976, **Guide to Colon Classification practical.** {CRRI ICHR}

Batty, C.D., 1966, **Introduction to Colon Classification**. {ICHR IIFT IIT JNU NASSDOC NMML SPA ZHL}

Navalani, K. and Gidwani, N.N., 1981, **Practical guide to Colon Classification**. {AIU IIT JNU NERC NIEPA}

Parkhi, R.S., 1950, **Principles of library classification with special reference to Colon and Decimal Classification**, Pt. 1 : General theory of classification. {CRRI}

Kaula, P.N., 1985, **A treatise on Colon Classification appended with a select bibliography on the scheme**. {NASSDOC NMML}

Anon, 1967, **Working papers for the symposia** : IASLIC conference, 6th, 1965, Trivandrum, Pt 1-3 : Colon Classification local documentation lists, library organisation and social science research, 1967; Pt. 4 : Colon Classification, local documentation lists, library organisation and social science research, 1967. [Indian Association of Special Libraries and Information Centres]. {NASSDOC SPA}

CLASSIFICATION SCHEMES : DECIMAL

Parkhi, R.S., 1945, **The Decimal and Colon Classifications** : A summary and a comparison. {NASSDOC}

Parkhi, R.S., 1964, **Decimal Classification and Colon Classification in perspective**. {CRRI IEG IIT ISI NAL NERC NMML}

Raju, A.A.N., 1984, **Decimal, Universal Decimal and Colon Classification** : A study in comparison. {ICA NASSDOC NERC NIEPA SPA}

See also Classification Schemes : Dewey Decimal; Classication Schemes :

Universal Decimal

CLASSIFICATION SCHEMES : DEWEY DECIMAL

Dewey, Melvil, 1936, **Abridged Decimal Classification and Relative Index**, 5th. edn.{DEPT ZHL}

Dewey, Melvil, 1959, **Abridged Dewey Decimal Classification and Relative Index**, 8th. edn. {USIS}

Dewey, Melvil, 1965, **Abridged Dewey Decimal Classification and Relative Index**, rev. edn. {USIS}

Dewey, Melvil, 1971, **Abridged Dewey Decimal Classification and Relative Index**, rev. edn. {USIS}

Biligiri, B.S. and Sulochna, C.R., 1973, **Classification for linguistics and languages** : A modified approach based on Decimal Classification. [Central Institute of Indian Languages, Mysore]. {ICHR ZHL}

Anon, 1966, **DDC descriptor frequencies**. [Defence Documentation Centre]. {IIT}

Parkhi, R.S., 1945, **The Decimal and Colon Classifications** : A summary and a comparison. {NASSDOC}

Pollard, A.F.C., 1926, **Decimal Bibliographical Classification of the Institut International de Bibliographies**. {BIS}

Parkhi, R.S., 1964, **Decimal Classification and Colon Classification in perspective**. {CRRI IEG IIT ISI NAL NERC NMML}

Raju, A.A.N., 1984, **Decimal, Universal Decimal and Colon Classification** : A study in comparison. {ICA NASSDOC NERC NIEPA SPA}

Dewey, Melvil, 1989, **Dewey Decimal Classification**, 20th edn. 4 vols, V. 1. : Introduction tables; V. 2. : Schedules 000-599; V. 3. : Schedules 600-990; V. 4. : Index manual, 20th edn. {NASSDOC}

Dewey, Melvil, 1982, **Dewey Decimal Classification** : 301-307, sociology : Expanded version based on edition 19. {NASSDOC}

Osborn, Jeanne, 1982, **Dewey Decimal Classification** : A study manual. {USIS}

Dewey, Melvil, 1935, **Dewey Decimal Classification and Relative Index,** 6th edn. {NAI}

Dewey, Melvil, 1942, **Dewey Decimal Classification and Relative Index.** 14th edn., 2 vols.{USIS ZHL}

Dewey, Melvil, 1951, **Dewey Decimal Classification and Relative Index**. 15th edn.{IEG IIT NAI USIS}

Dewey, Melvil, 1964, **Dewey Decimal Classification and Relative Index.** 16th edn. 2 vols. {CRRI NASSDOC NMML SPA USIS}

Dewey, Melvil, 1967, **Dewey Decimal Classification and Relative Index,** 17th edn., 2 vols. {CRRI NASSDOC NMML SPA USIS}

Dewey, Melvil, 1971, **Dewey Decimal Classification and Relative Index,** 18th edn., 3 vols. {IIMC ISI JNU NASSDOC NIEPA USIS}

Dewey, Melvil, 1979, **Dewey Decimal Classification and Relative Index,** 19th edn., 3 vols. {CRRI ICHR ISI JNU MHA NAI NASSDOC NMML USIS ZHL}

Sharma, Pandey S.K., 1979, **Dewey Decimal Classification for Indology** : Expansion and modification of Dewey Decimal Classification (18) for classifying Indological books with special reference to Indian philosophy and Indian religions. {DSSW ICHR IIC IIT INSA JNU MHA NIPCCD ZHL}

Baba, Abdul Majid, 1988, **Dewey Decimal Classification, Universal Decimal Classification and Colon Classification** : Development structure, comparison. {NASSDOC}

Sharma, Pandey Suraj Kant, 1976, **Expansion and modification of Dewey**

Decimal Classification (18) for classifying Indological books with special reference to Indian philosophy and Indian religions. {NASSDOC}

Dhyani, Pushpa, n.d., **Guide to Dewey Decimal Classification**. {DUL}

Anon, 1962, **Guide to use of Dewey Decimal Classification**. [Lake Placid Club Education Foundation]. {IIT USIS}

Bloomberg, Marty and Weber, Hans, 1976, **Introduction to classification and number building in Dewey**. {IIFT}

Battey, C.D., 1966, **Introduction to the Dewey Decimal Classification**. {IIFT IIT MFL SPA ZHL}

Chambers, Marjori, comp., 1968, **Introduction to Dewey Decimal Classification for British schools**. {DUL}

Batty, C.D. 1971, **Introduction to the eighteenth edition of the Dewey Decimal Classification**. {CRRI IIC JNU NIE USIS}

Qaisar, Mahmood Hasan, 1965, **Islamic sciences** : Expansion of Dewey Decimal Classification (16th edn.) for oriental libraries, {ZHL}

Stevenson, Gordon and Kramer-Greene, Judith, eds., 1983, **Melvil Dewey** : The man and the classification. {NASSDOC}

Stevenson, Gordon and Kramer-Greene, Judith, eds., n.d., **Melvil Dewey** : The man and the classification. {DUL}

Parkhi, R.S., 1950, **Principles of library classification with special reference to Colon and Decimal Classification**, Pt. 1 : General theory of classification. {CRRI}

Dewey, Melvil, 1976, **Selective Hindi Dewey Decimal Classification and Relative Index** tr. by Prabhu Narayan Gour. {DUL}

Gangadhara Rao, P., 1983, **Synthesis in D.D.C., 18th edn.** [Andhra University, Waltair]. {NASSDOC*}

See also Classification Schemes : Decimal; Classification Schemes : Universal Decimal

CLASSIFICATION SCHEMES : FACETED

Vickery, B.C., 1960, **Faceted classification**. [Association of Special Libraries and Information Bureaux]. {CRRI}

Croghan, Antony, 1968, **Faceted classification for an essay on the literature of the performing arts.** {DUL}

CLASSIFICATION SCHEMES : U.S. LIBRARY OF CONGRESS

Matthis, Raimund E. and Taylor, Desmond, 1971, **Adopting the Library of Congress classification system** : A manual of methods and techniques for application or conversion. {DUL}

La Montagne, Leo E., 1961, **American library classification with special reference to the Library of Congress**. {DUL}

Greenberg, Alan M., 1981, **Author index to Library of Congress classification** : Class P, Subclass PN, PR, PS, PZ. {BIS}

Williams, James G., et al, eds., 1972, **Classified Library of Congress subject headings**, 2 vols., V. 1: Classified list; V. 2: Alphabetical list. {IIT JNU NASSDOC NIH}

Immroth, John Philip, 1968, **Guide to Library of Congress classification**. {USIS}

Immroth, John Philip, 1971, **A guide to Library of Congress classification**, 2nd edn. {USIS}

Immroth, John Philip, 1980, **Guide to Library of Congress classification**, 3rd edn., by Lois Mai Chan. {USIS}
Chan, Lois Mai, 1980, **Immroth's guide to the Library of Congress Classification**, 3rd edn. {USIS}
Goodrum, Charles A. and Dalrymple, Helen W., 1982, **The Library of Congress,** 2nd edn. {IIC JNU NASSDOC NMML USIS}
Small, Herbert, 1982, **The Library of Congress** : Its architecture and decoration ed. by Henry Hope Reed. {USIS}
Gurney, Gene and Apple, Nick, 1981, **The Library of Congress** : A picture story of the world's largest library, rev. edn. {JNU}
Anon, 1979, **The Library of Congress** : A portrait of an institution. {USIS}
Cole, John, Y., ed., 1978, **The Library of Congress in perspective** {NASSDOC}
Anon, 1975, **U.S. Library of Congress subject headings**, 8th edn., 2nd vols. [Library of Congress, Subject Cataloguing Division]. {NASSDOC USIS}
Anon, 1980, **Library of Congress subject headings**, 9th edn. [U.S. Library of Congress, Subject Cataloguing Division]. {USIS}
Chan, Lois Mai, 1986, **Library of Congress subject headings** : Principles and application, 2nd edn. (Research Studies in Library Science, No. 19). {NASSDOC}
Anon, 1975, **Library of Congress subject headings** : Quarterly cumulative supplement to the 8th edn. [U.S. Library of Congress]. {NASSDOC}
Anon, 1982, **Library of Congress subject headings** : Quarterly cumulative supplements to the 9th edn., 1979-80. [Library of Congress]. {NASSDOC}
Martin, Nella Jane, 1948, **Subject headings used in the dictionary catalogues,** 5th edn. [U.S. Library of Congress]. {ZHL}
Schimmelpfeng, Richard H. and Cook, C. Donald, 1968, **The use of Library of Congress Classification** : Proceedings : Institute on the use of the Library of Congress classification, 1966, New York. [American Library Association]. {USIS}

CLASSIFICATION SCHEMES : UNIVERSAL DECIMAL

Rigby, Malcolm, 1981, **Automation and the UDC**, 1948-1980, 2nd edn. [International Federation for Documentation and Information]. {CRRI}
Rigby, M., 1974, **Computers and the UDC** : A decade of progress, 1963-1973. [International Federation for Documentation and Information]. {NIH}
Raju, A.A.N., 1984, **Decimal, Universal Decimal and Colon Classification** : A study in comparison. {ICA NASSDOC NERC NIEPA SPA}
Baba, Abdul Majid, 1988, **Dewey Decimal Classification, Universal Decimal Classification and Colon Classification** : Development structure, comparison. {NASSDOC}
Anon, 1956, **Extensions and corrections to the UDC**. [International Federation for Documentation and Information]. {IIT INSA}
Anon, 1963, **Guide to the Universal Decimal Classification.** (BS 1000 C : 1963). [British Standards Institution]. {AIU IIT JNU NASSDOC}
Perreault, Jean M., 1969, **Introduction to UDC**. {BIS IIT ISI JNU SPA}
Caless, T.W., et al, 1970, **Strategies for manipulating Universal Decimal Classification relationships for computer retrieval.** {JNU}
Perreault, Jean M., 1969, **Towards a theory for U.D.C.** : Essays aimed at structural understanding and operational improvement. {ICHR NASSDOC}
Anon, 1961, **UDC**, 3rd edn. [British Standards Institution]. {ICCR}
Bose, H., 1987, **U.D.C.** : Theory and practice. {JNU}
Foskett, A.C., 1973, **Universal Decimal Classification.** {ZHL}

Govrilova, S.A., 1979, **Universal Decimal Classification** : Its structure, application and tables : Revision procedure. [UNESCO; UNION, Moscow]. {NASSDOC}

Kyle, Barbara and Vickery, B.C., 1961, **The Universal Decimal Classification** : Present position and future developments. [UNESCO]. {ICA}

Anon, 1965, **Universal Decimal Classification** : Special subject edition for education. {DUL}

Anon, 1964, **Universal Decimal Classification** : Special subject edition for metallurgy. {DUL}

Sardana, J.L., 1983, **Universal Decimal Classification** : Structure and methodology. {BIS ICHR IIT JNU ZHL}

Anon, 1969, **Universal Decimal Classification** : Ten years supplement to abridged UDC editions, 1958-1968. [UNESCO; FID]. {ICA IIMC IIT NASSDOC}

Anon, 1958, **Universal Decimal Classification** : Trilingual abridged edition. {JNU}

See also Classification Schemes : Decimal; Classification Schemes : Dewey Decimal

CLASSIFIED CATALOGUE

See Catalogues : Classified

CLIPPINGS : BOOKS, NEWSPAPERS, ETC.

Howcraft, B. and Wagner, I., 1980, **Press cuttings** : Cooperative library guide. {ICA}

COLLEGE LIBRARIES

See Libraries : Universities and Colleges

COLON CLASSIFICATION

See Classification Schemes : Colon

COMMEMORATION VOLUMES

See under names, i.e., Deshpande, K.S.; Dewey, Melvil; Downs, Robert B.; Isaac, K.A.; Kamath, V.A.; Kaula, P.N.; Marshall, D.N.; Motilal (Master); Ranganthan, S.R.; Shera, Jesse H.; Sayers, William Charles Berwick, etc.

COMMERCE : INFORMATION SOURCES

Maltby, Arthur, ed., 1968, **Economics and commerce** : The sources of information and their organisation. {NASSDOC}

COMMERCIAL LIBRARIES

Lamp, J.P., 1955, **Commercial and technical libraries.** {BIS}

COMMUNICATION

Mortensen, C. David and Sereno, Kenneth K., 1973, **Advances in communication research**. {NASSDOC}

Ranganathan, S.R., 1951, **Classification and communication.** {ISI NERC}

Mathews, Anne J., 1983, **Communicate** : A librarian's guide to interpersonal relations. [American Library Association]. {USIS}

Rathbone, Robert R., 1972, **Communicating technical information.** {CRRI}

Bolt, A.B. and Wardle, M.E., 1970, **Communicating with a computer**. {NASSDOC}

Johnson, E.D., 1966, **Communication** : An introduction to the history of writing, printing, books and libraries, 3rd edn. {IIC MHA}

Johnson, E.D., 1973, **Communication** : An introduction to the history of writing, printing, books and libraries, 4th edn. {USIS}

De Reuck, Anthony and Knight, Julie, eds., 1967, **Communication in science** : Documentation and automation. [CIBA Foundation]. {MHA}

Penland, Patrick R., 1974, **Communication in science and technology**. {INSA}

McGarry, Keyin J., 1975, **Communication knowledge and the librarian**. {CRRI DUL NASSDOC}

Penland, Patrick R., 1972, **Communication manual for libraries.** {JNU}

Egan, Margret Elizabeth, 1954, **Communication of specialised information.** {JNU}

McGarry, K.J., and Burrel, T.W., 1973, **Communication studies**. {CRRI}

Jackson, Wills, 1953, **Communication theory**. {JNU}

Thayer, Lee, ed. and comp., 1967, **Communication theory and research** : Proceedings of the first international symposium. {NASSDOC}

Agrawal, S.P., gen ed., 1989, **Concepts in communication, informatics and librarianship**. (CICIL series). {JNU NASSDOC}

Anon, 1972, **Content Analysis** : A technique for systematic inference from communications. {NASSDOC}

Berelson, Bernard, 1971, **Content analysis in communication research.** {NASSDOC}

Budd, Richard W., et al, 1967, **Content analysis of communication.** {NASSDOC}

Abramson, Norman, 1985, **Data communication and information exchange network**. (ASTINFONET). [UNESCO]. {NASSDOC}

Ackoff, Rusell L., et al, 1976, **Designing national scientific and technological communication system**. {USIS}

Watson, James and Hill, Anne, 1986, **Dictionary of communication and media studies**. {JNU NASSDOC}

Fhessle, Barbara Ruth, 1965, **Focus on information and communication.** {JNU}

Pool, Ithiel de Sola, et al, eds., 1973, **Handbook of communication.** {NASSDOC}

Wiio, Osmo, 1984, **Information and communication system** : Introduction to the concepts of information, communication and research. {JNU}.

Orr, James Mconnell, 1977, **Libraries as communication systems.** {IIMC USIS}

McGarry, K.J., 1972, **Mass communications** : Selected readings for librarians. {NIPCCD}

Bhattacharya, I.S., 1962, **New trends in scientific communication**. [Indian Association of Special Libraries and Information Centres]. {SPA}

Casey, Robert S., 1958, **Oral communication of technical information.** {CRRI}

Foskett, D.J., 1984, **Pathways for communication** : Books and libraries in the information age. {AIU NIEPA}

Agrawal, Binod C., 1982, **Patterns of communication in international meeting** : A pilot study of tenth international congress of anthropological and ethnological sciences. {NASSDOC}

Powell, Judith W. and Lelieuvre, Robert B., 1979, **People work, communications dynamics for libraries**. [American Library Association]. {USIS}

Anon, 1976, **A register of communications research in Canada,** 1974-1975 : Status report. [Canadian Communication Research Information Centre, Ottawa]. {NASSDOC}

Williams, James G. and Pope, Elspeth, 1976, **Simulation activities in library,**

communication and information science, ed. by Patrick R. Penland. {NASSDOC}

King, Donald W., 1981, **Telecommunications and libraries** : A primer for librarians and information managers. {USIS}

See also Cybernatics; Mass Media; Content Analysis : Communications

COMMUNICATION IN EDUCATION

McGarry, K.J. and Burrel, T.W., 1973, **Communication studies**. {CRRI}

See also Education : Information Services

COMMUNICATION IN SCIENCE

De Reuck, Anthony and Knight, Julie, eds., 1967, **Communication in science** : Documentation and automation. [CIBA Foundation]. {MHA}

Penland, Patrick R., 1974, **Communication in science and technology**. {INSA}

Ackoff, Rusell L., et al, 1976, **Designing national scientific and technological communication system**. {USIS}

See also Scientific and Technical Information

COMMUNICATION OF TECHNICAL INFORMATION

Rathbone, Robert R., 1972, **Communicating technical information.** {CRRI}

Bolt, A.B. and Wardle, M.E., 1970, **Communicating with a computer**. {NASSDOC}

Penland, Patrick R., 1974, **Communication in science and technology**. {INSA}

Ackoff, Rusell L., et al, 1976, **Designing national scientific and technological communication system**. {USIS}

Casey, Robert S., 1958, **Oral communication of technical information.** {CRRI}

See also Scientific and Technical Information

COMMUNICATION RESEARCH

Mortensen, C. David and Sereno, Kenneth K., 1973, **Advances in communication research**. {NASSDOC}

Agrawal, S.P., gen ed., 1989, **Concepts in communication, informatics and librarianship**. (CICIL series). {JNU NASSDOC}

See also Content Analysis : Communication

COMMUNICATION RESEARCH : BIBLIOGRAPHY

Anon, 1976, **A register of communications research in Canada, 1974-1975** : Status report. [Canadian Communication Research Information Centre, Ottawa]. {NASSDOC}

COMMUNITY AND LIBRARIES

See Libraries and Community

COMMUNITY COLLEGE LIBRARIES

Wheeler, Helen R., 1968, **Basic book collection for the community college library.** {JNU}

Anon, 1976, **Community college libraries in the United States.** {USIS}

Vett, Fritz, 1975, **The community college library**. {DUL USIS}.

Wheeler, Helen Rippier, 1965, **The community college library** : A plan for action. {DUL USIS}

Allen, Kenneth W. and Allen, Loren, 1973, **Organisation and administration of the learning resources centre in the community college.** {USIS}

COMPARATIVE LIBRARIANSHIP

Gidwani, N.N., ed., 1973, **Comparative librarianship** : Essays in honour of Prof. D.N. Marshall. {ICHR IIC JNU NASSDOC NIPCCD NMML ZHL}. {NASSDOC}

Danton, J. Periam, 1973, **Dimensions of comparative librarianship.** [American Library Association]. {NASSDOC}

Simsova, S. and Mackee, Monique, 1970, **Handbook of comparative librarianship.** {NASSDOC}

Simsova, S. and Mackee, Monique, 1975, **Handbook of comparative librarianship,** 2nd edn. {BIS IICL ISI NIPCCD}

Mackee, Monique, 1983, **Handbook of comparative librarianship**, 3rd edn. {NASSDOC}

Chandler, George, ed., 1972, **International librarianship** : Surveys of recent developments in developing countries and in advanced librarianship submitted to the 1971 IFLA pre-session seminar for developing countries, August 24—September 1, 1971. [Library Association, London]. {NASSDOC}

Whatley, Allen, ed., 1974, **Proceedings** : International and comparative librarianship group conference, June 28-July 1, 1974, {NASSDOC}

Krzys, Richard, 1983, **World librarianship**. {IIT NMML}

See also International Librarianship

COMPUTER OUTPUT MICROFILM DEVICES

Avedon, Don M., 1971, **Computer output microfilm,** 2nd edn. [National Microfilm Association]. {USIS}

Saffady, William, 1979, **Computer output microfilm** : Its library applications. {JNU}

COMPUTER PROGRAMMES

Mossberg, Thomas, et al, 1976, **ADDLIB** : A packaged computer programme for processing, etc. {JNU NIH}

Spencer, Donlad D., ed., 1968, **Computer programmer's dictionary handbook.** {RTL}

Davis, Charles H. and Lundeen, Gerald W., 1974, **Illustrative computer programming for libraries**. {JNU}

COMPUTER PROGRAMMING

See Programming : Computers

COMPUTER SIMULATION

Abkin, Michael H. and Carrol, Tam W., 1976, **Computer library for agricultural systems simulation** : A progress report. {BIS}

Naylor, Thomas H., et al, 1968, **Computer simulation techniques.** {NASSDOC}

COMPUTERISATION

See Automation; Electronic Data Processing

COMPUTERS

Keren, Carl and Perlmutter Linda, 1985, **Applications of mini and micro computers in information, documentation and libraries.** {JNU NASSDOC}

Tedd, L.A., 1979, **Case studies in computer-based bibliographic information services**. {BCL}

Palmer, Richard Phillips, 1973, **Case studies in library computer systems**. {ISI USIS}

Anon, 1974, **Clinic on library applications of data processing**, 24th, 1974, Illinois. [University of Illinois at Urbana-Champaign]. {USIS}

Bolt, A.B. and Wardle, M.E., 1970, **Communicating with a computer**. {NASSDOC}

Wessel, Andrew E., 1975, **Computer-aided information retrieval**. {BIS CRRI NIH USIS}

Horn, Jack, n.d., **Computer and data processing** : Dictionary and guide. {RTL}

Tou, Julius T. and Wilcox, Richard H., eds., n.d., **Computer and information science** : Collected papers on learning, adaptation and control in information systems. {DUL}

Cox, N.S.M., 1966, **Computer and the library**. {IIT}

Madan, Som Nath, 1987, **Computer and library services**. {NASSDOC*}

Houghton, Bernard, ed., 1968, **Computer-based information retrieval systems**. {DUL INSA NASSDOC}

Anon, 1979, **Computer-based information services in medicines** : A feasibility study : On behalf of the University of Otago medical libraries. [Centerbury Medical Library]. {BCL}

Lynch, Michael Felix, 1974, **Computer-based information services in science and technology** : Principles and techniques. {BCL}

Henley, J.P., 1970, **Computer-based library and information systems**. {BIS IIT JNU NASSDOC NIH}

Henley, J.P., 1972, **Computer-based library and information systems**, 2nd edn. {DUL NIH}

Anon, 1981, **Computer-based national information systems** : Technology and public policy issues. [U.S. Office of Technology Assessment]. {USIS}

Methics, Lorraine M. and Watson, Peter G., 1976, **Computer-based reference service**. {JNU}

Fosdick, Howard, 1981, **Computer basics for librarians and information scientists**. {USIS}

Mahapatra, Piyushkanti, 1985, **Computer in library services**. {JNU NASSDOC NMML}

Abkin, Michael H. and Carrol, Tam W., 1976, **Computer library for agricultural systems simulation** : A progress report. {BIS}

Barron, D.W., 1971, **Computer operating systems**. {NASSDOC}

Katzan, Harry, 1971, **Computer organisation and the system/370**. {NASSDOC}

Avedon, Don M., 1971, **Computer output microfilm,** 2nd edn. [National Microfilm Association]. {USIS}

Saffady, William, 1979, **Computer output microfilm** : Its library applications. {JNU}

Spencer, Donlad D., ed., 1968, **Computer programmer's dictionary handbook**. {RTL}

Dodd, K.N., 1969, **Computer programming and languages**. {DUL}

Dial, O. Eugene, 1968, **Computer programming and statistics for basic research**. {NASSDOC}

Emerick, Paul L. and Wilkinson, Joseph W., 1970, **Computer programming for business and social science**. {NASSDOC}

Leeds, Herbert D. and Winberg, Gerald M., 1966, **Computer programming fundamentals,** 2nd edn. {NASSDOC}

Rajaraman, V., 1971, **Computer programming in Fortran IV**. {NASSDOC}

Anon, 1973, **Computer programming problems** : Batch-I. [National Computer Centre, Manchester]. {NASSDOC}

Wainwright, Jane, 1975, **Computer provision in British libraries**. {JNU}

Williams, Martha E., et al, comps. and eds., 1982, **Computer readable databases** : A directory and data sourcebook. 2 vols. [American Society for Information Science]. {USIS}

Hawkes, Nigel, 1971, **Computer revolution**. {NASSDOC}

Cardenas, Alfonso F., et al, eds., 1972, **Computer science**. {NASSDOC}

Forsyth, Alexandra I., et al, 1970, **Computer science** : Fortran language programming. {DUL}

Naylor, Thomas H., et al, 1968, **Computer simulation techniques**. {NASSDOC}

Swihart, Stanley J. and Heeley, Beryl F., 1973, **Computer systems in the library** : A handbook for managers and designers. {CRRI NASSDOC NIPCCD}

Kumar, P.S.G., 1987, **Computerisation in Indian libraries**. {NASSDOC}

Dolby, J.L., et al, 1969, **Computerised library catalogues** : Their growth, costs and utility. {IIT JNU NMML USIS}

Anon, 1983, **Computerised systems in library and information services**. {NASSDOC}

Philips, G.M. and Taylor, P.J., 1969, **Computers**. {DUL}

Sprowls, R. Clay, 1968, **Computers** : A programming problem approach, rev. edn. {DUL}

Taube, Mortimer, 1961, **Computers and common sense** : The myth of thinking machines. {JNU}

Anon, 1971, **Computers and computation**. {NASSDOC}

Eyre, John and Tonks, Peter, 1971, **Computers and systems** : Introduction for librarians. {IIT NASSDOC}

Rigby, M., 1974, **Computers and the UDC** : A decade of progress, 1963-1973. [International Federation for Documentation and Information]. {NIH}

Avebury, Lord, et al, eds., n.d., **Computers and the year 2000**. [National Computer Centre, Manchester]. {NASSDOC}

Chanana, Charanjit, 1973, **Computers in Asia.** {NASSDOC}

Bowles, Edmund A., ed., 1967, **Computers in humanistic research**. {NASSDOC}

Gopalakrishnan, P. and Narayanan, K.S., 1975, **Computers in India**. {NASSDOC}

Kochenburger, Ralph J. and Turcio, Corolyn J., 1974, **Computers in modern society**. {NASSDOC}

Anger, Arthur L., et al, 1972, **Computers science** : The PL/I language. {DUL}

Sterling, T.D. and Rollack, S.V., 1970, **Computing and computer science** : A first course with PL/I. {DUL}

Plaister, Jean M., 1982, **Computing in LASER regional library cooperation** : London and South Eastern library region. [Library Association, London]. {DUL}

Naur, Peter, 1974, **Concise survey of computer methods**. {NASSDOC}

Jordain, Philip B., 1969, **Condensed computer encyclopedia**. {IDSA}

Westin, Alen F. and Baker, Michal A., 1972, **Databanks in a free society** : Computers, record keeping and privacy : Report. [National Academy of Sciences, Washington]. {USIS}

Clifton, H.D., 1971, **Data processing systems design** : Case studies from the application of computers to business. {NASSDOC}

Rosove, Perry E., 1967, **Developing computer-based information systems.** {JNU}

Corbin, John, 1981, **Developing computer-based library systems.** {JNU}

Bird, E.A., 1972, **Electronic data processing computers for commercial students.** {NERC}

Campey, Lucille H., 1972, **Generating and printing indexes by computer.** [Association of Special Libraries and Information Bureaux]. {CRRI}

Negus, Ron, 1972, **Guide to Computer Bureau Services.** {NASSDOC}

Pritchard, Alan, 1969, **Guide to computer literature** : An introductory survey of the sources of information. {NASSDOC}

Conning, Arthur M., 1983, **Guide to the computerisation of population documentation storage and retrieval systems.** [United Nations]. {NASSDOC}

Anon, 1972, **Guide to selected computer-based information services.** [Association of Special Libraries and Information Bureaux]. {CRRI}

Davis, Charles H. and Lundeen, Gerald W., 1974, **Illustrative computer programming for libraries.** {JNU}

Hill, H.C., 1973, **Information processing and computer programming** : An introduction. {NIH}

Paice, D.B., 1977, **Information retrieval and the computer.** {BCL}

Mitchell, Ruth K., 1971, **Information science and computer basics.** {BIS}

Anon, n.d., **International standards for computers and information processing.** [International Organisation for Standardisation]. {BIS}

Tedd, L.A., 1977, **Introduction to computer-based library systems.** {JNU NIH}

Bergman, Samuel and Bruckner, Steven, 1972, **Introduction to computers and computer programming.** {DUL}

Artandi, Susan B., 1972, **Introduction to computers in information science.** {JNU}

Young, Micki Jo, et al, 1978, **Introduction to minicomputers in federal libraries.** [U.S. Library of Congress]. {USIS}

Baker, C.A., 1977, **An investigation of man-computer interaction in an online bibliographic information retrieval system.** {BCL}

Wolters, Marthin F., ed., 1972, **Key to the computer**, 2 vols. V. 1 : Text book; V. 2 : Training manual. {NASSDOC}

Woods, Lawrence A. and Pope, Nolan F., 1983, **Librarians' guide to microcomputer technology and applications.** {JNU NIEPA USIS}

Smith, G.L. and Meyer, R.S., eds., 1969, **Library use of computers** : Introduction. [Special Libraries Association, New York]. {IIT USIS}

Helms, Harry, ed., 1983, **McGraw Hill computer handbook.** {RTL}

Burton, Paul F., 1986, **Micro computer in library and information services** : An annotated bibliography. {JNU}

Walton, Robert A., 1983, **Microcomputers** : A planning and implementation guide for librarians and information professionals. {JNU}

Rorvig, Mark E., 1981, **Microcomputers and libraries** : A guide to technology, products and applications. [American Society for Information Science]. {USIS}

Anon, 1976, **Minicomputers and bibliographic information retrieval.** [British Library Lending Division]. {BCL}

Grosch, Audrey N., 1979-82, **Minicomputers in libraries**, 1979-80; 1981-82 {USIS}

Anon, 1975, **Papers** : Conference on use of computers in libraries and information centres, 1975, London. [Association of Special Libraries and Information Bureaux]. {CRRI}

Keren, Carl, and Perlmutter, Linda, n.d., **Proceedings** : International conference on the application of mini and micro computers in information, documentation and libraries, March 13-18, 1983, Tel Aviv. {IIT}

Sherman, Philip M., 1970, **Programming and coding digital computers.** {NASSDOC}

Weinberg, Gerald M., 1971, **Psychology of computer programming.** {NASSDOC}

Anon, 1983, **Report** : Asian regional seminar on information sources, systems and services in the social sciences, July 11-22, 1983, Philippines [UNESCO Regional Office, Bangkok]. {NASSDOC*}

Farr, M.A.L., et al, 1973, **Security for computer systems.** {NIPCCD}

Anon, 1982, **Use of computer in libraries** : Summary of the proceedings of a seminar held on March 15, 1982, New Delhi. {NASSDOC}

Anon, 1986, **Workshop on computer application to library and information activities.** [ILA NISSAT]. {JNU}

See also Automation; Computer Programmes; Information Storage and Rerieval Systems; Programming : Computers

COMPUTERS : BIBLIOGRAPHY

Bagley, D.E., 1966, **Computer in libraries** : A selected bibliography. {JNU}

Pritchard, Alan, 1969, **Guide to computer literature** : An introductory survey of the sources of information. {NASSDOC}

Anon, 1968-71, **International computer bibliography,** 1968; 1971. {NASSDOC}

COMPUTERS : DICTIONARIES

Horn, Jack, n.d., **Computer and data processing** : Dictionary and guide. {RTL}

Sippl, Charles J., 1966, **Computer dictionary and handbook**. {NASSDOC}

Sippl, Charles J. and Sippl, Roger J., 1983, **Computer dictionary and handbook,** 3rd edn. {NASSDOC RTL}

Blessum, William T. and Sippl, Charles J., 1972, **Computer glossary for medical and health sciences**. {NASSDOC}

Schmelz, Larry C. and Sippl, Charles J., 1972, **Computer glossary for students and teachers.** {NASSDOC}

Anderson, R.G., 1984, **Concise dictionary of data processing and computer terms,** 2nd edn. {NCERT}

Breuer, Hans, n.d., **Dictionary for computer languages.** {RTL}

Yadubaities, E.A., ed., 1981, **English-Russian glossary of computer systems and networks terminology**. {NASSDOC}

COMPUTERS : DIRECTORIES : GEOGRAPHICAL AREA : INDIA

Haleda; Prithvi, ed., 1983, **Computer directory of India, 1983.** {NASSDOC}

Haleda, Prithvi, ed., 1984, **Computer directory of India, 1984.** {NCERT}

COMPUTERS : PROGRAMMING

See Programming : Computers

CONFERENCES

See Meetings : Proceedings/Reports/Souvenirs

CONSERVATION
See Preservation, Restoration and Storage

CONTENT ANALYSIS : COMMUNICATION
Anon, 1972, **Content Analysis** : A technique for systematic inference from communications. {NASSDOC}
Berelson, Bernard, 1971, **Content analysis in communication research.** {NASSDOC}
Budd, Richard W., et al, 1967, **Content analysis of communication.** {NASSDOC}

CONTINUING EDUCATION
Ellis, Lee Robert, 1966, **Continuing education for adults through the American Public Library, 1833-1964**. [American Library Association]. {USIS}
Sardana, J.L., ed., 1984, **Continuing education for librarians** : Paper : All India seminar for librarians, February 13, 1984, New Delhi. [Indian Library Association]. {NASSDOC}
Stone, Elizabeth W., et al, 1974, **Continuing library and information science education** : Final report to the National Commission on Libraries and Information Science (with bibliography). {USIS}
Stone, Elizabeth W., 1974, **Continuing library education as viewed in relation to other continuing professional movements.** [American Society for Information Science]. {NIEPA}

COOPERATION : LIBRARY
See Library Cooperation

COPYING PROCESSES
See Reprography

COUNTY LIBRARIES
Scheuk, Gretchen Knief, 1954, **County and regional library development.** {NASSDOC}
Carnell, E.J., 1938, **County libraries** : Retrospect and forecast. {CRRI ZHL}
Anon, 1932, **County libraries in Great Britain and Ireland**. [Library Association, London]. {NASSDOC}
Cooke, A.S., ed., 1931, **County libraries manual.** [Library Association, London]. {NASSDOC}
Osborn, Egar and Sharr, F.A., 1950, **County library practice.** [Library Association, London]. {CRRI ZHL}
Sandre, Mildred W., 1942, **County library primer.** {JNU}
Long, Harriet Catherine, 1925, **County library service.** {JNU}
Macledo, Robert D., n.d., **County rural libraries** : Their policy and organisation. {JNU}

See also Regional Libraries

CYBERNETICS
Pask, Gordon, 1975, **Cybernetics of human learning and performance** : A guide to theory and research. {NASSDOC}

Ashby, W. Ross, 1964, **Introduction to cybernetics.** {NASSDOC}

See also Communication; Information Theory

CYRILLIC CHARACTERS : TRANSLITERATION

Anon, 1968, **International system for the transliteration of Slavic Cyrillic characters,** 2nd edn. (ISO/R 9-1968) (E). [International Organisation for Standardisation, Geneva]. {NASSDOC}

DAMAGE/LOSS/THEFT OF BOOKS

Bahr, Alic Harrison, n.d., **Book theft and library security systems**. {BIS JNU USIS}

Goswami, Badri Prasad, n.d., **Problems of misplacement, mutilation and theft of books in libraries**. {JNU}

DATA ARCHIVES

Rokhan, Stein, n.d., **Data archives for the social science**. {DSSW}

Nasatir, David, 1973, **Data archives for the social sciences** : Purposes, operations and problems. {ZHL}

Kapoor, S.K., et al, eds., n.d., **Proceedings** : Conference on organisation of data services in India and user education and training programmes, 13th, 1981, Waltair. [Indian Association of Special Libraries and Information Centres]. {BIS MMTC NIPCCD}

DATA LIBRARIES

See Data Archives

DATA PROCESSING

See Electronic Data Processing

See also Automation

DECIMAL CLASSIFICATION

See Classification Schemes : Decimal

DECISION LOGIC TABLES

McDaniel, Herman, ed., 1970, **Applications of decision tables** : A reader. {NASSDOC}

Anon, 1979, **Decision tables in data processing** : A report. [National Computer Centre, Manchester]. {NASSDOC}

DECISION MAKING

See Administration and Organisation

DELHI

See Geographical Area subdivision under main Descriptor, e.g., Libraries : Geographical Area : India : Delhi

DELHI LIBRARY BOARD

See also Delhi Public Library

DELHI PUBLIC LIBRARY

Anon, 1963, **Delhi Public Library** : Constitution, regulations of Delhi Library Board and rules of the library. [Delhi Library Board]. {NASSDOC}

Gardner, Frank M., 1957, **Delhi Public Library** : An evaluation report. {DSSW DUL}

Anon, 1976, **Delhi Public Library** : Silver jubilee souvenir, 27th October, 1976. {NASSDOC}

Swaran Kumar, 1963, **East and West**. : Delhi Public Library, India, as seen against the background of the Rochester Public Library. {NASSDOC*}

DELHI UNIVERSITY LIBRARY, DELHI

Anon, n.d., **Delhi University Library** : The opening of the new library by S. Radhakrishnan. {JNU}

Gupta, Shamsher, 1973, **Evaluation of Indian reference sources published during last ten years available in Delhi University Library**. (University of Delhi, Department of Library and Information Science, Sessional Project). {DUL}

DENMARK

See Geographical Area subdivision under main Descriptor, e.g., Libraries : Geographical Area : Denmark

DEPOSITORY LIBRARIES

Mechanic, Sylvia, 1971, **Annotated list of selected United States government publications available to depository libraries**. {NASSDOC}

Lane, Margaret T., 1981, **State publications and depository libraries** : A reference handbook. {USIS}

DESHPANDE, K.S.

Khan, H.A. and Ijari, S.R., 1990, **Current problems and trends in library and information services** : Professor K.S. Deshpande felicitation volume. {DUL}

DEVELOPING COUNTRIES

See Geographical Area subdivision under main Descriptor, e.g., Inter-Library Loans : Geographical Area : Developing Countries

DEWEY, MELVIL

Stevenson, Gordon and Kramer-Greene, Judith, eds., n.d., **Melvil Dewey** : The man and the classification. {DUL}

Stevenson, Gordon and Kramer-Greene, Judith, eds., 1983, **Melvil Dewey** : The man and the classification. {NASSDOC}

DEWEY DECIMAL CLASSIFICATION

See Classification Schemes : Dewey Decimal

DICTIONARIES/ENCYCLOPEADIAS/GLOSSARIES

Thompson, Elizabeth H., 1943, **ALA glossary of library terms**. [American Library Association]. {BIS CRRI ZHL}

Thompson, Elizabeth, H. 1971, **ALA glossary of library terms with a selection of terms in related fields**. [American Library Association]. {IIT NASSDOC}

Wedgeworth, R., et al, eds., 1980, **ALA world encyclopaedia of library and**

information services. [American Library Association]. {IIT NASSDOC NCERT NERC USIS}

Turner, Mary C., 1961, **Bookman's glossary**, 4th edn. {DUL}

Peters, Jean, ed., 1961, **The bookmen's glossary**. 5th edn. {NCERT}

Peters, Jean, ed., 1983, **The bookmen's glossary**. 61th edn. {NASSDOC}

Blessum, William T. and Sippl, Charles J., 1972, **Computer glossary for medical and health sciences**. {NASSDOC}

Schmalz, Larry C. and Sippl, Charles J., 1972, **Computer glossary for students and teachers.** {NASSDOC}

Anderson, R.G., 1984, **Concise dictionary of data processing and computer terms,**, 2nd edn. {NCERT}

Stokes, Adrian V., 1982, **Concise encyclopaedia of information technology**. {CRRI JNU NASSDOC RTC}

Tayyab, R. and Chanadana, K., comps., 1985, **A dictionary of acronyms and abbreviations in library and information science**, 2nd edn. [Canadian Library Association, Ottawa]. {NASSDOC}

Watson, James and Hill, Anne, 1986, **Dictionary of communication and media studies**. {JNU NASSDOC}

Camille, Claude, and Dehaine, Michel, 1970, **Dictionary of data processing.** {NASSDOC}

Wittmann, Alfred and Klos, Joel, 1977, **Dictionary of data processing,** 3rd. rev edn. {NASSDOC}

Rogers, Harold A., 1970, **Dictionary of data processing terms** : {UGC}

Trollhani, Lilian and Wittmann, Alfred, 1964, **Dictionary of information processing**, including fields of application. {RTL}

Rosenberg, Kenyon C. and Feinstein, Paul T., 1983, **Dictionary of library and educational technology,** 2nd rev edn. {NASSDOC}

Sharma, Pandey S.K. and Gupta, O.P., 1986, **Dictionary of library and information science** : English-Hindi; Hindi-English. {NASSDOC}

Gunjal, S.R. and Sangam, S.L., 1986, **Dictionary of library and information science** : English-Kannada. [University of Gulbarga, Gulbarga]. {NASSDOC}

Chopra, R.N., 1990, **Dictionary of library scinece.** {JNU}

El-Benhawy, Mohamad Amil, 1970, **Dictionary of library terms** : English-Arabic. {JNU}

Meadows, A.J., 1982, **Dictionary of new information technology**. {IIPA}

Gordon, M., et al, 1984, **Dictionary of new information technology acronym.** {JNU}

Kennlison, W.C. and Spilman, A.J.B., 1963, **Dictionary of printing paper making and book binding**. {DUL}

Goil, N.K., ed., 1973, **Dictionary of pseudonyms in Indian literature.** [Delhi Library Association]. {NASSDOC}

Clason, W.E., comp., 1973, **Elsevier's dictionary of library science, information and documentation**. {JNU ZHL}

Clason, W.E., comp., 1976, **Elsevier's dictionary of library science, information and documentation**, 2nd edn. {IIT}

Bry, Ilse, 1977, **Emerging field of socio-bibliography** : The collected essays of Ilse Bry, comp. and ed. by Lois Afflerback and Marga Franck {BCL IIT}

Woy, James, ed., 1980, **Encyclopaedia of business information sources.** {USIS}

Kruzas, Anthony Thomas, ed., 1974, **Encyclopaedia of information systems and services**. {MHA}

Kruzas, Anthony Thomas, ed., 1978, **Encyclopaedia of information system and services** : A guide to information storage and retrieval services, data base produces and publishers, online vendors, 3rd edn. {USIS}

Kruzas, Anthony Thomas, ed., 1981, **Encyclopaedia of information system and services** : An international guide to computer readable data bases, data base producers and publishers, online vendors and time sharing companies, 4th edn. {USIS}

Schmittroth, John, ed., 1982, **Encyclopaedia of information systems and services**, 5th edn. {USIS}

Eastlick, John T., ed., 1958, **Encyclopaedia of librarianship**. {SPA ZHL}

Landau, T., ed., 1958, **Encyclopaedia of librarianship**, 3rd edn. {SPA ZHL}

Landau, T., ed., 1967, **Encyclopaedia of librarianship**, rev. edn. {BIS CRRI DSSW IAMR IDSA IEG IIT MFL NASSDOC NCERT NIEPA}

Kent, Allen and Lancom, Harold, eds., n.d., **Encyclopaedia of library and information science**, 41 vols. {ACA IOSA IEG IIT INSA JNU NASSDOC NCERT NIH ZHL}

Anon, 1983, **Encyclopaedias and dictionaries of the world.** {NASSDOC}

Hayes, Robert M. and Becker, Joseph, 1971, **Glossary from handbook of data processing for libraries.** {USIS}

Askall, Glaister A., Geoffrey, 1960, **Glossary of the book** : Terms used in paper making, printing, binding book printing and publishing with notes on illuminated manuscripts bibliographies, private presses and printing societies. {DUL}

Anon, 1967, **Glossary of cataloguing terms**. (IS : 796-1966). [Indian Standards Institution]. {NAI NASSDOC}

Anon, 1964, **Glossary of cataloguing terms in Indian regional languages.** [Indian Association of Special Libraries and Information Centres]. {NASSDOC SPA}

Anon, 1963, **Glossary of classification terms.** (IS : 2550-1963). [Indian Standards Institutions]. {ISI NASSDOC}

Anon, 1976, **Glossary of documentation terms**. (BS : 5408-1976). [British Standards Institution]. {CRRI}

Buchanan, Brian W., 1976, **Glossary of indexing terms.** {BCL NASSDOC NERC}

Venkatappaiah, V., 1986, **Glossary of library and information science** : English-Telugu and Telugu-English. [Zilla Granthalaya Samstha, Machilipatnam]. {NASSDOC*}

Gour, P.N., 1980, **Glossary of library science technical terms**. {JNU NASSDOC RTL}

Barrett, W.J., 1961, **Glossary of photocopying terms.** {DUL}

Barrocal, Ramon, 1969, **A glossary of technical service terms for library science students.** [School of Library Science, Syracuse University]. {NASSDOC*}.

Anon, 1967, **Glossary of terms for wooden furniture.** (IS : 4415-1967). [Indian Standards Institution]. {NASSDOC}

Anon, 1974, **Glossary of terms relating to wooden furniture and fixtures**, rev. edn. (IS : 4415-1974). {NASSDOC}

Anon, 1986, **Glossary of terms used in the Public Libraries Department** : English-Telugu. [Government of Andhra Pradesh, Official Language Commission, Hyderabad]. {NASSDOC*}

Horsnell, Verina, 1974, **Intermediate lexicon for information science** : Feasibility study. [Polytechnic of North London]. {BCL JNU}

Rangra, V.K., 1982, **International dictionary of acronyms in data processing, library and information systems.** {CRRI MFL NASSDOC NMML}

Harrod, L.M., 1971, **Librarians' glossary of terms used in librarianship and the book crafts and reference book**, 3rd edn. {CRRI IIT JNU NASSDOC}

Harrod, L.M., 1977, **Librarians' glossary of terms used in librarianship, documentation and the book crafts and reference book**, 4th edn. {ICA IIC MMTC NCDC NCERT NERC NIH NMML ZHL}

Pipics, Zoltan, ed., 1969, **Librarians' practical dictionary in twenty-two languages.** {JNU}

Longley, Dennis and Shain, Michael, 1985, **Macmillan dictionary of information.** {NASSDOC}

Marshall, Faya Dix, 1979, **School librarians' encyclopedic dictionary.** {NIEPA}

See also Thesauri

DICTIONARIES/ENCYCLOPAEDIAS/GLOSSARIES : BIBLIOGRAPHY : GEOGRAPHICAL AREA : INDIA

Anon, 1964, **Bibliography of dictionaries and encyclopaedias in Indian languages.** [National Library, Calcutta]. {ZHL}

DICTIONARY CATALOGUES

See Catalogues : Dictionary

DIRECTORIES

Anon, 1979, **ALA membership directory, 1979-80.** [American Library Association]. {NASSDOC USIS}

Wilson, Brian J., ed., 1968-70, **ASLIB directory** : Information sources in medicine, the social sciences and the humanities. 2 vols. {IIT NASSDOC}

Codlin, Ellen M., ed., 1982, **ASLIB directory of information sources in the United Kingdom**, vol. 1: Science, Technology & Commerce, 5th edn. {JNU}

Dikshit, S.R. and Dikshit, S.D., comps., 1970-72, **All India booksellers and publishers directory, 1970, 1971, 1972.** {ICCR JNU NASSDOC}

Gupta, K.R., 1980-82, **All India directory of book trade**, vol. 1: Libraries; vol. 2; Booksellers and publishers {NASSDOC NCAER NCERT}

Anon, 1973, **American library directory**: A classified list of libraries in the U.S. and Canada with personnel and statistical data. {ICWA}

Anon, 1971, **American national standards for directories of libraries and information centres.** (ANSI Z39.5.-1971). [American National Standards Institute]. {NASSDOC}

Anon, 1987, **Bangladesh public library directory (1972-1986).** [Ministry of Education, Cultural Affairs Division, Directorate of Archives and Libraries, Bangladesh National Library, Colombo]. {NASSDOC}

Haleda, Prithvi, ed., 1983, **Computer directory of India, 1983.** {NASSDOC}

Haleda, Prithvi, ed., 1984, **Computer directory of India, 1984.** {NCERT}

Anon, 1977-79, **Directory**, 1977; 1979. [International Federation of Library Association and Institutions]. {NASSDOC}

Dadzie, E.W. and Strickland, J.T., n.d., **Directory of archives, libraries and schools of librarianship in Africa.** {IIMC}

Anon, 1968, **Directory of booksellers, publishers, libraries and librarians in India, 1968-69.** {SPA}

Khosla, Raj K., ed., 1973, **Directory of booksellers, publishers, libraries and librarians in India**, including who's who, 2nd edn, {ICA IDSA JNU NASSDOC NMML}

Sharma, Jai Kishore, 1973, **Directory of book trade in India**. JNU RTL}

Anon, n.d., **Directory of British publishers**, 1961; 1967. {DUL}

Kapoor, Pran, comp. and ed., 1979, **Directory of business Information research centres in India.** [National Industrial Documentation and Manpower Centre, New Delhi]. {NASSDOC}

Anon, 1971, **Directory of college and university libraries in New York State.** [University of the State of New York; State Education Department]. {JNU}

Anon, 1974, **Directory of co-operative libraries and documentation services.** [ICA, London]. {ICA}

Anon, 1976, **Directory of development documentation and information facilities in Asia and Pacific**. [UN Asian Development Institute, Bangkok]. {IEG IIFT NASSDOC}

Zidoemba, Dominique, 1977, **Directory of documentation, libraries and archives services in Africa**, 2nd edn. [UNESCO]. {JNU NASSDOC}

Anon, 1979, **Directory of educational documentation and information services**, 3rd edn., [UNESCO]. {NASSDOC NIPCCD}

Bhatia, Brajesh, and Goyal, M.M.L., 1971, **Directory of family planning and population libraries in India**. [National Institute of Family Planning]. {NIH}

Krishnamurty, P.G., 1980, **Directory of health science libraries and documentation centres in India**. [National Institute of Health and Family Welfare, New Delhi]. {NIH}

Dhir, S.C. and Anand, S.K., 1979, **Directory of health science libraries in South-Asia**. {NIH}

Barua, B.P. ed., 1986, **Directory of Indian public libraries** : A selected list of libraries. {NASSDOC}

Trivedi, Dinkar, ed., 1973, **Directory of Indian publishers**. [Federation of Publishers and Booksellers Association in India]. {IIPA NASSDOC RTL UGC}.

Anon, 1974, **A directory of information resources in the United States Federal Government, with a supplement of government sponsored information analysis centres**. [U.S. Library of Congress, National Referral Centre]. {USIS}

Anon, 1979, **Directory of information sources in Japan**. {JNU}

Anon, 1985, **Directory of institutions and organisations specialising in children's literature**. [International Board on Books for Young People; UNESCO]. {NASSDOC*}

Khan, Mohammad A.S., comp., 1983, **Directory of Islamic libraries and librarians**. [Islamic Library Association, California]. {ZHL}

Anon, 1979, **Directory of libraries and documentation centres in the United Nations system**. {JNU}

Anon, 1985, **Directory of libraries and information centres in Gujarat**. {Gujarat Granthalaya Seva Sangh, Ahmedabad]. {NASSDOC}

Anon, 1972, **A directory of libraries and library training programme in Thailand**. [UNESCO Regional Office for Education in Asia, Bangkok]. {NASSDOC NIEPA}

Collison, Robert, comp., 1970, **Directory of libraries and special collections on Asia and North Africa**. {NASSDOC NCERT NMML}

Goel, N.K., et al, 1964, **Directory of libraries and who's who in library profession in Delhi.** [Delhi Library Association]. {BIS CRRI DSSW ICCR ICWA

IEG IIC NMML ZHL}

Bhatia, S.K. and Surender Kumar, comps., 1988, **Directory of libraries in Delhi.** {ICA ICCR IIC IIPA JNU NIEPA NASSDOC}

Keeth, Kent H., comp., 1965, **A directory of libraries in Malaysia.** [University of Malaya Library, Kaula Lumpur]. {NASSDOC}

Mwinyimvua, E.A., comp. and ed., 1984, **Directory of libraries in Tanzania.** [National Central Library, Tanzania]. {NASSDOC}

Panwar, Bhanwar Singh and Vyas, Shree Dhar, 1970, **Directory of libraries, publishers and booksellers of Udaipur city and who's who.** {NMML RTL}

Khandwala, Vidyut K. and Naidu, M.K.R., eds., 1965, **Directory of libraries, publishers, booksellers in the city of Bombay**. [SNDT Women University Library]. {NASSDOC}

Gates, Hilary and Brookes, Alison, comps., 1986, **A directory of library and information retrieval software for micro-computers**, 2nd edn. {NASSDOC}

Chopra, H.R., Kumar, P.S.G. and Tejomurty, A., 1988, **Directory of library and information science schools in India**. {NASSDOC}

Berry, John N., ed., 1969, **Directory of library consultants**. {USIS}

Casby, Brinkley, comp., n.d., **Directory of library photo duplication services in the United States, Canada and Mexico**. {DUL}

Sharma, J.K., 1973, **Directory of library schools and lecturers in librarianship in Australia**. {NASSDOC*}

Anon, 1976, **Directory of medical libraries in the British Isles.** [Library Association, London, Medical Section]. {NIH}

Anon, 1988, **Directory of members**. [Micrographic Congress of India]. {NASSDOC}

Huen, P. Lim Pui, comp., 1973, **Directory of microfilm facilities in Southeast Asia**, 2nd edn. {JNU}

Hudson, Kenneth and Micholls, Ann, 1975, **Directory of museum**. {ICCR}

Sivaramamurti, C., 1959, **Directory of museums in India**. [Ministry of Scientific Research and Cultural Affairs, New Delhi]. {ICCR NASSDOC}

Buckner, B.C., comp., 1973, **Directory of population libraries and information centres in the United States**. [Carolina Population Centre, University of North Carolina]. {NIH RTL}

Anand Sagar, comp. and ed., 1986, **Directory of publishers and booksellers in India**, based on actual mailing. [Federation of Indian Publishers]. {NASSDOC}

Woodworth, David, comp., 1971, **Directory of publishers of British journals**. {NASSDOC}

Brownstone, David M. and Franck Irene M., 1982, **The directory of publishing.** {NASSDOC}

Chatterjee, Nihar Kanti, 1980, **Directory of research and special libraries in India and Sri Lanka**, 2 vols. {MMTC ZHL}

Kalia, D.R. and Surender Kumar, 1988, **Directory of scientific and technical libraries in India.** {DUL}

Tapingkae, A., 1974, **Directory of selected scholars and researchers in Southeast Asia.** [Regional Institute of Higher Education and Development, Singapore]. {NASSDOC}

Anon, 1986, **Directory of social science libraries, information centres and data bases in Sri Lanka.** [Sri Lanka Social Science Documentation Centre]. {NASSDOC}

Anon, 1962, **Directory of special and research libraries in India.** [Indian Association of Special Libraries and Information Centres]. {IIT ISI MFL NMML

ZHL}

Anon, 1985, **Directory of special and research libraries in India.** 2nd edn. [Indian Association of Special Libraries and Information Centres]. {ICCR ICWA IDSA IIPA NASSDOC NMML UGC}

Kruzas, Authony T., ed., 1963, **Directory of special libraries and information centres**. {ICCR ICWA IIPA}

Young, M.L. and Young, H.C., eds., 1974-79, **Directory of special libraries and information centres 1974; 1979**. {IIFT}

Young, M.L. and Young, H.C., eds., 1981-83, **Directory of special libraries and information centres 1981 to 1983**. {USIS}

Anon, 1976, **Directory of suppliers of library requisites**. [IDL Chemicals Limited, Hyderabad]. {NASSDOC*}

Anon, 1985, **Directory of United Nations databases and information systems** [United Nations Advisory Committee for Coordination of Information Systems]. {NASSDOC}

Anon, 1980, **Directory of United Nations information systems**, 2 vols. [United Nations Inter-Organisation Board of Information Systems, Geneva]. {MMTC RTL}

Anon, 1983 **Directory of World Bank depository libraries**. [International Bank for Reconstruction and Development] {NASSDOC}

Anon, 1985, **FID directory 1985-86**. [International Federation of Documentation and Information]. {NASSDOC}

Anon, n.d., **IFLA directory** : 1977; 1979; 1982-84; 1984-85; 1986-87; 1988-89. [International Federation of Library Associations and Institutions]. {NASSDOC}

Vashishth, C.P., ed., 1987, **ILA members directory**. [Indian Library Association]. {NASSDOC}

Ranganathan, S.R. and Das Gupta, S., 1951, **Indian library directory**, 3rd edn. [Indian Library Association]. {BIS INSA NASSDOC}

Joginder Singh and Sethi, A.R., eds., 1987, **Indian library directory**, 4th edn. [Indian Library Association]. {JNU NMML}

Anon, 1982, **Information trade directory** : An international directory of information products and services. {USIS}

Anon, 1978, **International bibliography of directories**, 6th edn. {NASSDOC}

Vaillancourt, Pauline M., 1980, **International directory of acronyms in library, information and computer sciences.** {NASSDOC USIS}

Goyal, S.P., 1973, **International directory of dealers of back-sets of periodicals.** {NASSDOC}

Cousineau, Marie Josee, comp., 1986, **International directory of libraries and documentation centres in terminology**. [Documentation Directorate, Ottawa]. {NASSDOC}

Anon, 1986, **International directory of library, archives and information science associations**, 2nd edn. [UNESCO General Information Programme; UNISIST]. {NASSDOC}

Gleiter, Karin, ed., 1975, **International directory of population information**, Pt. 2 : Address list. [Carolina Population Center, USA]. {NIH}

Anon, 1969, **International subscription agents** : An annotated directory, 2nd edn. [American Library Association]. {DUL}

Anon, 1962, **Library service yearbook and directory.** [Punjab Library Association]. {IIT}

Anon, n.d., **New India directory of libraries and educational institutions of India, Pakistan, Burma and Ceylon**. {AIU IIT}

Collison, Robert, n.d., **Scolma directory of libraries and special collections of Africa**, 2nd edn. {IIC IIT}

See also Guides/Handbooks/Manuals

DISPLAY SYSTEMS : INFORMATION
See Information Display Systems

DOCUMENTALISTS/INFORMATION SCIENTISTS/LIBRARIANS : EDUCATION AND TRAINING
See Documentation : Study and Teaching; Information Science : Study and Teaching; Library Education

DOCUMENTARY FILMS
See Moving Pictures : Documentary

DOCUMENTARY MOVING PICTURES
See Moving Pictures : Documentary

DOCUMENTATION : BIBLIOGRAPHY

Schutze, Gertrude, 1965, **Documentation source book.** {BIS DUL MHA NASSDOC NIH}

DOCUMENTATION : DICTIONARIES

Anon, 1976, **Glossary of documentation terms.** (BS : 5408-1976). [British Standards Institution]. {CRRI}

DOCUMENTATION : STUDY AND TEACHING

Brugghen, W. Van Den, 1975, **Syllabus for a documentation course.** [International Federation for Documentation and Information]. {BIS}

Anon, 1972, **World guide to library school and training course in documentation**. [UNESCO]. {ICA IIT JNU NASSDOC NERC NIEPA USIS}

DOCUMENTATION SERVICES

Shera, Jesse H., ed., n.d., **Advances in documentation and library science.** 3 vols. {BIS}

Anon, n.d., **Agricultural documentation** : Responsibilities of libraries and information services. {IIMC}

Weiner, Margery, 1974, **Answering any questions** : How to set up an information office. {BCL DUL}

Keren, Carl and Perlmutter, Linda, 1985, **Applications of mini and micro computers in information, documentation and libraries.** {JNU NASSDOC}

Sharma, Ram Saroop, ed., 1974, **Bibliography and documentation.** {ICHR IIT JNU NIPCCD}

Schuchmann, M., 1958, **Bibliography of standards on documentation.** {BIS ISI}

Anon, 1970, **Bibliography on documentation.** {JNU}

Vasarhelyi, Paul, n.d., **DARE Equal : UNESCO computerised data retrieval system for documentation in the social and human sciences.** {NASSDOC}

Agrawal, S.P., 1989, **Development of documentation in India** : Social science information. {BIS DSSW DUL ISI JNU NAL NASSDOC NERC NMML SPA ZHC}

Hussain, Khateeb M., 1973, **Development of information systems for education.**

{AIU INSA}

Konkar, S., 1985, **Dissemination services provided by special libraries in Pune.** [University of Poona, Pune]. {NASSDOC*}

Bradford, S.C., 1953, **Documentation.** {BCL BIS DUL MFL NAI SPA}

Ranganathan, S.R., ed., 1973, **Documentation** : Genesis and development. {AIU CRRI DUL ICA ICHR IIMC ISI JNU MFL MHA MMTC NASSDOC NIEPA NIPCCD NMML}

Whitehouse, Franck, 1971, **Documentation** : How to organise and control information processes in business and industry. {JNU}

Guha, Bimalendu, 1978, **Documentation and information** : Services, techniques and systems. {AIU BCL BIS IIMC ISI JNU MFL NASSDOC NCDC NERC NIEPA NIH NMML}

Guha, Bimalendu, 1988, **Documentation and information** : Services, techniques and systems, 2nd edn. {DUL ICA IIT JNU MHA NIH NIPCCD ZHL}

Sengupta, Benoyendra and Chatterjee, Mridula, 1977, **Documentation and information retrieval**. {DUL MHA ZHL}

Perry, J.W. and Kent, Allen, n.d., **Documentation and information retrieval** : An information to basic principle and cost analysis. {JNU}

Ranganathan, S.R., 1963, **Documentation and its facets** : Being a symposium of seventy papers by thirty-two authors. {BIS DUL DSSW IIFT JNU NMML SPA}

Shera, Jesse H., 1966, **Documentation and the organisation of knowledge**, ed. by D.J. Foskett. {DUL NASSDOC NMML USIS}

Aggarwal, J.C. and Agrawal, S.P., 1990, **Documentation encyclopaedia of UNESCO and education.** {NIEPA}

Shera, Jesse, H., et al, 1956, **Documentation in action**. {BIS DUL NASSDOC}

Kesavan, B.S. 1968, **Documentation in India**. {JNU}

Anon, 1961, **Documentation, indexing and retrieval of scientific information.** [US Committee on Government Operations]. {JNU}

Haworth, Carol S., 1964, **Documentation of semi-automatic bibliographic information retrieval**. {JNU}

Anon, 1980, **Documentation services in departmental libraries** : Papers : All India library convention, 2nd, March 3-6, 1980, New Delhi. [Government of India Librarians Association]. {CRRI NASSDOC NMML}

Asija, S., 1988, **Documentation services in India** : An overview of some selected documentation centres. {NASSDOC}

Schutze, Gertrude, 1965, **Documentation source book**. {BIS DUL MHA NASSDOC NIH}

Gray, Max, 1969, **Documentation standards**. {BIS DUL NIEPA}

Rubin, Martin L., ed., 1979, **Documentation standards and procedures for on-line systems**. {CRRI}

Anon, 1951, **Documentation techniques in the USA**. [Organisation for Economic Co-operation and Development, Paris]. {ISI}

Kempe, Mary E., 1977, **Documentation training needs in Eastern Africa**. {ICA}

Clason, W.E., comp., 1973, **Elsevier's dictionary of library science, information and documentation**. {JNU ZHL}

Anon, 1980, **Essential problems in terminology for informatics and documentation**. [International Federation for Documentation and Information]. {BIS CRRI}

Anon, 1978, **FID congress on new trends in documentation and information, 1978, Edinburg**. [International Federation of Documentation and Information]

{CRRI}

Kawatra, P.S., 1984, **Fundamentals of documentation** : With special reference to India. {DSSW DUL ICA ISI NCDC NMML}

Guinchat, Claire and Menou, Michel, 1983, **General introduction to the techniques of information and documentation work.** [UNESCO]. {JNU NMML}

Anon, 1976, **Glossary of documentation terms.** (BS : 5408-1976). [British Standards Institution]. {CRRI}

Elliott, C.K., 1971, **Guide to the documentation of psychology.** {NIH}

Anon, 1975, **Guidelines for the evaluation of training courses, workshops and seminars in scientific and technical information and documentation.** [UNESCO]. {NASSDOC}

Foubert, Charles Henri, 1982, **The IDOC documentation handbook.** [IDOC]. {NASSDOC}

Smith, J.C. and Hisson, N.J., 1965, **Information maintenance system documentation.** {JNU}

Jell, Hans and Machesney, Robert, 1965, **International bibliography of non-periodical literature on documentation and information.** {JNU}

Anon, 1972, **International standardisation of library and documentation techniques.** [UNESCO]. {ICA}

Anon, n.d., **International standards for documentation and terminology**, 3rd edn. [International Organisation for Standardisation]. {BIS}

Chakrabarti, A.K., 1980, **An introduction to documentation science.** {NASSDOC}

Mikhailov, A.I. and Giljarevaskij, R.S., n.d., **Introductory course in informatics/documentations.** [UNESCO]. {DUL NASSDOC}

Coblans, Herbert, 1974, **Librarianship and documentation** : An international perspective. {BIS ICHR ISI NASSDOC NERC}

Chandler, George, 1972, **Libraries, documentation and bibliography in the USSR, 1917-1971** : Survey and critical analysis of Soviet studies. {JNU NASSDOC}

Anon, 1964, **Looking forward in documentation.** [Association of Special Libraries and Information Bureaux]. {BIS}

Frank, O., ed., 1961, **Modern documentation and information practices** : A basic manual. [International Federation for Documentation and Information]. {BIS DUL ICA NASSDOC NIEPA}

Whatmore, Geoffrey, n.d., **Modern news library** : Documentation of current affairs in newspaper and broadcasting libraries. {IIMC}

Muhammad, Riaz, 1989, **Modern techniques of documentation and information work.** {NASSDOC}

Boaz, Martha, ed., 1959, **Modern trends in documentation.** {ISI}

Carter, Launor F., et al, 1967, **National document handling systems for science and technology.** {BIS IIMC NIH USIS}

Anon, n.d., **National Documentation Centre on Mass Communication** : Report. [Ministry of Information and Broadcasting, New Delhi]. {IIMC}

Mahajan, S.G. and Riswadker, M.R., 1984, **National seminar on social science documentation in India.** {JNU}

Loosjes, T.P., 1973, **On documentation of scientific literature.** {JNU}

Taraboi, Vasile, 1973, **Organisation, functioning and activities of national documentary information systems in the scientific, technical and economic fields.** [National Institute for Scientific and Technical Information and Documentation, Romania]. {BIS}

Boaz, Martha, ed., n.d., **Papers** : Symposium on modern trends in documentation, 1958, California. {CRRI}

Kashyap, S.C., 1986, **Parliaments and information dissemination**. {NASSDOC}

Stibic, V., 1983, **Personal documentation for professionals** : Means and methods. {JNU}

D'Olier, J.H. and Delmas, B., 1975, **Planning national infrastructures for documentation, libraries and archives** : Outline of a general policy. {DUL IIMC JNU NASSDOC NIEPA}

Penna, C.V. and Sewell, P.H., 1967, **The planning of library and documentation services**. [UNESCO]. {AIU ICA NIEPA SPA}

Anon, 1966, **Practical approach to information and data retrieval**. [Boston Industrial Education Institute]. {ISI}

Sood, S.P. and Jotwani, D., 1981, **Pralekhan** {JNU NASSDOC}.

Saunders, W.L., ed., 1966, **Provision and use of library and documentation services** : Some contributions. [University of Sheffield Postgraduate School of Librarianship]. {DUL JNU MHA NIH SPA USIS}

Scheele, Martin, 1961, **Punch-card methods in research and documentation with special reference to biology**. {CRRI DUL IIMC NASSDOC}

Anon, 1988, **Selective inventory of social science information and documentation services**, 3rd edn. [UNESCO Social and Human Sciences Documentation Centre]. {NASSDOC}

Agrawal, S.P., 1987, **Social science information and documentation** : Search and relevance in India. {BIS DUL JNU NASSDOC NIH NIEPA NMML ZHL}

Narula, Manju, 1973, **State of the art report on social science documentation in India**. {JNU}

Anon, 1974, **Status of documentation in India**. [Indian National Scientific Documentation Centre, New Delhi]. {JNU}

Anon, 1973, **Study on national structures for documentation and library services in countries with different levels of development, with particular reference to the needs of developing countries**. [UNESCO]. {ICA}

Brugghen, W. Van Den, 1975, **Syllabus for a documentation course**. [International Federation for Documentation and Information]. {BIS}

Wersig, Gernot and Neveling, Ulrich, comps., 1976, **Terminology of documentation**. [UNESCO]. {JNU NASSDOC NIPCCD ZHL}

Anon, 1970, **Training course in documentation techniques in Asia, July 20—August 21, 1970, Tokyo**. [Japanese National Commission for UNESCO]. {NASSDOC}

Anon, 1970, **Users of documentation**. {JNU}

Anon, 1975, **World guide to technical information and documentation services**, 2nd edn. [UNESCO]. {JNU NASSDOC}

See also Abstracting and Indexing Services; Information Services; Information Storage and Retrival Systems

DOWNS, ROBERT B.

Orne, Jerrold, ed., 1971, **Research librarianship** : Essays in honour of Robert B. Downs. {JNU NASSDOC USIS}

DUPLICATION OF CATALOGUING CARDS

See Catalogue Cards : Reproduction

EARLY PRINTED BOOKS
See Bibliography and Bibliographical Control : Early Printed Books

EAST AFRICAN SCHOOL OF LIBRARIANSHIP
Saith, S.S., 1968, **East African School of Librarianship.** [UNESCO]. {NASSDOC*}

ECOLOGY : ABSTRACTING AND INDEXING
Kesarwani, S.K. and Bhat, S.G. eds., n.d., **Abstracting, indexing and current awareness services in environmental science.** {INSA}

ECONOMIC ANALYSIS : LIBRARIES
Anon, n.d., **Economic analysis of special libraries with special reference to CSIR libraries**, memeo short bibliography. {NASSDOC}

ECONOMIC DEVELOPMENT : INFORMATION SERVICES
Anon, 1976, **Directory of development documentation and information facilities in Asia and Pacific**. [UN Asian Development Institute, Bangkok]. {IEG IIFT NASSDOC}

ECONOMICS : INFORMATION SOURCES
Maltby, Arthur, ed., 1968, **Economics and commerce** : The sources of information and their organisation. {NASSDOC}

EDUCATION : BIBLIOGRAPHY
Anon, 1972, **Education, library science, journalism** : A bibliography of doctoral dissertations, 1857-1970. [Inter-University Board of India and Ceylon, New Delhi]. {JNU NMML}
Hutchins, Robert M., 1954, **Great books** : The foundation of liberal education. {USIS}

EDUCATION : INFORMATION SERVICES
Anon, 1979, **Directory of educational documentation and information services**, 3rd edn., [UNESCO]. {NASSDOC NIPCCD}
Anon, 1983, **Educational information** : Problems, issues and strategies for resolving them : Report

EDUCATION AND LIBRARIES
See Libraries and Education

EDUCATION FOR LIBRARIANSHIP
See Library Education

EDUCATIONAL RESEARCH
Isaac, Stephen and Michael, William B, 1972, **Handbook in research and evaluation** : A collection of principles, methods and strategies useful in the planning, design and evaluation of studies in education and the behavioural sciences. {NASSDOC}

ELECTRONIC DATA PROCESSING

Avery, Louis and Hulthciss, S.C., 1962, **Advanced data processing in university library.** {JNU}

Awad, Elias M., 1966, **Automatic data processing** : Principle procedures. {JNU}

Saxon, James A. and Stayer, Wesley W., 1967, **Basic principles of data processing**. {JNU}

Anon, 1974, **Clinic on library applications of data processing**, 24th, 1974, Illinois. [University of Illinois at Urbana-Champaign]. {USIS}

Horn, Jack, n.d., **Computer and data processing** : Dictionary and guide. {RTL}

Williams, Martha E., et al, comps. and eds., 1982, **Computer readable databases** : A directory and data sourcebook. 2 vols. [American Society for Information Science]. {USIS}

Anderson, R.G., 1984, **Concise dictionary of data processing and computer terms,**, 2nd edn. {NCERT}

Westin, Alen F. and Baker, Michal A., 1972, **Databanks in a free society** : Computers, record keeping and privacy : Report. [National Academy of Sciences, Washington]. {USIS}

Abramson, Norman, 1985, **Data communication and information exchange network.** (ASTINFONET). [UNESCO]. {NASSDOC}

Schnake, M.A., 1973, **Data-processing concepts.** {NASSDOC}

Harper, William L., 1973, **Data processing documentation** : Standards, procedures and applications. {USIS}

Harvey, John, M., 1966, **Data-processing in public and university libraries.** {DUL IIT}

Clifton, H.D., 1971, **Data processing systems design** : Case studies from the application of computers to business. {NASSDOC}

Jolley, J.L., 1968, **Data university.** {JNU}

Bird, E.A., 1972, **Electronic data processing computers for commercial students.** {NERC}

De Rossi, Claude J., 1975, **Exploring the world of data processing.** {NASSDOC}

Rubin, Martin L., 1970-71, **Handbook of data management**, 6 vols, vol 1 : Introduction to the system life cycle; vol 2 : System life cycle standards; vol. 3 : System life cycle standards forms methods, by Peter Zuckerman; vol 4 : Advanced technology input and output; vol. 5 : Advanced technology systems concepts; vol. 6 : Data processing administration. {NASSDOC}

Hayes, Robert M. and Becker, Joseph, 1970, **Handbook of data processing for libraries** : A comprehensive guide to the use of modern data processing equipment in libraries. {CRRI IIT INSA NASSDOC NCAER NIH NMML USIS}

Hayes, Robert M. and Becker, Joseph, 1974, **Handbook of data processing for libraries**, 2nd edn. {BIS CRRI DUL ISI JNU USIS}

Rubin, Martin L., 1970-71, **Handbook of data processing management,** 6 vols. {NASSDOC}

Anon, 1970, **International seminar on electronic data processing in libraries, Regersburg**. {JNU}

Price, Wilson T., 1972, **Introduction to data processing**. {JNU}

Wendel, Thomas M. and Williams, William H., 1969, **Introduction to data processing and COBOL**. {NASSDOC}

Melin, Johns, **Libraries and data processing** : Where do we stand. {JNU}

Evans, Lynn, 1976, **Merging of databases for the production of secondary information publications** : Phase-1. {BCL}

Arnold, Robert R., et al, 1972, **Modern data processing,** 2nd edn. {NASSDOC}

Hall, James L. and Brown, Marjorie J., 1981, **On-line bibliographic databases** : An international directory, 2nd edn. [Association of Special Libraries and Information Bureaux]. {USIS}

Martin, James, 1982, **Principles of data-base management.** {NASSDOC}

Vanners, Robert G., 1965, **Principles of punched card data processing.** {JNU}

See also Artificial Intelligence; Online Data Processing; Programming : Computers

ELECTRONIC DATA PROCESSING : DICTIONARIES

Camille, Claude, and Dehaine, Michel, 1970, **Dictionary of data processing.** {NASSDOC}

Wittmann, Alfred and Klos, Joel, 1977, **Dictionary of data processing**, 3rd. rev edn. {NASSDOC}

Rogers, Harold A., 1970, **Dictionary of data processing terms** : {UGC}

Trollhani, Lilian and Wittmann, Alfred, 1964, **Dictionary of information processing**, including fields of application. {RTL}

Hayes, Robert M. and Becker, Joseph, 1971, **Glossary from handbook of data processing for libraries.** {USIS}

ELECTRONIC DATA PROCESSING : GEOGRAPHICAL AREA : GREAT BRITAIN

Anon, 1972, **Scope for automatic data processing in the British library**, 2 pts. [Department of Education and Science, Great Britain]. {NASSDOC}

ELECTRONIC DATA PROCESSING : GEOGRAPHICAL AREA : INDIA

Kapoor, S.K., et al, eds., 1981, **Organisation of data services in India.** [Indian Association of Special Libraries and Information Centres]. {NASSDOC}

ELECTRONIC DATA PROCESSING : PUBLIC ADMINISTRATION

Anon, 1973, **Automated information management in public administration** : Present development and impacts. [Organisation of Economic Co-operation and Development, Paris]. {TDA}

ENGINEERING : INFORMATION SERVICES

Anon, 1978, **Papers** : Seminar on information for engineering industry, February 10, 1978, New Delhi. [Association of Engineering Industry; Indian National Scientific Documentation Centre, New Delhi]. {BIS}

ENGINEERING : LIBRARIES

Mount, Ellis, 1975, **University science and engineering libraries** : Their operations, collections and facilities. {CRRI IIT}

EXCHANGES : PUBLICATIONS : LITERARY AND SCIENTIFIC

Anon, 1956, **Handbook on the international exchange of publications.** [UNESCO]. {CRRI IEG}

EXPERIMENTAL DESIGN

John, Peter W., 1971, **Statistical design and analysis of experiments.** {NASSDOC}

FACETED CLASSIFICATION
See Classification Schemes : Faceted

FARMINTON PLAN

Williams, Edwin Everitt, 1953. **Farminton plan handbook**. [Association of Research Libraries]. {USIS}

FEDERAL REPUBLIC OF GERMANY
See Germany

FESTSCHRIFT
See under names, i.e., Deshpande, K.S.; Dewey, Melvil; Downs, Robert B.; Isaac, K.A.; Kamath, V.A.; Kaula, P.N.; Marshall, D.N.; Motilal (Master); Ranganathan, S.R.; Shera, Jesse H.; Sayers, William Charles Berwick, etc.

FILES AND FILING : DOCUMENTATION
See Filing

FILING
Anon, 1980, **ALA filing rules**. [American Library Association]. {USIS}
Anon, 1942, **ALA rules for filing catalogue cards**. [American Library Association]. {CRRI IIT}
Seely, Pauline A., ed., 1968, **ALA rules for filing catalogue cards,** 2nd. edn. [American Library Association]. {BIS IIT JNU NIEPA NMML USIS}
Collison, Robert L., 1950, **Cataloguing arrangement and filing of special material in special libraries.** {NAL}
Alexs, Phillip, 1935, **Filing and preserving stock and records,** in libraries and other institutions including museums and art galleries. {JNU}
Anon, 1956, **Filing rules for dictionary catalogues of the Library of Congress.** [U.S. Library of Congress]. {IEC NASSDOC}
Continolo, G., n.d., **Modern filing methods and equipment.** {IIMC}
Duke, Richard D., 1961, **Personal filing system for the professional concerned with community planning.** {SPA}
Anon, 1962, **Practice for alphabetical arrangement**. (IS : 382-1952). [Indian Standards Institution]. {NAI NASSDOC}
Anon, n.d., **Specification for alphabetical arrangement and the filing order of numerals and symbols**. (BS 1749 : 1969). [British Standards Institution]. {CRRI NASSDOC}
Anon, n.d., **Specification for drawing filling equipment,** rev. edn. (IS : 2695-1974). [Indian Standards Institution]. {NASSDOC}

See also Alphabetization

FILING SYSTEMS
See Filing

FOLKLORE LIBRARIES
Mahapatra, Piyushkanti, 1966, **Folklore library**. {IIMC NASSDOC NMML}

FOREIGN TRADE LIBRARY
Sircar, Pankti, 1970, **Evaluation of the acquisition policy and procedure of periodicals in the Indian Institute of Foreign Trade Library and Rattan Tata**

Library. {DUL}

GILA

=Government of India Librarians Association (*now* Association of Government Librarians and Information Scientists)

GERMANY

See Geographical Area subdivision main Descriptor, e.g.,
Libraries : Geographical Area : Germany

GOVERNMENT LIBRARIES

Stockham, K.A., n.d., **The government and control of libraries**, 2nd edn. {DUL ICHR}

Narasimharao, K.V.V.L., 1988, **Handbook of AP Government Oriental Manuscripts Library and Research Institute.** [Andhra Pradesh Government Oriental Manuscripts Library and Institute, Hyderabad], {NASSDOC*}

Jain, M.K., 1990, **Handbook of government libraries.** {CRRI}

GOVERNMENT OF INDIA LIBRARIANS ASSOCIATION

See Association of Government Librarian and Information Science

GOVERNMENT PUBLICATIONS

Harleston, Robekah M. and Stoffle, Carla J., 1974, **Administration of government documents collections.** {USIS}

Anon, 1941, **Author entry for government publications.** [U.S. Library of Congress]. {NAI}

Pemberion, John E., 1982, **Bibliographic control of official publications.** {IIT}

Mc Lilvaine, Betsy, 1983, **A consumers', researchers' and students' guide to government publications**. {USIS}

Fry, Bernard, 1979, **Government publications** : Their role in the national programme for library and information services. [U.S. National Commission on Libraries and Information Science]. {USIS}

Schmeckebier, K.F. and Eastin, R.B., 1961, **Government publications and their use**, rev edn. {MFL}

Brown, Everett S., 1950, **Manual of government publications** : United States and foreign. {CRRI}

Wilcox, Jerome K., ed., 1940, **Manual on the use of the state publications.** [American Library Association]. {CRRI}

O'Hara, Frederick J., ed., 1973, **Reader in government documents.** {NASSDOC}

Lane, Margaret T., 1981, **State publications and depository libraries** : A reference handbook. {USIS}

GOVERNMENT PUBLICATIONS : GEOGRAPHICAL AREA : AUSTRALIA

Anon, n.d., **Australian government publications, 1974-82.** [National Library of Australia]. {NASSDOC}

GOVERNMENT PUBLICATIONS : GEOGRAPHICAL AREA : GREAT BRITAIN

Margen, A. Marry, ed., 1973, **British government publications** : An index to chairmen and authors, 1941-1960. [Library Association, London]. {NASSDOC}

Pemberton, John E., 1971, **British official publications.** {NASSDOC}

Anon, 1970-71, **Catalogue of government publications.** [HMSO, Great Britain].

{NASSDOC}

Rodgers, Frank, comp., 1971, **Serial publications in the British Parliamentary papers, 1900-1968** : A bibliography. [American Library Association]. {NASSDOC}

GOVERNMENT PUBLICATIONS : GEOGRAPHICAL AREA : INDIA

Anon, 1959, **Catalogue of Government of India civil publications** : Subject-wise arranged corrected up to 31st December, 1959. [Controller of Publications Delhi]. {NASSDOC NIPCCD}

Anon, n.d., **Catalogue of Government of India civil publications** : Subject-wise arranged corrected up to 31st December, 1959 : Supplement for the years 1968-70. [Controller of Publications, Delhi]. {IIFT ISI NASSDOC TDA}

Anon, 1977, **Catalogue of Government of India civil publications** : Subject-wise arranged, corrected up to 31st December, 1977, 8th supplement for the year 1977. {MMTC}

Anon, 1967, **Catalogue of publications issued by Government of Uttar Pradesh and obtainable from the book depot, Government Press, Allahabad, for the year ending, 1965-66** : Corrected up to September, 1966. {NASSDOC}

Mohinder Singh, 1982, **Government of India publications.** {MHA}

Fry, Bernard, 1979, **Government publications** : Their role in the national programme for library and information services. [U.S. National Commission on Libraries and Information Science]. {USIS}

Schmeckebier, K.F. and Eastin, R.B., 1961, **Government publications and their use**, rev edn. {MFL}

Mohinder Singh, 1967, **Government publications of India** : A survey of their nature, bibliographical control and distribution systems. {MFL NASSDOC NIPCCD}

Anon, 1967, **List of official publications not included in the general catalogue of Government of India publications issued during the period 1-1-1940 to 31-12-1960.** {NASSDOC}

GOVERNMENT PUBLICATIONS : GEOGRAPHICAL AREA : INDIA : UTTAR PRADESH

Anon, 1967, **Catalogue of publications issued by Government of Uttar Pradesh and obtainable from the book depot, Government Press, Allahabad, for the year ending, 1965-66** : Corrected up to September, 1966. {NASSDOC}

GOVERNMENT PUBLICATIONS : GEOGRAPHICAL AREA : USA

Mechanic, Sylvia, 1971, **Annotated list of selected United States government publications available to depository libraries.** {NASSDOC}

GREAT BRITAIN

See Geographical Area subdivision under main Descriptor, e.g., Information Services : Geographical Area : Great Britain

GREEK CHARACTERS : TRANSLITERATION

Anon, 1968, **International system for the transliteration of Greek characters into Latin characters.** (ISO/R 843-1968) (E). [International Organisation for Standardisation, Geneva]. {NASSDOC}

GUIDES/HANDBOOKS/MANUALS

Anon, 1979, **ALA handbook of organisation, 1979-80.** [American Library Association]. {NASSDOC USIS}

Anon, 1978, **BSO manual** : The development, rationale and use of broad system of ordering. [International Federation for Documentation and Information] {CRRI}

Sippl, Charles J., 1966, **Computer dictionary and handbook.** {NASSDOC}

Sippl, Charles J. and Sippl, Roger J., 1983, **Computer dictionary and handbook,** 3rd edn. {NASSDOC RTL}

Pacay, Philip, 1977, **ED art library manual** : A guide to resources and practice. {IIT}

Williams, Edwin Everitt, 1953. **Farminton plan handbook.** [Association of Research Libraries]. {USIS}

Pry, Barnard M. and Mohrarot, Foster E., 1963, **Guide to information sources in space science and technology.** {DUL}

Winchell, C.M., 1967, **Guide to reference books**, 8th edn. [American Library Association]. {JNU NASSDOC}

Dority, G. Kim, 1984, **Guide to reference books for small and medium sized libraries, 1970-82.** {NASSDOC}

Walford, A.J., ed., n.d., **Guide to reference material,** 3 vols. [Library Association, London]. {INSA NASSDOC NIPCCD ZHL}

Gidwani, N.N. and Navalani, K., 1974, **A guide to reference materials on India,** 2 vols. {INSA NAI NASSDOC NCAER NERC ZHL}

Kennedy, James R., ed., 1972, **Guide to reference sources on Africa, Asia, Latin America and the Caribbean, Middle East and North Africa and Russia and East Europe** : Selected and annotated. {NASSDOC}

Hewitt, A.R., 1957, **Guide to resources for Commonwealth studies in London, Oxford and Cambridge with bibliographical and other information.** {IEG JNU NIEPA}

Bardeh, Bertha R. and Denison, Barbara, n.d., **Guide to the SLA loan collection, classification schemes and subject heading lists.** [Special Libraries Association] {DUL}

Panchanathan, A., 1984, **Guide to Saraswati Mahal.** [Saraswati Mahal Library, Tanjore]. {NASSDOC*}

Maureen, J., 1966, **Guide to scientific periodicals** : Annotated bibliography. {DUL}

Anon, 1972, **Guide to selected computer-based information services.** [Association of Special Libraries and Information Bureaux]. {CRRI}

Mukherjee, A.K., 1979, **Guide to selected reference tools and Indological source materials** : Classified and annotated. {DUL NASSDOC}

Olle, James G., 1984, **A guide to sources of information in libraries.** {NASSDOC}

Anon, 1963, **Guide to the Universal Decimal Classification.** (BS 1000 C : 1963). [British Standards Institution]. {AIU IIT JNU NASSDOC}

Staveley, Ronald, ed., n.d., **Guide to unpublished research materials.** {IEG}

Gates, J.K., 1962, **Guide to the use of books and libraries.** {DUL IIT MFL}

Gates, J.K., 1969, **Guide to the use of books and libraries**, 2nd edn. {NIH USIS}

Gates, J.K., 1979, **Guide to the use of books and libraries**, 4th edn. {USIS}

Anon, 1962, **Guide to use of Dewey Decimal Classification.** [Lake Placid Club Education Foundation]. {IIT USIS}

Brimmer, Brenda, et al, 1962, **A guide to the use of United Nations documents, including reference to the specialised agencies and special U.N. bodies.** {MFL USIS}

Ashworth, W., ed., 1955, **Handbook of special librarianship and information work**. [Association of Special Libraries and Information Bureaux]. {BIS IEG}

Ashworth, W., ed., 1962, **Handbook of special librarianship and information work**. 2nd edn. [Association of Special Libraries and Information Bureaux]. {IIT SPA}

Ashworth, W., ed., 1967, **Handbook of special librarianship and information work**, 3rd edn. [Association of Special Libraries and Information Bureaux]. {MHA MMTC NASSDOC NIH}

Batten, W.E., ed., 1975, **Handbook of special librarianship and information work,** 4th edn. [Association of Special Libraries and Information Bureaux]. {CRRI IIT}

Anon, 1956, **Handbook on the international exchange of publications**. [UNESCO]. {CRRI IEG}

Von Busse, Gisela, ed., 1964, **Handbook on the international exchange of publications**. 3rd edn., [UNESCO]. {NASSDOC NMML}

Vanwijngaerden, Frans, ed., 1978, **Handbook on the international exchange of publications**. 4th edn., [UNESCO]. {JNU NASSDOC USIS}

Foubert, Charles Henri, 1982, **The IDOC documentation handbook**. [IDOC]. {NASSDOC}

Anon, 1982, **ISO standards handbook, 1982** : Information transfer. [UNESCO]. {NASSDOC}

Myers, Gerald E., 1977, **Insurance manual for libraries**. [American Library Association]. {BIS}

Balwinder, Kaur comp., n.d., **Librarians' guide to Indian periodicals published for free distribution**. {NASSDOC}

Taylor, L.J., ed., 1976, **Librarians' handbook** [Library Association London]. 2 vols. {JNU NASSDOC NIPCCD}

Press, Jaques Cattel, ed., 1979, **The Librarians' phone book**. {USIS}

Krishan Kumar, 1982, **Library manual**. {BIS DSSW ICA IIC IIFT IIMC IIT ISI JNU NCDC NERC NIH ZHL}

Ranganathan, S.R. and Sivaraman, K.M., 1951, **Library manual**. [Indian Library Association]. {BIS DSSW INSA NERC ZHL}

Ranganathan, S.R., 1966, **Library manual**, 2nd edn. {BIS CRRI DSSW ICHR IIT INSA MMTC NASSDOC NERC NIPCCD}

Toser, Marie A., 1964, **Library manual** : A study work manual of lessons on the use of books and libraries, 6th edn. {USIS}

Ranganathan, S.R., 1960, **Library manual for library authorities, librarians and honorary library workers**. {ICA}

Ranganathan, S.R., 1966, **Library manual for library authorities, librarians and honorary library workers**, 2nd edn. {BIS ISI JNU NIEPA NMML ZHL}

Anon, 1952, **Library trustees manual**. [Ohio Library Trustees Association]. {JNU}

Anon, 1961, **Reproductions reference guide**. 2nd edn. {NASSDOC}

Lowy, George, 1965, **Searcher's manual**. {IIT USIS}

Benz, Magdalena Krommer, 1977, **World guide to terminological activities**. {JNU}

See also Directories

HEBREW CHARACTERS : TRANSLITERATION

Anon, 1962, Transliteration of Hebrew (ISO/R 259-1962)(E) [International

Organisation for Standardisation, Geneva]. {NASSDOC}

HERALD OF LIBRARY SCIENCE (PERIODICAL)
Lal, S.S., comp., 1985, **Herald of Library Science** : Trend report, citation and index, 1962-83. {NASSDOC}

HORN BOOK MAGAZINE (PERIODICAL)
Miller, Bertha Mahony and Field, Elinor Whitney, eds., 1957, **Caldecott medal books**, with the artists' acceptance: Papers and related material chiefly from the Horn Book Magazine 1938-1957. {USIS}
Miller, Bertha M. and Field, Elinor W., eds., 1955, **Newbery medal books, with their authors' acceptance** : Papers and related material, chiefly from the Horn Book magazine, 1922-55. {USIS}

HUMANITIES
Asheim, Lester, 1957, **The humanities and the library** : Problems in the interpretation, evaluation and use of library materials. [American Library Association]. {AIU USIS}

HUMANITIES : BIBLIOGRAPHY
Hale, Barbara M., 1970, **Subject bibliography of the social sciences and humanities**. {IEG NASSDOC}

HUMANITIES : INFORMATION SERVICES
Stone, Sue, ed., 1980, **Humanities information research** : Proceedings of a seminar. {JNU}

HUNGARY
See Geographical Area subdivision under main Descriptor e.g., Libraries : Geographical Area : Hungary

IASLIC
=Indian Association of Special Libraries and Information Centres

ILA
=Indian Library Association

ISBN
=International Standard Book Numbering

ISDS
=International Serial Data System

ILLUSTRATED BOOKS : CHILDREN
See also Caldecott Medal Books

IMPERIAL LIBRARY OF THE MUGHALS
Aziz, Abdul, 1974, **The imperial library of the moghuls**. [Idarah-I Adabiyat-I Delhi]. {INSA NMML}

INDEXES AND INDEXING
Rowley, Jennifer E., 1982, **Abstracting and indexing.** {ISI JNU}

Rowley, Jennifer E., 1988, **Abstracting and indexing**, 2nd edn. {NASSDOC}

Kesarwani, S.K. and Bhat, S.G. eds., n.d., **Abstracting, indexing and current awareness services in environmental science.** {INSA}

Muhammad, Riaz, 1989, **Advanced indexing and abstracting practices.** {NASSDOC}

Greenberg, Alan M., 1981, **Author index to Library of Congress classification** : Class P, Subclass PN, PR, PS, PZ. {BIS}

Jones, Karen Spark, 1971, **Automatic keyword classification for information retrieval**. {BCL BIS NASSDOC}

Gautreaux, Agnes A. and Lally, Mary, comps., 1949, **Aviation subject headings** : A concise list for civil aviation libraries or collections. {DUL}

Anon, 1978, **BEPI** : Bibliography of English publications in India : An integrated author-title-subject index of scholarly and significant publications of the year, 1977-1978. {NASSDOC}

Anderson, M.D., 1971, **Book indexing**. {NASSDOC NIEPA}

Bochm, Eric H., 1967, **CUE system for bibliography and indexing**. {NASSDOC}.

Anon, 1977-82, **Canadian periodical index**, 1975; 1977 to 1982, formerly *Canadian index to periodicals and documentary films.* [Canadian Library Association]. {NASSDOC}

Narang, Rita, 1974, **Chain procedure** : An annotated bibliography. {JNU}

Garfield, E., 1979, **Citation indexing** : Its theory and application in science, technology and humanities. {NASSDOC NIH}

Voegelin, C.F. and Voegelin, F.M., 1977, **Classification and index of the world's languages**. {JNU}

Langridge, D.W., 1976, **Classification and indexing in the humanities**. {DUL JNU NASSDOC ZHL}

Vickery, B.C., 1959, **Classification and indexing in science**. {CRRI DUL IIT NAI}

Foskett, D.J., 1963, **Classification and indexing in the social sciences**. {DSSW IEG IIMC IIT NAI NASSDOC NIEPA SPA USIS}

Foskett, D.J., 1971, **Classification and indexing in the social sciences**, 2nd edn. {BIS ICA JNU NASSDOC}

Edwards, Tom, ed., 1982, **A comparative analysis of the major abstracting and indexing services for library and information science** : With notes on their coverage of archive material. [UNESCO]. {NASSDOC}

Anon, 1973, **A compressed term index language for library and information science.** [Association of Special Libraries and Information Bureaux]. {NASSDOC}

Atkins, Thomas V., ed., 1984, **Cross reference index**, 2nd edn. {USIS}

Anon, 1961, **Documentation, indexing and retrieval of scientific information.** [US Committee on Government Operations]. {JNU}

Bhattacharya, G., n.d., **A general theory of SIL, POPSI and CLASSAURUS** : Results of current classification research in India. {NASSDOC*}

Campey, Lucille H., 1972, **Generating and printing indexes by computer.** [Association of Special Libraries and Information Bureaux]. {CRRI}

Foskett, A.C., 1970, **Guide to personal indexes** : Using edgenotched and peek-a-boo cards, 2nd edn. {BIS IEG IIT JNU NASSDOC}

Anon, 1969, **Index of a publication.** (ISO/R 999-1969. (E). [International Organisation for Standardisation, Geneva]. {NASSDOC}

Harrod, Leonard Montague, ed., 1978, **Indexers on indexing** : Selection of articles published in the Indexer. {BIS}

Collison, Robert L., 1959, **Indexes and indexing.** {BIS CRRI IEG IIT MFL MHA

SPA}

Collison, Robert L., 1969, **Indexes and indexing** : Guide to the indexing of books and collections of books, periodicals, music recordings, films and other materials, with a reference section and suggestions for further reading, 3rd rev. edn. {USIS}

Collison, Robert L., 1972, **Indexes and indexing** : Guide to the indexing of books and collections of books, periodicals, music recordings, films and other materials, with a reference section and suggestions for further reading, 4th edn. {JNU NASSDOC NIPCCD NMML}

Prasher, R.G., 1990, **Index and indexing systems**. {JNU}

Knight, G. Norman, 1979, **Indexing, the art of** : A guide to the indexing of books and periodicals. {BCL NASSDOC}

Collison, Robert L., 1969, **Indexing books** : A manual of basic principles. {IEG IIT INSA NIPCCD}

Borko, Harold and Bernier, Charles L., 1978, **Indexing concepts and methods**. {BCL BIS}

Hunnisett, R.F., 1972, **Indexing for editors.** { NASSDOC NMML}

Soergel, Dagobert, 1974, **Indexing languages and thesauri** : Construction and maintenance. {CRRI IIT NASSDOC}

Devsare, H.K., n.d., **Indexing of children's magazines in Hindi with particular reference to its impact on society and social sciences**. (typed copy). {NASSDOC}

Rajan, T.N., 1981, **Indexing systems** : Concepts, models and techniques. [Indian Association of Special Libraries and Information Centres]. {BIS CRRI JNU MFL MMTC NASSDOC}

Anon, 1976, **Indexing systems** : IASLIC special course, November 1—December 14, 1976 : Course material. [Indian Association of Special Libraries and Information Centres]. {JNU}

Ramakrishnan, M.N., 1986, **Indexing systems and techniques**. {NASSDOC}

Janker, Frederic, 1964, **Indexing theory, indexing methods and search devices**. {IIT JNU USIS}

Spiker, Sina K., n.d., **Indexing your book** : A practical guide for authors. {DUL}

Sethi, A.R., and Moodgal, H.M.K., 1978, **Indian book review index,** 1975-76. {JNU NASSDOC}

Metcalfe, J., 1957, **Information indexing and subject cataloguing** : Alphabetical classified, coordinate, mechanical. {DUL IEG IIT}

Wilson, T.D., 1971, **Introduction to chain indexing**. {BCL ICHR IIT JNU NASSDOC}

Ramsden, Michael John, 1974, **An introduction to index language construction** : A programmed text. {BCL}

Anon, 1973, **Introduction to indexing and abstracting for technical information systems**. {TDA}

Richmond, Phyllis A., 1981, **Introduction to PRECIS for North American usage.** {USIS}

Corrigon, Phillip, 1967, **Introduction to sears list to subject heading.** {IIMC IIT}

Brown, A.G., 1976, **An introduction to subject indexing.** {ICA NIEPA NIH ZHL}

Brown, A.G., 1982, **Introduction to subject indexing** : A programmed text. 2nd edn. {IIT}

Williams, Raymond, 1976, **Keywords** : A vocabulary of culture and society {NMML}

Hutchins, W.J., 1975, **Languages of indexing and classification** : A linguistic study of structures and function. {DUL}

Anon, 1975, **Library of Congress subject headings**, 8th edn., 2nd vols. [Library of Congress, Subject Cataloguing Division]. {NASSDOC USIS}

Anon, 1975, **Library of Congress subject headings** : Quarterly cumulative supplement to the 8th edn. [U.S. Library of Congress]. {NASSDOC}

Anon, 1980, **Library of Congress subject headings**, 9th edn. [U.S. Library of Congress, Subject Cataloguing Division]. {USIS}

Anon, 1982, **Library of Congress subject headings** : Quarterly cumulative supplements to the 9th edn., 1979-80. [Library of Congress]. {NASSDOC}

Chan, Lois Mai, 1986, **Library of Congress subject headings** : Principles and application, 2nd edn. (Research studies in library science, No. 19). {NASSDOC}

Sears, Minnie Earl, 1944, **List of subject headings for small libraries including practical suggestings for the beginner in subject heading work**, 5th edn. {MHA}

Anon, 1911, **List of subject headings for use in dictionary catalogue**, 3rd rev. edn. [American Library Association]. {NAI}

Fox, Gertrude, 1964, **List of subject headings in home building and allied fields.** [National Housing Centre Library, Washington]. {SPA}

Carey, G.V., 1951, **Making an Index.** {IIT}

Quinn, J.H. and Aconib, H.M., 1937, **Manual of cataloguing and indexing.** {NAI}

Clarke, Archibald Leycester, 1933, **Manual of practical indexing including arrangement of subject catalogues.** {NAI}

Choudhary, Anil Roy, 1959, **National standards for cataloguing and indexing art museum objects and documents.** {ZHL}

Anon, 1976, **The planning of indexing and abstracting services in the social sciences** : Coverage overlap and content. [Bath University Library]. {BCL}

Lydall, G.O.E., 1955, **Practical guide to precis writing and indexing.** {DUL}

Agarwal, Shyam Sunder, 1971, **Pustakalaya soochikaran** : Ek adhyayan. [Madhya Pradesh Hindhi Granth Academy]. {NMML}

Anon, 1964, **Recommendations for the preparation of indexes for books, periodicals and other publications**, (BS 3700 : 1964). [British Standards Institution]. {CRRI NASSDOC}

Cleverdon, Cysil W., 1962, **Report on the testing and analysis of an investigation into the comparative efficiency of indexing systems.** {BIS IIT}

Anon, 1942, **Rules for indexing records.** [Imperial Record Department]. {NML}

Anon, n.d., **Rules for making alphabetical indexes.** [Indian Standards Institution]. {AIU NASSDOC}

Anon, n.d., **Rules for making alphabetical indexes,** rev. edn., (IS : 1275-1976). [Indian Standards Institution]. {NASSDOC}

Sherrie, Heather and Jones, Phyllis Mander, comps., 1950, **Short list of subject headings.** {CRRI}

East, H., 1979, **Some statistical indicators of UK abstracting and indexing services.** {BCL}

Girja Kumar and Krishan Kumar, 1976, **Soochikaran ke siddhant**, tr. by Prem Kumar Jayaswal. {BIS DUL NMML}

Cravan, Timothy, 1986, **String indexing.** {JNU NASSDOC}

Taube, Mortimer, n.d., **Studies in coordinate indexing.** {JNU}

Bikewell, Kenneth Graham Bartlett, 1978, **A study of indexers reactions to the PRECIS indexing system.** [Department of Library and Information Studies, Faculty of Humanities and Social Studies, Liverpool Polytechnic]. {BCL}

Metcalfe, J., 1959, **Subject classifying and indexing of libraries and literature.**

{IEG IIT MFL}

Rue, Eloise and Laplanie, Effie, 1952, **Subject heading for children's materials**. [American Library Association]. {ZHL}

Pettee, Julla, 1947, **Subject headings** : The history and theory of the alphabetical subject approach to books. {NAI}

Saifuddin, comp., 1962, **Subject headings** : A list with CC and DDC numbers. {NASSDOC}

Anon, 1951, **Subject headings** : A practical guide. [U.S. Library of Congress]. {CRRI USIS}

Anon, 1954, **Subject headings for financial libraries**. [Special Libraries Association, New York]. {ISI}

Martin, Nella Jane, 1948, **Subject headings used in the dictionary catalogues**, 5th edn. [U.S. Library of Congress]. {ZHL}

Quattlebaum, Marguerite V., ed., n.d., **Subject headings used in the dictionary catalogs of the Library of Congress from 1897 through December 1955,** 6th edn. [U.S. Library of Congress]. {BIS IEG USIS}

Quattlebaum, Marguerite V., ed., n.d., **Subject headings used in the dictionary catalogs of the Library of Congress from 1897 through December 1955** : Supplement to the 6th edn., January 1956-December 1959. [U.S. Library of Congress]. {IEG}

Quattlebaum, Marguerite V., ed., 1966, **Subject headings used in the dictionary catalogs of the Library of Congress,** 7th edn. [U.S. Library of Congress]. {USIS}

Anon, 1969, **Subject indices list.** [Central Reference Library, Calcutta]. {NASSDOC*]

Landry, Bertrand Clovis, 1971, **Theory of indexing** : Indexing theory as a model for information storage and retrieval. [Computer and Information Science Research Centre, Ohio State University]. {IIT}

Chan, Lois Mai, et al, eds., 1985, **Theory of subject analysis** : A source book. {NASSDOC}

Knight, G. Norman, ed., 1970, **Training in indexing** : A course. [Society of Indexers]. {IEG IIFT IIT NASSDOC}

Costello, John C., n.d., **Training manual and work book for use in abstracting and coordinate indexing**. [Battelle Memorial Institute, Ohio]. {BIS}

Varma, A.K., 1984, **Trends in subject indexing.** {NASSDOC NMML}

Anon, n.d., **USA standard** : Basic criteria for indexes, rev edn., (USAS Z 39. 4-1968). [American National Standards Institute]. {NASSDOC}

Burke, Remend A., 1952, **What is the index**. {NAI}

See also Chain Indexing; Pre Context Indexing Systems

INDEXES AND INDEXING : AUTOMATIC

Steven, Mary Elizabeth, 1965, **Automatic indexing** : A state of the art report. [U.S. National Bureau of Standards]. {USIS}

Campey, Lucille H., 1972, **Generating and printing indexes by computer.** [Association of Special Libraries and Information Bureaux]. {CRRI}

INDEXING : DICTIONARIES

Buchanan, Brian W., 1976, **Glossary of indexing terms**. {BCL NASSDOC NERC}

INDEXING : EDUCATION AND TRAINING
Knight, G. Norman, ed., 1970, **Training in indexing** : A course. [Society of Indexers]. {IEG IIFT IIT NASSDOC}
Costello, John C., n.d., **Training manual and work book for use in abstracting and coordinate indexing**. [Battelle Memorial Institute, Ohio]. {BIS}

INDEXING AND ABSTRACTING SERVICES
See Abstracting and Indexing Services
See also Abstracts and Abstracting; Indexes and Indexing

INDIA
See Geographical Area subdivision under main Descriptor, e.g., Information Services : Geographical Area : India

INDIA : BIBLIOGRAPHY
Anon, 1978, **BEPI** : Bibliography of English publications in India : An integrated author-title-subject index of scholarly and significant publications of the year, 1977-1978. {NASSDOC}
Kalia, D.R. and Jain, M.K., 1975, **A bibliography of bibliographies on India.** {ICA}
Vaswani, H.P., comp., 1964, **Books of India, 1963** : A reference catalogue of Indian book published in English in 1963. {NASSDOC}

INDIA : GOVERNMENT PUBLICATIONS
See Geovernment Publication : Geographical Area : India

INDIA OFFICE LIBRARY, LONDON
Arberry, A.J., 1967, **India Office Library** : A historical sketch, [Commonwealth Office, London]. {NASSDOC}
Arberry, A.J., 1938, **Library of the India Office** : A historical sketch. [India Office, London]. {NAI}

INDIAN ASSOCIATION OF SPECIAL LIBRARIES AND INFORMATION CENTRES
Banerjee, S.B., ed., 1980, **Indian Association of Special Libraries and Information Centres** : Perspective, performance, promise : Silver jubilee commemorative volume. [Indian Association of Special Libraries and Information Centres]. {JNU}

INDIAN INSTITUTE OF TECHNOLOGY LIBRARY, NEW DELHI
Humphrey, K.W., 1966, **Report on the library of the Indian Institute of Technology, New Delhi**. [Indian Institute of Technology]. {IIT}

INDIAN LIBRARY ASSOCIATION
Anon, 1983, **Fifty years of Indian Library Association, 1933-83** : Golden jubilee. [Indian Library Association]. {JNU MMTC ZHL}

INDIAN STANDARD INSTITUTION, NEW DELHI
See Bureau of Indian Standards

INDOLOGY : BIBLIOGRAPHY
Patil, P.K., 1972, **Bibliographical services for Indian studies** : A guide to printed sources of information. [Mysore Institute of Development Studies]. {NASSDOC}

INDUSTRY : INFORMATION SERVICES

Anon, 1975, **Seminar and exhibition on information for industry, 1975, Bangalore.** {CRRI}

INFORMATION DISPLAY SYSTEMS

Easterby, Ronald, ed., 1978, **Tasks, process and information display design** : NATO conference on visual presentation of information, September 4-8, 1978, Birmingham. {BIS}

INFORMATION NETWORKS

Anon, 1977, **Information networks for on-line bibliography retrieval.** [UNESCO]. {BIS}

Neelameghan, A., ed., 1979, **Ordering systems for global information networks** : Proceedings : International study conference on classification research, 3rd, January 6-11, 1975, Bombay, [FID/CR; Sarada Ranganathan Endowment for Library Science]. {BIS NASSDOC}

Dewe, A. and Deunelle, J., n.d., **Papers** : European conference on the contribution of users to planning and policy making for information systems and networks, 1978, Germany. {CRRI}

Kapoor, S.K., et al, eds., n.d., **Proceedings** : Conference on organisation of data services in India and user education and training programmes, 13th, 1981, Waltair. [Indian Association of Special Libraries and Information Centres]. {BIS MMTC NIPCCD}

INFORMATION NETWORKS LIBRARY
See Library Information Networks

INFORMATION RETRIEVAL SYSTEMS
See Information Storage and Retrieval Systems

INFORMATION SCIENCE

Tou, Julius T., ed., 1969, **Advances in information systems science**, 9 vols. {CRRI MHA DUL NASSDOC USIS}

Mittal, R.L., 1970, **Advances in library and information science.** {CRRI ICA NCAER NCDC}

Lucas, Henry C., 1976, **The analysis, design and implementation of information systems**. {TDA}

Meadow, Charles T., 1973, **Analysis of information systems.** {BIS CRRI DUL NIH NIPCCD USIS}

Anon, 1966-84, **Annual review of information science and technology**, 19 vols {CRRI NASSDOC USIS}

Keren, Carl and Perlmutter Linda, 1985, **Applications of mini and micro computers in information, documentation and libraries**. {JNU NASSDOC}

Bunch, Allan, 1984, **Basics of information work.** {JNU}

Neeland, Frances, 1967, **Bibliography on information science and technology for 1966**. {JNU}

Sardar, Z., 1988, **Building information systems in the Islamic world.** {NASSDOC}

McGarry, K.J., 1981, **Changing context of information** : An introductory analysis. {NIEPA}

Anon, 1982, **Changing information** : Concepts and technologies. {JNU USIS}

Slamecka, Vladimir, 1965, **Coming age of information technology** : Studies in coordinate indexing. {DUL}

Becker; Carol A., 1974, **Community information service** : A directory of public library involvement. {JNU}

Bunch, Allan, 1982, **Community information services** : Their origin, scope and development. {IIT}

Edwards, Tom, ed., 1978, **A comparative analysis of the major abstracting and indexing services for library and information science.** [UNESCO]. {NASSDOC}

Edwards, Tom, ed., 1982, **A comparative analysis of the major abstracting and indexing services for library and information science** : With notes on their coverage of archive material. [UNESCO]. {NASSDOC}

Stevens, Norman D., n.d., **Comparative study of three systems of information retrieval.** [Graduate School of Library Science, New Brunswick]. {BIS MHA}

Lancaster, F.W. and Smith, L.C., n.d., **Compatibility issues affecting information systems and services.** {JNU}

Wessel, Andrew E., 1975, **Computer-aided information retrieval.** {BIS CRRI NIH USIS}

Tou, Julius T. and Wilcox, Richard H., eds., n.d., **Computer and information science** : Collected papers on learning, adaptation and control in information systems. {DUL}

Houghton, Bernard, ed., 1968, **Computer based information retrieval systems.** {DUL INSA NASSDOC}

Anon, 1979, **Computer based information services in medicines** : A feasibility study : On behalf of the University of Otago medical libraries. [Centerbury Medical Library]. {BCL}

Lynch, Michael Felix, 1974, **Computer based information services in science and technology** : Principles and techniques. {BCL}

Henley, J.P., 1970, **Computer based library and information systems.** {BIS IIT JNU NASSDOC NIH}

Henley, J.P., 1972, **Computer based library and information systems,** 2nd edn. {DUL NIH}

Anon, 1981, **Computer based national information systems** : Technology and public policy issues. [U.S. Office of Technology Assessment]. {USIS}

Agrawal, S.P., gen ed., 1989, **Concepts in communication, informatics and librarianship.** (CICIL series). {JNU NASSDOC}

Pao, M.L., 1989, **Concepts of information retrieval.** {NASSDOC}

Borka, H., 1965, **Conceptual foundations of information systems.** {JNU}

Stokes, Adrian V., 1982, **Concise encyclopaedia of information technology.** {CRRI JNU NASSDOC RTC}

Naur, Peter, 1974, **Concise survey of computer methods.** {NASSDOC}

Anon, 1967, **Conference on mechanised information storage, retrieval and dissemination.** {NMML}

Linderman, Wilfred B., 1967, **Conference on the present status and future prospects of reference information work.** {JNU}

Saracevic, Tefko, and Wood, Judith B, 1981, **Consolidation of information** : A handbook on evaluation, restructuring and repackaging of scientific and technical information. [UNESCO]. {CRRI}

Hussain, Khateeb M., 1973, **Development of information systems for education.**

{AIU INSA}

Bhargava, G.D. and Tejomurty, A. eds., 1986, **Dimensions in library and information science**. {JNU}

Rowley, J.E. and Turner, C.M.D., 1978, **The dissemination of information**. {BCL DUL ISI NASSDOC ZHL}

Wilson, T.D. and Stephenson, J., 1969, **Dissemination of information** : An examination guidebook. {BIS DUL MFL NIPCCD}

Broadbent, K.P., 1980, **Dissemination of scientific information in the People's Republic of China**. [International Development Research Centre, Ottawa]. {NASSDOC}

Whitehouse, Franck, 1971, **Documentation** : How to organise and control information processes in business and industry. {JNU}

Guha, Bimalendu, 1988, **Documentation and information** : Services, techniques and systems, 2nd edn. {DUL ICA IIT JNU MHA NIH NIPCCD ZHL}

Sengupta, Benoyendra and Chatterjee, Mridula, 1977, **Documentation and information retrieval**. {DUL MHA ZHL}

Anon, 1961, **Documentation, indexing and retrieval of scientific information.** [US Committee on Government Operations]. {JNU}

Haworth, Carol S., 1964, **Documentation of semi-automatic bibliographic information retrieval**. {JNU}

Anon, 1963, **Does your firm need its own information service** : An enquiry into the economic advantages of an information service in small and medium-sized firms. [Organisation of Economic Cooperation and Development, Paris]. {TDA}

Vishwanathan, C.G., 1976, **Elements of information science**. {DUL NAI NIEPA}

Clason, W.E., comp., 1973, **Elsevier's dictionary of library science, information and documentation**. {JNU ZHL}

Garfield, Eugene, 1981, **Essays of an information scientist.** {CRRI JNU}

Barr, Keith and Line, Maurice, eds., 1975, **Essays on information and libraries**. {CRRI DUL ICA IIMC INSA JNU NASSDOC NIPCCD ZHL}

Anon, 1980, **Essential problems in terminology for informatics and documentation**. [International Federation for Documentation and Information]. {BIS CRRI}

Katzer, Zeffery, et al, 1978, **Evaluating information** : A guide for users of social science research. {NCAER}

Houghton, Bernard, 1977, **The evaluation of a programme designed for teaching on-line information retrieval techniques** : Final report for the period June-September 1976. [Liverpool Polytechnic, Department of Library and Information Studies]. {BCL}

Anon, 1978, **FID congress on new trends in documentation and information, 1978, Edinburg**. [International Federation of Documentation and Information] {CRRI}

Mason, Merilyn Gell, 1983, **The federal role in library and information services**. {USIS}

Moranjian, Lorig and Boss, Richard W., 1980, **Fee based information services**: A study of a growing industry. {IIT USIS}

Schutz, H., 1975, **Function and organisation of a national documentation centre in developing country**. [FID/DC Working Group]. {ICA JNU NASSDOC}

Booth, Grayce M., 1973, **Functional analysis of information processing** : A structured approach for simplifying systems design. {NASSDOC}

Guinchat, Claire and Menou, Michel, 1983, **General introduction to the**

techniques of information and documentation work. [UNESCO]. {JNU NMML}

Venkatappaiah, V., 1986, **Glossary of library and information science** : English-Telugu and Telugu-English. [Zilla Granthalaya Samstha, Machilipatnam]. {NASSDOC*}

Jagjit Singh, 1967, **Great ideas in information theory, language and cybernetics**. {INSA}

Davis, Charles H. and Ruse, James E., 1979, **Guide to information science.** {BCL JNU}

Lancaster, F.W., 1978, **Guidelines for the evaluation of information systems and services**. [UNESCO]. {JNU} .

Kaul, Neelima, comp., 1980, **Handbook of information scientists and librarians in India**. {BIS CRRI IIPA IIT ISI MMTC NASSDOC NCAER NIEPA NMML RTL}

Atherten, Pauline, 1977, **Handbook of information systems services**. {JNU}

Bakewell, K.G.B., n.d., **How to organise information** : A manager's guide to techniques and sources with a check list for secretaries and assistants. {JNU}

Wessel, Andrew E., 1979, **Implementation of complex information system.** {CRRI IIT USIS}

Anon, 1979, **Implication of modern information technology for national information policy and planning.** [UNESCO]. {NASSDOC}

Guha, B., ed., 1986, **In the library and information science horizon** : A collection of essays in honour of Dr. V.A. Kamath, presented by the Bombay Science Librarians Association (BOSLA). {JNU NASSDOC}

Jackson, Eugene B. and Jackson, Ruth L., 1978, **Industrial information systems** : A manual for higher management and their information officer, librarian/associates. {USIS}

Hammer, Donald P., ed., 1976, **The information age, its development, its impact.** {DUL USIS}

Kent, Allen, 1971, **Information analysis and retrieval**. {CRRI JNU MHA NASSDOC NIPCCD}

Singer, T.E.R., ed., n.d., **Information and communication practice in industry.** {IEG}

Anon, n.d., **Information and its dissemination**. [Institute of Petroleum, London]. {BIS}

Brittain, J.M., 1970, **Information and its users** : A review with special reference to the social sciences. {JNU NASSDOC}

Schutze, Gertrude, 1972, **Information and library science source book** : Supplement to documentation source book. {NERC}

Long, Nicholas, 1975, **Information and referral services** : Research findings. [U.S. Department of Health, Education and Welfare]. {NASSDOC}

Meltzer, Morton F., 1967, **The information center** : Management's hidden asset. [American Management Association]. {USIS}

Tolly, Roy D., 1979, **Information choice and policies** : Proceedings : American society for information science annual meeting, 42nd, October 14-18, 1979, Minneapoles. {USIS}

Lunin, Lois F., et al, 1981, **Information community** : An alliance for progress : Proceedings : ASIS annual meeting, 44th, 1981. {NASSDOC}

Kibirige, Harry M., 1983, **Information dilemma.** {NIEPA}

Pratt, Gordon, 1976, **Information economics** : Costs and prices of machine-readable information in Europe. [Association of Special Libraries and Information Bureaux]. {BCL}

Porat, Marc Uri, 1977, **The information economy** : Definition and measurement. {USIS}

Mclean, M., ed., 1985, **The information explosion** : The new electronic media in Japan and Europe. {NASSDOC}

Kohen, Manfred, ed., 1975, **Information for action** : From knowledge to wisdom. {JNU}

Howerton, Paul W., 1963, **Information handling** : First principles. {JNU}

Anon, 1966, **Information handling in the National Standard Reference Data System**. (NBS, Technical Note 290). [U.S. National Bureau of Standards]. {BIS}

Anthony, Lawrence James, ed., 1976, **Information in the 1980s** : Proceedings : ASLIB seminar for information planners and industry, May 13-14, 1976, Beaconfield. [Association of Special Libraries and Information Bureaux]. {BCL NASSDOC}

Anderla, Georges, 1986, **Information in 1985** : A forecasting study of information needs and resources. [Organisation for Economic Cooperation and Development]. {BCL BIS CRRI JNU MMTC}

Stamper, Ronald, 1973, **Information in business and administrative systems.** {DUL NASSDOC}

Freeman, Robert R., et al, eds., 1968, **Information in the language sciences** : Proceedings of the conference held at Airlic House, Warrenton, Virginia, March 4-6, 1966. {NASSDOC}

Metcalfe, J., 1957, **Information indexing and subject cataloguing** : Alphabetical classified, coordinate, mechanical. {DUL IEG IIT}

Anon, 1978-83, **Information Industry Market Place** : An international directory of information products and services, 1978; 1982; 1983. {USIS}

Breivick, Patrica Senn and Gel, E. Gordon, 1989, **Information literacy** : Revolution in the library. {NASSDOC}

Smith, J.C. and Hisson, N.J., 1965, **Information maintenance system documentation**. {JNU}

Mason, Donald, 1978, **Information management.** {IIT}

Taylor, Peter J. and Crown, Blaise, 1983, **Information management research in Europe** : Proceedings of the EURIMS conference, Paris. {JNU}

Anon, 1986, **Information market with special regard to social science information**. (FID studies in social science information and documentation). [Hungarian Academy of Science; International Federation for Documentation and Information]. {NASSDOC}

Steurat, Robert D., 1982 : **Information needs of the 80s.** {JNU}

Stater, Margaret, 1989, **Information needs of social scientists**. [British Library Research and Development Department]. {NASSDOC}

Anon, 1976, **Information policy for development** : National and international responsibilities. [UNESCO]. {NASSDOC}

Shera, Jesse H., 1958, **Information resources** : A challenge to American science and industry. {JNU}

Gyawali, Bharat M. and Standrodd, Garland L., n.d., **Information resources on Nepal.** {IEG}

Lamberton, Donald M., ed., 1974, **The information revolution : Annals.** [American Academy of Political and Social Science]. {USIS}

Debons, Anthony, ed., 1974, **Information science** : Search for identity. {INSA}

Anon, 1978, **Information science** : A unified view through a systems approach. [Indian Association of Special Libraries and Information Bureaux]. {DUL MMTC}

Mitchell, Ruth K., 1971, **Information science and computer basics.** {BIS}

Dhyani, Pushpa, 1990, **Information science and libraries.** {CRRI ICHR JNU ZHL}

Debons, Anthony and Larson, Arvid G., eds., n.d., **Information science in action** : System design, 2 vols. {DUL}

Anon, 1965, **Information sciences**. [U.S. Air Force Office of Scientific Research]. {JNU}

Chen, Ching-Chih and Hernon, Peter, 1982, **Information seeking** : Assessing and anticipating user needs. {JNU}

Bagg, Thomas C. and Stevens, Mary Elizabeth, 1961, **Information selection systems retrieving replica copies** : A state-of-art report. {JNU}

Taneja, Ram D., n.d., **Information service for the small enterprise** : Need, source and organisation. {BIS}

Norris, Willa, et al, 1972, **Information service in guidance for career development and planning**. {NIPCCD}

Foskett, D.J., 1967, **Information service in libraries.** {CRRI IEG JNU NAI}

Kashyap, Subhash C., 1988, **Information service in the Parliament of India.** {NASSDOC}

Collison, R.L., n.d., **Information services** : Their organisation and administration. {JNU}

Sharma, C.D. and Boonlia, Naresh, n.d., **Information services for college librarians.** {JNU}

Anon, 1977, **Information services for world trade centres.** [World Trade Centre Association]. {TDA}

Roy, A.K. and Kapoor, S.K., eds., 1982, **Information services in India** : Papers: IASLIC national seminar, 10th, December 21-24, 1982, Kanpur. [Indian Association of Special Libraries and Information Centres]. {ICA JNU MMTC NASSDOC NIPCCD}

Josey, E.J., ed., 1979, **The information society** : Issues and answers. [American Library Association]. {JNU}

Umapathy, K.S., 1978, **Information sources** : An international selective guide. {DUL ICA IIFT INSA}

Meachan, Mary, 1978, **Information sources in children's literature** : A practical reference guide. {NIPCCD}

Parper, C.C. and Turley, R.V., 1986, **Information sources in science and technology** : A practical guide to traditional and on-line use. {JNU}

Taube, Mortimer and Wooster, Harold, eds., 1958, **Information storage and retrieval** : Theory, system and devices. {CRRI DUL}

Becker, Joseph and Hayes, Robert M., 1963, **Information storage and retrieval** : Tools, elements, theories. {DUL ICA IEG MFL NASSDOC USIS}

Politt, A.S., 1989, **Information storage and retrieval systems** : Origin, development and applications. {NASSDOC}

Jahoda, Gerald, 1970, **Information storage and retrieval systems for individual researchers.** {ISI MHA USIS}

Kent, Allen and Galvin, Thomas J., eds., 1982, **Information technology** : Critical choices for library decision makers : Pittsburg conference on electronic information technology and its impact on library and information services, 1981, 4th, Pittsburg. {BIS CRRI IIT JNU USIS}

Anon, 1982, **Information technology and its impact on American education.** {USIS}

Anon, 1974, **Information technology in local government** : A survey of the development of urban and regional information systems in five European countries. [Organisation for Economic Cooperation and Development]. {BCL}

Smith, Robert Irvine and Combell, Bob, 1981, **Information technology revolution.** {NASSDOC}

Chartrand, Robert Lee and Morentz, James W., eds., 1979, **Information technology serving society.** {USIS}

Abramson, Norman, 1963, **Information theory and coding.** {INSA}

Anon, 1982, **Information trade directory** : An international directory of information products and services. {USIS}

Anon, 1982, **Information transfer,** 2nd edn. [International Organisation for Standardisation]. {CRRI MMTC}

Rowland, J.F.B., 1978, **Information transfer and use in chemistry** : Final report of the Chemical Information Review Committee. {BCL}

Lesko, Matthew, 1983, **Information U.S.A.** {USIS}

Houghton, Bernard, 1967, **Information work today** : Symposium on information work today, September, 1966, Liverpool. {ICA IIMC MHA}

Holloway, A.M., et al, 1976, **Information work with unpublished reports.** {NASSDOC}

El-Hadidy, Barbara and Horne, Estic E., 1984, **The infrastructure of an information society.** {JNU}

Horsnell, Verina, 1974, **Intermediate lexicon for information science** : Feasibility study. [Polytechnic of North London]. {BCL JNU}

Chandler, George, 1982, **International and national library and information services** : A review of some recent developments, 2 vols. {IIT NASSDOC NERC}

Jell, Hans and Machesney, Robert, 1965, **International bibliography of non-periodical literature on documentation and information.** {JNU}

Anon, 1986, **International directory of library, archives and information science associations**, 2nd edn. [UNESCO General Information Programme; UNISIST]. {NASSDOC}

Aiyepeku, Wilson O., 1983, **International socio-economic information systems** : An evaluating directory of DEVSIS-type programs. {NASSDOC}

Saracevic, Tefko, ed., 1970, **Introduction to information science.** {DUL NASSDOC}

Saracevic, Tefko, ed., 1970, **Introduction to information science.** {DUL NASSDOC}

Salton, Gerard and Mc Gill, Michael J., 1983, **Introduction to modern information retrieval.** {BIS}

Mikhailov, A.I. and Giljarevaskij, R.S., n.d., **Introductory course in informatics/documentations**. [UNESCO]. {DUL NASSDOC}

Anon, n.d., **Investigation concerning the SFS information service and its users**. [Finnish Standards Association]. {BIS}

Martyn, John, 1987, **Libraries and information centres in Britain**. [British Council, London]. {NASSDOC*}

Andersen, A., et al, 1985, **Libraries and information centres in the Soviet Union**. {NASSDOC*}

Anon, 1972, **Libraries and information technology** : A national system challenge : A report to the Council of Library Resources. [National Academy of Sciences, Washington]. {USIS}

Anon, 1976, **Library and information science manpower development in the Asian Region** : Report : Meeting of supervisors of library and documentation schools in the Asian region, Bangalore. {CRRI}

Anon, 1974, **Library and information service needs of the nation.** {JNU}

Agrawal, S.P., 1987, **Library and information services in India** : The current scenario. {NASSDOC}

Vernon, Ken, 1986, **Library and information services of management development institutions** : A practical guide. {NASSDOC}

Anon, 1968, **Library, information and archive work.** [Ministry of Labour, Great Britain]. {JNU}

Jones, Karen Sparck and Kay, Martin, 1973, **Linguistic and information science.** {DUL}

Weiss, Edward C., ed., 1977, **The many faces of information science.** {INSA JNU USIS}

Bourne, Charles P., 1966, **Methods of information handling.** {DUL IIMC IIT JNU NASSDOC}

Frank, O., ed., 1961, **Modern documentation and information practices** : A basic manual. [International Federation for Documentation and Information]. {BIS DUL ICA NASSDOC NIEPA}

Muhammad, Riaz, 1989, **Modern techniques of documentation and information work.** {NASSDOC}

Anon, 1986, **National policy on library and information system** : A presentation. [Government of India, Committee on National Policy on Library and Information System]. {NASSDOC*}

Anon, 1985, **New frontiers in library and information science**. [Zilla Granthalaya Samstha, Machilipatnam]. {NASSDOC*}

Taraboi, Vasile, 1973, **Organisation, functioning and activities of national documentary information systems in the scientific, technical and economic fields.** [National Institute for Scientific and Technical Information and Documentation, Romania]. {BIS}

De Grolier, Eric, 1979, **Organisation of information systems for government and public administration.** {BIS JNU}

Soergel, Dagobert, 1985, **Organising information** : Principle of database and retrieval. {JNU}

Kashyap, S.C., 1986, **Parliaments and information dissemination.** {NASSDOC}

Debons, Anthony and Cameron, William J., 1975, **Perspectives in information science**. {JNU}

Agarwal, S.N., et al, 1982, **Perspectives in library and information science** : Viswanathan festschrift. 2 vols. {AIU ICHR ISI JNU MMTC NASSDOC NCDC NIEPA NIPCCD SPA ZHL}

Luhn, Hans Peter, 1968, **Pioneer of information science** : Selected works. {JNU}

Anon, 1966, **Practical approach to information and data retrieval**. [Boston Industrial Education Institute]. {ISI}

Ravichandrarao, I.K., 1983, **Quantitative methods for library and information science.** {BIS ISI JNU NASSDOC}

Sharp, Harold S., 1964, **Readings in information retrieval**. {JNU}

Anon, n.d., **Responsibilities of libraries and information service.** [Organisation for European Economic Co-operation]. {BIS}

Slavens, Thomas P., ed., 1981, **Retrieval of information in the humanities and the social sciences**. {NIEPA}

Anon, 1971, **Review of national scientific and technical information policy** : Germany. [Organisation for Economic Co-operation and Development, Paris].

{CRRI ICA JNU}

Anon, 1988, **Selective inventory of social science information and documentation services**, 3rd edn. [UNESCO Social and Human Sciences Documentation Centre]. {NASSDOC}

Anon, 1979, **Selective list of activities in the field of information** : UNESCO Intergovernmental conference on scientific and technical information for development, 1979, Paris. {JNU}

Anon, 1967, **Seminar on library and information services for management.** [Liverpool College of Commerce]. {NMML}

Zemanck, H., 1972, **Skyline of information processing** : Proceedings of the 10th anniversary of IFIP, Amsterdom. {JNU}

Binwal, J.C., et al, ed., 1990, **Social science information** : Problems and prospects. {NASSDOC}

Agrawal, S.P., 1987, **Social science information and documentation** : Search and relevance in India. {BIS DUL JNU NASSDOC NIH NIEPA NMML ZHL}

Wessel, Andrew E., 1976, **The social use of information ownership and access.** {BCL NASSDOC USIS}

Schaetz, Chaire K., n.d., **Some characteristics of an efficient information retrieval system**. {JNU}

Kochen, Manfred, 1965, **Some problems in information science.** {JNU}

Prytherch, Ray, comp., 1983, **Sources of information librarianship and information science** : A grafton book. {NIH}

Harvey, John M., 1976, **Specialised information centres.** {BCL CRRI ICA USIS}

Kent, Allen, 1965, **Specialised information centres.** {JNU}

Hug, William E., ed., 1974, **Strategies for change in information programs.** {DUL USIS}

Boaz, Martha, ed., 1981, **Strategies for meeting the information needs of society in the year 2000.** {USIS}

Kaimann, Richard A., 1973, **Structured information files.** {NASSDOC}

Machlup, Fritz and Mansfield, Una, n.d., **Study of information** : Inter- disciplinary messages. {JNU}

Anon, n.d., **Study of the information in the Philippine population programs.** [Population Center Foundation of the Philippines]. {NIH}

Foskett, A.C., 1971, **The subject approach to information**, 2nd edn. {IIMC INSA ISIL JNU NASSDOC ZHL}

Foskett, A.C., 1977, **Subject approach to information**, 3rd edn. {JNU NMML}

Wellisch, Hans and Wilson, Thomas D., n.d., **Subject retrieval in the seventies** : New directions. {ICHR}

Houghton, Bernard, 1972, **Technical information sources** : A guide to patent specification, standards and technical reports literature. {BIS}

Vickery, B.C., 1970, **Techniques of information retrieval**. {AIU BCL IEG IIMC INSA JNU}

Anon, 1980, **Technology in support of library science and information service.** [Sarada Ranganathan Endowment for Library Science, Bangalore]. {BIS}

Kent, Allen, 1962, **Textbook on mechanised information retrieval.** {CRRI}

Anon, 1979, **Theoretical problems of informatics** : Forecasting of the development of scientific information activities. [International Federation for Documentation and Information]. {CRRI}

Anon, 1981, **Theoretical problems of information** : Criteria of the quality of information systems and processes : Collection of papers. [International

Federation for Documentation and Information]. {BIS}

Anon, 1979, **Theoretical problems of information** : New trends in information and its terminology. [International Federation for Documentation and Information]. {CRRI}

Harbo, Ols, ed., 1980, **Theory and applications of information research** : Proceedings : International research forum on information science, 2nd, August 3-6, 1977, Copenhagen. {BCL}

Trezza, Alphonse F., 1982, **Toward a federal library and information services network** : A proposal. {USIS}

Fairthorne, Robert Arthur, 1961, **Towards information retrieval.** {JNU}

Barquin, Raman C. and Mead, Graham P., n.d., **Towards the information society.** {DUL}

Rubinoff, Morris, ed., 1965, **Towards a national information system** : Second annual national colloquium on information retrieval. {IIT}

Anon, 1975, **Toward a national program for library and information services** : Goals for action. [U.S. National Commission on Libraries and Information Science]. {USIS}

Lancaster, F.W., 1978, **Toward paperless information system.** {BCL DUL IIFT ISI ISIL USIS}

Hills, Philip J., ed., 1982, **Trends in information transfer.** {ISI NASSDOC}

Ghosh, G.B. and Banerjee, B.N., 1974, **Trends of information service in India.** {AIU CRRI ICHR NASSDOC NERC NIH NIPCCD ZHL}

Anon, 1978, **UNISIST** : A study on the application of scientific and technological information in development. [UNESCO]. {JNU}

Rayward, W. Boyd, 1975, **The universe of information**. [International Federation of Documentation and Information]. {CRRI}

Anon, 1969, **World guide to technical information and documentation services.** [UNESCO]. {CRRI NMML}

Anon, 1975, **World guide to technical information and documentation services,** 2nd edn. [UNESCO]. {JNU NASSDOC}

Wilson, John H., ed., 1973, **A world of information** : American society for information science meeting, 35th, October 23-26, 1972, Washington, D.C. {USIS}

INFORMATION SCIENCE : BIBLIOGRAPHY

Lamberton, D.M., ed., 1971, **Economics of information and knowledge** : Selected readings. {NASSDOC}

INFORMATION SCIENCE : STUDY AND TEACHING

Foskett, D.J., 1976, **NATIS** : Preliminary survey of education and training programmes at university level in information and library science. [UNESCO]. {NIEPA}

See also Library Education

INFORMATION SCIENTISTS : EDUCATION AND TRAINING

See also Library Education

INFORMATION SERVICES

Anthony, Lawrence James, ed., 1976, **ASLIB seminar for information planners and industry, May 13-14, 1976, Boaconfield.** {BCL NASSDOC}

Bunch, Allan, 1982, **Community information services** : Their origin, scope and development. {IIT}

Mason, Merilyn Gell, 1983, **The federal role in library and information services.** {USIS}

Moranjian, Lorig and Boss, Richard W., 1980, **Fee based information services**: A study of a growing industry. {IIT USIS}

Anon, 1982, **Future development of libraries and information services.** [Department of Education and Science, Great Britain]. {ISI}

Anon, 1980, **Handbook for information systems and services.** [UNESCO] {IDSA}

Long, Nicholas, 1975, **Information and referral services** : Research findings. [U.S. Department of Health, Education and Welfare]. {NASSDOC}

Meltzer, Morton F., 1967, **The information center** : Management's hidden asset. [American Management Association]. {USIS}

Kibirige, Harry M., 1983, **Information dilemma.** {NIEPA}

Anon, 1978-83, **Information industry market place** : An international directory of information products and services, 1978; 1982; 1983. {USIS}

Mason, Donald, 1978, **Information management.** {IIT}

Taneja, Ram D., n.d., **Information service for the small enterprise** : Need source and organisation. {BIS}

Norris, Willa, et al, 1972, **Information service in guidance for career development and planning.** {NIPCCD}

Foskett, D.J., 1967, **Information service in libraries.** {CRRI IEG JNU NAI}

Kashyap, Subhash C., 1988, **Information service in the Parliament of India.** {NASSDOC}

Collison, R.L., n.d., **Information services** : Their organisation and administration. {JNU}

Sharma, C.D. and Boonlia, Naresh, n.d., **Information services for college librarians.** {JNU}

Anon, 1977, **Information services for world trade centres.** [World Trade Centre Association]. {TDA}

Roy, A.K. and Kapoor, S.K., eds., 1982, **Information services in India** : Papers: IASLIC national seminar, 10th, December 21-24, 1982, Kanpur. [Indian Association of Special Libraries and Information Centres]. {ICA JNU MMTC NASSDOC NIPCCD}

Josey, E.J., ed., 1979, **The information society** : Issues and answers. [American Library Association]. {JNU}

Umapathy, K.S., 1978, **Information sources** : An international selective guide. {DUL ICA IIFT INSA}

Murdick, Robert G. and Ross, Jod E., 1977, **Information system for modern management.** {ICA}

Anon, 1982, **Information trade directory** : An international directory of information products and services. {USIS}

Anon, 1982, **Information transfer,** 2nd edn. [International Organisation for Standardisation]. {CRRI MMTC}

Rowland, J.F.B., 1978, **Information transfer and use in chemistry** : Final report of the Chemical Information Review Committee. {BCL}

Houghton, Bernard, 1967, **Information work today** : Symposium on information work today, September, 1966, Liverpool. {ICA IIMC MHA}

Holloway, A.M., et al, 1976, **Information work with unpublished reports.** {NASSDOC}

Chandler, George, 1982, **International and national library and information**

services : A review of some recent developments, 2 vols. {IIT NASSDOC NERC}

Gessford, J.E., 1980, **Modern information systems.** {NIH}

Penna, C.V., et al, eds., 1977, **National library and information services** : Handbook for planners. {CRRI DUL IIT INSA JNU NASSDOC NCAER NIEPA}

Anon, 1982, **Papers** : IASLIC seminar on information services in India, 1982, Kanpur. [Indian Association of Special Libraries and Information Centres]. {CRRI}

Kapoor, S.K., ed., 1979, **Papers and proceedings** : IASLIC conference, 8th, December 26-29, 1978, Madras, Pt I : Standardisation of techniques and procedures for information handling; Pt II : Library and information system for rural development. [Indian Association of Special Libraries and Information Centres]. {BIS NIPCCD}

Gehrke, U., 1975, **Planning for a national information and documentation system** : Kenya. [UNESCO]. {NASSDOC}

Jones, Clara Station, ed., 1978, **Public library information and referral service.** {USIS}

Overhagem, Carl F.J. and Herman, R. Joyce, eds., 1965, **Report** : Planning conference on information transfer experiments, September 3, 1965, Massachusetts. {USIS}

Anon, n.d., **Responsibilities of libraries and information service.** [Organisation for European Economic Co-operation]. {BIS}

Anon, n.d., **Specification for bibliographic information interchange format for magnet tape.** (BS 4748 : 1971). [British Standards Institution]. {CRRI}

Hug, William E., ed., 1974, **Strategies for change in information programs.** {DUL USIS}

Anon, 1965, **Working papers and proceedings** : IASLIC seminar, 2nd, 1965, Chandigarh : Part-I : Users and library information services. [Indian Association of Special Libraries and Information Centres]. {SPA}

See also Reference Services : Libraries; subdivision 'Information Services' under specific subjects, e.g., Social Sciences : Information Services; Technology : Information Services, etc.

INFORMATION SERVICES : GEOGRAPHICAL AREA : CANADA

Anon, 1969, **Scientific and technical information in Canada**. [Science Council of Canada]. {JNU}

INFORMATION SERVICES : GEOGRAPHICAL AREA : GREAT BRITAIN

Codlin, Ellen M., ed., 1982, **ASLIB directory of information sources in the United Kingdom**, vol. 1: Science, Technology & Commerce, 5th edn. {JNU}

Burkett, J., ed., 1965, **Special library and information services in the United Kingdom**, 2nd edn. [Library Association, London]. {NIEPA}

INFORMATION SERVICES : GEOGRAPHICAL AREA : INDIA

Sengupta, B., 1981, **Indian reference and information services**. {ICA NIH}

Astall, Raland, 1966, **Special libraries and information bureau** : An examination guidebook. {BIS ICA IIC IIFT IIT MFL NMML SPA}

Saha, J., 1969, **Special libraries and information services in India and in the U.S.A.** {IEG IIT NASSDOC}

Ghosh,.G.B. and Banerjee, B.N., 1974, **Trends of information service in India.** {AIU CRRI ICHR NASSDOC NERC NIH NIPCCD ZHL}

INFORMATION STORAGE AND RETRIEVAL SYSTEMS

Shera, Jesse H., ed., n.d., **Advances in documentation and library science.** 3 vols. {BIS}

Meadow, Charles T., 1973, **Analysis of information systems.** {BIS CRRI DUL NIH NIPCCD USIS}

Jones, Karen Spark, 1971, **Automatic keyword classification for information retrieval.** {BCL BIS NASSDOC}

Hagler, Ronald, and Simmons, Peter, 1982, **Bibliographic record and information technology.** {DUL JNU}

Tedd, L.A., 1979, **Case studies in computer based bibliographic information services.** {BCL}

Wolman, Yecheskel, 1983, **Chemical information** : A practical guide to utilisation. {CRRI}

Stevens, Norman D., n.d., **Comparative study of three systems of information retrieval.** [Graduate School of Library Science, New Brunswick]. {BIS MHA}

Wessel, Andrew E., 1975, **Computer-aided information retrieval.** {BIS CRRI NIH USIS}

Houghton, Bernard, ed., 1968, **Computer based information retrieval systems.** {DUL INSA NASSDOC}

Henley, J.P., 1970, **Computer based library and information systems.** {BIS IIT JNU NASSDOC NIH}

Henley, J.P., 1972, **Computer based library and information systems,** 2nd edn. {DUL NIH}

Anon, 1981, **Computer based national information systems** : Technology and public policy issues. [U.S. Office of Technology Assessment]. {USIS}

Stokes, Adrian V., 1982, **Concise encyclopaedia of information technology.** {CRRI JNU NASSDOC RTC}

Saracevic, Tefko, and Wood, Judith B, 1981, **Consolidation of information** : A handbook on evaluation, restructuring and repackaging of scientific and technical information. [UNESCO]. {CRRI}

Henderson, M.M., et al, **Cooperation, convertibility and compatibility among information systems** : A literature review. {BIS}

Vasarhelyi, Paul, n.d., **DARE Equal : UNESCO computerised data retrieval system for documentation in the social and human sciences.** {NASSDOC}

Anon, 1976, **DEVSIS** : The preliminary design of an international information system for the development sciences. [International Development Research Centre, DEVSIS Study Team, Ottawa]. {NASSDOC}

Hussain, Khateeb M., 1973, **Development of information systems for education.** {AIU INSA}

Rowley, J.E. and Turner, C.M.D., 1978, **The dissemination of information.** {BCL DUL ISI NASSDOC ZHL}

Wilson, T.D. and Stephenson, J., 1969, **Dissemination of information** : An examination guide book. {BIS DUL MFL NIPCCD}

Montgomery, K. Leon, 1975, **Document retrieval systems** : Factors effecting search time. {DUL IIT NASSDOC USIS}

Guha, Bimalendu, 1988, **Documentation and information** : Services, techniques and systems, 2nd edn. {DUL ICA IIT JNU MHA NIH NIPCCD ZHL}

Sengupta, Benoyendra and Chatterjee, Mridula, 1977, **Documentation and information retrieval.** {DUL MHA ZHL}

Perry, J.W. and Kent, Allen, n.d., **Documentation and information retrieval** : An information to basic principle and cost analysis. {JNU}

Ranganathan, S.R., 1963, **Documentation and its facets** : Being a symposium of seventy papers by thirty-two authors. {BIS DUL DSSW IIFT JNU NMML SPA}

Salton, Gerard, 1975, **Dynamic information and library processing.** {CRRI DUL ICHR INSA ISI NASSDOC USIS}

Bird, E.A., 1972, **Electronic data processing computers for commercial students.** {NERC}

Kent, Allen, et al, eds., 1967, **Electronic handling of information** : Testing and evaluation. {DUL INSA}

Kruzas, Anthony Thomas, ed., 1974, **Encyclopaedia of information systems and services.** {MHA}

Kruzas, Anthony Thomas, ed., 1978, **Encyclopaedia of information system and services** : A guide to information storage and retrieval services, database produces and publishers, online vendors, 3rd edn. {USIS}

Kruzas, Anthony Thomas, ed., 1981, **Encyclopaedia of information system and services** : An international guide to computer readable databases, database producers and publishers, online vendors and time sharing companies, 4th edn. {USIS}

Schmittroth, John, ed., 1982, **Encyclopaedia of information systems and services**, 5th edn. {USIS}

Anon, n.d., **Final report on mechanised information services in the university library** : Phase-I : Planning. 13 pts. Pt 1 : Mechanised information services in the university library : Introduction and summary; Pt 2 : Summary of symposium on mechanised information services in the university library; Pt 3 : Inventory of available databases; Pt 4 : Standards for cataloguing of magnetic tape material; Pt 5 : Nature of typical databases; Pt 6 : Evaluation of generalised file management systems; Pt 7 : Experience with Library of Congress rare tapes; Pt 8 : Experimental on-line mathematics citation database; Pt 9 : Development programme for a centre for information services; Pt 10 : Preliminary specifications (hardware and software) for a centre for information and documentation services (Interim report); Pt 11 : On the development of social science information; Pt 12 : Joint design and development of library systems; and Pt 13 : Library and human memory. [Institute of Library Research, University of California]. {BIS}

Carey, R.J.P., 1966, **Finding and using technical information.** {MHA}

Kolatkar, Ram S., 1970, **Finding the facts** : Newspaper information retrieval system. {IIMC JNU NIPCCD}

Booth, Grayce M., 1973, **Functional analysis of information processing** : A structured approach for simplifying systems design. {NASSDOC}

Kochen, Manfred, ed., 1967, **The growth of knowledge** : Readings on organisation and retrieval of knowledge. {NIEPA USIS}

Anon, 1972, **Guide to selected computer based information services.** [Association of Special Libraries and Information Bureaux]. {CRRI}

Atherton, Pauline, 1978, **Handbook for information systems and services.** [UNESCO]. {ICA IIMC NASSDOC NIEPA TDA USIS}

Chandler, G., 1967, **How to find out** : A guide to sources of information for all, arranged by the Dewey Decimal Classification, 2nd edn. {MHA}

Alexander, C. and Burke, A.J., 1958, **How to locate educational information and data,** 4th edn. {NIEPA}

Wessel, Andrew E., 1979, **Implementation of complex information system.**

{CRRI IIT USIS}
Jackson, Eugene B. and Jackson, Ruth L., 1978, **Industrial information systems** : A manual for higher management and their information officer, librarian/associates. {USIS}
Kent, Allen, 1971, **Information analysis and retrieval.** {CRRI JNU MHA NASSDOC NIPCCD}
Anon, n.d., **Information and its dissemination.** [Institute of Petroleum, London]. {BIS}
Doednikoff, Basic, 1973, **Information retrieval.** {JNU}
Van Rijsbergen, C.J., 1979, **Information retrieval,** 2nd edn. {BCL CRRI DUL IEG MMTC NIH}
Metcalfe, John, 1976, **Information retrieval** : British and American. {JNU}
Scheeter, George, 1967, **Information retrieval** : A critical view. {JNU}
Heaps, H.S., 1978, **Information retrieval** : Computational and theoretical aspects. {BCL CRRI NIH}
Sharp, John Raymond, 1970, **Information retrieval** : Notes for students. {BCL}
Paice, D.B., 1977, **Information retrieval and the computer.** {BCL}
Kent, Allen, ed., 1960, **Information retrieval and machine translation.** {CRRI DUL}
Doyle, Lauren B., 1975, **Information retrieval and processing.** {BIS CRRI DUL IIMC ISI NASSDOC NIH USIS}
Jones, Karen Spark, ed., 1981, **Information retrieval experiment.** {BIS IIMC IIT}
Haltery, Loweld H. and McCormik, Edmaral M., 1962, **Information retrieval management.** {JNU}
Lancaster, F.W. and Fayen, E.G., 1973, **Information retrieval on-line.** {DUL INSA ISI NASSDOC USIS}
Oddy, R.N., et al, eds., 1981, **Information retrieval research.** {IIMC JNU NASSDOC}
Lancaster, F.W., 1968, **Information retrieval systems** : Characteristics, testing and evaluation. {TDA}
Lancaster, F.W., 1979, **Information retrieval systems** : Characteristics, testing and evaluation, 2nd edn. {CRRI DUL IIT USIS}
Anon, 1970, **Information retrieval systems** : Subject authority list, 7th edn. [American Petroleum Institute]. {IIT}
Barhydt, Gordon, C. and Schmidt, Charles T., n.d., **Information retrieval thesaurus of education terms.** {AIU}
Chen, Ching-Chih and Hernon, Peter, 1982, **Information seeking** : Assessing and anticipating user needs. {JNU}
Chen, Ching-Chih and Hernon, Peter, 1982, **Information seeking** : Assessing and anticipating user needs. {JNU}
Taube, Mortimer and Wooster, Harold, eds., 1958, **Information storage and retrieval** : Theory, system and devices. {CRRI DUL}
Becker, Joseph and Hayes, Robert M., 1963, **Information storage and retrieval** : Tools, elements, theories. {DUL ICA IEG MFL NASSDOC USIS}
Politt, A.S., 1989, **Information storage and retrieval systems** : Origin, development and applications. {NASSDOC}
Jahoda, Gerald, 1970, **Information storage and retrieval systems for individual researchers.** {ISI MHA USIS}
Murdick, Robert G. and Ross, Jod E., 1977, **Information system for modern management.** {ICA}

Vickery, B.C., 1973, **Information systems.** {DUL ICA ISI MMTC NASSDOC}
Burch, John G., et al, 1979, **Information systems** : Theory and practice. {JNU NIPCCD TDA}
Shera, J.H., et al, 1975, **Information systems in documentation.** {CRRI DLU JNU}
Weisman, Herman M., 1972, **Information systems, services and centres.** {CRRI DUL NASSDOC USIS}
Kent, Allen and Galvin, Thomas J., eds., 1982, **Information technology** : Critical choices for library decision makers : Pittsburg conference on electronic information technology and its impact on library and information services, 1981, 4th, Pittsburg. {BIS CRRI IIT JNU USIS}
Anon, 1982, **Information technology and its impact on American education.** {USIS}
Anon, 1974, **Information technology in local government** : A survey of the development of urban and regional information systems in five European countries. [Organisation for Economic Cooperation and Development]. {BCL}
Smith, Robert Irvine and Combell, Bob, 1981, **Information technology revolution.** {NASSDOC}
Chartrand, Robert Lee and Morentz, James W., eds., 1979, **Information technology serving society.** {USIS}
Aiyepeku, Wilson O., 1983, **International socio-economic information systems** : An evaluating directory of DEVSIS-type programs. {NASSDOC}
Anon, n.d., **International standards for computers and information processing.** [International Organisation for Standardisation]. {BIS}
Salton, Gerard and Mc Gill, Michael J., 1983, **Introduction to modern information retrieval.** {BIS}
Rowley, J.E., 1979, **Mechanised in-house information systems.** {BCL CRRI NIPCCD}
Anon, 1976, **Minicomputers and bibliographic information retrieval.** [British Library Lending Division]. {BCL}
Arnold, Robert R., et al, 1972, **Modern data processing,** 2nd edn. {NASSDOC}
Gessford, J.E., 1980, **Modern information systems.** {NIH}
Carter, Launor F., et al, 1967, **National document handling systems for science and technology.** {BIS IIMC NIH USIS}
Holmes, P.L., 1978, **On-line information retrieval** : An introduction and guide to British library's short term experimental information network project, Vol. 1 : Experimental use of non-medical information services; Vol. 2 : Experimental use of medical information services. [British Library]. {BCL}
Hall, J.L., comp., 1977, **On-line information retrieval, 1965-76** : A bibliography with a guide to on-line databases and systems. [Association of Special Libraries and Information Bureaux]. {BCL CRRI NASSDOC}
Houghton, Bernard and Convey, John, 1977, **On-line information retrieval systems** : An introductory manual to principles and practices. {BCL CRRI DUL NIH}
Vickery, B.C., 1965, **On retrieval system theory,** 2nd edn. {CRRI DUL IIT}
Perlman, M., ed., 1977, **Organisation and retrieval of economic knowledge** : Proceedings of the conference held by the International Economic Association. {NASSDOC}
Taraboi, Vasile, 1973, **Organisation, functioning and activities of national documentary information systems in the scientific, technical and economic**

fields. [National Institute for Scientific and Technical Information and Documentation, Romania]. {BIS}

De Grolier, Eric, 1979, **Organisation of information systems for government and public administration**. {BIS JNU}

Mabbs, A.W., 1974, **Organisation of intermediate records storage**. [UNESCO]. {NIEPA NMML}

Needham, C.D., 1966, **Organising knowledge in libraries** : An introduction to classification and cataloguing. {IIC MFL SPA ZHL}

Needham, C.D., 1971, **Organising knowledge in libraries** : An introduction to information retrieval, 2nd rev edn. {ICA IIFT NASSDOC}

Anon, 1981, **Papers** : Conference on electronic information technology and its impact on library and information service, 4th, 1981, Pittsburg. {IIT}

Anon, 1973, **Papers** : Conference on informatics, 1973, Durham. [Association of Special Libraries and Information Bureaux]. {CRRI}

Horsnell, Verina, ed., 1974, **Papers** : Conference on informatics, 1974, Oxford. [Association of Special Libraries and Information Bureaux]. {CRRI}

Anon, 1981, **Papers** : DRTC annual seminar on information analysis and consolidation, 1981, Bangalore. [Documentation Research and Training Centre, Bangalore]. {CRRI}

Anon, 1980, **Papers** : DRTC refresher seminar on data accessibility and dissemination, 1980, Bangalore. [Documentation Research and Training Centre, Bangalore]. {CRRI}

Anon, 1982, **Papers** : IASLIC seminar on information services in India, 1982, Kanpur. [Indian Association of Special Libraries and Information Centres]. {CRRI}

Anon, 1980, **Papers** : Workshop on computer techniques in information processing. [University of Delhi, Department of Library and Information Science]. {AIU}

Kapoor, S.K., ed., 1979, **Papers and proceedings** : IASLIC conference, 8th, December 26-29, 1978, Madras, Pt I : Standardisation of techniques and procedures for information handling; Pt II : Library and information system for rural development. [Indian Association of Special Libraries and Information Centres]. {BIS NIPCCD}

Anon, 1966, **Practical approach to information and data retrieval**. [Boston Industrial Education Institute]. {ISI}

Kochen, Manfred, 1974, **Principles of information retrieval**. {CRRI DUL ISI MHA USIS}

Anon, 1957, **Proceedings** : International study conference on classification for information retrieval, 1957, {IEC IIT}

Anon, 1980, **Proceedings** : Seminar on international cooperative information systems, July 9-13, 1979. [International Development Research Centre]. {CRRI USIS}

Anon, 1983, **Report** : Asian regional seminar on information sources, systems and services in the social sciences, July 11-22, 1983, Philippines [UNESCO Regional Office, Bangkok]. {NASSDOC*}

Simon, Herbert A. and Siklossy, Leurent, 1972, **Representation and meaning** : Experiments with information processing systems. {NASSDOC}

Slavens, Thomas P., ed., 1981, **Retrieval of information in the humanities and the social sciences**. {NIEPA}

Mc Garry, K.J. and Burrell, T.W., 1972, **Semantics in the organisation of knowledge** : A programmed text for students in information retrieval. {NASSDOC}

Anon, 1970, **System scope for library automation and generalised information**

storage and retrieval at Stanford University. {IIT}

Vickery, B.C., 1970, **Techniques of information retrieval.** {AIU BCL IEG IIMC INSA JNU}

Kent, Allen, 1962, **Textbook on mechanised information retrieval.** {CRRI}

Anon, 1979, **Theoretical problems of informatics** : Forecasting of the development of scientific information activities. [International Federation for Documentation and Information]. {CRRI}

Anon, 1981, **Theoretical problems of information** : Criteria of the quality of information systems and processes : Collection of papers. [International Federation for Documentation and Information]. {BIS}

Landry, Bertrand Clovis, 1971, **Theory of indexing** : Indexing theory as a model for information storage and retrieval. [Computer and Information Science Research Centre, Ohio State University]. {IIT}

Rubinoff, Morris, ed., 1965, **Towards a national information system** : Second annual national colloquium on information retrieval. {IIT}

Hills, Philip J., ed., 1982, **Trends in information transfer.** {ISI NASSDOC}

Anon, 1980, **UNISIST guide for the establishment and evaluation of services for selective dissemination of information.** [UNESCO]. {CRRI}

Anon, 1980, **UNISIST guide to standards for information handling.** [UNESCO]. {BIS DUL MMTC}

Anon, 1978, **UNISIST guidelines for the evaluation of information systems and services.** [UNESCO]. {BIS}

Howerton, P.W., 1963, **Vistas in information handling** : The augmentation of man's intellect by machine. {MHA}

See also Electronic Data Processing; Indexes and Indexing : Automatic; Libraries : Automation; SMART (Information Retrieval System); SYNTOL (Information Retrival System); Selective Dissemination of Information

INFORMATION STORAGE AND RETRIEVAL SYSTEMS : CHEMISTRY

Peaks, Gilbert L., et al, 1957, **Progress report in chemical literature retrieval.** {CRRI}

INFORMATION STORAGE AND RETRIEVAL SYSTEMS : MEDICINE

See also MEDLARS

INFORMATION STORAGE AND RETRIEVAL SYSTEMS : POPULATION

Conning, Arthur M., 1983, **Guide to the computerisation of population documentation storage and retrieval systems.** [United Nations]. {NASSDOC}

INFORMATION STORAGE AND RETRIEVAL SYSTEMS : TECHNOLOGY

Anon, 1982, **Information technology and its impact on American education.** {USIS}

Anon, 1974, **Information technology in local government** : A survey of the development of urban and regional information systems in five European countries. [Organisation for Economic Cooperation and Development]. {BCL}

Smith, Robert Irvine and Combell, Bob, 1981, **Information technology revolution.** {NASSDOC}

Chartrand, Robert Lee and Morentz, James W., eds., 1979, **Information technology serving society.** {USIS}

Maltha, D.J., 1976, **Technical literature search and the written report**. {BCL}

INFORMATION THEORY

Jagjit Singh, 1967, **Great ideas in information theory, language and cybernetics**. {INSA}

Abramson, Norman, 1963, **Information theory and coding**. {INSA}

Jelinek, Frederick, 1968, **Probabilistic information theory** : Discrete and memoryless models. {INSA}

Anon, 1981, **Theoretical problems of information** : Criteria of the quality of information systems and processes : Collection of papers. [International Federation for Documentation and Information]. {BIS}

Anon, 1979, **Theoretical problems of information** : New trends in information and its terminology. [International Federation for Documentation and Information]. {CRRI}

Anon, 1964, **Transactions** : Prague conference on information theory, statistical decision function, random processes, June 3, 1962. {INSA}

INITIALISMS

See Acronyms

INSTRUCTIONAL MEDIA CENTRE

Davis, Harold S., ed., 1971, **Instructional Media Centre** : Bold new venture. {USIS}

INTELLECTUAL FREEDOM

See Censorship

INTERLIBRARY LOANS

Thomson, Sarah Katharin, 1970, **Interlibrary loan involving academic libraries**. [American Library Association]. {NASSDOC}

Thomson, Sarah Katharin, 1979, **Interlibrary loan procedure manual**. [American Library Association]. {DUL NASSDOC USIS}

Anon, 1962, **International inter-library lending** : A review of the literature. [International Federation of Library Associations and Institutions]. {NASSDOC}

Kent, Allen, ed., 1974, **Resource sharing in libraries** : Why, how when : Next action steps. {IIT INSA NASSDOC}

Anon, n.d., **Working papers and proceedings of the three symposia**, I : General vs special classification schemes; II : Inter library loan and exchange of materials in India; III : Social science documentation in India : IASLIC seminar, 3rd, 1964, Lucknow; [Indian Association of Special Libraries and Information Centres]. {NASSDOC SPA}

INTERLIBRARY LOANS : GEOGRAPHICAL AREA : DEVELOPING COUNTRIES

Vervliet, H.D.L., 1979, **Resource sharing of libraries in developing countries** : Proceedings : IFLA/UNESCO pre-session seminar for librarians from developing countries, August 30-September 3, 1977, [Antwerp University]. {NASSDOC}

INTERNATIONAL BOOK NUMBERING SYSTEM

Anon, 1972, **ISBN** : International standard book numbering (incorporating the recommendations for implementing the Standard Book Numbering Scheme). [Standard Book Numbering Agency, London]. {NASSDOC}

INTERNATIONAL FEDERATION OF LIBRARY ASSOCIATIONS AND INSTITUTIONS

Anon, 1977-79, **Directory**, 1977; 1979. [International Federation of Library Association and Institutions]. {NASSDOC}

Anon, 1987, **IFLA and the Third World** : The IFLA core on the advancement of librarianship in the Third World. (ALP). {NASSDOC}

Anon, 1988, **IFLA annual** : Proceedings of the general conferences; Annual reports. [International Federation of Library Associations and Institutions]. {NASSDOC}

Anon, n.d., **IFLA directory** : 1977; 1979; 1982-84; 1984-85; 1986-87; 1988-89. [International Federation of Library Associations and Institutions]. {NASSDOC}

Anon, 1986, **IFLA statutes, rules of procedure terms of reference.** [International Federation of Library Associations and Institutions] {NASSDOC}

INTERNATIONAL LIBRARIANSHIP

Gidwani, N.N., ed., 1973, **Comparative librarianship** : Essays in honour of Prof. D.N. Marshall. {ICHR IIC JNU NASSDOC NIPCCD NMML ZHL}

Chandler, George, ed., 1972, **International librarianship** : Surveys of recent developments in developing countries and in advanced librarianship submitted to the 1971 IFLA pre-session seminar for developing countries, August 24—September 1, 1971. [Library Association, London]. {NASSDOC}

See also Comparative Librarianship; Library Science

INTERNATIONAL SERIAL DATA SYSTEM

Mullis, A.A., ed., 1983, **ISDS manual**. (International Serial Data System). {NASSDOC}

INTERNATIONAL STANDARD BOOK NUMBERING SYSTEM

Anon, 1972, **ISBN** : International standard book numbering (incorporating the recommendations for implementing the Standard Book Numbering Scheme). [Standard Book Numbering Agency, London]. {NASSDOC}

INTERVIEWING

Atkinson, Jean, 1968, **Handbook for interviewers** : A manual for Government social survey interviewing staff, describing practice and procedures on structured interviewing. {NASSDOC}

Gorden, Raymond L., 1969, **Interviewing** : Strategy, techniques and tactics. {NASSDOC}

ISAAC, K.A.

Devarajan, G. and Rahelamma, A.V., 1990, **Library computerisation in India** : Isaac festschrift. {JNU}

ISLAMIC LIBRARIES : BIBLIOGRAPHY

Anon, n.d., **Islamic libraries**, mimeo short bibliography. {NASSDOC}

ISLAMIC LIBRARIES : DIRECTORY

Khan, Mohammad A.S., comp., 1983, **Directory of Islamic libraries and librarians**. [Islamic Library Association, California]. {ZHL}

ISRAEL

See Geographical Area subdivision under main Descriptor, e.g., Library Education : Geographical Area : Israel

JAMMU AND KASHMIR

See Geographical Area subdivision under main Descriptor, e.g., Libraries : Geographical Area : India: Jammu and Kashmir

JAPAN

See Geographical Area subdivision under main Descriptor, e.g., References Services : Libraries : Geographical Area : Japan

JAWAHARLAL NEHRU UNIVERSITY LIBRARY SYSTEM

Anon, 1976, **Management services** : Report on the library system of the Jawaharlal Nehru University. [Institute of Secretariat Training and Management, New Delhi]. {JNU ZHL}

JOHN NEWBERY MEDAL BOOKS

See Newbery Medal Books

JOURNAL OF APPLIED PHYSICS (PERIODICAL)

Libetz, Ben Anni, 1964, **Citations for physics literature** : Experimental issue : Citations of Journal of Applied Physics : The physical review. {DUL}

JOURNALISM : BIBLIOGRAPHY

Anon, 1972, **Education, library science, journalism** : A bibliography of doctoral dissertations, 1857-1970. [Inter-University Board of India and Ceylon, New Delhi]. {JNU NMML}

KAMATH, V.A.

Guha, B., ed., 1986, **In the library and information science horizon** : A collection of essays in honour of Dr. V.A. Kamath, presented by the Bombay Science Librarians Association (BOSLA). {JNU NASSDOC}

KARNATAKA

See Geographical Area subdivision under main Descriptor, e.g., Public Libraries : Geographical Area : India : Karnataka

KAULA, P.N.

Bhargava, G.D. and Tejomurty, A. eds., 1986, **Dimensions in library and information science**. {JNU}

KHUDA BAKSH ORIENTAL PUBLIC LIBRARY

O'Connor, V.C. Scott, 1920, **Eastern library**. {ZHL}

O'Connor, V.C. Scott, 1977, **Eastern library** : An introduction to the Khuda Bakhsh Oriental Public Library, 2nd edn. {JNU NMML}

O'Connor, V.C. Scott, 1985, **An eastern library** : An introduction to the Khuda Bakhsh Oriental Public Library, 3rd edn. {NASSDOC*}

O'Connor, V.C. Scott, 1950, **Ek mashriqui kutubkhana** : Kutub- khana Khuda

Bakhsh, tr. by Mubarizuddin Rifat. {NMML}

KNOWLEDGE

Boulding, Kenneth E. and Senesh, Lawrence, 1983, **Optimum utilisation of knowledge** : Making knowledge serve human betterment. {NMML}

Bliss, Henry Evelyn, 1929, **Organisation of knowledge and system of the sciences**. {DUL}

Bliss, Henry Evelyn, 1939, **Organisation of knowledge in libraries and the subject-approach to books,** 2nd edn. {BIS IEG USIS}

Needham, C.D., 1966, **Organising knowledge in libraries** : An introduction to classification and cataloguing. {IIC MFL SPA ZHL}

Mechluip, Fritz, 1972, **Production and distribution of knowledge in the United States.** {NASSDOC}

Wilson, Patrick, 1977, **Public knowledge and private ignorance** : Towards a library and information policy. {CRRI USIS}

McGarry, K.J. and Burrell, T.W., 1972, **Semantics in the organisation of knowledge** : A programmed text for students in information retrieval. {NASSDOC}

Bulick, Stephen, 1982, **Structure and subject interaction** : Toward a sociology of knowledge in the social sciences. {BIS}

LATIN AMERICA

See Geographical Area subdivision under main Descriptor, e.g., Public Libraries : Geographical Area : Latin America

LAW : LIBRARY

See Library Legislation

LAW LIBRARIES

Anon, 1968, **Report** Jessup, Libby, F., et al, 1962, **Manual of procedures for private law libraries.** [American Association of Law Libraries]. {USIS}

LEH UNIVERSITY LIBRARY

Flannery, Anne and Mack, James D., 1966, **Mechanised circulation system, Leh University Library**. {JNU}

LIBRARIANS

See Librarians and Librarianship

See also Library Science as a Profession

LIBRARIANS : BIOGRAPHY

Khosla, Raj K. and Gaur, M.K., eds., 1967, **Men of library science and libraries in India**. {SPA USIS}

Landau, T., 1972, **Who's who in librarianship and information science,** 2nd edn. {JNU}

See also under names, e.g., Ranganathan, S.R.,

LIBRARIANS : CONGRESS

See Meetings : Proceedings/Reports/Souvenirs

LIBRARIANS : EDUCATION AND TRAINING
See Library Education

LIBRARIANS : IN-SERVICE TRAINING

Sardana, J.L., ed., 1984, **Continuing education for librarians** : Paper : All India Seminar for Librarians, February 13, 1984, New Delhi, [Indian Library Association]. {NASSDOC}

Anon, 1967, **Proceedings** : Seminar of university librarians in India, 1967, Jaipur. [Rajasthan University]. {DUL IIT}

Anon, 1984, **Reading material** : Orientation seminar on planning and management for senior administrators of public library services, February 6-10, 1984, New Delhi. {NASSDOC NIEPA}

Anon, 1977, **Report** : Orientation course for the libraries of cooperative training colleges and apex level organisations/institutions in India, June 1977, New Delhi. [National Council for Cooperative Training, New Delhi]. {ICA}

LIBRARIANS : PROFESSIONAL ETHICS

Anon, 1984, **Papers** : IASLIC national seminar, 11th, November 26-29, 1984, Hyderabad, I : Toward a code of professional ethics; II : Document delivery, reproduction, translation. [Indian Association of Special Libraries and Information Centres]. {NASSDOC}

LIBRARIANS : SALARIES, PENSIONS, ETC.

Anon, 1974, **Report** : University Grants Commission committee on scales of pay and qualification, etc., for library staff in universities and colleges. [University Grants Commission, New Delhi]. {NIEPA}

LIBRARIANS AND LIBRARIANSHIP

Muthuswamy, A.T., 1969, **ABC of library science.** {NASSDOC}

Voight, Melvin J. and Harris, Michael J., 1970-86, **Advances in librarianship**, 14 vols. {IEG NASSDOC NCAER NIH NMML USIS}

Minaikit, Nonglak, 1968, **Annotated bibliography on librarianship in Thailand.** {JNU}

Anon, 1985, **Bachelor degree in library and information science** : A handbook. [Andhra Pradesh Open University, Hyderabad]. {NASSDOC}

Wijasuriya, D.E.K. and Huck-Tee, Lim, 1975, **Barefoot librarian** : Library development in Southeast Asia with special reference to Malaysia. {NIEPA}

White, Carl M., ed., 1964, **Bases of modern librarianship** : A study of library theory and practice in Britain, Canada, Denmark, the Federal Republic of Germany and the United States. {IIT JNU NIPCCD NMML SPA}

Yrumpeter, Marg C. and Rounds, Richards, 1985, **Basic budgeting practices for librarians**. {JNU}

Spivack, Jane, F., 1982, **Careers in information.** {USIS}

Anon, 1961, **The changing pattern of librarianship**. [Library Association, London]. {ICA}

Shiart-Shibbs, B., 1985, **Changing technology and education for librarianship and information science.** {NASSDOC}

Smith, Josephine Metcalfe, 1968, **A chronology of librarianship**. {USIS}

Thorton, John L., 1941, **Chronology of librarianship**. {CRRI}

Jackson, Miles M., ed., 1970, **Comparative and international librarianship** : Essays on themes and problems. {AIU IIT}

Gidwani, N.N., ed., 1973, **Comparative librarianship** : Essays in honour of Prof.

D.N. Marshall. {ICHR IIC JNU NASSDOC NIPCCD NMML ZHL}

Chene, Steven Seapho, 1976, **Comparative study of librarian's job satisfaction** : Cataloguer and reference librarians in university libraries. {JNU}

Jackson, Miles M., ed., 1981, **Contemporary developments in librarianship** : An international handbook. [Library Association, London]. {IIT NASSDOC}

Sardana, J.L., ed., 1984, **Continuing education for librarians** : Paper : All India seminar for librarians, February 13, 1984, New Delhi. [Indian Library Association]. {NASSDOC}

Danton, J. Periam, 1973, **Dimensions of comparative librarianship.** [American Library Association]. {NASSDOC}

Thomas, Diana M., 1981, **Effective reference librarian**. {IIT ISI NASSDOC}

Anon, 1975, **Essays and studies in librarianship**. {NASSDOC}

Foskett, D.J. and Palmer, B.I., 1961, **Essays in librarianship** : In memory of William Charles Berwick Sayers. {MFL}

Mangla, P.B., et al, eds., 1983, **Fifty years of librarianship in India** : Past present and future : Papers : All India Library Conference, 29th, December 5-9, 1983. [Indian Library Assocation] {MMTC NASSDOC ZHL}

Harrison, K.C., 1964, **First steps in librarianship.** {CRRI ICHR IIT MFL SPA}

Sewell, P.H., ed., 1963, **Five year work in librarianship.** [Library Association, London]. {IIT}

Wasserman, Paul, ed., 1972, **Frontiers in librarianship** : Proceedings of Change Institute, 1969. [Change Institute, University of Maryland]. {JNU NIPCCD}

Mukherjee, A.K., 1969, **Fundamentals of special librarianship and documentation**. [Indian Association of Special Libraries and Information Centres]. {AIU DUL IIT}

Singh, R.S.P., 1981, **Glimpses of librarianship**. {JNU}

Neelameghan, A., ed., 1977, **Guidelines for formulation of a policy on education, training and development of library and information personnel** : All India seminar on library and information science education, October 3-8, 1977, Delhi. [Indian Statistical Institution]. {NASSDOC}.

Simsova, S. and Mackee, Monique, 1970, **Handbook of comparative librarianship**. {NASSDOC}

Simsova, S. and Mackee, Monique, 1975, **Handbook of comparative librarianship,** 2nd edn. {BIS IICL ISI NIPCCD}

Mackee, Monique, 1983, **Handbook of comparative librarianship**, 3rd edn. {NASSDOC}

Ashworth, W., ed., 1955, **Handbook of special librarianship and information work.** [Association of Special Libraries and Information Bureaux]. {BIS IEG}

Ashworth, W., ed., 1962, **Handbook of special librarianship and information work**. 2nd edn. [Association of Special Libraries and Information Bureaux]. {IIT SPA}

Ashworth, W., ed., 1967, **Handbook of special librarianship and information work**, 3rd edn. [Association of Special Libraries and Information Bureaux]. {MHA MMTC NASSDOC NIH}

Batten, W.E., ed., 1975, **Handbook of special librarianship and information work,** 4th edn. [Association of Special Libraries and Information Bureaux]. {CRRI IIT}

Thompson, James, 1968, **History of the principles of librarianship.** {IIT}

Goyal, Satpaul, ed, n.d., **Indian librarianship**. {JNU}

Sharma, Ravindra N., ed., 1981, **Indian librarianship** : Perspectives and prospects.

{IEG NASSDOC}

Debons, Anthony, 1981, **Information professional** : Survey of an emerging field. {IIT JNU USIS}

Garnoosky, Leon, ed., n.d., **International aspects of librarianship**. {IEG}

Jackson, Miles M., ed., 1981, **International handbook of contemporary developments in librarianship.** {USIS}

Gates, J.K., 1968, **Introduction to librarianship.** {IIT MFL NCAER ZHL}

Gates, J.K., 1976, **Introduction to librarianship,** 2nd edn. {USIS}

Gardner, Frank M., 1951, **Letters to a younger librarian**. {DUL NASSDOC}

Savage, Ernest A., 1942, **The librarian and his committee.** {CRRI}

Ganguly, N., 1933, **Librarian and library administration**. {NAI}

Jahoda, Gerald and Braunagel, J.S., 1980, **Librarian and reference queries** : A systematic approach. {CRRI ISI USIS}

Lyle, Guy R., 1970, **Librarian speaking** : Interview with university librarians. {JNU USIS}

Harrod, L.M., 1971, **Librarians' glossary of terms used in librarianship and the book crafts and reference book**, 3rd edn. {CRRI IIT JNU NASSDOC}

Harrod, L.M., 1977, **Librarians' glossary of terms used in librarianship, documentation and the book crafts and reference book**, 4th edn. {ICA IIC MMTC NCDC NCERT NERC NIH NMML ZHL}

Taylor, L.J., ed., 1976, **Librarians' handbook** [Library Association London]. 2 vols. {JNU NASSDOC NIPCCD}

Ghazi, Muhammad Ismail, 1963, **A librarian's musing.** {JNU}

Pipics, Zoltan, ed., 1969, **Librarians' practical dictionary in twenty-two languages**. {JNU}

De Hart, Florence E, 1979, **Librarian's psychological commitments** : Human relations in librarianship. {INSA NIPCCD USIS}

Gujarati, B.S., 1964, **Librarianship.** {NERC NIPCCD ZHL}

Tomlinson, N., 1963, **Librarianship.** {NIH}

Umapathy Setty, K. 1977, **Librarianship** : Change or status quo. {CRRI JNU}

Irwin, Raymond, 1949, **Librarianship** : Essays on applied bibliography. {CRRI}

Atkinson, Frank, 1974, **Librarianship** : Introduction to the profession. {ICA USIS}

Mukherjee, A.K., 1966, **Librarianship** : Its philosophy and history. {BIS IIT NASSDOC NIH SPA}

Sharma, Ravindra N., ed., 1981, **Librarianship** : Perspectives and prospects. {AIU NIEPA}

Hutchings, F.G.B., 1969, **Librarianship** : A short manual with special reference to developing countries. {IIMC SPA}

Jayaswal, P.K., 1990, **Librarianship and bureaucratic organisation** : A study in the sociology of library profession in India. {JNU NASSDOC}

Coblans, Herbert, 1974, **Librarianship and documentation** : An international perspective. {BIS ICHR ISI NASSDOC NERC}

Abdul Haq, A.M. and Aman, Mohammad M., 1977, **Librarianship and the Third World** : An annotated bibliography of selected literature on developing nations, 1960-1975. {NASSDOC}

Myson, William, 1963, **Librarianship as a career**. {ICA}

Anon, n.d., **Librarianship as a profession,** mimeo short bibliography. {NASSDOC}

Chopra, H.R., 1984, **Librarianship as a profession** : A study of socio-economic background and professional orientation of the libraries in Delhi : Thesis. [Punjab University]. {NASSDOC}

Asheim, Lester, 1966, **Librarianship in developing countries.** {NIPCCD}
Bhargava, G.D.,1977, **Librarianship in India and abroad** : Retrospect and prospect. {CRRI ICA IIT JNU NASSDOC NCAER NIEPA NIPCCD ZHL}
Lancaster, F.W., 1982, **Libraries and librarians in an age of electronics.** {USIS}
McColvin, L.R., 1909, **Library staff.** {IIT}
Conroy, Barbara, 1978, **Library staff development and continuing education** : Principles and practices. {USIS}
Nichols, H., 1979, **Local studies librarianship.** {NIH}
Tauber, Maurice Falcolm, 1967, **Louis Round Wilson** : Librarian and administrator. {USIS}
Picken, F.M. and Mathews, D.A., 1979, **Medical librarianship** : Outlines of modern librarianship. {NIH USIS}
Sabor, Josefa E., 1969, **Methods of teaching librarianship.** [UNESCO]. {IIMC JNU NASSDOC NIEPA NIPCCD}
Bhattacharya, K.K., 1979, **Modern trends in librarianship in India.** {IIMC IIT NMML}
Wassermann, Paul, 1972, **The new librarianship** : A challenge for change. {USIS}
Sellen, B.C., ed., 1984, **New options for librarians.** {NASSDOC*}
Mohanrajan, P.A., ed., 1984, **New trends in international librarianship.** {NASSDOC NMML}
Hussain, Mahmud, 1974, **Of libraries and librarians.** [University of Karachi]. {ZHL}
Shiflett, Orvin Lee, 1981, **Origins of American academic librarianship.** {JNU}
Wallace, Sarah Leslie, 1956, **Patrons are people** : How to be a model librarian, 2nd rev edn. [American Library Association]. {DUL USIS}
Broadffield, A., 1949, **Philosophy of librarianship.** {CRRI IEG IIT}
Simsova, Sylva, 1982, **Primer of comparative librarianship.** {IIT}
Jain, T.C., 1971, **Professional associations and development of librarianship** : Case studies. [Library Association, London; American Library Association]. {AIU NASSDOC NCAER}
Saunders, W.L., ed., 1966, **Provision and use of library and documentation services** : Some contributions. [University of Sheffield Postgraduate School of Librarianship]. {DUL JNU MHA NIH SPA USIS}
Reilly, Jane A., 1981, **The public librarian as adult learners' advisor** : An innovation in human services. {USIS}
Robbins-Carter, Jane, ed., 1982, **Public librarianship** : A reader. {USIS}
Hoadley, Irene Braden and Clark, Alice S., eds., 1974, **Quantitative methods in librarianship** : Standards, research and management. {IIT ISI JNU}
Cave, Roderick, 1976, **Rare book librarianship.** {NASSDOC}
Simpson, Murray, C.T., 1976, **Rare book librarianship** : A select annotated bibliography. {JNU}
West, Celeste and Katz, Elizabeth, eds., 1972, **Revolting librarians.** {USIS}
Ennis, Philip H. and Winger, Howard W., eds., 1962, **Seven questions about the profession of librarianship** : Proceedings of the 26th Annual Conference of the Graduate Library School. {IEG}
Shera, J.H., 1970, **Sociological foundations of librarianship.** {IEG NASSDOC NIEPA NMML ZHL}
Prytherch, Ray, comp., 1983, **Sources of information librarianship and information science** : A grafton book. {NIH}
Ruggles, Melville J. and Swank, Paynard C., 1962, **Soviet libraries and librarianship** : Report of the visit of the delegation of U.S. librarians to the Soviet

Union, May-June, 1961 under the U.S.-Soviet cultural exchange agreement. [American Library Association]. {NASSDOC NMML}

Worth, Wilfred Ash, 1979, **Special librarianship**. {JNU}

Anon, 1985, **Special librarianship**. [Andhra Pradesh Open University, Hyderabad]. {NASSDOC*}

Stewart, James D., 1947, **Tabulation of librarianship** : Classified tables for the arrangement of all material relating to library economy. {CRRI}

Rawski, Conrad H. and Towaid, A., eds., 1973, **Theory of librarianship** : Papers in honour of Jesse H. Shera. {NASSDOC*}

Burkett, Jack, ed., 1968, **Trends in special librarianship**. {IEG IIT MMTC}

Landau, T., 1972, **Who's who in librarianship and information science,** 2nd edn. {JNU}

Krzys, Richard, 1983, **World librarianship**. {IIT NMML}

Rajagopalan, T.S., ed., 1988, **Year's work in Indian librarianship, 1987**. [Indian Library Association]. {NASSDOC}

Kohn, Rita T. and Tepper, Krysta, 1981, **You can do it** : Manual for librarians. {USIS}

Clarke, J.D., 1963, **Your future as a librarian.** {IIFT}

LIBRARIANS AND LIBRARIANSHIP : GEOGRAPHICAL AREA : ASIA

Anon, 1977, **National information system** : Library and information science manpower development in Asian region : Meeting of supervisors of library and documentation schools in the Asian region, Bangalore. [UNESCO; DRTC]. {JNU}

LIBRARIANS AND LIBRARIANSHIP : GEOGRAPHICAL AREA : ASIA : SOUTH EAST

Anwar, H., 1985, **Issues in South East Asian librarianship** : A selection of papers and articles. {NASSDOC}

LIBRARIANS AND LIBRARIANSHIP : GEOGRAPHICAL AREA : AUSTRALIA

Borcharat, D.H. and Horacek, J.I., 1975, **Librarianship in Australia, New Zealand and Oceania.** {NASSDOC}

LIBRARIANS AND LIBRARIANSHIP : GEOGRAPHICAL AREA : GREAT BRITAIN

Whatley, H.A., ed., 1972, **British librarianship and information science**, 1966-70. {JNU NMML}

Wasserman, Paul, ed., 1972, **Frontiers in librarianship** : Proceedings of Change Institute, 1969. [Change Institute, University of Maryland]. {JNU NIPCCD}

Saunders, W.L., ed., 1967, **Librarianship in Britain today**. [Library Association, London]. {IIT}

LIBRARIANS AND LIBRARIANSHIP : GEOGRAPHICAL AREA : INDIA

Datta, N., 1985, **Academic status for university and college librarians in India.** {JNU}

Subbaiah, R., 1988, **Agricultural librarianship in India**. {NASSDOC}

Anon, 1975, **Faculty status for university and college librarian in India** : Basic documents. {JNU NASSDOC ZHL}

Anon, 1983, **Fifty years of Government of India Librarians Association.** [Government of India Librarians Association]. {NASSDOC NMML}

Mangla, P.B., et al, eds., 1983, **Fifty years of librarianship in India** : Past, present and future : Papers : All India library conference, 29th, December 5-9, 1983. [Indian Library Association]. {MMTC NASSDOC ZHL}

Kaul, Neelima, comp., 1980, **Handbook of information scientists and librarians in India**. {BIS CRRI IIPA IIT ISI MMTC NASSDOC NCAER NIEPA NMML RTL}

Misra, Jogesh, 1979, **History of libraries and librarianship in modern India since 1850**. {JNU NERC NMML}

Sogani, Kamal Chand and Vijay Narain, eds., 1973, **Librarian and libraries** : In the memory of the Master Moti Lal ji and his Shri Sanmati Pustakalaya. {JNU NASSDOC}

Chopra, H.R., 1989, **Librarianship as a profession in India**. {NASSDOC}

Bhargawa, G.D., 1977, **Librarianship in India and abroad** : Retrospect and prospect. {CRRI ICA IIT JNU NASSDOC NCAER NIEPA NIPCCD ZHL}

Datta, Bimal Kumar, 1970, **Libraries and librarianship of ancient and medieval India**. {IIC IIT JNU NAI NERC NMML}

LIBRARIANS AND LIBRARIANSHIP : GEOGRAPHICAL AREA : INDIA : DELHI

Goel, N.K., et al, 1964, **Directory of libraries and who's who in library profession in Delhi**. [Delhi Library Association]. {BIS CRRI DSSW ICCR ICWA IEG IIC NMML ZHL}

LIBRARIANS AND LIBRARIANSHIP : GEOGRAPHICAL AREA : THAILAND

Minaikit, Nonglak, 1968, **Annotated bibliography on librarianship in Thailand.** {JNU}

Ambhnwong, Suthilak, 1967, **Libraries and librarianship in Thailand**. {JNU}

LIBRARIANS AND LIBRARIANSHIP : GEOGRAPHICAL AREA : THIRD WORLD

Abdul Haq, A.M. and Aman, Mohammad M., 1977, **Librarianship and the Third World** : An annotated bibliography of selected literature on developing nations, 1960-1975. {NASSDOC}

LIBRARIES

Tripathi, S.M., 1983, **Adhunik granthalaya** : Vyavastha avam sanchalan ke mooltatva. {NASSDOC}

Tiwari, Bhaskar Nath, n.d., **Adult education and libraries.** {AIU}

Trinkner, Charles L., 1962, **Better libraries make better schools**. {JNU}

King, Marion, 1954, **Books and people** : Five decades of New York's oldest library. {NAI}

Sigel, Efrem, et al, 1982, **Books, libraries and electronics** : Essays on the future of written communication. {USIS}

Boyd, Jessie, et al, 1941, **Books, libraries and you**, {ZHL}

Boyd, Jessie, et al, 1965, **Books, libraries and you** : A handbook on the use of reference books and the reference resources of the library, 3rd edn. {USIS}

Eastlick, John T., ed., 1971, **The changing environment of libraries** : Papers delivered at the 1970-71 colloquim series. [American Library Association]. {USIS}

Bonn, George S. and Faibisoff, Sulvia, eds., 1978, **Changing times, changing libraries.** {USIS}

Fleet, Anne, 1973, **Children's libraries**. {DUL}

Abkin, Michael H. and Carrol, Tam W., 1976, **Computer library for agricultural systems simulation** : A progress report. {BIS}

Anon, 1948, **Descriptive list of professional and non-professional duties in**

libraries : Preliminary draft. [American Library Association]. {USIS}

Hicks, Warren B. and Tillin, Alma, 1970, **Developing multi-media libraries.** {JNU}

Morton, E.H., 1974, **Development of library services** : Trinidad and Tobago. [UNESCO]. {ISI}

Anon, 1977-79, **Directory**, 1977; 1979. [International Federation of Library Association and Institutions]. {NASSDOC}

Anon, 1974, **Directory of co-operative libraries and documentation services.** [ICA, London]. {ICA}

Blagden, John, 1980, **Do we really need libraries?** {NIPCCD}

Christien, Roger, 1978, **The electronic library** : Bibliographic databases, 1978-79, 2nd rev. edn. {USIS}

Thompson, James, 1982, **End of libraries.** {IIT}

Lancaster, F.W. and Cleverdon, C.W., eds., 1977, **Evaluation and scientific management of libraries and information centres.** {NIEPA}

Wallace, Sarah Leslie, ed., 1962, **Friends of the library** : Organisation and activities. [American Library Association]. {NASSDOC USIS}

Anon, 1982, **Future development of libraries and information services.** [Department of Education and Science, Great Britain]. {ISI}

Anon, 1982, **Future of libraries** : Panel discussion by librarians, administrators, faculty and students : Papers from the millionth volume celebration. [New York State University]. {NASSDOC}

Stockham, K.A., n.d., **The government and control of libraries**, 2nd edn. {DUL ICHR}

Overton, C. David, 1951, **Gramophone recording library**. {CRRI}

Sharma, Chandra Kant, 1978, **Granthalaya mein sandhrab seva**. {JNU NMML}

Anon, 1982, **Granthalaya pragati** : Souvenir : Andhra Pradesh libraries conference, December 10-12, 1982, Tirupati. [Andhra Pradesh Public Library Association]. {NASSDOC*}

Ranganathan, S.R. and Nagar, M.L., 1951, **Granthalaya pratikriya**. {JNU}

Agarwal, Shyam Sunder, 1978, **Granthalaya sangathan**. {BIS}

Anon, 1974, **Granthalaya shastra paribhasha kosh**. {NASSDOC NMML}

Hobson, Anthony, 1970, **Great libraries**. {NMML USIS}

Strauss, William, et al, 1968, **Guide to laws and regulation on federal libraries** : A compilation and analysis. {USIS}

Gates, J.K., 1962, **Guide to the use of books and libraries.** {DUL IIT MFL}

Gates, J.K., 1969, **Guide to the use of books and libraries**, 2nd edn. {NIH USIS}

Gates, J.K., 1979, **Guide to the use of books and libraries**, 4th edn. {USIS}

Anon, 1976, **Guidelines for newspaper libraries.** [American Newspaper Publishers Association]. {USIS}

Gupta, B.M., et al, eds., 1984-89, **Handbook of libraries, archives and information centres in India**, 8 vols. : Vol. 1 : Libraries and archives; Vol. 2 : Libraries and archives; Vol. 3 : Information policy system and network; Vol. 4 : Asia-Pacific co-operative information systems and networks and programmes; Vol. 5 : Information technology industry and networks; Vol. 6 : International co-operative information systems, network and programmes; Vol. 7 : Science and technology information systems and centres; Vol. 8 : Social sciences information systems and centres. {DSIW IDSA JNU NASSDOC NCAER NMML}

Marshall, D.N., 1983, **History of libraries** : Ancient and mediaeval. {JNU}

Misra, Jogesh, 1979, **History of libraries and librarianship in modern India since 1850**. {JNU NERC NMML}

Johnson, Elmer D., 1965, **History of libraries in the Western world**. {NASSDOC}

Currie, Dorothy H., 1965, **How to organise a children's library**? {DUL}

Morton, Leslie T., 1979, **How to use a medical library**? {NIH}

Naude, Gabriel, 1961, **Instructions concerning erecting of a library**. {DUL}

Myers, Gerald E., 1977, **Insurance manual for libraries**. [American Library Association]. {BIS}

Anon, 1986, **International directory of library, archives and information science associations**, 2nd edn. [UNESCO General Information Programme; UNISIST]. {NASSDOC}

Anon, 1963, **International library directory** : A world directory of libraries. {ICWA}

Deshpande, K.S., 1958, **Land of libraries** : Story of a study tour of the USA. [Gurudev Literary Association, Hubli]. {AIU ZHL}

Sogani, Kamal Chand and Vijay Narain, eds., 1973, **Librarian and libraries** : In the memory of the Master Moti Lal ji and his Shri Sanmati Pustakalaya. {JNU NASSDOC}

Gerard, David E., ed., 1970, **Libraries and the arts** : A symposium of papers and discussions at the seminar held in the College of Librarianship, September 1-6, 1969, Wales. {NASSDOC}

Benge, Ronald C., 1970-75, **Libraries and cultural change, 1970; 1975**. {AIU IIT MMTC NASSDOC USIS}

Marshall, Margaret R., n.d., **Libraries and literature for teenagers**. {ICHR}

Karunakarnan Nayar, 1947, **Libraries and mass education**. [Sri Setha Parvathi Bayi Library, Kottayam]. {NASSDOC*}

Hobbs, John L., 1984, **Libraries and the materials of local history**. {CRRI NAI}

Shera, Jesse H., 1965, **Libraries and the organisation of knowledge**. {IIT USIS}

Kaufman, Paul, 1969, **Libraries and their users** : Collected papers in library history. [Library Association, London]. {NIPCCD}

Dutta, D.N., 1975, **Libraries and their uses**. {ICA IIT}

Goodell, John S. and Kemper, Robert E., eds., 1975, **Libraries and work sampling**. {BIS}

Brawne, Michael, 1970, **Libraries architecture and equipment**. {IIT ZHL}

Anon, 1971, **Libraries as educational tools**. [Sri Venkateswara University, Tirupati]. {JNU}

Knight, Douglas M. and Nourse, E. Shapley, eds., 1969, **Libraries at large** : Tradition, innovation and the national interest : The resource book based on the materials of the National Advisory Commission on Libraries. {JNU USIS}

Vosper, Robert and Koops, William R.H., 1977, **Libraries for all** : A world of books and their readers : World congress on libraries for all, 50th, 1977, Brussels. [International Federation of Library Association and Institutions]. {IIT}

McColvin, Lionel R., 1961, **Libraries for children**. {DUL}

Lewis, M. Joy, 1969, **Libraries for the handicapped**. {DUL}

Calderhead, Particia, ed., 1972, **Libraries for professional practice**. {CRRI IIT}

Chandler, George, 1966, **Libraries in the modern world**. {AIU IIC SPA}

Luczynska, Alfreda and Krystyna, Remerowa, comps., n.d., **Libraries in Poland**. {BIS}

Anon, 1974, **Libraries in the political science** : Georg Legh and German librarianship, 1933-53, tr. by Marta L. Dosa {JNU}

Estabrook, Leigh, ed., 1977, **Libraries in post-industrial society**. {IIT}

Gerard, David, 1978, **Libraries in society**. {IIT NIEPA}

Licklider, J.C., 1965, **Libraries of the future**. {JNU NMML SPA USIS}

Kujoth, Jean Spealman, 1969, **Libraries, readers and book selection.** {USIS}

Petru, William C., ed., 1967, **Library** : Introduction for library assistants. [Special Library Association, New York]. {IIT}

Harrison, K.C., 1963, **Library and the community**. {MFL}

Harrison, K.C., 1977, **The library and the community**, 3rd rev. edn. {USIS}

Harrison, K.C., 1966, **Library and the community**. {ICA}

Sahai, Shrinath, 1973, **Library and the community**. {JNU NASSDOC NMML}

Anon, 1985, **Library and the community** : Units 1-9. [Andhra Pradesh Open University, Hyderabad]. {NASSDOC*}

Hernon, Peter, et al, 1973, **Library and library related publications** : A directory of publishing opportunities in journals, serials and annuals. {NASSDOC}

Penland, Partick R. and Mathai, Aleyamma, 1978, **Library as a learning service centre**. {JNU}

Collison, Robert L., 1869, **Library assistance to readers.** [DUL MHA}

Ranganathan, S.R., 1950, **Library development plan** : Thirty-year programme for India. [University of Delhi]. {BIS MFL NERC SPA}

Wright, Gordon H., ed., 1966, **Library in colleges of commerce and technology.** {DUL IIT}

Cowles, Betty M. and Orr, Robert W., 1952, **Library instruction manual,** 3rd edn. {ZHL}

Moon, Eric and Nyren, Karl, eds., 1970, **Library issues** : The sixties. {ICHR USIS}

Krishan Kumar, 1982, **Library manual.** {BIS DSSW ICA IIC IIFT IIMC IIT ISI JNU NCDC NERC NIH ZHL}

Ranganathan, S.R. and Sivaraman, K.M., 1951, **Library manual**. [Indian Library Association]. {BIS DSSW INSA NERC ZHL}

Ranganathan, S.R., 1966, **Library manual**, 2nd edn. {BIS CRRI DSSW ICHR IIT INSA MMTC NASSDOC NERC NIPCCD}

Toser, Marie A., 1964, **Library manual** : A study work manual of lessons on the use of books and libraries, 6th edn. {USIS}

Anon, 1962, **Library service yearbook and directory**. [Punjab Library Association]. {IIT}

Ranganathan, S.R. and Neelameghan, A., 1966, **Library services for all**. [Mysore Library Association, Bangalore]. {BIS SPA}

Sanders, Brenda M., n.d., **Library services in hospitals** : A survey of their present provision and possible future development in the Southeast Metropolitan region. {DUL}

Anon, 1978, **Library services in rural areas**. [Library Advisory Council, Wales]. {NIEPA}

Sharr, F.A., 1962, **Library services in a sparsely populated area**. [UNESCO]. {NASSDOC*}

Buckland, Michael K., 1963, **Library services in theory and context**. {IIT}

Martin, William, ed., 1975, **Library service to the disadvantaged.** {NIPCCD}

Ray, Sheila G., 1982, **Library service to schools.** {JNU}

Ray, Colin, 1979, **Library service to schools and children.** {JNU NIPCCD}

Godden, Irene P., 1984, **Library technical service** : Operations and management. {JNU}

Harrod, Leonard Montague, 1969, **Library work with children** : With special reference to developing countries. {DUL}

Anon, 1978, **Maintaining library services** : A study in six countries. [Education and Science Department, Great Britain]. {IIMC NIEPA}

Steele, Colin, 1976, **Major libraries of the world** : A selective guide. {NMML}
Anon, 1933, **Manual of library routine.** {JNU}
Joncich, M.I. and Lancaster, F.W., 1977, **Measurement and evaluation of library services.** {IIT USIS}
Boorer, David, 1967, **Mental hospital library**. {DUL}
Guthman, Judith, ed., 1969, **Metropolitan libraries** : The challenge and the promise. [American Library Association]. {USIS}
Whatmore, Geoffrey, n.d., **Modern news library** : Documentation of current affairs in newspaper and broadcasting libraries. {IIMC}
Hussain, Mahmud, 1974, **Of libraries and librarians**. [University of Karachi]. {ZHL}
Bliss, Henry Evelyn, 1939, **Organisation of knowledge in libraries and the subject-approach to books,** 2nd edn. {BIS IEG USIS}
Ranganathan, S.R., 1963, **Organisation of libraries**, 3rd edn. {JNU NIH}
Allen, Joan, 1961, **Organisation of small libraries** : A manual of educational institutions in tropical countries. {JNU NIEPA}
Mittal, S.R., 1964, **Organising village library** : A guide book for social education workers and village librarians. [National Council for Educational Research and Training, New Delhi]. {ICA ISI NIPCCD}
Anon, 1982, **Papers** : All India seminar on libraries and the book trade, February 1982, New Delhi. [Indian Library Association]. {IIMC IIT JNU ZHL}
Anon, 1966, **Papers** : Seminar on work flow in libraries, November 21-24, 1966, New Delhi; 3 vols., Vol. 1 : Special libraries; Vol II : University libraries; Vol. III : Government libraries. [Indian National Scientific Documentation Centre, New Delhi]. {NASSDOC NMML SPA}
Anon, n.d., **Papers** : Symposium on new technology in libraries : Prospects and problems for libraries in the Gulf States, 1982, Teheran. [Ministry of Petroleum and Minerals, Teheran]. {CRRI}
Foskett, D.J., 1984, **Pathways for communication** : Books and libraries in the information age. {AIU NIEPA}
Overton, David, 1983, **Planning the administrative library**. {DUL}
McKee, B., 1989, **Planning library service**. {NASSDOC}
D'Olier, J.H. and Delmas, B., 1975, **Planning national infrastructures for documentation, libraries and archives** : Outline of a general policy. {DUL IIMC JNU NASSDOC NIEPA}
Datta, Bimal Kumar, 1956, **A practical guide to library procedure.** {NASSDOC}
Datta, Bimal Kumar, 1962, **Practical guide to library procedure.** {CRRI DUL IIT NERC SPA ZHL}
Moreland, Carroll C. and Usmani, M. Adil, eds., n.d., **Proceedings** : Seminar on the purpose and function of library in national education, April 7-10, 1961, Nazimabad. [Society for the Promotion and Improvement of Libraries]. {NASSDOC*}
Tiwari, Bhaskar Nath, n.d., **Prodh siksha aur pustakalaya**. {NIEPA NIPCCD}
Anon, 1963, **Protecting the library and its resources** : A guide to physical protection and insurance : Report on a study conducted by Gage Babcock and Associates, Incorporated. [American Library Association]. {DUL IIT NASSDOC IIT}
Sharma, Pandey S.K., **Pustakalaya aur hum** {RTL}
Shastri, Dwarka Prasad, 1958, **Pustakalaya aur sandarbh seva.** {BIS DUL}
Vajpayee, Hanuman Prasad, 1958, **Pustakalaya Karyapadhati.** {JNU}
Bagari, N.D., 1973, **Pustakalaya paddhati**. {DUL}
Shastri, Dwarka Prasad, 1959, **Pustakalaya parichay.** {BIS}

Shastri, Dwarka Prasad, 1974, **Pustakalaya parichay**, 2nd edn. {BIS NMML}
Shastri, A., 1967, **Pustakalaya-Prakriya, Patna.** {NMML}
Vashishth, C.P., ed., 1986, **Quality in libraries**. [Indian Library Association]. {NASSDOC*}
Chen, Ching-Chih, ed., 1978, **Quantitative measurement and dynamic library service.** {BIS IIT}
Anon, n.d., **Responsibilities of libraries and information service.** [Organisation for European Economic Co-operation]. {BIS}
Anon, 1974, **The right to read and the nation's libraries**. [American Association of School Libraries, Children's Services Division; Public Library Association; American Library Association]. {USIS}
Anon, 1978, **Role of libraries in socio-economic development** : Papers : All India library convention, 1st, February 13, 1978, Delhi. [Government of India Librarians Association]. {NASSDOC}
Anon, 1965, **Role of the library in the development of the community** : Society for the promotion and improvement of libraries seminar, April 12-18, 1964, Karachi. [Hamdard National Foundation, Karachi]. {NASSDOC}
Lancaster, F.W., 1980, **The role of the library in an electronic society** : Proceedings : Library applications of data processing clinic, 1979, Illinois. [University of Illinois at Urbana-Champaign]. {USIS}
Anon, 1971, **Role of the library in national reconstruction** : Society for the promotion and improvement of libraries seminar, October 30—November 3, 1967, Rawalpindi. [Hamdard National Foundation, Karachi]. {NASSDOC}
Foskett, D.J., 1964, **Science, humanism and libraries**. {IIT JNU}
Turock, Betty J., 1982, **Serving the older adult** : A guide to library programs and information sources. {USIS}
Kister, Kenneth F., 1968, **Social issues and library problems** : Case studies in the social science. {NMML}
Anon, 1970, **Standards for library functions at the state level**, rev edn., [American Association of State Libraries, Standards Revision Committee. {USIS}
Angelo, Douglas St., et al, 1971, **State library policy** : Its legislative and environmental contexts. {USIS}
Anon, 1964, **Student use of libraries** : An inquiry into the needs of students, libraries and the educational process. [American Library Association]. {USIS}
Anon, 1960, **Studying the community** : A basis for planning library adult education services. (Library Community Project). [American Library Association]. {USIS}
Thomas, P.A., 1971, **Task analysis of library operations**. [Association of Special Libraries and Information Bureaux]. {DUL IIT}
Daniel, Gore, 1978, **To know a library** : Essays and annual report, 1975-76. {JNU}
Jordan, Robert Thayer, 1970, **Tomorrow's library** : Direct access and delivery. {USIS}
Anon, 1987, **Trends 1985-86** : Report to the Council by the Secretary General. [International Federation of Library Associations and Institutions]. {NASSDOC*}
Sharma, C.D., 1978, **Use of libraries** : A guide to better use of libraries and their resources. {CRRI ICA IIT MMTC NASSDOC NCAER NCDC NIPCCD NMML}
Smith, Paul, 1980, **Use of libraries and the literature of human geography**. {SPA}
Baker, E.A., ed., n.d., **Uses of libraries.** {AIU}
Aldrich, Ella V., 1960, **Using books and libraries**, 4th edn. {ZHL}
Aldrich, Ella V., 1967, **Using books and libraries**, 5th edn. {DUL NASSDOC USIS}

Whittaker, Kenneth, 1965, **Using libraries**. {CRRI IIT MFL}

Whittaker, Kenneth, 1972, **Using libraries** : An information guide for students and general users, 3rd edn. {ICA}

Brogan, Gerald E. and Buck, Jeanne T., 1969, **Using libraries effectively**. {ICA}

Esdaile, Arundell, n.d., **World's great libraries,** 1934-1937 2 vols. {NAI}

Anon, 1963, **Your library** : Readers guide to Karnatak University Library, Dharwar. {NASSDOC}

Katz, William A., 1979, **Your library** : A reference guide. {USIS}

Katz, William A., 1984, **Your library** : A reference guide, 2nd edn. {JNU NASSDOC}

Lolley, John L., 1974, **Your library** : What's in it for you. {CRRI}

Barnes, Melvyn, 1978, **Youth library work** : Exploratory essays, 2nd edn. {IIT}

See also Libraries and Librarianship

LIBRARIES : ADMINISTRATION AND ORGANISATION

See Administration and Organisation

LIBRARIES : AUTOMATION

Kimber, Richard T., 1968, **Automation in libraries.** {AIU BIS IIT ISI JNU NASSDOC NCAER NIH SPA}

Kimber, Richard T., 1974, **Automation in libraries**, 2nd edn. {USIS}

Singh, S.P., 1975, **Automation in libraries.** {ICHR NASSDOC NIPCCD SPA}

Anon, 1974, **Clinic on library applications of data processing**, 24th, 1974, Illinois. [University of Illinois at Urbana-Champaign]. {USIS}

Almasy, Elina, et al, 1976, **Comparative survey analysis** : An annotated bibliography, 1967-1978. {NASSDOC}

Barron, D.W., 1971, **Computer operating systems.** {NASSDOC}

Katzan, Harry, 1971, **Computer organisation and the system/370**. {NASSDOC}

Avedon, Don M., 1971, **Computer output microfilm,** 2nd edn. [National Microfilm Association]. {USIS}

Saffady, William, 1979, **Computer output microfilm** : Its library applications. {JNU}

Swihart, Stanley J. and Heeley, Beryl F., 1973, **Computer systems in the library** : A handbook for managers and designers. {CRRI NASSDOC NIPCCD}

Anon, 1979, **Decision tables in data processing** : A report. [National Computer Centre, Manchester]. {NASSDOC}

Rosove, Perry E., 1967, **Developing computer based information systems.** {JNU}

Sen, N.B., ed., 1965, **Development of libraries in new India**. {ICA IIC IIT NASSDOC SPA}

Davis, Charles H. and Lundeen, Gerald W., 1974, **Illustrative computer programming for libraries**. {JNU}

Davis, Charles H. and Lundeen, Gerald W., 1981, **Illustrative computer programming for libraries** : Selected examples for information specialists, 2nd edn. {NASSDOC USIS}

Balmforth, C.L. and Cox, N.S., eds., 1971, **Interface** : Library automation with special reference to computing activity. {JNU NASSDOC}

Saffady, William,1983, **Introduction to automation for librarians.** [American Library Association]. {USIS}

Ashby, W. Ross, 1964, **Introduction to cybernetics.** {NASSDOC}

Wendel, Thomas M. and Williams, William H., 1969, **Introduction to data**

processing and COBOL. {NASSDOC}

Rice, James, 1984, **Introduction to library automation.** {NASSDOC NMML}

Markuson, B.E., 1964, **Libraries and automation.** {IIT}

Lancaster, F.W., 1982, **Libraries and librarians in an age of electronics**. {USIS}

Heiliger, Edward M. and Henderson, Paul B., 1971, **Library automation** : Experience, methodology and technology of the library as an information system. {AIU INSA JNU NASSDOC NIPCCD NMML}

Reynolds, Dennis, 1985, **Library automation** : Issues and applications. {JNU NASSDOC NMML}

Salmon, Stephen R., ed., 1969, **Library automation** : A state of art review : Papers : Pre-conference institute on library automation, 1967, San Francisco. [American Library Association]. {USIS}

Butler, Brett and Martin, Susan K. eds., 1975, **Library automation-II** : The state of art : Papers : Pre-conference institute on library automation, June 22-23, 1973, Las Vegas. [American Library Association, Information Science and Automation Division]. {USIS}

Lucy,.Te-Chu Lee, 1985, **Library automation and information science** : A collection of essays. {NASSDOC}

Anon, 1970, **Library automation at the New York Public Library and the Association of New York Libraries for Technical Services**. [LARC]. {USIS}

Salmon, Stephen R., 1975, **Library automation systems**, 2nd edn. {CRRI JNU NIH}

Daiute, Robert J. and Gorman, Kenneth A., 1974, **Library operations research** : Computer programming for circulation. {USIS}

Smith, G.L. and Meyer, R.S., eds., 1969, **Library use of computers** : Introduction. [Special Libraries Association, New York]. {IIT USIS}

Anon, 1979, **Problems and failures in library automation** : Clinic on library applications of data processing, 1978, Illinois. [University of Illinois at Urbana-Champaign]. {USIS}

Anon, 1980, **The professional librarian's reader in library automation and technology**. {JNU USIS}

Lancaster, F.W., 1980, **The role of the library in an electronic society** : Proceedings : Library applications of data processing clinic, 1979, Illinois. [University of Illinois at Urbana-Champaign]. {USIS}

Pruett, Nancy Jones, 1986, **Scientific and technical libraries**, 2 vols. {JNU}

Strauss, Lucille J., et al, 1964, **Scientific and technical libraries** : Their organisation and administration. {BIS CRRI IIT INSA}

Strauss, Lucille J., et al., 1972, **Scientific and technical libraries** : Their organisation and administration, 2nd edn. {BIS ISI INSA JNU}

Anon, 1985, **Scientific and technological information for development**. [United Nations Information Systems]. {JNU}

Anon, 1982, **Use of computer in libraries** : Summary of the proceedings of a seminar held on March 15, 1982, New Delhi. {NASSDOC}

Anon, 1966, **Working papers for the symposia** : IASLIC conference, 5th, 1963, Pune, Pt. I : Document and data processing in academic research and special libraries in India; Pt. II : Problems and prospects of library associations in India. [Indian Association of Special Libraries and Information Centres]. {NASSDOC}

See also Automation; MARC System

LIBRARIES : BIBLIOGRAPHY : GEOGRAPHICAL AREA : THAILAND
Minaikit, Nonglak, 1968, Annotated bibliography on librarianship in Thailand. {JNU}

LIBRARIES : BRANCHES, DELIVERY STATIONS, ETC.
Mortimore, Arthur D., 1966, **Branch libraries.** {ICA}
Sharp, Henry A., 1938, **Branch libraries** : Modern problems and administration. {JNU}
Enser, A.G.S., 1950, **Branch library practice.** {CRRI}

LIBRARIES : CENTRALISATION
See also Centralised Processing : Libraries

LIBRARIES : CIRCULATION/LOANS
Dranov, Paula, 1977, **Automated library circulation systems.** {IIT}
Fry, George, et al, 1961, **Circulation systems selection manual for college and university libraries.** {JNU}
Wegman, Edward, 1982, **International circulation of books.** [UNESCO]. {NASSDOC}
Anon, 1961, **Study of circulation control systems** : Public libraries, college and university libraries, special libraries. (Library Technology Project). [American Library Association]. {DUL IIT USIS}

See also Charging System : Libraries

LIBRARIES : COMMERCIAL
See Commercial Libraries

LIBRARIES : COMMUNICATION SYSTEMS
Becker, Joseph, ed., 1971, **Interlibrary communications and information networks.** {JNU}

LIBRARIES : COUNTY
See County Libraries
See also Regional Libraries

LIBRARIES : DEPOSITORY
See Depository Libraries

LIBRARIES : DIRECTORIES
See under Directories

LIBRARIES : GEOGRAPHICAL AREA : AFRICA
Dadzie, E.W. and Strickland, J.T., n.d., **Directory of archives, libraries and schools of librarianship in Africa**. {IIMC}
Zidoemba, Dominique, 1977, **Directory of documentation, libraries and archives services in Africa**, 2nd edn. [UNESCO]. {JNU NASSDOC}
Collison, Robert, n.d., **Scolma directory of libraries and special collections of Africa**, 2nd edn. {IIC IIT}

LIBRARIES : GEOGRAPHICAL AREA: ASIA : SOUTH EAST

Zidoemba, DominiqAnders, Mary Edna, 1976, **Libraries and library services in the Southeast** : A report of the Southeastern states cooperative library survey, 1972-74. {BIS ISI}

LIBRARIES : GEOGRAPHICAL AREA : AUSTRALIA

Balnaves, John, 1956, **Australian libraries.** {NASSDOC}

LIBRARIES : GEOGRAPHICAL AREA : BURMA

See Libraries : Geographical Area : Myanmar

LIBRARIES : GEOGRAPHICAL AREA : CANADA

Jackson, Sidney L,. et al, eds., 1976, **A century of service** : Librarianship in United States and Canada. [American Library Association]. {USIS}

LIBRARIES : GEOGRAPHICAL AREA : CEYLON

See Labraries : Geographical Area : Sri Lanka

LIBRARIES : GEOGRAPHICAL AREA : DENMARK

White, Carl M., ed., 1964, **Bases of modern librarianship** : A study of library theory and practice in Britain, Canada, Denmark, the Federal Republic of Germany and the United States. {IIT JNU NIPCCD NMML SPA}

LIBRARIES : GEOGRAPHICAL AREA : FINLAND

Anon, 1971, **Libraries in Finland**. [Finnish Library Association, Helsinki]. {NASSDOC*}

LIBRARIES : GEOGRAPHICAL AREA : FRANCE

Ferguson, John, 1971, **Libraries in France**. {NASSDOC}

LIBRARIES : GEOGRAPHICAL AREA : GERMANY

White, Carl M., ed., 1964, **Bases of modern librarianship** : A study of library theory and practice in Britain, Canada, Denmark, the Federal Republic of Germany and the United States. {IIT JNU NIPCCD NMML SPA}

LIBRARIES : GEOGRAPHICAL AREA : GREAT BRITAIN

Benewick, Anne J., 1974, **Asian and African collections in British libraries** : Problems and prospects. {DUL NMML}

White, Carl M., ed., 1964, **Bases of modern librarianship** : A study of library theory and practice in Britain, Canada, Denmark, the Federal Republic of Germany and the United States. {IIT JNU NIPCCD NMML SPA}

Mc Colvin, Lionel R. and Revie, James, 1949, **British libraries**. {MHA}

Esdaile, Arundell, 1946, **British Museum Library**. {NAL NMML}

Anon, 1932, **County libraries in Great Britain and Ireland**. [Library Association, London]. {NASSDOC}

Irwin, Raymond, 1966, **English library** : Sources and history. {JNU}

Sutton, S.C., 1967, **Guide to the India Office Library** : With a note on the India Office Records. [India Office Library]. {NMML}

Sutton, S.C., 1968, **Guide to the India Office Library** : With a note on the India Office Records, 2nd edn. [India Office Library]. {IEG IIT JNU MFL NASSDOC

NMML RTL}

Parish, Charles, 1966, **History of the Birmingham Library**. {JNU}

Harrison, K.C., n.d., **Libraries in Britain**. {IEG}

McColvin, Lianol R., 1961, **Libraries in Britain**. {NASSDOC}

Arberry, A.J., 1938, **Library of the India Office** : A historical sketch. [India Office, London]. {NAI}

Ellis, Alec, 1971, **Library services for young people in England and Wales, 1830-1970**. {DUL}

Burkett, J., ed., 1965, **Special library and information services in the United Kingdom**, 2nd edn. [Library Association, London]. {NIEPA}

LIBRARIES : GEOGRAPHICAL AREA : GREAT BRITAIN : OXFORD

Gibson, Strickland, 1914, **Some Oxford libraries**. {JNU}

LIBRARIES : GEOGRAPHICAL AREA : HONGKONG

Kan, Lai-Bing, comp., 1963, **Libraries in Hongkong** : A directory {ICWA}

LIBRARIES : GEOGRAPHICAL AREA : HUNGARY

Kerlsztury D., n.d., **Famous Hungarian libraries**. [National Szecheni Library]. {NASSDOC}

Kiss, Jeno, 1972, **Libraries in Hungary**. [National Szechenyi Library, Budapest]. {NASSDOC}

LIBRARIES : GEOGRAPHICAL AREA : INDIA

Mookerjee, S.K., 1969, **Development of libraries and library science in India**. {ICA IIC IIT NASSDOC NERC NIH NIPCCD NMML}

Sen, N.B., ed., 1965, **Development of libraries in new India**. {ICA IIC IIT NASSDOC SPA}

Agrawal, S.P., 1989, **Development of library services in India** : Social science information. {BIS DUL ISI JNU NASSDOC NERC NMML ZHL}

O'Connor, V.C. Scott, 1920, **Eastern library**. {ZHL}

O'Connor, V.C. Scott, 1977, **Eastern library** : An introduction to the Khuda Bakhsh Oriental Public Library, 2nd edn. {JNU NMML}

O'Connor, V.C. Scott, 1985, **An eastern library** : An introduction to the Khuda Bakhsh Oriental Public Library, 3rd edn. {NASSDOC*}

Ohdedar, A.K., 1966, **Growth of the library in modern India, 1498-1836**. {ICHR IIT NMML ZHL}

Gupta, B.M., et al, eds., 1984-89, **Handbook of libraries, archives and information centres in India**, 8 vols. : Vol. 1 : Libraries and archives; Vol. 2 : Libraries and archives; Vol. 3 : Information policy system and network; Vol. 4 : Asia-Pacific co-operative information systems and networks and programmes; Vol. 5 : Information technology industry and networks; Vol. 6 : International co-operative information systems, network and programmes; Vol. 7 : Science and technology information systems and centres; Vol. 8 : Social sciences information systems and centres. {DSIW IDSA JNU NASSDOC NCAER NMML}

Misra, Jogesh, 1979, **History of libraries and librarianship in modern India since 1850**. {JNU NERC NMML}

George, K.M., 1985, **Indian libraries** : Trends and prospectives. {JNU NMML}

Kipp, Laurence, 1961, **Indian libraries and India Wheat Loan Education Exchange Programme** : A report. {JNU}

Kumar, P.S.G., 1977, **Indian library chronology**. {BIS JNU NERC NIPCCD}

Ranganathan, S.R. and Das Gupta, S., 1951, **Indian library directory**, 3rd edn. [Indian Library Association]. {BIS INSA NASSDOC}

Trehan, G.L., 1981, **Inside library India** : North meets South. {JNU NASSDOC}

Trehan, G.L., 1975, **Learning and libraries in ancient India** : A study. {JNU}

Datta, Bimal Kumar, 1970, **Libraries and librarianship of ancient and medieval India**. {IIC IIT JNU NAI NERC NMML}

Anon, 1951, **Libraries in India**. [Ministry of Education, New Delhi]. {BIS NMML}

Anon, 1960, **Libraries in India**. [Ministry of Education, New Delhi]. {MHA NASSDOC}

Rajagopalan, T.S. and Ramaswami, K., n.d., **Libraries serving the CSIR complex**. [Indian National Scientific Documentation Centre]. {IIT NASSDOC}

Girja Kumar, 1986, **Library development in India**. {JNU NMML}

Chakravarty, N.C., 1962, **Library movement in India**. {NASSDOC}

Kaula, P.N., ed., 1968, **Library movement in India**. [Delhi Library Association]. {CRRI}

Sharma, Jagdish Saran, 1986, **Library movement in India and abroad**. {JNU}

Khosla, Raj K. and Gaur, M.K., eds., 1967, **Men of library science and libraries in India**. {SPA USIS}

Anon, n.d., **New India directory of libraries and educational institutions of India, Pakistan, Burma and Ceylon**. {AIU IIT}

Ranganathan, S.R., 1944, **Post-war reconstruction of libraries in India**. [Punjab Library Association, Lahore]. {ZHL}

Trehan, G.L., et al, 1982, **Prospects of library services in India** : A study. {JNU}

Sarada, K., 1986, **Rural library services in India**. {NASSDOC*}

Saha, J., 1969, **Special libraries and information services in India and in the U.S.A.** {IEG IIT NASSDOC}

Anon, 1966, **Working papers for the symposia** : IASLIC conference, 5th, 1963, Pune, Pt. I : Document and data processing in academic research and special libraries in India; Pt. II : Problems and prospects of library associations in India. [Indian Association of Special Libraries and Information Centres]. {NASSDOC}

Anon, 1966, **Working papers of the two symposia** : IASLIC seminar, 4th 1966, Hyderabad, Pt. 1 : Procurement of government publications and technical reports; Pt. 2 : Devaluation : Its impact on the development of libraries in India. [Indian Association of Special Libraries and Information Centres]. {NASSDOC SPA}

LIBRARIES : GEOGRAPHICAL AREA : INDIA : BARODA

See Libraries : Geographical Area : India : Gujarat : Baroda

LIBRARIES : GEOGRAPHICAL AREA : INDIA : BOMBAY

See Libraries : Geographical Area : India : Maharashtra : Bombay

LIBRARIES : GEOGRAPHICAL AREA : INDIA : CALCUTTA

See Libraries Geographical Area : India : West Bengal : Calcutta

LIBRARIES : GEOGRAPHICAL AREA : INDIA : DELHI

Goel, N.K., et al, 1964, **Directory of libraries and who's who in library profession in Delhi**. [Delhi Library Association]. {BIS CRRI DSSW ICCR ICWA IEG IIC NMML ZHL}

Bhatia, S.K. and Surender Kumar, comps., 1988, **Directory of libraries in Delhi**.

{ICA ICCR IIC IIPA JNU NIEPA NASSDOC}

Bhatia, S.K., ed., 1979, **Libraries in Delhi** : A comprehensive list. {AIU IIT}

LIBRARIES : GEOGRAPHICAL AREA : INDIA : DIRECTORIES
See under Directories

LIBRARIES : GEOGRAPHICAL AREA : INDIA : GUJARAT : BARODA

Dutt, Newton Mohun, 1928, **Baroda and its libraries**. [Central Library, Baroda]. {NAI NASSDOC}

Kudelkar, Janardan S., n.d., **The Baroda library movement** : A short account of the origin and growth of the Central Library Department of the Baroda State. [Central Library, Baroda]. {NASSDOC}

LIBRARIES : GEOGRAPHICAL AREA : INDIA : JUMMU AND KASHMIR

Anon, 1976, **Report** : Committee on the re-organisation of libraries, research centres and museums for the government of Jammu and Kashmir. [Punjab Agricultural University, Ludhiana]. {NASSDOC*}

LIBRARIES : GEOGRAPHICAL AREA : INDIA : KERALA

Ramanujam Nair, P., 1974, **Library movement in Kerala** : The need for reform and legislation. {NERC}

LIBRARIES : GEOGRAPHICAL AREA : INDIA : MAHARASHTRA : BOMBAY

Khandwala, Vidyut K. and Naidu, M.K.R., eds., 1965, **Directory of libraries, publishers, booksellers in the city of Bombay**. [SNDT Women University Library]. {NASSDOC}

LIBRARIES : GEOGRAPHICAL AREA : INDIA : UTTAR PRADESH : ALIGARH

Razvi, M.H., 1973, **Aligarh Muslim University library** : An approach paper on Fifth Five Year Plan including statistical analysis. {JNU}

LIBRARIES : GEOGRAPHICAL AREA : INDIA : UTTAR PRADESH : ALLAHABAD

Ranganathan, S.R., 1947, **Library development plan for Allahabad University**. {AIU NASSDOC}

LIBRARIES : GEOGRAPHICAL AREA : INDIA : WEST BENGAL

Kabir, Abulfazal M. Fazle, 1987, **Libraries of Bengal 1700-1947**. {NMML}

LIBRARIES : GEOGRAPHICAL AREA : INDIA : WEST BENGAL : CALCUTTA

Kapoor, S.K. ed., 1977, **Library scene in Calcutta** : Seminar on the occasion of the 100th meeting of the IASLIC study circle, February 26-27, 1977. [Indian Association of Special Libraries and Information Centres]. {NASSDOC*}

LIBRARIES : GEOGRAPHICAL AREA : MALAYSIA

Wijasuriya, D.E.K. and Huck-Tee, Lim, 1975, **Barefoot librarian** : Library development in Southeast Asia with special reference to Malaysia. {NIEPA}

Keeth, Kent H., comp., 1965, **A directory of libraries in Malaysia.** [University of Malaya Library, Kaula Lumpur]. {NASSDOC}

Huck-Tee, Edward Lim, 1970, **Libraries in West Malaysia and Singapore** : A short history. [University of Malaysia, Kuala Lumpur]. {CRRI NASSDOC}

LIBRARIES : GEOGRAPHICAL AREA : MYANMAR

Anon, n.d., New India directory of libraries and educational institutions in India, Pakistan, Burma and Ceylon. {AIU IIT}

LIBRARIES : GEOGRAPHICAL AREA : NEPAL

Pandey, B.D., 1979, **Report of expert consultative services rendered to Cooperative Training Centre in Nepal for organising their library and documentation services**. [International Cooperation Alliance Regional Office and Education Centre for South-East Asia, New Delhi]. {ICA}

LIBRARIES : GEOGRAPHICAL AREA : NETHERLANDS

Anon, 1962, **Libraries in the Netherlands.** [Netherlands Librarians Association]. {NASSDOC}

Burkett, Jack, 1963, **Special libraries and documentation centres in the Netherlands** {IIT JNU NASSDOC SPA}

LIBRARIES : GEOGRAPHICAL AREA : NEW YORK

See Libraries : Geographical Area : USA : New York

LIBRARIES : GEOGRAPHICAL AREA : NEW ZEALAND

Fenwick, Sara Innis, 1975, **Library services for children in New Zealand schools and public libraries** : A report. [New Zealand Library Association]. {JNU}

LIBRARIES : GEOGRAPHICAL AREA : OXFORD

See Libraries : Geographical Area : Great Britain : Oxford

LIBRARIES : GEOGRAPHICAL AREA : PACIFIC : NORTH WEST

Kroll, Morton, 1961, **College, university and special libraries of the Pacific North West**. {JNU}

LIBRARIES : GEOGRAPHICAL AREA : PAKISTAN

Anon, 1975, **Library development in Pakistan** : Resume and recommendation : National seminar, February 7-9, 1974, Lahore. [Society for the Promotion and Improvement of Libraries]. {NASSDOC*}

Khan, Sadiq Ali, 1982, **Library services in Pakistan** : Being the proceedings of the departments of library science. . . . {JNU}

Anon, n.d., **New India directory of libraries and educational institutions of India, Pakistan, Burma and Ceylon.** {AIU IIT}

LIBRARIES : GEOGRAPHICAL AREA : POLAND

Luczynska, Alfreda and Krystyna, Remerowa, comps., n.d., **Libraries in Poland.** {BIS}

LIBRARIES : GEOGRAPHICAL AREA : RUSSIA

Horecky, Paul L., **Libraries and bibliographic centres in the Soviet Union**. {IEG}

Chandler, George, 1972, **Libraries, documentation and bibliography in the USSR, 1917-1971** : Survey and critical analysis of Soviet studies. {JNU NASSDOC}

Francis, Simon, ed., 1971, **Libraries in the USSR**. {NASSDOC}

Kodiyan, Cicily, 1987, **Libraries in the USSR**. [USSR Embassy in India, New Delhi].

{NASSDOC}

Ruggles, Melville J. and Swank, Paynard C., 1962, **Soviet libraries and librarianship** : Report of the visit of the delegation of U.S. librarians to the Soviet Union, May-June, 1961 under the U.S.-Soviet cultural exchange agreement. [American Library Association]. {NASSDOC NMML}

Anon, 1983, **The State Lenin Library of USSR**. {NASSDOC*}

LIBRARIES : GEOGRAPHICAL AREA : SCANDINAVIA

Harrison, K.C., 1969, **Libraries in Scandinavia**, 2nd edn. {IIT}

LIBRARIES : GEOGRAPHICAL AREA : SINGAPORE

Huck-Tee, Edward Lim, 1970, **Libraries in West Malaysia and Singapore** : A short history. [University of Malaysia, Kuala Lumpur]. {CRRI NASSDOC}

LIBRARIES : GEOGRAPHICAL AREA : SRI LANKA

Anon, n.d., **New India directory of libraries and educational institutions of India, Pakistan, Burma and Ceylon**. {AIU IIT}

LIBRARIES : GEOGRAPHICAL AREA : SWEDEN

Anon, 1962, **Hospital library in Sweden**, tr. by Frykman. {DUL}

LIBRARIES : GEOGRAPHICAL AREA : THAILAND

Anon, 1972, **A directory of libraries and library training programme in Thailand**. [UNESCO Regional Office for Education in Asia, Bangkok]. {NASSDOC NIEPA}

Ambhnwong, Suthilak, 1967, **Libraries and librarianship in Thailand**. {JNU}

LIBRARIES : GEOGRAPHICAL AREA : THAILAND : BIBLIOGRAPHY

See Libraries : Bibliography : Geographical Area : Thailand

LIBRARIES : GEOGRAPHICAL AREA : TRINIDAD AND TOBAGO

Morton, E.H., 1974, **Development of library services** : Trinidad and Tobago. [UNESCO]. {ISI}

LIBRARIES : GEOGRAPHICAL AREA : USA

Kalia, D.R., **American libraries** : Lessons for developing countries. (Mimeographed). {NASSDOC*}

White, Carl M., ed., 1964, **Bases of modern librarianship** : A study of library theory and practice in Britain, Canada, Denmark, the Federal Republic of Germany and the United States. {IIT JNU NIPCCD NMML SPA}

Jackson, Sidney L., et al, eds., 1976, **A century of service** : Librarianship in United States and Canada. [American Library Association]. {USIS}

Hamer, Philip M., ed., 1961, **A guide to archives and manuscripts in the United States**. [U.S. National Historical Publications Commission]. {USIS}

Lydenberg, H.M., 1932, **History of the New York Public Library**. {NAI}

Moore, Everett L., 1964, **Issues of freedom in American libraries**. [American Library Association]. {USIS}

Anon, 1977, **Libraries and the life of the mind in America** : Addresses delivered at the centennial celebration of the American Library Association, [American Library Association]. {IIT NIPCCD USIS}

Plotnik, Arthur, 1975, **Library life — American style** : A journalist's field report.

{USIS}

Anon, 1974, **The right to read and the nation's libraries**. [American Association of School Libraries, Children's Services Division; Public Library Association; American Library Association]. {USIS}

Saha, J., 1969, **Special libraries and information services in India and in the U.S.A.** {IEG IIT NASSDOC}

LIBRARIES : GEOGRAPHICAL AREA : USA : DIRECTORIES

See under Directories

LIBRARIES : GEOGRAPHICAL AREA : USA : NEW YORK

Plotnik, Arthur, King, Marion, 1954, **Books and people** : Five decades of New York's oldest library. {NAI}

Lydenberg, H.M., 1932, **History of the New York Public Library.** {NAI}

Anon, 1963, **Special libraries of Greater New York**, 10th edn. [Special Libraries Association, New York]. {DUL}

LIBRARIES : GEOGRAPHICAL AREA : USSR

See Libraries : Geographical Area : Russia

LIBRARIES : LAW

See Law Libraries

LIBRARIES : MEDICAL

See Medical Libraries

LIBRARIES : NATIONAL

See National Libraries

LIBRARIES : NEWSPAPERS

See Newspapers/Periodicals/Press Clippings : Libraries

LIBRARIES : PERSONNEL MANAGEMENT

See Library Personnel

See also Administration and Organisation

LIBRARIES : PUBLIC RELATIONS

See Public Relations in Libraries

LIBRARIES : REGIONAL

See Regional Libraries

LIBRARIES : SAFETY MEASURES

Bahr, Alic Harrison, n.d., **Book theft and library security systems**. {BIS JNU USIS}

LIBRARIES : SCHOOL

See School Libraries

LIBRARIES : SCIENTIFIC
See Scientific Libraries

LIBRARIES : SHELVING
Gawrecki, Drahoslav, 1968, **Compact library shelving**. [American Library Association]. {DUL NASSDOC USIS}

LIBRARIES : SOCIETIES, ETC
See Library Associations

LIBRARIES : SPECIAL
See Special Libraries

LIBRARIES : SPECIAL COLLECTIONS
See Special Collection in Libraries
See also Map Collections; Special Libraries

LIBRARIES : TECHNICAL
See Technical Libraries

LIBRARIES : UNIVERSITIES AND COLLEGES
See Academic Libraries

LIBRARIES AND ADULT EDUCATION
Thomas. Carl, et al, 1950, **Adult education activities for public libraries**. [UNESCO]. {IEG ZUL}
Tiwari, Bhaskar Nath, n.d., **Adult education and libraries**. {AIU}
Ellis, Lee Robert, 1966, **Continuing education for adults through the American Public Library, 1833-1964**. [American Library Association]. {USIS}
Anon, 1985, **Libraries in social education** : Report of the national seminar on libraries in social education, 6th, September 26—October 5, 1955, 2nd ed. [Indian Adult Education Association]. {NIPCCD}
Monroe, Margaret Ellen, 1963, **Library adult education** : The biography of an idea. {USIS}
Houle, Cyril O., ed., 1951, **Libraries in adult and fundamental education** : Report of the Malmo Seminar. [UNESCO]. {IEG NASSDOC ZHL}
Houle, Cyril O., ed., 1957, **Libraries in adult and fundamental education** : Report of the Malmo Seminar, (Hindi Translation). [Indian Adult Education Association]. {NIEPA}
Tiwari, Bhaskar Nath, n.d., **Prodh siksha aur pustakalaya**. {NIEPA NIPCCD}
Anon, 1960, **Studying the community** : A basis for planning library adult education services. (Library Community Project). [American Library Association]. {USIS}

LIBRARIES AND THE COMMUNITY
Benge, Ronald Charles, 1979, **Culture crisis and libraries in the Third World**. {IIT}
Harrison, K.C., 1963, **Library and the community**. {MFL}
Harrison, K.C., 1966, **Library and the community**. {ICA}
Harrison, K.C., 1977, **The library and the community**, 3rd rev. edn. {USIS}
Sahai, Shrinath, 1973, **Library and the community**. {JNU NASSDOC NMML}
Anon, 1985, **Library and the community** : Units 1-9. [Andhra Pradesh Open University, Hyderabad]. {NASSDOC*}
Shera, J.H., 1970, **Sociological foundations of librarianship**. {IEG NASSDOC

NIEPA NMML ZHL}

LIBRARIES AND EDUCATION

Ernest, Roe, 1966, **Teachers, librarians and children** : A study of libraries in education. {IIT}

LIBRARIES AND EDUCATION : BIBLIOGRAPHY

Tauber, Maurice F. and Orne, Jerrold, eds., 1976, **Education and libraries** : Selected papers. {AIU USIS}

LIBRARIES AND EDUCATION : GEOGRAPHICAL AREA : INDIA

Ranganathan, S.R., 1973, **New education and school library** : Experience of half a century. {DUL ICA JNU NIEPA}

LIBRARIES AND STATE

Benton, Milored, comp., 1973, **Federal library resources** : A user's guide to research collections. {USIS}

Mason, Merilyn Gell, 1983, **The federal role in library and information services**. {USIS}

Stockham, K.A., n.d., **The government and control of libraries**, 2nd edn. {DUL ICHR}

Wellisch, J.B., et al, 1974, **Public library and federal policy**. {NIPCCD}

LIBRARY ADMINISTRATION AND ORGANISATION

See Administration and Organisation

LIBRARY ADULT EDUCATION

See Libraries and Adult Education

LIBRARY ARCHITECTURE

Wheeler, Joseph L. and Githens, Alfred Morton, 1941, **The American public library building** : Its planning and design with special reference to its administration and service. [American Library Association]. {USIS}

Duchein, Michel, 1977, **Archive buildings and equipment**. {DUL}

Werner, Mevissen, 1958, **Buchereibau** : Public library building. {DUL}

Anon, 1980, **Buildings for small public libraries** : Remodelled and adapted including new designs for branches. [American Library Association]. {DUL}

Anon, 1964, **Code of practice relating to primary elements in the design of buildings for archives**. (IS : 2663-1964). [Indian Standards Institution]. {NASSDOC}

Anon, 1960, **Code of practice relating to primary elements in the design of library buildings**. (IS : 1553-1960). [Indian Standards Institution]. {NASSDOC}

Hanley, E.R., 1939, **College and university library building**. [American Library Association]. {IIT}

Gerould, James Thayer, n.d., **College library building** : Its planning and equipment. {DUL}

Anon, 1957, **Design for elementary libraries**. [Department of School, City of South Bend]. {JNU}

Newbury, K.M., ed., n.d., **Design in the library**. [Library Association London]. {ISI}

Myller, Rolf, 1966, **The design of the small public library**. {USIS}

Cohen, Aaron and Cohen, Elaine, 1979, **Designing and space planning for libraries** : A behavioural guide. {BIS NASSDOC USIS}

Orr, N.M., 1972, **Designing library buildings for activity**. {CRRI ICA ICHR ISI

MMTC NASSDOC}
Plaster, C.D., 1939, **Floor and floor coverings**. [American Library Association]. {NAI}
Pierce, William S., 1980, **Furnishing the library interior**. {BIS USIS}
Soule, Charles C., n.d., **How to plan a library building for library work.** {IEG}
Anon, n.d., **Impact of technology on the library building**. [Educational Facilities Laboratories, New Delhi]. {AIU}
Brooks, James and Draper, James, 1979, **Interior design for libraries**. [American Library Association]. {USIS}
Brawne, Michael, 1970, **Libraries architecture and equipment**. {IIT ZHL}
Khandwala, Vidyut K., ed., 1982, **Library architecture**. [Indian Association of Special Libraries and Information Centres]. {MMTC NIEPA}
Sharma, H.D., 1972, **Library building and furniture with special reference to college libraries**. {CRRI ICA ICHR INSA MF - NASSDOC NIEPA NIH NIPCCD ZHL}
Deprospo, Ernest R., 1969, **Library building consultant role and responsibility**. {IIT}
Reynolds, J.D., ed., 1967, **Library buildings.** {DUL}
Berriman, S.G., 1969, **Library buildings, 1967 1968**. {DUL}
Trezza, Alphonse F., ed., 1967, **Library buildings** : Innovation for changing needs : Proceedings. {AIU}
Kaula, Prithvi N., 1971, **Library buildings** : Planning and design. {ICA IIMC IIT NASSDOC NIEPA NIH NIPCCD ZHL}
Shaw, Robert J., ed., 1967, **Library buildings for the future** : Proceedings. Library buildings institute and American libraries trustee association workshop, 1965, Detroit. {DUL}
Thompson, Anthony, 1963, **Library buildings of Britain and Europe**. {CRRI IIT NASSDOC}
Poole, Frazer G., ed., 1965, **The library environment** : Aspects of interior planning : Proceedings : Library equipment institute, 2nd, 1964, St. Louis. {JNU USIS}
Boaz, Martha, ed. 1951, **Living library** : Planning public library buildings for cities of 100,000 or less. {CRRI}
Herbert, Ward, ed., 1976, **New library buildings** : Architect-librarian assessment, 1973-74. {DUL}
Langmead, Staphen and Beckman, Margaret, 1970, **New library design** : Guidelines to planning academic library buildings. {AIU BIS CRRI IIT JNU NIPCCD USIS}
Metcalf, Keyes D., 1965, **Planning academic and research library buildings**. {BIS IIT NASSDOC NIH USIS}
Thompson, Godfrey, 1977, **Planning and design of library buildings**, 2nd edn. {CRRI}
Ellsworth, Ralph Eugene, 1960, **Planning college and university library** : A book for campus planners and architects. {USIS}
Galvin, Hoyt R. and Devereaux, Kathryn A., eds., 1955, **Planning a library building**. {DUL}
Roth, Harold, L., ed., 1964, **Planning library buildings for service** : Proceedings : Library building and equipment institute, July 6-8, 1961, Kent. [American Library Association]. {BIS DUL}
Ellsworth, Ralph E., 1973, **Planning manual for academic library buildings**. {JNU}

Jast, L. Stanley, 1928, **Planning of great library**. {ZHL}

Burchard, John E., et al, eds., 1949, **Planning the university library building** : A summary of discussions by librarians, architects and engineers. {NASSDOC ZHL}

Anon, 1959, **Plans for six public library buildings**. [American Library Association]. {USIS}

Schunk, Russell J., 1945, **Pointers for public library building planners.** {DUL}

Katz, William A. and Swarf, Roderick G., eds., 1964, **Problems in planning library facilities**, Consultants, architects, plans and critiques : Proceedings : Library building institute, July 12-13, 1963, Chicago. [American Library Association]. {BIS DUL NASSDOC*}

Anon, 1977, **Recommendations relating to primary elements in the design of library buildings**. [Indian Standards Institution]. {NASSDOC}

Galvin, Hoyt R. and Van Buren, Martin, 1959, **The small public library building**, 2nd edn. [UNESCO]. {CRRI IEG IIMC IIT BIS NASSDOC NERC ZHL}

Rajwant Singh, 1984, **University library buildings in India**. {AIU BIS DUL IIT JNU MMTC NASSDOC NIEPA}

LIBRARY ARCHITECTURE : GEOGRAPHICAL AREA : EUROPE

Thompson, Anthony, 1963, **Library buildings of Britain and Europe**. {CRRI IIT NASSDOC}

LIBRARY ARCHITECTURE : GEOGRAPHICAL AREA : GREAT BRITAIN

Thompson, Anthony, 1963, **Library buildings of Britain and Europe**. {CRRI IIT NASSDOC}

LIBRARY ARCHITECTURE : GEOGRAPHICAL AREA : INDIA

Anon, 1980, **Papers** : Seminar on library buildings in India, February 11-13, 1980, New Delhi. [National Information System for Science and Technology, New Delhi]. {BIS CRRI IIT}

Rajwant Singh, 1984, **University library buildings in India**. {AIU BIS DUL IIT JNU MMTC NASSDOC NIEPA}

LIBRARY ARCHITECTURE : GEOGRAPHICAL AREA : USA

Wheeler, Joseph L. and Githens, Alfred Morton, 1941, **The American public library building** : Its planning and design with special reference to its administration and service. [American Library Association]. {USIS}

LIBRARY ASSOCIATIONS

Fang, Josephine Riss and Songe, Alice H., 1973, **Handbook of national and international library associations**. [American Library Association]. {NASSDOC USIS}

Fang, Josephine Riss and Nauta, Paul, eds., 1985, **International guide to library and information science education** : A reference source for educational programmes in the information fields world-wide. [International Federation of Library Associations and Institutions]. {NASSDOC}

Kapoor, S.K., et al, eds., 1980, **Papers** : IASLIC seminar, 9th, October 23-26, 1980, Nagpur, I : Role of information centres in technology transfer; II : Role of State-level and national library association in library development in India. [Indian Association of Special Libraries and Information Centres]. {CRRI INSA JNU NASSDOC}

Jain, T.C., 1971, **Professional associations and development of librarianship** : Case studies. [Library Association, London; American Library Association]. {AIU NASSDOC NCAER}

Anon, 1966, **Working papers for the symposia** : IASLIC conference, 5th, 1963, Pune, Pt. I : Document and data processing in academic research and special libraries in India; Pt. II : Problems and prospects of library associations in India. [Indian Association of Special Libraries and Information Centres]. {NASSDOC}

See also Name of the Association, e.g., Indian Library Association; Library Association, London

LIBRARY BUILDINGS

See Library Architecture

LIBRARY CATALOGUES

See Catalogues and Cataloguing

LIBRARY CHARGING SYSTEMS

See Charging Systems : Libraries

LIBRARY CLASSIFICATION

See Classification Schemes

LIBRARY CONFERENCES

See Meetings : Proceedings/Reports/Souvenirs

LIBRARY CONSULTANTS

Berry, John N., ed., 1969, **Directory of library consultants.** {USIS}

See also Caldecott Medal Books

LIBRARY COOPERATION

Weber, David C., 1976, **Century of cooperative programme among academic libraries.** {BIS}

Metcalf, Keyes D., 1964, **Co-operation among Mainne libraries** : A report prepared for the larger libraries of Maine. {DUL}

Stenstrom, Ralph H., 1970, **Cooperation between types of libraries, 1940-1968** : An annotated bibliography. [American Library Association]. {NASSDOC}

Henderson, M.M., et al, **Cooperation, convertibility and compatibility among information systems** : A literature review. {BIS}

Anon, n.d., **Cooperative cataloguing manual for the use of contributing libraries.** [U.S. Library of Congress]. {DUL}

Kenney, Brigitte L., 1959, **Cooperative centralised processing** : A report of the establishment and first year of operation of the South West Mission Library Service. {DUL}

Luquire, W., 1986, **Coordinating cooperative collection development** : A national prospective. {JNU NASSDOC}

Myrick, William J., 1975, **Coordination** : Concept or reality. {DUL}

Anon, 1967, **Inter-library cooperation** : A sampling of inter-library cooperation programmes. [American Library Association; Committee on Inter Library

Co-operation]. {DUL}

Anon, 1962, **Inter-library cooperation in England and Wales**. [H.M.S.O., London]. {NASSDOC}

Thomson, Sarah Katharin, 1970, **Interlibrary loan involving academic libraries**. [American Library Association]. {NASSDOC}

Thomson, Sarah Katharin, 1979, **Interlibrary loan procedure manual**. [American Library Association]. {DUL NASSDOC USIS}

Agrawal, S.P., ed., 1984, **Inter-Library Resources Centre** : Holding of periodicals. {NASSDOC}

Anon, 1975, **Inter-Library Resources Centre** : Indian Council of Social Science Research—Jawaharlal Nehru University. [Indian Council of Social Science Research]. {NASSDOC}

Bishop, Enid and Waller, Jean M., eds. 1972, **International co-operation in orientalist librarianship**. {JNU NMML}

Anon, 1962, **International inter-library lending** : A review of the literature. [International Federation of Library Associations and Institutions]. {NASSDOC}

Chandler, George, ed., 1972, **International librarianship** : Surveys of recent developments in developing countries and in advanced librarianship submitted to the 1971 IFLA pre-session seminar for developing countries, August 24—September 1, 1971. [Library Association, London]. {NASSDOC}

Savary, M.J., 1968, **Latin American cooperative acquisitions programme**. {IIFT}

Kartashou, N.S., ed., 1983, **Lenin and library cooperation**. {NASSDOC*}

Jefferson, G., 1966-1977, **Library co-operation, 1966; 1968; 1977.** {AIU ICA IIT NIH}

Humphry, John A., 1963, **Library co-operation** : Brown university study of university school community library coordination in the State of Rhode Island. {DUL}

Verma, Subash Chandra, 1977-78, **Library co-operation in India, 1977; 1978**. {NASSDOC}

Bryan, J.F.W., et al, 1956, **Library co-operation in the North West** : A report. {DUL}

Kent, A. and Galuin, T.J., 1977, **Library resource sharing.** {ISI JNU NIH}

Hamilton, Beth A. and Ernst, William B. Jr., eds., 1977, **Multitype library cooperation**. {NASSDOC USIS}

Houghton, A.G. and Nixon, M., 1976, **National transport system for inter-library loan**. {JNU}

Anon, 1963, **Prospects for library co-operation in New York city** : Planning for more effective utilisation of reference and research resources submitted by Nelson Associations Incorporated, New York. {DUL}

Kent, Allen, ed., 1974, **Resource sharing in libraries** : Why, how when : Next action steps. {IIT INSA NASSDOC}

Vervliet, H.D.L., 1979, **Resource sharing of libraries in developing countries** : Proceedings : IFLA/UNESCO pre-session seminar for librarians from developing countries, August 30-September 3, 1977, [Antwerp University]. {NASSDOC}

Gorst, S.M., 1953, **Scheme for the organisation of co-operative libraries**. [Plunkett Foundation for Co-operative Studies]. {ICA}

Silva, M., ed., 1985, **Sharing of information** : South Asian initiatives. {NASSDOC*}

Anon, 1971, **Study of characteristics, costs and magnitude of inter-library loans in academic libraries**. [Association of Research Libraries, Washington]. {JNU}

Estes, Rice, 1953, **Study of seven academic libraries in Brooklyn and their cooperative potential.** {JNU}

Anon, 1982, **Study report on the feasibility of an international data bank for the non-aligned countries**. [UNESCO]. {NASSDOC}

Oehlerts, Donald E., 1962, **Study to determine the feasibility of establishing a cooperative technical processing program and direct transmission of interlibrary loans**. {DUL}

Hunt, K.G., 1955, **Subject specialisation and cooperative book purchase in the libraries of Great Britain**. {DUL}

Willemin, Silvere, 1966, **Technique of union catalogue** : A practical guide. [UNESCO]. {IIMC NASSDOC NERC}

Morehouse, H.G., 1966, **Telefascimile services between libraries with the xerox management telescopier**. {JNU}

See also Farminton Plan; Inter Library Loans; Library Information Networks; Union Catalogues

LIBRARY COOPERATION : BIBLIOGRAPHY

Stenstrom, Ralph H., 1970, **Cooperation between types of libraries, 1940-1968** : An annotated bibliography. [American Library Association]. {NASSDOC}

LIBRARY COOPERATION : GEOGRAPHICAL AREA : DEVELOPING COUNTRIES

Vervliet, H.D.L., 1979, **Resource sharing of libraries in developing countries** : Proceedings : IFLA/UNESCO pre-session seminar for librarians from developing countries, August 30-September 3, 1977, [Antwerp University]. {NASSDOC}

LIBRARY COOPERATION : GEOGRAPHICAL AREA : GREAT BRITAIN

Anon, 1962, **Inter-library cooperation in England and Wales**. [H.M.S.O., London]. {NASSDOC}

Hunt, K.G., 1955, **Subject specialisation and cooperative book purchase in the libraries of Great Britain**. {DUL}

LIBRARY COOPERATION : GEOGRAPHICAL AREA : INDIA

Agrawal, S.P., ed., 1984, **Inter-Library Resources Centre** : Holding of periodicals. {NASSDOC}

Anon, 1975, **Inter-Library Resources Centre** : Indian Council of Social Science Research — Jawaharlal Nehru University. [Indian Council of Social Science Research]. {NASSDOC}

Verma, Subash Chandra, 1977-78, **Library co-operation in India, 1977; 1978.** {NASSDOC}

LIBRARY COOPERATION : GEOGRAPHICAL AREA : NON-ALIGNED COUNTRIES

Anon, 1982, **Study report on the feasibility of an international data bank for the non-aligned countries**. [UNESCO]. {NASSDOC}

LIBRARY COOPERATION : GEOGRAPHICAL AREA : USA

Anon, 1963, **Prospects for library co-operation in New York city** : Planning for more effective utilisation of reference and research resources submitted by Nelson Associations Incorporated, New York. {DUL}

LIBRARY DECORATION

Brooks, James and Draper, James, 1979, **Interior design for libraries.** [American Library Association]. {USIS}

See also Library Environment; Library Furniture/Equipment; Library Furnishings

LIBRARY DISPLAYS

See Library Exhibits

LIBRARY EDUCATION

Danton, J. Periam, 1970, **Between MLS and PHD** : A study of sixth year specialist programmes in accredited library schools. {DUL}

Sardana, J.L., ed., 1984, **Continuing education for librarians** : Paper : All India seminar for librarians, February 13, 1984, New Delhi. [Indian Library Association]. {NASSDOC}

Stone, Elizabeth W., et al, 1974, **Continuing library and information science education** : Final report to the National Commission on Libraries and Information Science (with bibliography). {USIS}

Stone, Elizabeth W., 1974, **Continuing library education as viewed in relation to other continuing professional movements**. [American Society for Information Science]. {NIEPA}

Baker, Robert, K., 1981, **Doing library research** : An introduction for community college students. {USIS}

Lubrans, John, ed., 1974, **Educating the library user**. {USIS}

Tauber, Maurice F. and Orne, Jerrold, eds., 1976, **Education and libraries** : Selected papers. {AIU USIS}

Schur, H. and Saunders, W.L., 1968, **Education and training for scientific and technological library and information work.** {IIT SPA}

Schur, H., 1973, **Education and training of information specialists.** {BCL CRRI ICA}

Evans, A.J., et al, 1977, **Education and training of users of scientific and technical information** : UNISIST guide for teachers. [UNESCO]. {BCL ISI NASSDOC}

Berelson, Bernard, ed., n.d., **Education for librarianship.** {AIU IEG}

Danton, J. Periam, 1949, **Education for librarianship.** [UNESCO]. {IEG NASSDOC}

New, Peter G., 1978, **Education for librarianship** : Decisions in organising a system of professional education. {NIEPA}

Chakraverty, N.C., 1966, **Education for librarianship** : A survey. [Indian Association of Special Libraries and Information Centres]. {SPA}

Anon, 1965, **Education for librarianship in India**. [Indian Association of Special Libraries and Information Centres]. {IIT MFL NASSDOC}

Srivastava, A.P., 1969, **Education for library science and documentation** : Iran. [UNESCO]. {NASSDOC*}

Anon, 1972, **Education, library science, journalism** : A bibliography of doctoral dissertations, 1857-1970. [Inter-University Board of India and Ceylon, New Delhi]. {JNU NMML}

Mc Collough, Ethel Farguhar and Van Buren, Maud, 1931, **Essentials in library education**. [American Library Association]. {NASSDOC*}

Houghton, Bernard, 1977, **The evaluation of a programme designed for teaching on-line information retrieval techniques** : Final report for the period June-September 1976. [Liverpool Polytechnic, Department of Library and Information Studies]. {BCL}

Rees, Alan M., et al, n.d., **Feasibility study for continuing education of medical librarians** : Interim report. {DUL}

Shera, Jesse H., 1972, **Foundations of education for librarianship.** {AIU IIFT ISI NIPCCD USIS ZHL}

Barrocal, Ramon, 1969, **A glossary of technical service terms for library science students**. [School of Library Science, Syracuse University]. {NASSDOC*}.

Anon, 1982, **Guidelines for curriculum development in records management and administration of modern archives**. [UNESCO]. {NASSDOC}

Anon, 1978, **Guidelines for curriculum development on information studies.** [UNESCO]. {NASSDOC*}

Shankman, Florence V. and Kranyik, Robert, 1964, **How to teach reference and research skills.** {JNU}

Anon, 1987, **Hundred years of library education.** [Nagpur University, Department of Library and Information Science, Nagpur]. {NASSDOC}

Kumar, P.S.G., ed., 1987, **Hundred years of library education and its future** : Pre-seminar volume : ILA-IASLIC-GILA-IATLIS library education centenary seminar, October 10-12, 1987, Nagpur. [Nagpur University, Department of Library and Information Science, Nagpur]. {NASSDOC}

Swanson, Don R., ed., 1965, **Intellectual foundations of library education.** {IIT}

Fang, Josephine Riss and Nauta, Paul, eds., 1985, **International guide to library and information science education** : A reference source for educational programmes in the information fields world-wide. [International Federation of Library Associations and Institutions]. {NASSDOC}

Palmer, B.I., 1962, **Itself an education**. [Library Association, London]. {IIT}

Palmer, B.I., 1971, **Itself an education** : Six lectures on classification, 2nd edn. [Library Association, London]. {NASSDOC NMML}

Aggarwal, D.S., 1985, **Lectures on universe of knowledge.** {NMML}

Monroe, Margaret Ellen, 1963, **Library adult education** : The biography of an idea. {USIS}

Mangla, P.B., ed., 1981, **Library and information science education in India** : Papers and recommendations of an All India seminar held at the Department of Library Science, University of Delhi, during October 3-8, 1977, {AIU ICA JNU NASSDOC NIEPA}

Tirkha, R.N. and Arneja, M.S., 1983, **Library development oriented education.** {ICA}

Malhan, Inder Vir and Kapoor, Shabad, 1982, **Library education** : A bibliography. {IIT JNU NASSDOC}

Kohl, David F., 1986, **Library education and professional issues** : A handbook for library management. {JNU NASSDOC}

Bonn, G.S., 1966, **Library education and training in developing countries.** {ICA NIEPA}

Porsons, C.J., 1973, **Library use in further education.** {DUL}

Anderson, Ursula, 1977, **Management training for libraries**. [Library Association, London]. {NIEPA NIPCCD}

Sabor, Josefa E., 1969, **Methods of teaching librarianship**. [UNESCO]. {IIMC

JNU NASSDOC NIEPA NIPCCD}

Foskett, D.J., 1976, **NATIS** : Preliminary survey of education and training programmes at university level in information and library science. [UNESCO]. {NIEPA}

Dean, John, 1972, **Planning library education programmes :** A study of the problems involved in the management and operation of library schools in the developing countries. {MFL NIEPA}

Casteleyn, Mary, 1981, **Planning library training programmes.** {NIEPA}

Anon, 1986, **Profession education and training for library and information work** : A review. [Library Association, London]. {NASSDOC}

Carroll, Frances Laverne, 1981, **Recent advances in school librarianship.** {NIEPA}

Gleaves, Edwin S. and Tucker, John Mark, 1983, **Reference service and library education** : Essays in honour of Neel Chaney. {JNU}

Anon, 1986, **Report** : Seminar on library education, December 1-4, 1965, Bombay. [Shreemati Nathibai Damodar Thachery Women's University, Bombay]. {AIU NASSDOC}

Reagon, Agnes Lytton, 1959, **Study of factors influencing college students to become librarians.** {JNU}

Brugghen, W. Van Den, 1975, **Syllabus for a documentation course.** [International Federation for Documentation and Information]. {BIS}

Wynar, Bohdan S., 1962, **Syllabus for research methods in librarianship.** {DUL}

Borko, Harold, ed., 1973, **Targets for research in library education.** [American Library Association]. {USIS}

Grimshaw, Ernest, 1960, **Teacher librarian.** {JNU}

Douglas, M.P., 1949, **Teacher librarians handbook.** [American Library Association]. {DUL NIEPA ZHL}

Ernest, Roe, 1966, **Teachers, librarians and children** : A study of libraries in education. {IIT}

Hostrop, Richard W., 1968, **Teaching and the community college library.** {JNU}

Finn, David, et al, 1978, **Teaching manual for tutor-librarians.** {JNU}

Branscomb, Harvie, 1940, **Teaching with books** : A study of college libraries. [American Library Association]. {ZHL}

Branscomb, Harvie, 1964, **Teaching with books** : A study of college libraries. {DUL}

Anon, 1978, **UNISIST guidelines for formulating policy on education, training and development of library and information personnel.** [UNESCO]. {BIS}

Anon, 1975, **UNISIST guidelines for the organisation of training courses, workshops and seminars in scientific and technical information and documentation.** [UNESCO]. {BIS}

Sellen, Betty Carol, ed., 1980, **What else can you do with a library degree.** {IIT}

Anon, 1972, **World guide to library school and training course in documentation.** [UNESCO]. {ICA IIT JNU NASSDOC NERC NIEPA USIS}

Bramley, Gerald, 1975, **World trends in library education.** {AIU IIT NERC NIEPA USIS}

See also Librarians : In-Service Training; Library Schools

LIBRARY EDUCATION : BIBLIOGRAPHY

Malhan, Inder Vir and Kapoor, Shabad, 1982, **Library education** : A bibliography.

{IIT JNU NASSDOC}

LIBRARY EDUCATION : GEOGRAPHICAL AREA : AFRICA

Saith, S.S., 1968, **East African School of Librarianship.** [UNESCO]. {NASSDOC*}

LIIBRARY EDUCATION : GEOGRAPHICAL AREA : ASIA

Bowden, Russel E., ed., 1980, **Library education programme in developing countries with special reference to Asia** : UNESCO pre-IFLA conference seminar on library education programme in developing countries, August 15-18, 1980, Philippines. [Library Association, London]. {IIT NASSDOC}

Anon, 1970, **Training course in documentation techniques in Asia**, July 20—August 21, 1970, Tokyo. [Japanese National Commission for UNESCO]. {NASSDOC}

LIBRARY EDUCATION : GEOGRAPHICAL AREA : ASIA : SOUTH EAST

Anon, 1965, **Papers** : Seminar on library science in Southeast Asia, December 18-20, 1964, Bangkok. [Association of Southeast Asian Institutions of Higher Learning]. {NASSDOC NIEPA}

LIBRARY EDUCATION : GEOGRAPHICAL AREA : DEVELOPING COUNTRIES

Bonn, G.S., 1966, **Library education and training in developing countries.** {ICA NIEPA}

Bowden, Russel E., ed., 1980, **Library education programme in developing countries with special reference to Asia** : UNESCO pre-IFLA conference seminar on library education programme in developing countries, August 15-18, 1980, Philippines. [Library Association, London]. {IIT NASSDOC}

LIBRARY EDUCATION : GEOGRAPHICAL AREA : GREAT BRITAIN

Taylor, Peter J., ed., 1976, **Library and information studies in the United Kingdom and Ireland, 1950-1974** : An index to theses. [Association of Special Libraries and Information Bureaux]. {NASSDOC}

Anon, 1968, **A report on the supply and training of librarians.** [Department of Education and Science, Great Britain]. {NIEPA}

LIBRARY EDUCATION : GEOGRAPHICAL AREA : INDIA

Mookerjee, S.K., 1969, **Development of libraries and library science in India.** {ICA IIC IIT NASSDOC NERC NIH NIPCCD NMML}

Anon, 1965, **Education for librarianship in India**. [Indian Association of Special Libraries and Information Centres]. {IIT MFL NASSDOC}

Anon, 1973, **First All India workshop on the methods of teaching and evaluation in library science, May 15-30, 1973, Delhi.** {DUL}

Majeed Khan, M.A., 1982, **Handbook of library science education in India.** [Andhra Pradesh Library Association, Hyderabad]. {NASSDOC}

Mangla, P.B., ed., 1981, **Library and information science education in India** : Papers and recommendations of an All India seminar held at the Department of Library Science, University of Delhi, during October 3-8, 1977, {AIU ICA JNU NASSDOC NIEPA}

Khurshid, A., 1987, **Library education in India, Pakistan and Iran.** {NASSDOC*}

Anon, 1977, **Papers** : Seminar on library and information science education in India, 1977, New Delhi. {JNU}

LIBRARY EDUCATION : GEOGRAPHICAL AREA : IRAN
Khurshid, A., 1987, **Library education in India, Pakistan and Iran.** {NASSDOC*}

LIBRARY EDUCATION : GEOGRAPHICAL AREA : ISRAEL
Carnóvsky, Leon, n.d., **Report on a programme of library education in Israel.** (Technical assistance : Special report, No. 1). [UNESCO]. {IEG NASSDOC}

LIBRARY EDUCATION : GEOGRAPHICAL AREA : PAKISTAN
Khurshid, A., 1987, **Library education in India, Pakistan and Iran.** {NASSDOC*}

LIBRARY EDUCATION : GEOGRAPHICAL AREA : THAILAND
Anon, 1972, **A directory of libraries and library training programme in Thailand.** [UNESCO Regional Office for Education in Asia, Bangkok]. {NASSDOC NIEPA}

LIBRARY EDUCATION : RESEARCH
Borko, Harold, ed., 1973, **Targets for research in library education.** [American Library Association]. {USIS}

LIBRARY EMPLOYEES
Anon, 1973, **Manpower in the field of documentation and library services.** [UNESCO]. {CRRI ICA}

LIBRARY EMPLOYEES : GEOGRAPHICAL AREA : INDIA
Anon, 1968, **Working papers for the symposia** : IASLIC seminar, 5th, October 7-9, 1968, Durgapur, Pt. I : Selective dissemination of information for India; Pt. II : Functions and problems of library personnel in special libraries of India. [Indian Association of Special Libraries and Information Centres]. {NASSDOC}

LIBRARY ENVIRONMENT
Poole, Frazer G., ed., 1965, **The library environment** : Aspects of interior planning : Proceedings : Library equipment institute, 2nd, 1964, St. Louis. {JNU USIS}

LIBRARY EQUIPMENT/FURNITURE
See Library Furniture/Equipment

LIBRARY EVALUATION
Gardner, Frank M., 1957, **Delhi Public Library** : An evaluation report. {DSSW DUL}
Anon, 1969, **Final report** : Project for evaluating the benefits from university libraries. [University of Durham]. {NIEPA}
Lancaster, F.W., 1988, **If you want to evaluate your library.** [Library Association, London]. {NASSDOC}
Goldhor, Herbert, ed., n.d., **Measurement and evaluation** : Papers presented at a conference conducted by the University of Illinois, Graduate School of Library Science, September 10-12, 1967. {DUL}
Joncich, M.I. and Lancaster, F.W., 1977, **Measurement and evaluation of library services.** {IIT USIS}
Beeler, M. Fancher, et al, 1974, **Measuring the quality of library service.** {NIEPA USIS}

Kunz, Werener, 1977, **Methods of analysis and evaluation of information needs** : A critical review. {JNU}

Chen, Ching-Chih, ed., 1978, **Quantitative measurement and dynamic library service.** {BIS IIT}

LIBRARY EXHIBITS

Coplan, Kate, 1974, **Effective library exhibits** : How to prepare and promote good displays, 2nd edn. {CRRI USIS}

Garvey, Mona, 1969, **Library displays** : Their purpose, construction and use. {USIS}

Mathur, Lalit Mohan, 1970, **Principles and techniques of educational library displays and exhibits**. {IIT NMML}

LIBRARY EXTENSION

Craster, H.H.E., 1941, **Bedlican library extension scheme.** {NAL}

LIBRARY FINANCE

Yrumpeter, Marg C. and Rounds, Richards, 1985, **Basic budgeting practices for librarians**. {JNU}

Martin, Murray, S., 1978, **Budgetary control in academic libraries.** {AIU DUL}

Lee, Sul H., 1973, **Planning programming budgeting system** : Implications for library management. {JNU}

Guruswamy Naidu, N., 1990, **Public library finance.** {CRRI}

Adamson, Edith, 1962, **Public library finance** : A literature review. {JNU}

Tejomurty, A., 1981, **University library finances in Madhya Pradesh** : A comparative study. {NASSDOC}

LIBRARY FURNISHINGS

Poole, Frazer G. and Trezza, Alphonse F., eds., 1969, **The procurement of library furnishings** : Specifications BID documents and evaluation : Proceedings : Library equipment institute, 3rd, 1966, New York. [American Library Association]. {USIS}

LIBRARY FURNITURE/EQUIPMENT

Anon, 1967, **Glossary of terms for wooden furniture.** (IS : 4415-1967). [Indian Standards Institution]. {NASSDOC}

Anon, 1974, **Glossary of terms relating to wooden furniture and fixtures**, rev. edn. (IS : 4415-1974). {NASSDOC}

Anon, 1963, **Library furniture and equipment**. [American Library Association]. {DUL IIT NASSDOC ZHL}

Landau, T., 1963, **Library furniture and equipment**. {IIT NMML ZHL}

Poole, Frazer G. and Trezza, Alphonse F., eds., 1969, **The procurement of library furnishings** : Specifications BID documents and evaluation : Proceedings : Library equipment institute, 3rd, 1966, New York. [American Library Association]. {USIS}

LIBRARY INFORMATION NETWORKS

Bommer, Michael R.W. and Chorba, Ronald W., 1982, **Decision-making for library management**. {JNU NIEPA}

Luquire, W., ed., 1984, **Experiences of library network administrators** : Papers based on the symposium 'From our past : Towards 2000'. {NASSDOC}

Murdick, Robert G. and Ross, Jod E., 1977, **Information system for modern management.** {ICA}

Vickery, B.C., 1973, **Information systems**. {DUL ICA ISI MMTC NASSDOC}

Burch, John G., et al, 1979, **Information systems** : Theory and practice. {JNU NIPCCD TDA}

Sherrod, John, 1975, **Information systems and networks** : Eleventh annual symposium {JNU}

Newman, Simon M., 1965, **Information systems compatibility**. {JNU}

Anon, 1976, **Information systems design for socio-economic development** : Retrospect and prospect. [International Federation for Documentation and Information]. {JNU}

Radford, K.J., 1978, **Information systems for strategic decisions.** {DUL}

Shera, J.H., et al, 1975, **Information systems in documentation.** {CRRI DUL JNU}

Anon, 1979, **Information systems in UK agriculture.** [UK Agriculture Information Review Committee; British Library Research and Development Department]. {BCL}

Weisman, Herman M., 1972, **Information systems, services and centres**. {CRRI DUL NASSDOC USIS}

Genaway, David, C., 1984, **Integrated online library systems** : Principles, planning and implementation. {NASSDOC}

Becker, Joseph, ed., 1971, **Interlibrary communications and information networks.** {JNU}

Thiagrajan, R., 1978, **Lecture notes** : NISSAT training course on systems analysis for information sciences, December 12-23, 1978, New Delhi. [Department of Science and Technology, New Delhi]. {BIS}

Burkett, Jack, 1983, **Library and information network in the United Kingdom**. [Association of Special Libraries and Information Bureaux]. {CRRI JNU}

Martin, Susan K., 1978, **Library networks, 1978-79.** {IIT USIS}

Anon, 1976, **Life sciences information network**. [National Library of Australia]. {JNU}

Christ, Alam G.L., n.d., **MINIS, MICROS and terminals for libraries and information services**. {JNU}

Rouse, William B., 1980, **Management of library networks** : Policy analysis, implementation and control. {IIT}

Mortin-Labatut, Girele and Sly, Mureen, 1982, **Manual for the preparation of records in development information systems**. [International Development Research Centre]. {NASSDOC}

Anon, 1976, **NATIS** : Design and planning of national information systems. [UNESCO]. {NASSDOC*}

Anon, 1976, **NATIS** : National information policy. {NASSDOC*}

Foskett, D.J., 1976, **NATIS** : Preliminary survey of education and training programmes at university level in information and library science. [UNESCO]. {NIEPA}

Krishnamurty, P.G., 1979, **National information base for health population and family welfare in India** : Manual for preparation of input for computerised bibliographic information base. [National Institute of Health and Family Welfare, New Delhi]. {NIH}

Anon, 1977, **National information system** : Library and information science manpower development in Asian region : Meeting of supervisors of library and documentation schools in the Asian region, Bangalore. [UNESCO; DRTC]. {JNU}

Anon, 1985, **National Information System for Science and Technology (NISSAT)** : Detailed project report, (1985-1990). [Ministry of Science and Technology, New Delhi]. {NASSDOC}

Anon, n.d., **National information system for social sciences**, typed Short bibliography. {NASSDOC}

Neelameghan, A., ed., 1979, **Ordering systems for global information networks** : Proceedings : International study conference on classification research, 3rd, January 6-11, 1975, Bombay, [FID/CR; Sarada Ranganathan Endowment for Library Science]. {BIS NASSDOC}

Kapoor, S.K. and Ghosh, S.B., eds., 1977, **Planning of national information network** : 11th, IASLIC conference at Dharwar, 1977. {JNU}

Kent, Allen and Galvin, Thomas J., eds., 1979, **Structure and governance of library networks** : Proceedings of the 1978 conference in Pittsburg. {JNU}

Anon, 1977, **Third European congress on information systems and networks overcoming the language barrier, Luxembourg**. {JNU}

Williams, Patrick and Pearce, Joan T., 1978, **The vital network** : A theory of communication and society. {USIS}

Anon, 1987, **Women's information network for Asia and Pacific**. [United Nations Economic and Social Commission for Asia and Pacific, Bangkok]. {NASSDOC}

LIBRARY LAWS

Ranganathan, S.R., 1963, **Five laws of library science**. {BIS CRRI IIT MHA NAI NCAER NMML SPA ZHL}

Sivaswami Iyyar, P.S., 1931, **The five laws of library science**. [Madras Library Association, Madras]. {NASSDOC*}

Shypla, Bana Bihari, 1984, **Fundamental theories in abstracting and fundamental laws in library science**. {JNU}

Ranganathan, S.R., 1955, **Heading and canons.** {BIS IEG ISI}

Atherton, Pauline A., 1973, **Putting knowledge to work** : American view of Ranganathan's Five Laws of Library Science. {AIU IIMC JNU NIEPA USIS}

LIBRARY LEGISLATION

Jain, H.C., 1972, **Law library administration and reference.** {CRRI MMTC}

Ranganathan, S.R., 1953, **Library legislation**. [Madras Library Association]. {BIS IEG}

Mittal, R.L., 1971, **Public library law** : An international survey. {ICA NASSDOC NMML}

Gradiner, Frank M., 1971, **Public library legislation** : A comparative study. [UNESCO]. {JNU NASSDOC NIEPA}

Angelo, Douglas St., et al, 1971, **State library policy** : Its legislative and environmental contexts. {USIS}

LIBRARY LEGISLATION : GEOGRAPHICAL AREA : INDIA

Venkatappaiah, V. and Vashishth, C.P., 1990, **Indian library legislation,** 2 vols., Vol. 1 : Union Library Bills and Acts; Vol. 2 : State Library Bills and Acts. {NASSDOC}

Sadhu, S.H. and Saraf, B.N., 1967, **Library legislation in India** : A historical and comparative study. {BIS ICA IIMC NASSDOC NERC SPA}

Rout, R.K., 1986, **Library legislation in India** : Problems and prospects.

{NASSDOC*}

Anon, 1975, **Rampur Raza Library Bill**. [Lok Sabha, New Delhi]. {JNU}

LIBRARY LEGISLATION : GEOGRAPHICAL AREA : INDIA : ANDHRA PRADESH

Narasimhan, P.V.A. and Majeed Khan, M.A., 1980, **Andhra Pradesh Public Libraries Act, 1960 with latest amendments and commentaries.** [Andhra Pradesh Public Library Association]. {NASSDOC*}

LIBRARY LEGISLATION : GEOGRAPHICAL AREA : INDIA : PUNJAB

Hakam Singh, 1962 **Library legislation in the Punjab.** [Punjab Library Literary Circle]. {IIT}

LIBRARY MOVEMENT

Kudelkar, Janardan S., n.d., **The Baroda library movement** : A short account of the origin and growth of the Central Library Department of the Baroda State. [Central Library, Baroda]. {NASSDOC}

Raju, A.A.N., 1988, **History of library movement in Andhra Pradesh, 1900-1956.** {NASSDOC*}

Mahajan, S.G., 1984, **History of public library movement in Maharashtra.** {JNU NASSDOC*}

Mahajan, S.G., 1979, **History of the public library movement in western Maharashtra, 1805-1921** : Thesis. (Poona University). {NASSDOC}

Kumar, P.S.G., 1977, **Indian library chronology**. {BIS JNU NERC NIPCCD}

Olle, James G., 1967, **Library history** : An examination guide book, 2nd rev edn. {ICHR IIT}

Goschen, Viscount, n.d., **Library movement.** {AIU}

Chakravarty, N.C., 1962, **Library movement in India.** {NASSDOC}

Kaula, P.N., ed., 1968, **Library movement in India.** [Delhi Library Association]. {CRRI}

Sharma, Jagdish Saran, 1986, **Library movement in India and abroad.** {JNU}

Ramanujam Nair, P., 1974, **Library movement in Kerala** : The need for reform and legislation. {NERC}

Hobbs, John L., 1962, **Local history and the library**. {IIC NMML SPA}

Shastri, A., 1967, **Pustakalaya andolan, Bihar.** {NMML}

LIBRARY NETWORKS

See Library Information Networks

LIBRARY OF CONGRESS

See US Library of Congress

LIBRARY OF CONGRESS CLASSIFICATION

See Classification Schemes : Library of Congress

LIBRARY ORIENTATION

Kirkendall, Carolyn A., ed., 1981, **Directions for the decade** : Library instruction in the 1980's : Conference on library orientation for academic libraries, 10th, May 8-9. 1980. [Eastern Michigan University]. {USIS}

Lubrans, John, ed., 1974, **Educating the library user.** {USIS}

Anon, 1930, **Library instruction** : Junior and senior high schools. {ZHL}

Cowles, Betty M. and Orr, Robert W., 1952, **Library instruction manual,** 3rd edn.

{ZHL}

Mac Cafferty, Maxine, n.d., **Papers** : EUSIDIC conference on user education, 1976, Graz. {CRRI}

Girja Kumar and Krishan Kumar, 1983, **Philosophy of user education**. {DUL IIT ISI JNU NASSDOC NIEPA ZHL}

Lubrans, John, ed., 1978, **Progress in educating the library user**. {CRRI IIT}

Mac Cafferty, Maxine, 1977, **User education** : Towards a better use of information resources. {BCL}

Fjallbrant, Nancy and Malley, Ian, 1984, **User education in libraries**. {DUL JNU NASSDOC NIEPA}

Stone, Phillip J., 1968, **User's manual for the general inquirer**. {NASSDOC}

See also Library Users and User Study

LIBRARY ORIENTATION : BIBLIOGRAPHY

Lockwood, Deborah, L., comp., 1979, **Library instruction** : A bibliography. {NIPCCD}

LIBRARY PERSONNEL

Datta, N., 1985, **Academic status for university and college librarians in India**. {JNU}

Anon, 1981, **Background papers** : Sub-regional workshop for cooperative librarians and documentation officers for South East Asia, April 14-29, 1981, Los Banos. [ICA Regional Office and Education Centre for South East Asia, New Delhi]. {ICA}

Anon, 1970, **Biographical directory of librarians in the United States and Canada**, 5th edn. {NASSDOC}

Anon, 1975, **Faculty status for university and college librarian in India** : Basic documents. {JNU NASSDOC ZHL}

Harrod, Leonard Mortague and Prytherch, R.J., ed., 1984, **Harrod's librarians' glossary and reference book**. {NCERT}

Boss, Richard W., 1983, **The library manager's guide to automation**, 2nd edn. {NASSDOC USIS}

Anon, 1973, **Manpower in the field of documentation and library services**. [UNESCO]. {CRRI ICA}

Anon, 1969, **Manual for new members of the staff**. [County Library]. {JNU}

Schramm, Wilbur, 1973, **Men, messages and media** : A look at human communication. {NASSDOC}

Khosla, Raj K. and Gaur, M.K., eds., 1967, **Men of library science and libraries in India**. {SPA USIS}

Wallace, Sarah Leslie, 1956, **Patrons are people** : How to be a model librarian, 2nd rev edn. [American Library Association]. {DUL USIS}

Anon, 1982, **Personnel administration for libraries** : A bibliographic essay. [American Library Association]. {BIS DUL}

Martin, Lowell, 1946, **Personnel administration in libraries**. {JNU}

Stebbins, K.B., 1966, **Personnel administration in libraries**, 2nd edn. rev. by P.G. Mohrhardt. {JNU NIH USIS}

Herbert, Clara W., 1939, **Personnel administration in public libraries**. [American Library Association]. {CRRI}

Maloney, R. Kay, ed., 1977, **Personnel development in libraries**. [Bureau of

Library and Information Science Research, Rutgers University Graduate School of Library Science]. {NIPCCD USIS}

Katz, Bill and Fraley, Ruth A., eds., 1986, **Personnel issues in reference services**, {JNU NASSDOC}

Savage, A.W., 1977, **Personnel management.** {JNU}

Khanna, J.K., 1981, **Personnel management in libraries**. {BIS IIFT IIMC ISI JNU NIEPA ZHL}

Juggal Kishore, 1981, **Personnel management in libraries**. {JNU}

Cowley, John, 1982, **Personnel management in library**. {DUL IIT}

Goswami, Badri Prasad, 1972, **Personnel motivation and work efficiency in libraries**. {NASSDOC}

Anon, 1966, **Personnel organisation and procedure** : A manual suggested for use in public libraries, 2nd edn. [American Library Association]. {DUL USIS}

Anon, 1951, **Position classification and salary administration in libraries.** [American Library Association]. {IIT}

Anon, 1974, **Professional and non-professional duties in libraries**, 2nd edn. [Research and Development Committee, Library Association, London]. {IIT ZHL}

West, Celeste and Katz, Elizabeth, eds., 1972, **Revolting librarians**. {USIS}

Anon, 1989, **Roles and responsibilities of librarians and library technicians** : Report. [Canada Library Association, Ottawa].

Mery, Richard E., 1975, **Staff communication in libraries**. {JNU}

Jones, Noragh and Jordon, Peter, 1982, **Staff management in library and information work**. {IIT NASSDOC NIH}

Durey, Peter, 1976, **Staff management in university and college libraries**, ed. by G. Chandler. {ISI}

Prytherch, R., ed., 1986, **Staff training in libraries** : The British experience. {NASSDOC}

Anon, 1976, **Staffing of public libraries** : A report. [Department of Education and Science, Great Britain]. {BIS IIT ZHL}

Downs, Robert B., 1958, **Status of American college and university librarian.** {JNU}

Anon, 1967, **Study of 1967 annual salaries of members of Special Library Association**. [Personnel Committee of Special Libraries Association]. {JNU}

Fay, Adra M., 1950, **Supervising library personnel**. {DUL}

Ward, Patricia Layzell, 1966, **Women and librarianship** : An investigation into certain problems of library staffing. {DUL}

LIBRARY PLANNERS

Anon, 1960, **Guidelines for library planners.** [American Library Association]. {IIT}

See also Library Planning

LIBRARY PLANNING

Hamburg, Morris, et al, 1974, **Library planning and decision-making systems.** {DUL NIEPA}

Vosper, Robert and Newskirk, Leone I., 1976, **National and international library planning**. {DUL}

Jast, L. Stanley, 1928, **Planning of great library**. {ZHL}

Penna, C.V. and Sewell, P.H., 1967, **The planning of library and documentation services.** [UNESCO]. {AIU ICA NIEPA SPA}

Penna, C.V., 1970, **Planning of library and documentation services**, 2nd edn. [UNESCO]. {IIMC INSA MFL NASSDOC NCAER NERC NIH NIPCCD NMML TDA}
Comey, A.C. and McNamara, Katherine, 1937, **State and national planning.** {ISI}

See also Library Planners

LIBRARY PRIZES
See also Caldecott Miedal Books

LIBRARY PROGRAMMES
Anderson, Florence, 1963, **Library programme, 1911-61.** {ZHL}
Robotham, John S. and Lafleur, Lydia, 1976, **Library programmes** : How to select, plan and produce them. {USIS}
Robotham, John S. and Lafleur, Lydia, 1981, **Library programmes** : How to select, plan and produce them, 2nd edn. {USIS}
Edsall, Marian S., 1980, **Library promotion handbook.** {IIT USIS}

See also Public Relations in Libraries

LIBRARY PUBLICITY
Eliott, Charles A., 1951, **Library publicity and service.** {DUL MHA}
Mathur, Lalit Mohan, 1970, **Principles and techniques of educational library displays and exhibits.** {IIT NMML}

See also Public Relations in Libraries

LIBRARY READERS
See under Library Users and User Study

LIBRARY RESOURCES
Lee, C.P., 1971, **Library resources** : How to research and write a paper? {IIMC IIT NASSDOC NCAER}

See also Union Catalogues

LIBRARY RESOURCES : BIBLIOGRAPHY : GEOGRAPHICAL AREA : USA
Downs, Robert B., n.d., **American library resources** : A bibliographical guide: Supplement: 1961-1970. {NASSDOC}

LIBRARY RESOURCES : GEOGRAPHICAL AREA : BURMA
See Library Resources : Gographical Area : Myanmar

LIBRARY RESOURCES : GEOGRAPHICAL AREA : GREAT BRITAIN
Hewitt, A.R., 1957, **Guide to resources for Commonwealth studies in London, Oxford and Cambridge with bibliographical and other information.** {IEG JNU NIEPA}

LIBRARY RESOURCES : GEOGRAPHICAL AREA : MYANMAR : RANGOON
Calder, Rose E., et al, comps., **A guide to library resources in Rangoon.** {IEG}

LIBRARY RESOURCES : GEOGRAPHICAL AREA : USA

Osburn, Charles B., ed., 1979, **Academic research and library resources :** Changing patterns in America. {DEPT IIT JNU NIPCCD}

LIBRARY RESOURCES : GEOGRAPHICAL AREA : USA : BIBLOGRAPHY

See Library Resources : Bibliography : Geographical Area : USA

LIBRARY SCHOOLS : GEOGRAPHICAL AREA : AFRICA

Dadzie, E.W. and Strickland, J.T., n.d., **Directory of archives, libraries and schools of librarianship in Africa**. {IIMC}

LIBRARY SCHOOLS : GEOGRAPHICAL AREA : NEW JERSEY

See Library Schools : Geographical Area : USA : New Jersey

LIBRARY SCHOOLS : GEOGRAPHICAL AREA : USA : NEW JERSEY

Gardin, J.C., 1985, **New Jersey graduate school of library science.** 2 vols. {IIT}

LIBRARY SCIENCE

Shera, Jesse H., ed., n.d., **Advances in documentation and library science.** 3 vols. {BIS}

Mittal, R.L., 1970, **Advances in library and information science.** {CRRI ICA NCAER NCDC}

Shukla, Lalita S., 1974, **Basic foundations of library science.** {CRRI JNU ZHL}

Danton, J. Periam, 1970, **Between MLS and PHD** : A study of sixth year specialist programmes in accredited library schools. {DUL}

Pathak, Vijay, and Ramaiah, L.S. 1986, **Bibliography of research in library and information in India**. {NMML}

Whatley, H.A., ed., 1972, **British librarianship and information science,** 1966-70. {JNU NMML}

Eastlick, John T., ed., 1971, **The changing environment of libraries** : Papers delivered at the 1970-71 colloquim series. [American Library Association]. {USIS}

Khan, H.A. and Ijari, S.R., 1990, **Current problems and trends in library and information services** : Professor K.S. Deshpande felicitation volume. {DUL}

Sharma, C.D. and Vyas, Kailash, 1983, **Developing horizons in library and information science**, 2 vols. {AIU IIT ISI JNU NASSDOC NMML SPA}

Anon, 1972, **Education, library science, journalism** : A bibliography of doctoral dissertations, 1857-1970. [Inter-University Board of India and Ceylon, New Delhi]. {JNU NMML}

Kent, Allen and Lancom, Harold, eds., n.d., **Encyclopaedia of library and information science**, 41 vols. {ACA IOSA IEG IIT INSA JNU NASSDOC NCERT NIH ZHL}

Rajagopalan, T.S., comp., 1973, **Essays in library science**, 3rd edn. {JNU}

Ranganathan, S.R., 1963, **Five laws of library science.** {BIS CRRI IIT MHA NAI NCAER NMML SPA ZHL}

Sivaswami Iyyar, P.S., 1931, **The five laws of library science.** [Madras Library Association, Madras]. {NASSDOC*}

Wallace, Sarah Leslie, ed., 1962, **Friends of the library** : Organisation and activities. [American Library Association]. {NASSDOC USIS}

Shypla, Bana Bihari, 1984, **Fundamental theories in abstracting and**

fundamental laws in library science. {JNU}

Sharma, Madhusudan, 1990, **Fundamentals of library and information science.** {NMML}

Sharma, J.S., 1977, **Fundamentals of library science** : A modern approach. {ICA ISI JNU ZHL}

Gour, P.N., 1980, **Glossary of library science technical terms.** {JNU NASSDOC RTL}

Anon, 1974, **Granthalaya shastra paribhasha kosh.** {NASSDOC NMML}

Misra, Jogesh, 1979, **History of libraries and librarianship in modern India since 1850.** {JNU NERC NMML}

Kumar, P.S.G., 1977, **Indian library chronology.** {BIS JNU NERC NIPCCD}

Fang, Josephine Riss and Songe, Alice H., 1976, **International guide to library, archival and information science associations.** {USIS}

Butler, Pierce, 1961, **Introduction to library science.** {AIU IIT MFL}

Shera, Jesse H., 1976, **Introduction to library science** : Basic elements of library science. {DUL}

Mott, Thomas H. Jr., et al, 1972, **Introduction to PL-1 programming for library and information science.** {BCL IIT JNU}

Gupta, Pawan K. and Usha Pawan, 1986, **Library and information science** : Current trends in India. {JNU}

Stephen, Parker J., 1984, **Library and information science and archive administration** : A guide to building a basic collection for library schools. {JNU}

Mangla, D.B., ed., 1981, **Library and information science education in India;** Papers and recommendations of an All India Seminar held at the Department of Library and Information Science, University of Delhi, during October 3-8, 1977. {AIU ICA JNU NASSDOC NIEPA}

Anon, n.d., **Library and information science journals in India**; typed short bibliography. {NASSDOC}

Agrawal, S.P., ch. ed., 1985, **Library and information science literature** : SSDC resources. {NASSDOC}

Anon, 1972, **Library and information sciences** : An ERIC bibliography [Educational Resources Information Centre]. {NASSDOC}

Anon, 1974, **Library and information service needs of the nation.** {JNU}

Vashishth, C.P., ed., 1989, **Library and information services in India** : Assessment and effectiveness. [Indian Library Association]. {NASSDOC}

Agrawal, S.P., 1987, **Library and information services in India** : The current scenario. {NASSDOC}

Ranganathan, S.R., 1969, **Library science based service.** {NERC}

Cohen, Nathan M., et al, 1963, **Library science dissertations, 1925-1960** : An annotated bibliography of doctoral studies. {USIS}

Chandrasekharan, K., 1953, **Library science in India.** [Madras Library Association]. {BIS SPA}

Anon, 1963, **Library science in India today** : A symposium. [Bengal Library Association, Calcutta]. {NASSDOC*}

Anon, 1965, **Library science in Indian universities** : Report. [University Grants Commission, New Delhi]. {ICA IIC JNU NASSDOC NIEPA}

Venkatappaiah, V., comp., n.d., **Library science literature in Andhra Pradesh, 1924-1989.** {NASSDOC*}

Magnoti, Shirley, 1982, **Library science research, 1974-79.** {DUL}

Kaula, P.N., ed., 1965, **Library science today** : Ranganathan festschrift. {BIS CRRI

ICHR IIT INSA MFL NIH SPA ZHL}

Duff, Brown James, 1949, **Manual of library economy**. {JNU}

Duff, Brown James, 1977, **Manual of library economy**, ed. by R.N. Lock. {BIS CRRI DUL MFL MHA NIH SPA}

Anon, 1985, **Manual of library management**. [Physical Research Laboratory, Ahmedabad]. {JNU}

Dutta, D.N., 1978, **Manual of library management.** {DUL IIT}

Headicar, B.M., 1935, **Manual of library organisation.** {NAI}

Anon, 1933, **Manual of library routine.** {JNU}

Venkatappaiah, V., ed., 1979, **March of library science** : Kaula festschrift : Papers presented in honour of Prof. P.N. Kaula. {CRRI ICA ICHR IIC IIFT INSA ISI JNU NCAER NIEPA ZHL}

Iyengar, T.K.S., 1977, **New dimensions in library science.** {CRRI DUL ICHR IIT ISI NIEPA}

Anon, 1969, **Papers** : IASLIC conference on library profession in India : Its status and responsibilities and standardised library practices and job classification, 1969, Bombay. [Indian Association of Special Libraries and Information Centres]. {CRRI}

Agarwal, S.N., et al, 1982, **Perspectives in library and information science** : Viswanathan festschrift. 2 vols. {AIU ICHR ISI JNU MMTC NASSDOC NCDC NIEPA NIPCCD SPA ZHL}

Ranganathan, S.R., 1948, **Preface to library science.** {BIS}

Anon, 1977, **Proceedings and papers** : IASLIC seminar on library scene in Calcutta, 1977, Calcutta. [Indian Association of Special Libraries and Information Centres]. {JNU}

Collison, R.L., ed., 1966, **Progress in library science.** {CRRI IEG IIFT NIH NMML}

Shastri, Dwarka Prasad, 1959, **Pustakalaya parichay**. {BIS}

Shastri, Dwarka Prasad, 1974, **Pustakalaya parichay**, 2nd edn. {BIS NMML}

Atherton, Pauline A., 1973, **Putting knowledge to work** : American view of Ranganathan's Five Laws of Library Science. {AIU IIMC JNU NIEPA USIS}

Ennis, Philip H. and Winger, Howard W., eds., 1962, **Seven questions about the profession of librarianship** : Proceedings of the 26th Annual Conference of the Graduate Library School. {IEG}

Prytherch, Ray, comp., 1983, **Sources of information librarianship and information science** : A grafton book. {NIH}

Sharma, J.S., 1965, **Substance of library science.** {ICHR IIC IIT MFL NIH NERC SPA}

Gardin, J.C., 1965, **SYNTOL**, ed. by Susan Artandi, 2 vols. [New Jersy Graduate School of Library Science]. {IIT MFL}

See also Comparative Librarianship

LIBRARY SCIENCE : ACRONYMS

Chakrabarti, Bhubaneswar and Chakraborty, A.R. 1983, **Acronyms, initialisms and abbreviations in library and information science** : An annotated guide. {NASSDOC}

Rangra, V.K., 1982, **International dictionary of acronyms in data processing, library and information systems.** {CRRI MFL NASSDOC NMML}

Vaillancourt, Pauline M., 1980, **International directory of acronyms in library, information and computer sciences.** {NASSDOC USIS}

See also Acronyms

LIBRARY SCIENCE : BIBLIOGRAPHY

Anon, 1966, **Bibliography on work-flow in libraries.** [Council of Scientific and Industrial Research, New Delhi]. {INSDOC NASSDOC}.

Prasher, R.G., 1971, **Indian library literature** : An annotated bibliography. {ICHR NASSDOC NIPCCD NMML}

Anon, 1949-83, **Library literature** : An index to library and information science, 1949-51 to 1982-83. {NASSDOC USIS}

Ranganathan, S.R., 1969, **Library science based service.** {NERC}

Cohen, Nathan M., et al, 1963, **Library science dissertations**, 1925-1960 : An annotated bibliography of doctoral studies. {USIS}

Broadus, Robert N., 1973, **Selecting materials for libraries.** {USIS}

LIBRARY SCIENCE : DICTIONARIES AND ENCYCLOPEADIAS

Yong, Heartsill, et al, eds., 1983, **The ALA glossary of library and information science.** [American Library Association]. {USIS}

Thompson, Elizabeth H., 1943, **ALA glossary of library terms.** [American Library Association]. {BIS CRRI ZHL}

Thompson, Elizabeth, H. 1971, **ALA glossary of library terms with a selection of terms in related fields.** [American Library Association]. {IIT NASSDOC}

Wedgeworth, R., et al, eds., 1980, **ALA world encyclopaedia of library and information services.** [American Library Association]. {IIT NASSDOC NCERT NERC USIS}

Camille, Claude, and Dehaine, Michel, 1970, **Dictionary of data processing.** {NASSDOC}

Wittmann, Alfred and Klos, Joel, 1977, **Dictionary of data processing,** 3rd. rev edn. {NASSDOC}

Rogers, Harold A., 1970, **Dictionary of data processing terms** : {UGC}

El-Benhawy, Mohamad Amil, 1970, **Dictionary of library terms** : English-Arabic. {JNU}

Hayes, Robert M. and Becker, Joseph, 1971, **Glossary from handbook of data processing for libraries.** {USIS}

Gour, P.N., 1980, **Glossary of library science technical terms.** {JNU NASSDOC RTL}

Barrocal, Ramon, 1969, **A glossary of technical service terms for library science students.** [School of Library Science, Syracuse University]. {NASSDOC*}.

Harrod, L.M., 1971, **Librarians' glossary of terms used in librarianship and the book crafts and reference book,** 3rd edn. {CRRI IIT JNU NASSDOC}

Harrod, L.M., 1977, **Librarians' glossary of terms used in librarianship, documentation and the book crafts and reference book,** 4th edn. {ICA IIC MMTC NCDC NCERT NERC NIH NMML ZHL}

LIBRARY SCIENCE : PERIODICALS

See Serials

LIBRARY SCIENCE : RESEARCH

Rolland, E. Stevens, ed., n.d., **Historical and bibliographical methods in library research.** {ICHR}

Downs, Robert B., 1966, **How to do library research?** {ICA IIT JNU NIH USIS}

Lee, C.P., 1971, **Library resources** : How to research and write a paper. {IIMC IIT

NASSDOC NCAER}

Cohen, Nathan M., et al, 1963, **Library science dissertations, 1925-1960** : An annotated bibliography of doctoral studies. {USIS}

Bundy, Mary Lee and Wasserman, Paul, eds., 1970, **Reader in research methods for librarianship**. {USIS}

LIBRARY SCIENCE : SOCIETIES, ETC.
See Library Associations

LIBRARY SCIENCE : STATISTICAL METHODS
See Library Statistics

LIBRARY SCIENCE : STUDY AND TEACHING
See Library Education

LIBRARY SCIENCE : TERMINOLOGY

Cross, Otti, n.d., **Library terms**. {ISI}

LIBRARY SCIENCE AS A PROFESSION

Spivack, Jane, F., 1982, **Careers in information.** {USIS}

Anon, 1969, **Papers** : IASLIC conference on library profession in India : Its status and responsibilities and standardised library practices and job classification, 1969, Bombay. [Indian Association of Special Libraries and Information Centres]. {CRRI}

LIBRARY STATISTICS

Anon, 1966, **Library statistics** : A handbook of concepts, definitions and terminology. [American Library Association, Statistics Coordinating Project]. {USIS}

John, Peter W., 1971, **Statistical design and analysis of experiments.** {NASSDOC}

Carpenter, Ray L. and Vasu, Ellan Storey, 1979, **Statistical methods for librarians**. {ISI}

Sardana, J.L. and Sehgal, R.L., 1982, **Statistical methods for librarians.** {ICHR ISI JNU NASSDOC}

Fisher, Ronald A., 1970, **Statistical methods for research workers,** 14th edn. {NASSDOC}

Agrawal, S.P., ch. ed., 1985, **Statistics and data sources**, Pt. 1 : SSDC sources. {NASSDOC}

Eckard, Helen Mary, n.d., **Statistics of public libraries**, 1960-61. {JNU}

LIBRARY SURVEYS

Line, Maurice, B., 1969, **Library surveys** : An introduction to their use, planning, procedure and presentation. {CRRI IIT NASSDOC USIS}

Line, Maurice B., 1982, **Library surveys** : An introduction to their use, planning, procedure and presentation, 2nd edn. {JNU NASSDOC}

LIBRARY USER EDUCATION
See Library Orientation

LIBRARY USERS AND USER STUDY

Buckland, Michael K., 1975, **Book availability and the library user**. {JNU

NASSDOC USIS}

Lubrans, John, ed., 1974, **Educating the library user**. {USIS}

Evans, A.J., et al, 1977, **Education and training of users of scientific and technical information** : UNISIST guide for teachers. [UNESCO]. {BCL ISI NASSDOC}

Anon, 1989, **Effective methods of promoting reading habits in Asia and the Pacific**. [Asian Cultural Centre for UNESCO, Tokyo]. {NASSDOC*}

Benton, Milored, comp., 1973, **Federal library resources** : A user's guide to research collections. {USIS}

Brittain, J.M., 1970, **Information and its users** : A review with special reference to the social sciences. {JNU NASSDOC}

Chen, Ching-Chih and Hernon, Peter, 1982, **Information seeking** : Assessing and anticipating user needs. {JNU}

Waples, Douglas and Carnovsky, Leon, 1939, **Libraries and readers in the State of New York**. {NASSDOC*}

Dutta, D.N. 1975, **Libraries and their uses.** {ICA IIT}

Cowley, John, ed., 1975, **Libraries in higher education** : The user approach to service. {INSA NIEPA}

Kujoth, Jean Spealman, 1969, **Libraries, readers and book selection.** {USIS}

Girja Kumar and Krishan Kumar, 1983, **Philosophy of user education.** {DUL IIT ISI JNU NASSDOC NIEPA ZHL}

Mikhailov, A.I., n.d., **Problems of information user needs**. [International Federation for Documentation and Information]. {CRRI DUL}

Lubrans, John, ed., 1978, **Progress in educating the library user**. {CRRI IIT}

Anon, 1965, **Reaching readers** : The library's responsibility and opportunity : Papers with a summary of discussions and recommendations. Regional conference workshop for librarians, 6th, December 6-13, 1964, Albay. {NASSDOC}

Anon, 1965, **User and library information service**. [Indian Association of Special Libraries and Information Centres]. {IIFT}

Mac Cafferty, Maxine, 1977, **User education** : Towards a better use of information resources. {BCL}

Fjallbrant, Nancy and Malley, Ian, 1984, **User education in libraries**. {DUL JNU NASSDOC NIEPA}

Fjallbrant, Nancy, 1977, **User education programmes in Swedish academic libraries** : A study of developments in the year 1973-77. {JNU}

Ford, Geoffrey, 1979, **User studies** : An introduction guide and select bibliography. [Centre for Research of User Studies, University of Sheffield, Sheffield]. {NASSDOC}

Anon, 1981, **User surveys and evaluation of library services** [Association of Research Libraries, Washington]. {NASSDOC}

Stone, Phillip J., 1968, **User's manual for the general inquirer**. {NASSDOC}

Anon, 1970, **Users of documentation**. {JNU}

See also Library Orientation

LIFE SCIENCES : INFORMATION SERVICES

Anon, 1976, **Life sciences information network**. [National Library of Australia]. {JNU}

LOANS : INTERLIBRARY
See Interlibrary Loans

LOGIC STRUCTURE TABLES
See Decision Logic Tables

MARC
=Machine Readable Catalogue

MARC SYSTEM
Avram, Henriette D., et al, 1968, **The MARC II format** : A communications format for bibliographic data, 2 vols. [U.S. Library of Congress]. {USIS}
Avram, Henriette D., et al, 1968, **The MARC pilot project** : Final report on a project. [US Library of Congress]. {USIS}
Jeffreys, A.E. and Wison, T.D., 1970, **UK MARC project** : Proceedings of seminar organised by the cataloguing and indexing group of the Library Association at the University of Southampton, March 28-30, 1976. {NASSDOC}

MARC SYSTEM : GEOGRAPHICAL AREA : GREAT BRITAIN
Anon, 1975, **UK MARC manual**. {Bibliographic Services Division, British Library, London]. {JNU}
Anon, 1980, **UK MARC manual**, 2nd edn. [Bibliographic Services Division, British Library, London]. {BIS}

MEDLARS
=Medical Literature Analysis and Retrieval System

MACHINE READABLE BIBLIOGRAPHIC DATA
Coward, R.E. and Yelland, H., eds., 1975, **Interchange of bibliographic information in machine readable form** : Papers given at the Western European seminar, May 12-16, 1974, England. [Library Association, London]. {BCL}
Dierickx, Harold and Hopkinson, Alan, eds., 1981, **Reference manual for machine-readable bibliographic descriptions**, 2nd rev edn. [UNESCO]. {NASSDOC}

MACHINE READABLE CATALOGUE SYSTEM
See MARC System

MACHINE TRANSLATING
Kent, Allen, ed., 1960, **Information retrieval and machine translation**. {CRRI DUL}
Garvin, Paul L., 1972, **On machine translation** : Selected papers. {USIS}

MADHYA PRADESH
See Geographical Area subdivision under Main Descriptors, e.g., Academic Libraries : Geographical Area : India : Madhya Pradesh

MAHARAJA SAYAJIRAO UNIVERSITY OF BARODA
Sudame, G.R., 1972, **Study of the effect of library use on academic achievement of post-graduate students in the M.S. University of Baroda.**

{NASSDOC}

MALAYSIA

See Geographical Area subdivision under Main Descriptor, e.g., Libraries : Geographical Area : Malaysia

MANAGEMENT : BIBLIOGRAPHY

Vernon, D.C., 1975, **Use of management and business literature.** {MMTC}

MANAGEMENT : INFORMATION SYSTEM

Murdick, Robert G. and Ross, Jod E., 1977, **Information system for modern management.** {ICA}

MANUSCRIPTS

Kane, Lucile M., 1966, **Guide to the care and administration of manuscripts,** 2nd edn. [American Association for State and Local History]. {NMML}

Hammond, George P., 1972, **Guide to the manuscript collections of the Bancroft Library**, 2 Vols. {JNU}

Strassberg, Richard, 1974, **Manual of archival and manuscript processing procedures**. {DUL}

Bordin, Ruth B. and Warner, Robert M., 1966, **Modern manuscript library.** {NMML}

Crutchky, Brooke, 1967, **Preparation of manuscripts and correction of proofs.** {DUL}

Gupta, R.D., 1970, **Preserving manuscripts and other research material in the Braj area of India,** (reprinted from the Bulletin of the British Association of Orientalists). [Vrindaban Research Institute]. {NMML}

See also Archives; Museums

MANUSCRIPTS : CATALOGUES

Anon, 1980, **Catalogue of special collections in National Library, Baghdad.** [National Library, Baghdad]. {NASSDOC}.

MANUSCRIPTS : CONSERVATION AND RESTORATION

Agrawal, O.P., 1984, **Conservation of manuscripts and painting of South-East Asia**. {NMML}

Barrow, W.J., 1972, **Manuscripts and documents** : Their deterioration and restoration. {NASSDOC NMML}

Gupta, R.D., 1970, **Preserving manuscripts and other research material in the Braj area of India,** (reprinted from the Bulletin of the British Association of Orientalists). [Vrindaban Research Institute]. {NMML}

MANUSCRIPTS : SANSKRIT

Shah, Ambalal P., ed., n.d. **Catalogue of Sanskrit and Prakrit manuscripts,** 4 parts. [Lalbhai Dalpatbhai Institute of Indology]. {INSA}

MAP COLLECTIONS : GEOGRAPHICAL AREA : CANADA

Carrington, David K., comp., 1970, **Map collection in the United States and Canada** : A directory, 2nd edn. [Special Libraries Association, New York]. {USIS}

Carrington, David K. and Stephenson, Richard W., comps., 1978, **Map collections**

in the United States and Canada : A directory, 3rd edn. [Special Libraries Association, New York]. {USIS}

MAP COLLECTIONS : GEOGRAPHICAL AREA : USA
Carrington, David K., comp., 1970, **Map collection in the United States and Canada** : A directory, 2nd edn. [Special Libraries Association, New York]. {USIS}
Carrington, David K. and Stephenson, Richard W., comps., 1978, **Map collections in the United States and Canada** : A directory, 3rd edn. [Special Libraries Association, New York]. {USIS}

MAP LIBRARIES
See Map Collections

MARSHALL, D.N.
Gidwani, N.N., ed., 1973, **Comparative librarianship** : Essays in honour of Prof. D.N. Marshall. {ICHR IIC JNU NASSDOC NIPCCD NMML ZHL}

MASS COMMUNICATION
See Mass Media

MASS MEDIA
McGarry, K.J., 1972, **Mass communications** : Selected readings for librarians. {NIPCCD}

MASS MEDIA : BIBLIOGRAPHY
McGarry, K.J., 1972, **Mass communications** : Selected readings for librarians. {NIPCCD}

MASS MEDIA : DICTIONARIES
Watson, James and Hill, Anne, 1986, **Dictionary of communication and media studies**. {JNU NASSDOC}

MASS MEDIA : INFORMATION SERVICES
Anon, n.d., **National Documentation Centre on Mass Communication** : Report. [Ministry of Information and Broadcasting, New Delhi]. {IIMC}

MASS MEDIA : LIBRARIES
Duggal, K.S., 1982, **Indian broadcast media yearbook.** {NASSDOC}
Tiihonen, Pertti, n.d., **Influence of television on the use of libraries.** {IIMC}
Davis, Harold S., ed., 1971, **Instructional Media Centre** : Bold new venture. {USIS}
Wisdom, Aline C., 1974, **Introduction to library services for library media technical assistants.** {ICA}
Cabeceiras, James, 1978, **Multimedia library** : Materials selection and use. {IIFT JNU NIPCCD}
Cabeceiras, James, 1982, **Multimedia library** : Materials selection and use, 2nd edn. {NIEPA}
Enright, B.J., 1972, **New media and the library in education.** {IIT NIH}
Brown, James W., 1976, **New media in public libraries** : Survey of current practices. {USIS}

MECHANICAL ENGINEERING : INFORMATION SERVICES

Wall, Rayond Alwyn, ed., 1974, **Papers** : Seminar on mechanical engineering information : Provision and use, March 27-29, 1974, Loughborough. {BCL}

MEDIA LIBRARIES

See Mass Media : Libraries

MEDICAL LIBRARIES

Anon, 1976, **Directory of medical libraries in the British Isles.** [Library Association, London, Medical Section]. {NIH}

Morton, Leslie T., 1979, **How to use a medical library.** {NIH}

Picken, F.M. and Mathews, D.A., 1979, **Medical librarianship** : Outlines of modern librarianship. {NIH USIS}

Thornton, John L., 1963, **Medical librarianship** : Principles and practice. {DUL}

MEDICAL LITERATURE ANALYSIS AND RETRIEVAL SYSTEM

Anon, 1968, **Evaluation of the MEDLARS demand research services.** [U.S. National Library of Medicine]. {USIS}

Charen, Thelma, 1975, **Technical notes** : MEDLARS indexing instructions. [National Library of Medicine, Maryland]. {CRRI}

MEDICINE : INFORMATION SERVICES

Anon, 1979, **Computer based information services in medicines** : A feasibility study : On behalf of the University of Otago medical libraries. [Centerbury Medical Library]. {BCL}

MEETINGS : PROCEEDINGS/REPORTS/SOUVENIRS

Anon, 1980, **ALA year book**: A review of library events, 1979. [American Library Association] {IIT JNU USIS}

Anon, 1986, **APINESS** : Report : UNESCO/AASSREC regional meeting of experts to develop Asia Pacific Information Network in Social Sciences, May 12-16, 1986, Bangkok. {NASSDOC}

Anon, 1947, **ASLIB meeting on planning and equipment of special libraries, April 6, 1946, London**. {CRRI}

Anthony, Lawrence James, ed., 1976, **ASLIB seminar for information planners and industry, May 13-14, 1976, Boaconfield.** {BCL NASSDOC}

Randall, William, ed., 1944, **Acquisition and cataloguing of books** : Papers presented before the library institute at the University of Chicago, July 29 to August 9, 1940. {JNU NAI ZHL}

Bloomfield, B.C., 1972, **Acquisition and provision of foreign books by national and university libraries in the United Kingdom :** Papers of the Morecamb conference, April 16, 1972. {NMML}

Anon, 1960, **American libraries** : Report : U.S. field seminar on library reference services for Japanese librarians, June 1960. [International House of Japan]. {DUL NASSDOC}

Anon, 1983, **Asian regional seminar on information sources, systems and services in the social sciences, July 11-22, 1983, Philippines**. [Unesco Regional Office, Bangkok]. {NASSDOC}

Gangadhara Rao, P. and Raghavan, Q.S., eds., 1986, **Assessment of public library development in India** : Seminar papers. [University of Madras,

Department of Library and Information Science]. {NASSDOC}

Luhn, H.P., 1963, **Automation and scientific communication** : Short papers contributed to the theme sessions of the 26th annual meeting of the American Documentation Institute at Chicago. {JNU}

Anon, 1981, **Background papers** : Sub-regional workshop for cooperative librarians and documentation officers for South East Asia, April 14-29, 1981, Los Banos. [ICA Regional Office and Education Centre for South East Asia, New Delhi]. {ICA}

Anon, 1977, **Bibliography** : Reports from the International Conference on Education, 1975. [UNESCO]. {ICA}

Mangla, P.B., ed., 1985, **Building library collections and national policy for library** : Seminar papers : All India library conference, 30th, January 28-31, 1985, Jaipur. [Indian Library Association]. {NASSDOC}

Anon, 1976, **Capital provision for university libraries** : Report of a working party. [University Grants Commission, London]. {IIT JNU NIEPA ZHL}

Anon, 1986, **Challenges of new technologies** : All India library convention, 6th September 1-4, Shimla, [Government of India Librarians Association]. {NMML}

Eastlick, John T., ed., 1971, **The changing environment of libraries** : Papers delivered at the 1970-71 colloquim series. [American Library Association]. {USIS}

Bakewell, K.G.B., ed., 1968, **Classification for information retrieval** : Papers presented at an intensive course held in September 1967 at the School of Librarianship. [Liverpool College of Commerce]. {NIH}

Packer, Katherine H. and Phillips, Delores, eds., 1969, **Code and the cataloguer** : Proceedings of the colloquium on the Anglo-American Cataloguing Rules held at the School of Library Science, University of Toronto on March 31 and April 1, 1967. {NASSDOC}

Thayer, Lee, ed. and comp., 1967, **Communication theory and research** : Proceedings of the first international symposium. {NASSDOC}

Anon, 1975, **Conference number and souvenir** : All India library conference, 22nd, January 17-20, 1976, Delhi. [Indian Library Association]. {NASSDOC}

Sardana, J.L., ed., 1984, **Continuing education for librarians** : Paper : All India seminar for librarians, February 13, 1984, New Delhi. [Indian Library Association]. {NASSDOC}

Stone, Elizabeth W., et al, 1974, **Continuing library and information science education** : Final report to the National Commission on Libraries and Information Science (with bibliography). {USIS}

Anon, 1988, **Convention and exposition** : Micrographic Congress (India), 2nd, January 20-22, 1988, New Delhi. {NASSDOC}

Anon, n.d., **Convention papers** : All India library convention, 5th, May 23-26, 1985, Hardwar. [Government of India Librarians Association]. {NASSDOC}

Anon, 1986, **Course material** : Workshop on computer application to library and information activities, 2nd, September 8-13, 1986, Ahmedabad. [ILA; Physical Research Laboratory, Ahmedabad]. {NASSDOC}

Anon, 1976, **Delhi Public Library** : Silver jubilee souvenir, 27th October, 1976. {NASSDOC}

Singer, Howard W. and Smith, Richard Daniel, eds., 1970, **Deterioration and preservation of library materials** : Conference of the Graduate Library School, 34th, August 4-6, 1969, Chicago. {AIU CRRI IIT INSA JNU NASSDOC NMML}

Anon, 1954, **Development of public libraries in Africa** : Ibadan seminar. [UNESCO]. {IEG NASSDOC ZHL}

Anon, 1952, **Development of public libraries in Latin America** : The Sao Paulo conference. [UNESCO]. {IEG NASSDOC ZHL}

Anon, 1985, **Development of research and information system in the Third World** : Report of the proceedings: Research and information system for the non-aligned and other developing countries, 2nd, November 20-22, 1985, New Delhi. [RISNODC]. {NASSDOC}

Anon, 1967, **Developments in classification** : DRTC annual seminar, 2 vols. [Documentation Research and Training Centre]. {NASSDOC}

Koops, William R.H. and Stellingwerff, Johannes, eds., 1977, **Developments in collection building in university libraries in Western Europe**: Symposium on . . ., March 31-April 2, 1976, Amsterdam. {IIT}

Kirkendall, Carolyn A., ed., 1981, **Directions for the decade** : Library instruction in the 1980's : Conference on library orientation for academic libraries, 10th, May 8-9. 1980. [Eastern Michigan University]. {USIS}

Anon, 1980, **Documentation services in departmental libraries** : Papers : All India library convention, 2nd, March 3-6, 1980, New Delhi. [Government of India Librarians Association]. {CRRI NASSDOC NMML}

Anon, 1983, **Educational information** : Problems, issues and strategies for resolving them : Report of a regional workshop. [National Institute for Educational Research]. {NIEPA}

Anon, 1957, **Exchange of ideas** : East and West meet the challenge : Final report : Seminar on the international exchange of publications in the Indo-Pacific area, 1957, Tokyo. {IEG}

Mangla, P.B., et al, eds., 1983, **Fifty years of librarianship in India** : Past, present and future : Papers : All India library conference, 29th, December 5-9, 1983. [Indian Library Association]. {MMTC NASSDOC ZHL}

Anon, 1972, **Final report** : International congress on the universal availability of publications. [UNESCO]. {NASSDOC}

Anon, 1982, **Final report** : International congress on the universal availability of publications. [UNESCO]. {NASSDOC}

Mosher, Frederic J., ed., 1954, **Freedom of book selection** : Proceedings : Conference on intellectual freedom, 2nd, June 20-21, 1953. [American Library Association]. {AIU USIS}

Wasserman, Paul, ed., 1972, **Frontiers in librarianship** : Proceedings of Change Institute, 1969. [Change Institute, University of Maryland]. {JNU NIPCCD}

Fussler, Herman, ed., 1954, **Functions of the library in the modern college** : Conference of the Graduate Library School, 19th, 1954, Chicago. {IIT SPA}

Anon, 1982, **Future of libraries** : Panel discussion by librarians, administrators, faculty and students : Papers from the millionth volume celebration. [New York State University]. {NASSDOC}

Neelameghan, A., ed., 1977, **Guidelines for formulation of a policy on education, training and development of library and information personnel** : All India seminar on library and information science education, October 3-8, 1977, Delhi. [Indian Statistical Institution]. {NASSDOC}.

Kumar, P.S.G., ed., 1987, **Hundred years of library education and its future** : Pre-seminar volume : ILA-IASLIC-GILA-IATLIS library education centenary seminar, October 10-12, 1987, Nagpur. [Nagpur University, Department of Library and Information Science, Nagpur]. {NASSDOC}

Anon, 1988, **IFLA annual** : Proceedings of the general conferences; Annual reports. [International Federation of Library Associations and Institutions]. {NASSDOC}

Anon, 1987, **IFLA round-table on research on reading, August 13-15, 1987, Manchester** : Preparatory meeting before Brighton Congress. {NASSDOC*}

Anon, 1966, **INSDOC seminar on work-flow in libraries**, November 21-24, 1966, New Delhi, 3 pts. Pt-1 : Special libraries; Pt-2 : University libraries; Pt-3 : Government libraries. {BIS}

Anon, 1976, **Indexing systems** : IASLIC special course, November 1—December 14, 1976 : Course material. [Indian Association of Special Libraries and Information Centres]. {JNU}

Anthony, Lawrence James, ed., 1976, **Information in the 1980s** : Proceedings : ASLIB seminar for information planners and industry, May 13-14, 1976, Beaconfield. [Association of Special Libraries and Information Bureaux]. {BCL NASSDOC}

Freeman, Robert R., et al, eds., 1968, **Information in the language sciences** : Proceedings of the conference held at Airlic House, Warrenton, Virginia, March 4-6, 1966. {NASSDOC}

Taylor, Peter J. and Crown, Blaise, 1983, **Information management research in Europe** : Proceedings of the EURIMS conference, Paris. {JNU}

Anon, n.d., **Information processing** : Proceedings : International conference on information processing. {JNU}

Anon, 1960, **Information processing** : Proceedings : International conference on information processing. {JNU}

Roy, A.K. and Kapoor, S.K., eds., 1982, **Information services in India** : Papers: IASLIC national seminar, 10th, December 21-24, 1982, Kanpur. [Indian Association of Special Libraries and Information Centres]. {ICA JNU MMTC NASSDOC NIPCCD}

Sherrod, John, 1975, **Information systems and networks** : Eleventh annual symposium {JNU}

Kent, Allen and Galvin, Thomas J., eds., 1982, **Information technology** : Critical choices for library decision makers : Pittsburg conference on electronic information technology and its impact on library and information services, 1981, 4th, Pittsburg. {BIS CRRI IIT JNU USIS}

Coward, R.E. and Yelland, H., eds., 1975, **Interchange of bibliographic information in machine readable form** : Papers given at the Western European seminar, May 12-16, 1974, England. [Library Association, London]. {BCL}

Dimitrov, Th. and Maruli, L., 1982, **International documents for 80's** : Their role and use : Proceedings : World symposium on international documentation, 2nd, 1980, Brussels. {JNU NMML}

Chandler, George, ed., 1972, **International librarianship** : Surveys of recent developments in developing countries and in advanced librarianship submitted to the 1971 IFLA pre-session seminar for developing countries, August 24—September 1, 1971. [Library Association, London]. {NASSDOC}

Anon, 1972, **Issues in library administration** : Papers presented at the U.S.-Japan conference on libraries and information science in higher education, 2nd, 1972. {JNU}

Gerard, David E., ed., 1970, **Libraries and the arts** : A symposium of papers and discussions at the seminar held in the College of Librarianship, September 1-6, 1969, Wales. {NASSDOC}

Anon, 1977, **Libraries and the life of the mind in America** : Addresses delivered at the centennial celebration of the American Library Association, [American Library Association]. {IIT NIPCCD USIS}

Vosper, Robert and Koops, William R.H., 1977, **Libraries for all** : A world of books and their readers : World congress on libraries for all, 50th, 1977, Brussels. [International Federation of Library Association and Institutions]. {IIT}

Houle, Cyril O., ed., 1951, **Libraries in adult and fundamental education** : Report of the Malmo Seminar. [UNESCO]. {IEG NASSDOC ZHL}

Houle, Cyril O., ed., 1957, **Libraries in adult and fundamental education** : Report of the Malmo Seminar, (Hindi Translation). [Indian Adult Education Association]. {NIEPA}

Anon, 1985, **Libraries in social education** : Report of the national seminar on libraries in social education, 6th, September 26—October 5, 1955, 2nd ed. [Indian Adult Education Association]. {NIPCCD}

Kumar, P.S.G., ed., 1988, **Library and information manpower development** : Papers and proceedings : Nagpur Seminar. {NASSDOC}

Mangla, P.B., ed., 1981, **Library and information science education in India** : Papers and recommendations of an All India seminar held at the Department of Library Science, University of Delhi, during October 3-8, 1977, {AIU ICA JNU NASSDOC NIEPA}

Anon, 1976, **Library and information science manpower development in the Asian Region** : Report : Meeting of supervisors of library and documentation schools in the Asian region, Bangalore. {CRRI}

Salmon, Stephen R., ed., 1969, **Library automation** : A state of art review : Papers : Pre-conference institute on library automation, 1967, San Francisco. [American Library Association]. {USIS}

Butler, Brett and Martin, Susan K. eds., 1975, **Library automation-II** : The state of art : Papers : Pre-conference institute on library automation, June 22-23, 1973, Las Vegas. [American Library Association, Information Science and Automation Division]. {USIS}

Shaw, Robert J., ed., 1967, **Library buildings for the future** : Proceedings. Library buildings institute and American libraries trustee association workshop, 1965, Detroit. {DUL}

Anon, 1975, **Library development in Pakistan** : Resume and recommendation : National seminar, February 7-9, 1974, Lahore. [Society for the Promotion and Improvement of Libraries]. {NASSDOC*}

Bowden, Russel E., ed., 1980, **Library education programme in developing countries with special reference to Asia** : UNESCO pre-IFLA conference seminar on library education programme in developing countries, August 15-18, 1980, Philippines. [Library Association, London]. {IIT NASSDOC}

Poole, Frazer G., ed., 1965, **The library environment** : Aspects of interior planning : Proceedings : Library equipment institute, 2nd, 1964, St. Louis. {JNU USIS}

Anon, 1983, **Library in the information revolution** : Proceedings : Congress of South-East Asian librarians, 6th, May 30 - June 3, 1983, Singapore. {JNU}

Anon, 1967, **Library resources on East Asia** : Reports and working papers for the 10th meeting of the committee on American library resources. [Association for Asian Studies]. {JNU}

Kapoor, S.K. ed., 1977, **Library scene in Calcutta** : Seminar on the occasion of the 100th meeting of the IASLIC study circle, February 26-27, 1977. [Indian Association of Special Libraries and Information Centres]. {NASSDOC*}

Khan, Sadiq Ali, 1982, **Library services in Pakistan** : Being the proceedings of the departments of library science. . . . {JNU}

Goldhor, Herbert, ed., n.d., **Measurement and evaluation** : Papers presented at a conference conducted by the University of Illinois, Graduate School of Library Science, September 10-12, 1967. {DUL}

Vashishth, C.P., ed., 1987, **Modernisation in libraries** : Seminar Papers : All India Library Conference, 33rd, December 28-31, 1987, Tiruchirapalli. [Indian Library Association]. {NASSDOC}

Anon, 1977, **National information system** : Library and information science manpower development in Asian region : Meeting of supervisors of library and documentation schools in the Asian region, Bangalore. [UNESCO; DRTC]. {JNU}

Anon, 1963, **National libraries** : Their problems and prospects : Symposium on national libraries in Europe, September 8-27, Vienna. [UNESCO]. {AIU BIS CRRI IEG IIMC MFL NASSDOC NIEPA NIPCCD}

Anon, 1972, **National Library Bill, 1972** : Report and evidence : India, Lok Sabha, Joint Committee on the National Library Bill. {AIU NMML}

Anon, 1984, **Need for National Information Policy** : Its parameters : Papers : Convention and conference of the Society for Information Science, 4th, December 27-28, 1984, Madras. {NASSDOC*}

Stone, Elizabeth W., ed., 1971, **New directions in staff development moving from ideas to action** : The papers : Microworkshop on staff development, June 28, 1970, Detroit. [American Library Association]. {USIS}

Anon, 1986, **New Education Policy** : Libraries and information system : Papers and proceedings. [NCERT; Raja Rammohan Roy Library Foundation, Calcutta]. {NMML}

Vashishth, C.P., ed., 1986, **New education policy vis-a-vis library development** : Papers presented in the seminar held at New Delhi on February 13, 1986. [Indian Library Association]. {NASSDOC}

Neelameghan, A., ed., 1979, **Ordering systems for global information networks** : Proceedings : International study conference on classification research, 3rd, January 6-11, 1975, Bombay, [FID/CR; Sarada Ranganathan Endowment for Library Science]. {BIS NASSDOC}

Perlman, M., ed., 1977, **Organisation and retrieval of economic knowledge** : Proceedings of the conference held by the International Economic Association. {NASSDOC}

Anon, 1978, **Papers** : All India public library convention, November, 16-18, 1978, New Delhi. [Delhi Library Association, Delhi]. {MMTC NMML}

Anon, 1981, **Papers** : All India seminar on agricultural library and information services, December 29-January 16, 1980. [Andhra Pradesh Agricultural University, Hyderabad; Indian Council of Agricultural Research, New Delhi]. {IIMC}

Anon, 1982, **Papers** : All India seminar on libraries and the book trade, February 1982, New Delhi. [Indian Library Association]. {IIMC IIT JNU ZHL}

Anon, 1982, **Papers** : All India seminar on library resources in university education and research, 1982, Hyderabad. [Osmania University Library, Hyderabad]. {ZHL}

Anon, 1983, **Papers** : All India seminar on national policy for library and information science education, 1983, Nagpur. {NASSDOC}

Anon, 1981, **Papers** : Conference on electronic information technology and its impact on library and information service, 4th, 1981, Pittsburg. {IIT}

Anon, 1973, **Papers** : Conference on informatics, 1973, Durham. [Association of Special Libraries and Information Bureaux]. {CRRI}

Horsnell, Verina, ed., 1974, **Papers** : Conference on informatics, 1974, Oxford. [Association of Special Libraries and Information Bureaux]. {CRRI}

Anon, 1975, **Papers** : Conference on informatics, 1975, Cambridge. [Association of

Special Libraries and Information Bureaux]. {CRRI}

Anon, 1975, **Papers** : Conference on use of computers in libraries and information centres, 1975, London. [Association of Special Libraries and Information Bureaux]. {CRRI}

Anon, 1981, **Papers** : DRTC annual seminar on information analysis and consolidation, 1981, Bangalore. [Documentation Research and Training Centre, Bangalore]. {CRRI}

Anon, 1983, **Papers** : DRTC refresher seminar, 1983, Bangalore. [Documentation Research and Training Centre, Bangalore]. {JNU}

Anon, 1980, **Papers** : DRTC refresher seminar on data accessibility and dissemination, 1980, Bangalore. [Documentation Research and Training Centre, Bangalore]. {CRRI}

Mac Cafferty, Maxine, n.d., **Papers** : EUSIDIC conference on user education, 1976, Graz. {CRRI}

Dewe, A. and Deunelle, J., n.d., **Papers** : European conference on the contribution of users to planning and policy making for information systems and networks, 1978, Germany. {CRRI}

Anon, 1978, **Papers**: FID congress on new trends in documentation and information, 1978, Edinburg. {CRRI}

Anon, 1968, **Papers** : FID pre-congress seminar on education and training : Theory and provision with a look at new developments and an example of the challenges confronting information workers, 1978, Edinburg. [International Federation for Documentation and Information]. {NASSDOC}

Anon, 1972, **Papers** : IASLIC conference, 9th, 1972, Calcutta. [Indian Association of Special Libraries and Information Centre]. {IIT INSA JNU MMTC}

Anon, 1975, **Papers** : IASLIC conference, 10th, 1975, Lucknow, Pt. A. : Library documents aspects of utilisation; Pt. B. : Procurement of periodicals : Current problems in India [Indian Association of Special Libraries and Information Centres]. {IIMC}

Chakraborty, A.R. and Kapoor, S.K., eds., 1983, **Papers** : IASLIC conference, 14th, December 26-29, 1983, New Delhi, I : Information flow in non R and D context; II : Grey literature. [Indian Association of Special Libraries and Information Centres]. {JNU MMTC NASSDOC NCAER NIEPA NIPCCD}

Anon, 1969, **Papers** : IASLIC conference on library profession in India : Its status and responsibilities and standardised library practices and job classification, 1969, Bombay. [Indian Association of Special Libraries and Information Centres]. {CRRI}

Kapoor, S.K. and Ghosh, S.B., eds., 1977, **Papers** : IASLIC conference on planning of national information network, 11th, November 2-5, 1977, Dharwar. [Indian Association of Special Libraries and Information Centres]. {CRRI ISI JNU NIEPA NIPCCD}

Anon, 1966, **Papers** : IASLIC national seminar, 4th, 1966, Hyderabad. [Indian Association of Special Libraries and Information Centres]. {NASSDOC}

Anon, 1984, **Papers** : IASLIC national seminar, 11th, November 26-29, 1984, Hyderabad, I : Toward a code of professional ethics; II : Document delivery, reproduction, translation. [Indian Association of Special Libraries and Information Centres]. {NASSDOC}

Anon, 1970, **Papers** : IASLIC seminar, 6th, November 2-5, 1970, Bangalore. [Indian Association of Special Libraries and Information Centres]. {BIS JNU NMML}

Anon, 1976, **Papers** : IASLIC seminar, 7th, December 28-31, 1976, Burdwan. [Indian Association of Special Libraries and Information Centres]. {BIS JNU

NASSDOC}

Kapoor, S.K., et al, eds., 1980, **Papers** : IASLIC seminar, 9th, October 23-26, 1980, Nagpur, I : Role of information centres in technology transfer; II : Role of State-level and national library association in library development in India. [Indian Association of Special Libraries and Information Centres]. {CRRI INSA JNU NASSDOC}

Anon, 1982, **Papers** : IASLIC seminar on information services in India, 1982, Kanpur. [Indian Association of Special Libraries and Information Centres]. {CRRI}

Anon, n.d., **Papers** : IASLIC symposium on the development of libraries in India under the Third Five Year Plan with particular reference to special libraries, January 23-25, 1960, Calcutta. [Indian Association of Special Libraries and Information Centres]. {BIS}

Anon, 1987, **Papers** : IFLA General Conference, 53rd, August 16-21, 1987, Bringhton. [International Federation of Library Associations and Institutions]. {NASSDOC*}

Ingram, K.E. and Jefferson, Albert A., 1976, **Papers** : International library conference on libraries and the challenge of change, April 24-29, 1976, Kingsten. [Jamaica Library Association]. {IIT}

Anon, 1980, **Papers** : National conference, 1980, Tirupati. [Indian Association of Academic Librarians]. {ZHL}

Stueart, Robert D. and Johnson, Richard D., 1979, **Papers** : National conference on new horizons for academic libraries, November 8-11, 1978, Boston, {IIT}

Gangadhara Rao, P. and Raghavan, Q.S., eds., 1986, **Papers** : National seminar on assessment of public library development in India, March 3-6, 1986, Madras. [University of Madras, Department of Library Science; University Grants Commission, New Delhi]. {NASSDOC}

Kumar, P.S.G., ed., 1985, **Papers** : National seminar on library and information manpower development, December 6-9, 1985, Nagpur. [Nagpur University, Department of Library and Information Science; University Grants Commission, New Delhi]. {NASSDOC}

Anon, 1986, **Papers** : National seminar on library and information science education in India : New perspective, December 10-12, 1986, Trivandrum. [Kerala State Committee on Science, Technology and Environment]. {NASSDOC}

Anon, 1978, **Papers** : Seminar on information for engineering industry, February 10, 1978, New Delhi. [Association of Engineering Industry; Indian National Scientific Documentation Centre, New Delhi]. {BIS}

Anon, 1977, **Papers** : Seminar on library and information science education in India, 1977, New Delhi. {JNU}

Anon, 1980, **Papers** : Seminar on library buildings in India, February 11-13, 1980, New Delhi. [National Information System for Science and Technology, New Delhi]. {BIS CRRI IIT}

Anon, 1965, **Papers** : Seminar on library science in Southeast Asia, December 18-20, 1964, Bangkok. [Association of Southeast Asian Institutions of Higher Learning]. {NASSDOC NIEPA}

Wall, Rayond Alwyn, ed., 1974, **Papers** : Seminar on mechanical engineering information : Provision and use, March 27-29, 1974, Loughborough. {BCL}

Anon, 1979, **Papers** : Seminar on reference sources on South Asia, 1979, Jaipur. {JNU}

Anon, 1961, **Papers** : Seminar on the rendering of Indic names, 1960-61, Calcutta. [Indian Association of Special Libraries and Information Centres]. {NASSDOC}

Anon, 1979, **Papers** : Seminar on the role of the National Library of India, November 23, 1978, Calcutta. [National Library Employee's Association, Calcutta]. {NASSDOC}

Anon, 1975, **Papers** : Seminar on thesaurus in information systems, December 1-5, 1975, Bangalore. [DRTC, Bangalore; Indian National Scientific Documentation Centre, New Delhi]. {BIS CRRI DUL IIMC ZHL}

Anon, 1966, **Papers** : Seminar on work flow in libraries, November 21-24, 1966, New Delhi; 3 vols., Vol. 1 : Special libraries; Vol II : University libraries; Vol. III : Government libraries. [Indian National Scientific Documentation Centre, New Delhi]. {NASSDOC NMML SPA}

Boaz, Martha, ed., n.d., **Papers** : Symposium on modern trends in documentation, 1958, California. {CRRI}

Anon, n.d., **Papers** : Symposium on new technology in libraries : Prospects and problems for libraries in the Gulf States, 1982, Teheran. [Ministry of Petroleum and Minerals, Teheran]. {CRRI}

Motiwale, Sushila A. and Jagtar Singh, eds., 1986, **Papers** : UGC sponsored national seminar on documentation services in university and college libraries, January 12-14, 1986, Jabalpur. {NASSDOC}

Anon, 1980, **Papers** : Workshop on computer techniques in information processing. [University of Delhi, Department of Library and Information Science]. {AIU}

Venkatappaiah, V., ed., 1989, **Papers** : Workshop on norms, guidelines and standards for public libraries. [Zilla Granthalaya Samstha, Eluru]. {NASSDOC*}

Kapoor, S.K., ed., 1979, **Papers and proceedings** : IASLIC conference, 8th, December 26-29, 1978, Madras, Pt I : Standardisation of techniques and procedures for information handling; Pt II : Library and information system for rural development. [Indian Association of Special Libraries and Information Centres]. {BIS NIPCCD}

Anon, 1984, **Papers and proceedings** : Round table discussion on the concepts of Australian national bibliography, 1983, South Wales. {JNU}

Pearson, J.D., ed., 1971, **Papers on oriental library collections submitted to a library panel** : International congress of orientalists, 27th, August 17, 1967, Ann Arbor, Michigan. {NMML}

Chandel, A.S., ed., 1987, **Planning in library resource sharing** : Proceedings : Seminar on coordination in resource sharing held at Isabella Thouburn College, Lucknow. {NASSDOC}

Roth, Harold, L., ed., 1964, **Planning library buildings for service** : Proceedings : Library building and equipment institute, July 6-8, 1961, Kent. [American Library Association]. {BIS DUL}

Anon, 1979, **Problems and failures in library automation** : Clinic on library applications of data processing, 1978, Illinois. [University of Illinois at Urbana-Champaign]. {USIS}

Katz, William A. and Swarf, Roderick G., eds., 1964, **Problems in planning library facilities**, Consultants, architects, plans and critiques : Proceedings : Library building institute, July 12-13, 1963, Chicago. [American Library Association]. {BIS DUL NASSDOC*}

Anon, 1935, **Proceedings** : All India library conference, 2nd, 1935, Lucknow. [Indian Library Association]. {NASSDOC}

Anon, 1942, **Proceedings** : All India library conference, 5th, April 4-6, 1942, Bombay. [Indian Library Association]. {NASSDOC}

Anon, 1946, **Proceedings** : All India library conference, 7th, January 25-28, 1946,

Baroda. [Indian Library Association]. {NASSDOC}

Krishan Kumar and Vashishth, C.P., eds., 1980, **Proceedings** : All India library conference, 26th, March 6-9, 1980, New Delhi. [Indian Library Association]. {NASSDOC}

Anon, 1987, **Proceedings** : All India library conference, 32nd, 1987. [Indian Library Association]. {NASSDOC}

Anon, 1988, **Proceedings** : All India library conference, 34rd, 1988. [Indian Library Association]. {NASSDOC}

Anon, 1989, **Proceedings** : All India library conference, 35th, 1989. [Indian Library Association] {NASSDOC}

Anon, n.d., **Proceedings** : All India library convention. [Government of India Librarians Association]. {NMML}

Anon, 1927, **Proceedings** : Anniversary conference of Library Association, 15th, 1927, Edinburg. [Library Association, London]. {NASSDOC}

Kent, Allen and Galvin, Thomas J., eds., 1978, **Proceedings** : Conference on the on-line revolution in libraries, 1978, Pittsburg. {JNU}

Kapoor, S.K., et al, eds., n.d., **Proceedings** : Conference on organisation of data services in India and user education and training programmes, 13th, 1981, Waltair. [Indian Association of Special Libraries and Information Centres]. {BIS MMTC NIPCCD}

Whatley, Allen, ed., 1974, **Proceedings** : International and comparative librarianship group conference, June 28-July 1, 1974, {NASSDOC}

Amarsinghe, N., ed., 1987, **Proceedings** : International conference of directors of national libraries of Asia and Oceania, 3rd, November 18-23, Colombo. {NASSDOC}

Keren, Carl, and Perlmutter, Linda, n.d., **Proceedings** : International conference on the application of mini and micro computers in information, documentation and libraries, March 13-18, 1983, Tel Aviv. {IIT}

Radhakrishnan, S., and Iyengar, T.K.S., eds., 1977, **Proceedings** : International conference on technical information services for developing countries, March, 1977, Madras. [International Council of Scientific Unions, Committee of Science and Technology in Developing Countries]. {BCL BIS CRRI IIT JNU}

Perti, R.K., ed., 1987, **Proceedings** : International seminar on conservation of traditional records, paper and allied materials. [National Archives of India]. {NAT}

Anon, 1957, **Proceedings** : International study conference on classification for information retrieval, 1957, {IEC IIT}

Atherton, Pauline, ed., 1965, **Proceedings** : International study conference on classification research, 2nd, September 14-18, 1969, Elsinore. {BIS IIT}

Perreault, Jean M. and Dohlberg, Ingetraut, eds., 1983, **Proceedings** : International study conference on classification research : Universal classification, 4th, June 28-July 2, 1982, Ausburg. {BIS}

Anon, 1988, **Proceedings** : National seminar on strategies for survival by Nigerian academic and research libraries during austere times, November 9-11, 1987, Ibadan. [Nigerian Association of Agricultural Librarians and Documentalists; Nigerian Librarian Association, Academic and Research Libraries Section]. {NASSDOC*}

Anon, 1966, **Proceedings** : National symposium on information display, 7th, Technical session. [Society for Information Display]. {JNU}

Anon, 1987, **Proceedings** : Regional seminar on measurement and application of micrographics, 3rd, 1987, Pune. {NASSDOC}

Anon, 1967, **Proceedings** : Seminar of university librarians in India, 1967, Jaipur. [Rajasthan University]. {DUL IIT}

Dowing, J.C. and Sharp, N.F., 1969, **Proceedings** : Seminar on the Anglo-American Cataloguing Rules, 1967. [Library Association, London]. {ZHL}

Anon, 1980, **Proceedings** : Seminar on international cooperative information systems, July 9-13, 1979. [International Development Research Centre]. {CRRI USIS}

Moreland, Carroll C. and Usmani, M. Adil, eds., n.d., **Proceedings** : Seminar on the purpose and function of library in national education, April 7-10, 1961, Nazimabad. [Society for the Promotion and Improvement of Libraries]. {NASSDOC*}

Anon, 1982, **Proceedings and list of government of Indian libraries of Delhi**: All India library convention, 3rd, February 10-12, 1982, New Delhi. [Government of India Librarians Association]. {CRRI NASSDOC}

Anon, 1977, **Proceedings and papers** : IASLIC seminar on library scene in Calcutta, 1977, Calcutta. [Indian Association of Special Libraries and Information Centres]. {JNU}

Anon, 1981, **Proceedings and papers** : International conference on delivery mechanisms for engineering and technological information, November 3-5, 1980, Budapest. {BIS}

Anon, 1969, **Proceedings of the General Council** : IFLA annual. [International Federation of Library Association and Institutions]. {NASSDOC}

Anon, 1982, **Public libraries in developing society and planning for national information system** : Seminar papers : All India library conference, 28th, October 20-23, 1982, Lucknow. [Indian Library Association]. {ICA NASSDOC NIPCCD ZHL}

Rayward, W. Boyd, ed., 1978, **The public library** : Circumstances and prospects : Papers presented at the 39th Annual Conference. {IIT USIS}

Carnovsky, Leon, 1968, **Public library in the urban setting** : The thirty second conference of the Graduate Library School, July 31-August 2, 1967. {NMML}

Anon, 1965, **Reaching readers** : The library's responsibility and opportunity : Papers with a summary of discussions and recommendations. Regional conference workshop for librarians, 6th, December 6-13, 1964, Albay. {NASSDOC}

Anon, 1947, **Report** : ASLIB meeting on planning and equipment of special libraries, April 6, 1946, London. [Association of Special Libraries and Information Bureaux]. {CRRI}

Anon, 1961, **Report** : Advisory committee for libraries. [Ministry of Education, New Delhi]. {NASSDOC}

Anon, 1989, **Report** : Asia Pacific information network in social science : Regional advisory group (APINESS/RAG) meeting. [UNESCO Principal Regional Office for Asia and the Pacific, Bangkok]. {NASSDOC}

Anon, 1987, **Report** : Asia Pacific POPIN experts working group on population information networking. [U.N. Economic and Social Commission for Asia and the Pacific, Bangkok]. {NASSDOC}

Anon, 1983, **Report** : Asian regional seminar on information sources, systems and services in the social sciences, July 11-22, 1983, Philippines [UNESCO Regional Office, Bangkok]. {NASSDOC*}

Anon, 1976, **Report** : Australia committee on inquiry on public libraries. {JNU}

Anon, 1978, **Report** : Committee appointed by the Government of Andhra Pradesh to review the working of the Andhra Pradesh Public Library Act, 1960, and to suggest amendments to the act. [Government of Andhra Pradesh, Hyderabad]. {NASSDOC*}

Anon, 1982, **Report** : Committee appointed for developing the Tagore Memorial Library, Vijayawada. [Zilla Granthalaya Samstha, Machilipatnam]. {NASSDOC*}

Anon, 1978, **Report** : Committee on private libraries. [Government of Andhra Pradesh, Hyderabad]. {NASSDOC*}

Anon, 1976, **Report** : Committee on the re-organisation of libraries, research centres and museums for the government of Jammu and Kashmir. [Punjab Agricultural University, Ludhiana]. {NASSDOC*}

Anon, 1984, **Report** : Expert working group on development of population information centres and networks, June 20-23, 1984. [U.N. Economic and Social Commission for Asia and the Pacific]. {NASSDOC}

Anon, 1963, **Report** : International conference on cataloguing principles, October 9-14, 1961, Paris. [International Federation of Library Associations and Institutions]. {IIT ISI NIEPA NMML}

Anon, 1960, **Report** : National Archives committee on archival legislation. [National Archives of India, New Delhi]. {MFL}

Anon, 1970, **Report** : National Library committee to enquire into the strained relations among the members of staff, 1969. [National Library, Calcutta]. {JNU}

Anon, 1968, **Report** : National Library reviewing committee, 1968. [National Library, Calcutta]. {JNU}

Anon, 1977, **Report** : Orientation course for the libraries of cooperative training colleges and apex level organisations/institutions in India, June 1977, New Delhi. [National Council for Cooperative Training, New Delhi]. {ICA}

Overhagem, Carl F.J. and Herman, R. Joyce, eds., 1965, **Report** : Planning conference on information transfer experiments, September 3, 1965, Massachusetts. {USIS}

Anon, 1985, **Report** : Regional seminar on curriculum development in information studies, September 17-21, 1985, Bangkok. [UNESCO]. {NASSDO*}

Anon, 1985, **Report** : Seminar on documentation and information systems for vocational training, November 5-16, 1985, Pattaya, Thailand. [International Labour Office; Asian and Pacific Skill Development Programme, Islamabad]. {NASSDOC}

Anon, 1986, **Report** : Seminar on library education, December 1-4, 1965, Bombay. [Shreemati Nathibai Damodar Thachery Women's University, Bombay]. {AIU NASSDOC}

Anon, 1972, **Report** : Seminar on public library system, 1972, Bangalore. {JNU}

Anon, 1981, **Report** : Sub-regional workshop for cooperative librarians and documentation officers for S.E. Area, April, 14-29, 1981, Los Banos. [ICA Regional Office and Education Centre for South-East Asia, New Delhi]. {ICA NASSDOC}

Anon, 1974, **Report** : University Grants Commission committee on scales of pay and qualification, etc., for library staff in universities and colleges. [University Grants Commission, New Delhi]. {NIEPA}

Anon, 1958, **Report** : University Grants Commission library committee. [University Grants Commission, New Delhi]. {SPA}

Khandwala, Vidyut K. and Sales-Pontes, A. Hilda, 1982, **Report** : Western regional conference on library architecture, October 8-10, 1980, Bombay. [Indian Association of Special Libraries and Information Centres]. {JNU NASSDOC}

Anon, 1974, **Report** : Working meeting on Asian resources for a population library network, September 13-15, 1973, Bangkok. [UN Economic Commission for Asia and the Far East]. {NIH}

Anon, 1966, **Report** : Working group on libraries, 1964, New Delhi. [Planning Commission, New Delhi]. {AIU CRRI JNU MFL MHA NASSDOC NCAER NERC NIEPA NIPCCD NMML}

Anon, 1980, **Report** : Workshop on road research and information for South East Asia, 1980, Melbourne. {CRRI}

Mumfort, Erid, et al, eds., 1985, **Research methods in information systems** : Proceedings of the IFIP WG 8.2 colloquium, Manchester Business School, September 1-3, 1984. {NASSDOC}

Vervliet, H.D.L., 1979, **Resource sharing of libraries in developing countries** : Proceedings : IFLA/UNESCO pre-session seminar for librarians from developing countries, August 30-September 3, 1977, [Antwerp University]. {NASSDOC}

Eaton, F. Thelma and Strout, Donald Everett, eds., 1959, **Role of classification in the modern American library** : Papers presented at an institute conducted by the University of Illinois, Graduate School of Library Science, 1959. {DUL}

Anon, 1978, **Role of libraries in socio-economic development** : Papers : All India library convention, 1st, February 13, 1978, Delhi. [Government of India Librarians Association]. {NASSDOC}

Anon, 1965, **Role of the library in the development of the community** : Society for the promotion and improvement of libraries seminar, April 12-18, 1964, Karachi. [Hamdard National Foundation, Karachi]. {NASSDOC}

Lancaster, F.W., 1980, **The role of the library in an electronic society** : Proceedings : Library applications of data processing clinic, 1979, Illinois. [University of Illinois at Urbana-Champaign]. {USIS}

Anon, 1971, **Role of the library in national reconstruction** : Society for the promotion and improvement of libraries seminar, October 30—November 3, 1967, Rawalpindi. [Hamdard National Foundation, Karachi]. {NASSDOC}

Zemanck, H., 1972, **Skyline of information processing** : Proceedings of the 10th anniversary of IFIP, Amsterdom. {JNU}

Jenssen, Gudbrand, n.d., **A small country in the world of standards** : ANSINBS symposium on international standards information and ISONET. {BIS}

Ranganathan, S.R. and Girja Kumar, 1960, **Social science research and libraries** : Papers and summary proceedings of the library seminar on research in the social science, January 2-4, 1959. {NMML}

Anon, 1967, **Social science research and library development** : Summary proceedings. [Indian Council of World Affairs; Indian School of International Studies]. {NASSDOC*}

Anon, 1979, **Souvenir** : AP libraries conference, 1st, 1979, Hyderabad. {NASSDOC*}

Anon, 1980, **Souvenir** : AP libraries conference, 2nd, 1980, Narasaropet. {NASSDOC*}

Anon, 1982, **Souvenir** : AP libraries conference, 3rd, 1982, Tirupati. {NASSDOC*}

Anon, n.d., **Souvenir** : All India library conference, 14th, 1964, Indore. [Indian Library Association]. {NASSDOC}

Anon, 1965, **Souvenir** : All India library conference, 15th, 1965, Mysore. [Indian Library Association]. {NASSDOC}

Anon, 1966, **Souvenir** : All India library conference, 16th, 1966, Chandigarh. [Indian Library Association]. {NASSDOC}

Anon, 1973, **Souvenir** : All India library conference, 20th, 1973, Hyderabad. [Indian

Library Association]. {NASSDOC}

Anon, 1975, **Souvenir** : All India library conference, 21st, 1975, Bhubneswar. [Indian Library Association]. {NASSDOC}

Anon, 1976, **Souvenir** : All India library conference, 22nd, 1976, New Delhi. [Indian Library Association]. {NASSDOC}

Anon, 1978, **Souvenir** : All India library conference, 24th, 1978, Bangalore. [Department of Public Libraries, Bangalore; Indian Library Association]. {NASSDOC}

Augustine, C.A., ed., 1979, **Souvenir** : All India library conference, 25th, May 14-18, 1979, Trivandrum. [Indian Library Association]. {ICA}

Anon, 1980, **Souvenir** : All India library conference, 26th, March 6-9, 1980, New Delhi, [Indian Library Association]. {ICA}

Anon, 1981, **Souvenir** : All India library conference, 27th, January 9-12, 1981, Hyderabad; Indian Library Association. [Academy of Library Science and Documentation, Hyderabad]. {ICA NASSDOC}

Anon, 1985, **Souvenir** : All India library conference, 31st, 1985, Baroda. [Indian Library Association]. {NASSDOC}

Anon, n.d., **Souvenir** : All India library conference, 32nd, Anantpur. [Indian Library Association]. {NASSDOC}

Anon, 1987, **Souvenir** : All India library conference, 33rd, 1987, Tiruchirapalli. [Indian Library Association]. {NASSDOC}

Anon, 1988, **Souvenir** : All India library conference, 1988, Calcutta. [Indian Library Association]. {NASSDOC}

Anon, 1989, **Souvenir** : All India library conference, 1989, Pune. [Indian Library Association]. {NASSDOC}

Anon, 1987, **Souvenir** : Golden jubilee celebration. [Department of Library and Information Science, Andhra University]. {NASSDOC}

Anon, 1981, **Souvenir** : IASLIC all India conference, 13th, 1981, Waltaire. [Indian Association of Special Libraries and Information Centres]. {NASSDOC}

Anon, 1967, **Souvenir** : IASLIC conference, 7th, December 27-30, 1967, Delhi. [University of Delhi]. {NASSDOC}

Anon, 1980, **Souvenir** : IASLIC national seminar, 9th, 1980, Nagpur [IASLIC]. {NASSDOC}

Anon, 1984, **Souvenir** : IASLIC national seminar, 11th, 1984, Hydrabad [IASLIC]. {NASSDOC*}

Anon, 1987, **Souvenir** : Library education centenary celebration. [Nagpur University]. {NASSDOC*}

Anon, 1962, **Standards of public library service in England and Wales** : Report of the working party appointed by the Minister of Education in March, 1961. {NASSDOC}

Verona, Eva, 1971, **Statement of principles adopted at the international conference on cataloguing principles,** October 1961, Paris. [IFLA Committee on Cataloguing, London]. {NASSDOC}

Kent, Allen and Galvin, Thomas J., eds., 1979, **Structure and governance of library networks** : Proceedings of the 1978 conference in Pittsburg. {JNU}

Metcalf, Keyes D., ed., 1960, **Studies in library administrative problems** : Eight reports from a seminar on library administration. {DUL USIS}

Harbo, Ols, ed., 1980, **Theory and applications of information research** : Proceedings : International research forum on information science, 2nd, August 3-6, 1977, Copenhagen. {BCL}

French, Ruth, ed., n.d., **Toward a better cataloguing code**. {IEG}

Rubinoff, Morris, ed., 1965, **Towards a national information system** : Second annual national colloquium on information retrieval. {IIT}

Anon, 1964, **Transactions** : Prague conference on information theory, statistical decision function, random processes, June 3, 1962. {INSA}

Jeffreys, A.E. and Wison, T.D., 1970, **UK MARC project** : Proceedings of seminar organised by the cataloguing and indexing group of the Library Association at the University of Southampton, March 28-30, 1976. {NASSDOC}

Anon, 1974, **U.N. report** : Working meeting on Asian resources for a Population Library Information Network, September 13-15, 1973, Bangkok. [U.N. Economic Commission for Asia and the Far East]. {NIH}

Anon, 1959, **University and college libraries** : Containing the report and the proceedings of the Seminar on 'from publisher to reader' held on March 4-7, 1966. [University Grants Commission, New Delhi]. {DUL NASSDOC}

Lincoln, Cynthia Mary, ed., 1976, **University libraries as information centres** : Proceedings of IATUL sixth meeting, 1975. {DCL}

Anon, 1982, **Use of computer in libraries** : Summary of the proceedings of a seminar held on March 15, 1982, New Delhi. {NASSDOC}

Schimmelpfeng, Richard H. and Cook, C. Donald, 1968, **The use of Library of Congress Classification** : Proceedings : Institute on the use of the Library of Congress classification, 1966, New York. [American Library Association]. {USIS}

Kumar, P.S.G., ed., 1989, **Working documents** : Workshop on norms, guidelines and standards for library and information science education. [Nagpur University Department of Library and Information Science, Nagpur]. {NASSDOC}

Anon, 1968, **Working of central museums** : Report : Central museums review committee, 1968, New Delhi. {AIU}

Anon, 1979, **Working papers** : All India library conference, 25th, May 14-18, 1979, Trivandrum. [Indian Library Association]. {ICA NCDC NMML}

Anon, 1980, **Working papers** : Seminar on library buildings in India, February 11-13, 1980, New Delhi. [NISSAT].

Anon, 1964, **Working papers** : Seminar on use of microforms and space management in libraries. [Sri Venkateshwar University Library, Tirupati].

Anon, 1970, **Working papers and proceedings** : DRTC seminar on cataloguing, 1970, Bangalore. [Documentation Research and Training Centre, Bangalore]. {NASSDOC}

Anon, 1971, **Working papers and proceedings** : DRTC seminar on reference service. [Documentation Research and Training Centre, Bangalore]. {NASSDOC}

Anon, 1967, **Working papers and proceedings** : IASLIC conference, 4th, 1967, Dhanbad. [Indian Association of Special Libraries and Information Centres]. {SPA}

Anon, 1965, **Working papers and proceedings** : IASLIC seminar, 2nd, 1965, Chandigarh : Part-I : Users and library information services. [Indian Association of Special Libraries and Information Centres]. {SPA}

Anon, n.d., **Working papers and proceedings of the three symposia**, I : General vs special classification schemes; II : Inter library loan and exchange of materials in India; III : Social science documentation in India : IASLIC seminar, 3rd, 1964, Lucknow; [Indian Association of Special Libraries and Information Centres]. {NASSDOC SPA}

Anon, 1966, **Working papers for the symposia** : IASLIC conference, 5th, 1963, Pune, Pt. I : Document and data processing in academic research and special libraries in India; Pt. II : Problems and prospects of library associations in India.

[Indian Association of Special Libraries and Information Centres]. {NASSDOC}

Anon, 1967, **Working papers for the symposia** : IASLIC conference, 6th, 1965, Trivandrum, Pt 1-3 : Colon Classification local documentation lists, library organisation and social science research, 1967; Pt. 4 : Colon Classification, local documentation lists, library organisation and social science research, 1967. [Indian Association of Special Libraries and Information Centres]. {NASSDOC SPA}

Anon, 1966, **Working papers of the two symposia** : IASLIC seminar, 4th 1966, Hyderabad, Pt. 1 : Procurement of government publications and technical reports; Pt. 2 : Devaluation : Its impact on the development of libraries in India. [Indian Association of Special Libraries and Information Centres]. {NASSDOC SPA}

Anon, 1968, **Working papers for the symposia** : IASLIC seminar, 5th, October 7-9, 1968, Durgapur, Pt. I : Selective dissemination of information for India; Pt. II : Functions and problems of library personnel in special libraries of India. [Indian Association of Special Libraries and Information Centres]. {NASSDOC}

MICROFILM SERVICES

Huen, P. Lim Pui, comp., 1973, **Directory of microfilm facilities in Southeast Asia**, 2nd edn. {JNU}

Ballou, Hubbard, W., ed., 1968, **Guide to micro reproduction equipment,** 4th edn. [National Microfilm Association]. {NASSDOC}

MICROFILMS/MICROFICHES

Anon, 1966, **Code of practice for the processing of microfilms**, Silver halide. (IS : 3083-1966). [Indian Standards Institution]. {NASSDOC}

Anon, 1965, **Code of practice for storage and use of microfilms of permanent value.** (IS : 3130-1965). [Indian Standards Institution]. {NASSDOC}

Avedon, Don M., 1971, **Computer output microfilm,** 2nd edn. [National Microfilm Association]. {USIS}

Saffady, William, 1979, **Computer output microfilm** : Its library applications. {JNU}

Huen, P. Lim Pui, comp., 1973, **Directory of microfilm facilities in Southeast Asia**, 2nd edn. {JNU}

Zemsky, Robert, 1979, **Microfiche reader.** {USIS}

Dranov, Paula, 1976, **Microfilm** : The librarians' view, 1976-77. {USIS}

Anon, 1975-83, **Microfilming of technical drawings and other drawing office equipments** : Pt-1 : operation procedures (ISO 3272/I-1983); Pt-II : Quality criteria and control (ISO 3272/II-1978); Pt-III : Unitized 35 mm microfilm carriers (ISO 3272/III-1975). [International Organisation for Standardisation, Geneva]. {NASSDOC}

Majumdar, Gopal Kumar, 1974, **Newspaper microfilming** : A plea for newsprint documentation. {NASSDOC ZHL}

Anon, 1975, **Recommendations for the processing and storage of silver gelatin-type microfilm.** (BS : 1153 : 1975). [British Standards Institution]. {CRRI}

Anon, 1955, **Recommendations for the storage of microfilm.** (BS : 1153 : 1955). [British Standards Institution]. {CRRI NASSDOC NMML}

See also Audio-Visuals

MICROFISCHES

See Microfilms/Microfisches

MICROFORMS

Veaner, Allen B., 1970, **Evaluation of micropublications** : A handbook for librarians. [American Library Association]. {NASSDOC}

Ballou, Hubbard, W., ed., 1968, **Guide to micro reproduction equipment,** 4th edn. [National Microfilm Association]. {NASSDOC}

Anon, n.d., **A guide to micrographics**. [Bhabha Atomic Research Centre; Micrographic Congress of India]. {NASSDOC*}

Anon, 1978, **MIMC microforms annual, 1977-78**. [Microform International Marketing Corporation]. {NASSDOC}

Folcarelli, Ralph F., et al, 1982, **The microform connection** : A basic guide for libraries. {USIS}

Teague, S.J., 1977, **Microform librarianship**. {NASSDOC}

Teague, S.J., 1979, **Microform librarianship**, 2nd edn. {IDA ZHL}

Anon, 1970, **Microform retrieval equipment guide**. [Bastuibak Archives and Records Service, Washington]. {BIS}

Ladd, Dorothy P. and Gabriel, Michael R., 1980, **Microform revolution in libraries**. {BIS}

Teague, S. John, 1985, **Microform, video and electronic media librarianship.** {NMML}

Anon, n.d., **Microforms annual, 1982-83** : An international guide to microforms. {NASSDOC}

Anon, n.d., **Microforms annual, 1984-85** : An international guide to microforms. {NASSDOC}

Joshi, M., 1985, **Microforms as an alternative to physical growth in libraries**. [University of Poona, Pune]. {NASSDOC*}

Spreitzer, Francis, ed., 1985, **Microforms in libraries**. [American Library Association]. {NASSDOC}

Diaz, Albert J., ed., 1975, **Microforms in libraries** : A reader. {BIS JNU USIS}

Llewellyn, Raney M., ed., 1936, **Microphotography for libraries**. {DUL}

Gunther, A., 1962, **Microphotography in the library**. [UNESCO]. {IDA NASSDOC}

Lewis, Chester M. and Affen, Hauser William H., 1956, **Microrecording** : Industrial and library applications. {DUL}

Anon, 1958, **Microtext and microreading**. [County Technical Library Service, Hertfordshire]. {DUL}

Williams, Bernard J.S., 1970, **Miniaturised communications** : A review of microforms. [Library Association, London]. {NASSDOC}

Fleischer, Eugene B., 1978, **Style manual for citing microform and non-print media.** [American Library Association]. {BIS}

MICROFORMS : BIBLIOGRAPHY

Reichmann, Felix and Tharpe, Josephine M., 1972, **Bibliographic control of microforms**. {ISI JNU}

Veaner, Allen B., ed., 1977, **Studies in micropublishing**, 1853-1976. {USIS}

MICROPHOTOCOPY

Llewellyn, Raney M., ed., 1936, **Microphotography for libraries**. {DUL}

Gunther, A., 1962, **Microphotography in the library**. [UNESCO]. {IDA NASSDOC}

See also Microfilms/Microfisches

MOBILE LIBRARIES

Gringhuis, Drik, n.d., **Here comes the book mobile.** {JNU}

Eastwood, C.R., 1967, **Mobile libraries and other public library transport**. [Association of Assistant Librarians, London]. {BIS}

MOTILAL (MASTER)

Sogani, Kamal Chand and Vijay Narain, eds., 1973, **Librarian and libraries** : In the memory of the Master Moti Lal ji and his Shri Sanmati Pustakalaya. {JNU NASSDOC}

MOVING PICTURES : DOCUMENTARY : CATALOGUES

Anon, 1955, **Descriptive catalogue of documentary films.** [Films Division, Government of India]. {NAL}

MUNICIPAL COLLEGE LIBRARIES

See Community College Libraries

MUSEUMS

Agrawal, O.P., 1977, **Care and preservation of museum objects.** {NASSDOC}

Singh A.P., 1987, **Conservation and museum techniques.** {NMML}

See also Archives

MUSEUMS : GEOGRAPHICAL AREA : INDIA

Anon, 1968, **Working of central museums** : Report : Central museums review committee, 1968, New Delhi. {AIU}

MUSIC : CATALOGUING

See Cataloguing of Music and Musical Instruments

MYANMAR

See under Geographical Area subdivision under main Descriptors, e.g., Library Resources : Geographical Area : Myanmar

NATIONAL ARCHIVES OF INDIA, NEW DELHI

Momoh, O.A., 1975, **Catalogue of new accessions in the headquarter's library, National Archives of India, April 1966 to March 1974**. {NAI}

NATIONAL ARCHIVES OF UNITED STATES

See US National Archives

NATIONAL BIBLIOGRAPHY

Lewis, P.R., 1982, **The fall and rise of national bibliography**. [Sarada Ranganathan Endowment for Library Science, Bangalore]. {NASSDOC*}

Anon, 1970, **Guide to national bibliographical centres.** [UNESCO]. {DUL IIMC NASSDOC USIS}

Anon, 1979, **Guidelines for national bibliographic agency and national bibliography**. [UNESCO]. {NASSDOC}

Anon, 1967, **A survey of the contents of existing national bibliographies.**

[UNESCO]. {NASSDOC*}

Pomassel, Gerhand, 1975, **Synoptic tables concerning the current national bibliographies**. {NASSDOC}

NATIONAL BIBLIOGRAPHY : GEOGRAPHICAL AREA : AUSTRALIA

Anon, n.d., **Australian national bibliography**, 1974-80. [National Library of Australia]. {NASSDOC}.

Anon, 1984, **Papers and proceedings** : Round table discussion on the concepts of Australian national bibliography, 1983, South Wales. {JNU}

NATIONAL BIBLIOGRAPHY : GEOGRAPHICAL AREA : BANGLADESH

Anon, 1975, **Bangladesh national bibliography**. {NASSDOC}

NATIONAL BIBLIOGRAPHY : GEOGRAPHICAL AREA : GREAT BRITAIN

Anon, 1950-83, **British national bibliography**, 1950-54 to 1973; 1975 to 83, 2 vols. [British Library Bibliographic Services Division]. {NASSDOC}

Gorman, Michael, and Linford, John E., 1971, **Description of the BNB/MARC record** : A manual of practice. {JNU}

NATIONAL BIBLIOGRAPHY : GEOGRAPHICAL AREA : INDIA

Lewis, P.R., 1982, **The fall and rise of national bibliography**. [Sarada Ranganathan Endowment for Library Science, Bangalore]. {NASSDOC*}

Anon, 1958-77, **Indian National Bibliography**. [Central Reference Library, Calcutta]. {DSSW INSA NASSDOC}

Anon, 1958-62, **Indian National Bibliography** : Cumulated Index 1958-62. [Central Reference Library, Calcutta]. {NASSDOC}

Kesavan, B.S., ed., 1978, **National bibliography of Indian literature 1901-1953,** 4 vols. [Sahitya Akademi, New Delhi]. {DSSW INSA MFL NASSDOC}

NATIONAL BIBLIOGRAPHY : GEOGRAPHICAL AREA : LATIN AMERICA

Zimmerman, Irena, 1971, **Current national bibliographies of Latin America** : A state-of-the-art study. [Centre for Latin America, University of Florida]. {NASSDOC}

NATIONAL BIBLIOGRAPHY : GEOGRAPHICAL AREA : NEW ZEALAND

Anon, 1978, **New Zealand national bibliography**, 1978. [National Library of New Zealand]. {NASSDOC}

NATIONAL BOOK LEAGUE

Morpurgo, J.E., 1969, **Book and journal services for doctors and nurses** : An interim report on a National Book League investigation. {DUL}

NATIONAL DOCUMENTATION CENTRE ON MASS COMMUNICATION, NEW DELHI

Anon, n.d., **National Documentation Centre on Mass Communication** : Report. [Ministry of Information and Broadcasting, New Delhi]. {IIMC}

NATIONAL LENDING LIBRARY FOR SCIENCE AND TECHNOLOGY

Houghton, Bernard, 1972, **Out of the dinosaurs** : The evolution of the National Lending Library for Science and Technology. {NASSDOC}

See also Public Liibraries : Geographical Area : Great Britain

NATIONAL LIBRARIES

Dudley, Edward, ed., 1983, **Development of national library and information service.** [Library Association, London]. {NIEPA}

Chandler, George, 1982, **International and national library and information services** : A review of some recent developments, 2 vols. {IIT NASSDOC NERC}

Anon, 1963, **National libraries** : Their problems and prospects : Symposium on national libraries in Europe, September 8-27, Vienna. [UNESCO]. {AIU BIS CRRI IEG IIMC MFL NASSDOC NIEPA NIPCCD}

Penna, C.V., et al, eds., 1977, **National library and information services** : Handbook for planners. {CRRI DUL IIT INSA JNU NASSDOC NCAER NIEPA}

Verma, Subash Chandra, 1985, **National library and information system**. {NASSDOC NMML}

Allison, Anne Manne and Allan, Ann, eds., 1979, **National library network**. {IIT}

Anon, 1969, **National Library of Medicine classification** : A scheme for the shelf arrangement of books in the field of medicine and its related sciences, 3rd edn. [U.S. National Library of Medicine]. {USIS}

Al-Nahari, Abdulaziz Mohamed, 1984, **Role of national libraries in developing countries with special reference to Saudi Arabia**. {NMML}

NATIONAL LIBRARIES : GEOGRAPHICAL AREA : DEVELOPING COUNTRIES

Al-Nahari, Abdulaziz Mohamed, 1984, **Role of national libraries in developing countries with special reference to Saudi Arabia**. {NMML}

NATIONAL LIBRARIES : GEOGRAPHICAL AREA : EUROPE

Anon, 1963, **National libraries** : Their problems and prospects : Symposium on national libraries in Europe, September 8-27, Vienna. [UNESCO]. {AIU BIS CRRI IEG IIMC MFL NASSDOC NIEPA NIPCCD}

NATIONAL LIBRARIES : GEOGRAPHICAL AREA : INDIA

Kesavan, B.S., 1961, **India's national library**. [National Library, Calcutta]. {IIT JNU MFL ZHL}

Majumdar, 1987, **India's national library** : Systematisation. [National Library, Calcutta]. {NASSDOC}

Anon, 1972, **National Library Bill, 1972** : Report and evidence : India, Lok Sabha, Joint Committee on the National Library Bill. {AIU NMML}

Kaula, P.N., 1970, **National library of India** : Critical study. {AIU ICHR IIC IIFT IIMC IIT ISI NERC NIEPA NIH NIPCCD NMML SPA ZHL}

Nagaraj, M.N. and Ghosh, A.K., eds., 1978, **The National Library of India, 1903-1978** : A pictorial history released on the occasion of platinum jubilee of the National Library, Calcutta. [National Library, Calcutta]. {NASSDOC}

Ranganathan, S.R., 1946, **National library system** : A plan for India. {ZHL}

Anon, 1978, **National library week souvenir, 1976.** [Kerala Library Association, Trivandrum]. {ICA JNU MMTC}

Anon, 1979, **Papers** : Seminar on the role of the National Library of India, November 23, 1978, Calcutta. [National Library Employee's Association, Calcutta]. {NASSDOC}

Anon, 1970, **Report** : National Library committee to enquire into the strained relations among the members of staff, 1969. [National Library, Calcutta]. {JNU}

Anon, 1968, **Report** : National Library reviewing committee, 1968. [National Library,

Calcutta]. {JNU}

NATIONAL LIBRARIES : GEOGRAPHICAL AREA : JAPAN

Anon, n.d., **National Diet Library** : Organisation, functions and activities. [National Diet Library, Japan]. {AIU}

NATIONAL LIBRARIES : GEOGRAPHICAL AREA : SAUDI ARABIA

Al-Nahari, Abdulaziz Mohamed, 1984, **Role of national libraries in developing countries with special reference to Saudi Arabia**. {NMML}

NATIONAL LIBRARY BILL, 1972

Anon, 1972, **National Library Bill, 1972** : Report and evidence : India, Lok Sabha, Joint Committee on the National Library Bill. {AIU NMML}

NEPAL

See Geographical Area subdivision under main Descriptor, e.g., Libraries : Geographical Area : Nepal

NEPAL : BIBLIOGRAPHY

Gyawali, Bharat M. and Standrodd, Garland L., n.d., **Information resources on Nepal**. {IEG}

NETWORKS : INFORMATION

See Information Networks

NEWBERY, JOHN

See also Newbery Medal Books

NEWBERY MEDAL BOOKS

Miller, Bertha M. and Field, Elinor W., eds., 1955, **Newbery medal books, with their authors' acceptance** : Papers and related material, chiefly from the Horn Book magazine, 1922-55. {USIS}

NEW JERSEY

See Geographical Area subdivision under main Descriptor, e.g., Library Schools : Geographical Area : USA : New Jersey

NEW YORK

See Geographical Area subdivision under main Descriptor, e.g., Libraries : Geographical Area : USA : New York

NEW YORK PUBLIC LIBRARY

Lydenberg, H.M., 1932, **History of the New York Public Library.** {NAI}

Anon, 1970, **Library automation at the New York Public Library and the Association of New York Libraries for Technical Services.** [LARC]. {USIS}

NEW YORK REVIEW OF BOOKS (PERIODICAL)

Nobile, Philip, 1974, **Intellectual skywriting** : Literary politics and the New York Review of Books. {USIS}

NEWSPAPERS/PERIODICALS/PRESS CLIPPINGS : LIBRARIES

Anon, 1976, **Guidelines for newspaper libraries.** [American Newspaper Publishers Association]. {USIS}

Anon, 1983, **Guidelines for presentation of abstract sheets in serial publications**. (IS : 10455-1983). [Indian Standards Institution]. {CRRI}

Anon, 1983, **IENS press handbook**. [Indian and Eastern Newspaper Society, New Delhi]. {JNU}

Whatmore, Geoffrey, n.d., **Modern news library** : Documentation of current affairs in newspaper and broadcasting libraries. {IIMC}

Whatmore, Geoffrey, 1964, **News information** : Organisation of press cuttings in the libraries of newspapers and broadcasting services. {IIMC IIT NMML SPA}

Anon, n.d., **Newspaper libraries**, mimeo short bibliography. {NASSDOC}

Majumdar, Gopal Kumar, 1974, **Newspaper microfilming** : A plea for newsprint documentation. {NASSDOC ZHL}

Howcraft, B. and Wagner, I., 1980, **Press cuttings** : Cooperative library guide. {ICA}

Anon, 1918, **Rules for press listing**. [Imperial Record Department]. {NAI}

NON-BOOK MATERIALS

Shashi Bala, 1982, **Non-book material available in Nehru Memorial Museum and Library** : A brief survey. {NMML}

Riddle, Jean, et al, 1970, **Non-book materials** : The organisation of integrated collections. [Canadian Library Association]. {NERC USIS}

Riddle, Jean, et al., 1979, **Non-book materials** : The organisation of integrated collections, 2nd edn. [Canadian Library Association]. {NERC USIS}

Weihs, Jean, 1989, **Non-book materials** : The organisation of integrated collections, 3rd edn. [Canadian Library Association]. {NASSDOC}

Anon, 1973, **Non-book materials cataloguing rules** : Integrated code of practice and draft revision of the Anglo-American Cataloguing Rules. [Library Association Media Cataloguing Rules Committee; National Council for Educational Technology, London]. {NASSDOC}

Fothergill, Richard and Butchart, I., 1972, **Non-book materials in libraries** : A practical guide. {ISIR}

Daily, Jay E., 1972, **Organising non-print materials** : A guide for librarians. {ICHR IIT JNU NASSDOC ZHL}

See also Audio-Visuals

NON-BOOK MATERIALS : CATALOGUING

See Cataloguing of Non Book Materials

OFFICIAL PUBLICATIONS

See Government Publications

ONLINE DATA PROCESSING

Rubin, Martin L., ed., 1979, **Documentation standards and procedures for on-line systems.** {CRRI}

Anon, n.d., **Final report on mechanised information services in the university library** : Phase-I : Planning. 13 pts. Pt 1 : Mechanised information services in the university library : Introduction and summary; Pt 2 : Summary of symposium on mechanised information services in the university library; Pt 3 : Inventory of available databases; Pt 4 : Standards for cataloguing of magnetic tape material; Pt 5 : Nature of typical databases; Pt 6 : Evaluation of generalised file management systems; Pt 7 : Experience with Library of Congress rare tapes; Pt 8 : Experimental on-line mathematics citation database; Pt 9 : Development programme for a centre for information services; Pt 10 : Preliminary specifications (hardware and software) for a centre for information and documentation services (Interim report); Pt 11 : On the development of social science information; Pt 12 : Joint design and development of library systems; and Pt 13 : Library and human memory. [Institute of Library Research, University of California]. {BIS}

Anon, 1977, **Information networks for on-line bibliography retrieval.** [UNESCO]. {BIS}

Lancaster, F.W. and Fayen, E.G., 1973, **Information retrieval on-line**. {DUL INSA ISI NASSDOC USIS}

Genaway, David, C., 1984, **Integrated online library systems** : Principles, planning and implementation. {NASSDOC}

Baker, C.A., 1977, **An investigation of man-computer interaction in an online bibliographic information retrieval system**. {BCL}

Hoover, Ryan E., ed., 1980, **The library and information manager's guide to on-line services**. {USIS}

Hall, James L. and Brown, Marjorie J., 1981, **On-line bibliographic databases** : An international directory, 2nd edn. [Association of Special Libraries and Information Bureaux]. {USIS}

Mildreth, C.R., ed., 1989, **On line catalogue**. [Library Association, London. {NASSDOC}

Fayen, Emily Gallup, 1973, **The online catalogue** : Improving public access to library materials. {USIS}

Harter, Stephen P., 1986, **On-line information retrieval** : Concepts, principles and techniques. {JNU}

Holmes, P.L., 1978, **On-line information retrieval** : An introduction and guide to British library's short term experimental information network project, Vol. 1 : Experimental use of non-medical information services; Vol. 2 : Experimental use of medical information services. [British Library]. {BCL}

Hall, J.L., comp., 1977, **On-line information retrieval, 1965-76** : A bibliography with a guide to on-line databases and systems. [Association of Special Libraries and Information Bureaux]. {BCL CRRI NASSDOC}

Houghton, Bernard and Convey, John, 1977, **On-line information retrieval systems** : An introductory manual to principles and practices. {BCL CRRI DUL NIH}

Kent, Allen and Galvin, Thomas J., eds., 1978, **The on-line revolution in libraries** : Proceedings of the 1977 conference in Pittsburgh. {JNU}

Sieburth, J.F., 1988, **Online search services in the academic library** : Planning, management and operation. [American Library Association]. {NASSDOC}

Hoover, Ryan, E., ed., 1982, **On-line search strategies**. {USIS}

Henry, W.M., 1980, **Online searching**. {IIT}

Byerly, Greg, 1983, **Online searching** : A dictionary and bibliographic guide. {NASSDOC USIS}

Maloney, James J., ed., 1983, **Online searching technique and management**. [American Library Association]. {USIS}

OPERATIONS RESARCH

Duckworth, Walter E., 1962, **Guide to operational research.** {NASSDOC}

Churchman, C. West, et al, 1969, **Introduction to operations research.** {NASSDOC}

White, Douglas, et al, 1969, **Operational research techniques,** Vol. 1 : Introduction. {NASSDOC}

Swanson, Don R. and Bookstein, Abraham, eds., 1972, **Operations research** : Implications for libraries. {NASSDOC}

Taha, Handy A., 1971, **Operations research** : An introduction. {NASSDOC}

House, William C., 1972, **Operations research** : An introduction to modern applications. {NASSDOC}

Rowley, J. E. and Rowley, Petter J., 1981, **Operations research** : A tool for library management. [American Library Association]. {USIS}

OPTICAL CHARACTER RECOGNITION DEVICES

Groenewegena, H.W. and Marshall, J., 1976, **Optical character recognition** : Use of OCR techniques in decentralised data collection for bibliographic information systems. [International Development Research Centre, Ottawa]. {NASSDOC}

ORIENTAL LIBRARY

See Special Libraries

OXFORD

See Geographical Area subdivision under main Descriptor, e.g., Libraries : Geographical Area : Great Britain : Oxford

PRECIS

=Pre Context Indexing System

PAKISTAN

See Geographical Area subdivision under main Descriptor, e.g., Books and Reading : Geographical Area : Pakistan

PERIODICALS

See Serials

See also Newspapers/Periodicals/Press Clippings : Libraries

PERSONALIA

See under names, e.g., Ranganathan, S.R.,

PHONORECORDS : CATALOGUING

See Cataloguing of Phonorecords

PHOTOCOPYING SERVICES IN LIBRARIES

Whitestone, Patricia, 1977, **Photocopying in libraries** : The librarians speak. {IIT}

PHYSICAL VERIFICATION IN LIBRARIES

See Stock Verification in Libraries

PICTURES

Ireland, Norma Olin, 1952, **Picture file in school, college and public libraries**, rev edn. {ZHL}

PRE CONTEXT INDEXING SYSTEMS

Bikewell, Kenneth Graham Bartlett, 1978, **A study of indexers reactions to the PRECIS indexing system**. [Department of Library and Information Studies, Faculty of Humanities and Social Studies, Liverpool Polytechnic]. {BCL}

PRESERVATION, RESTORATION AND STORAGE

Mehta, S.P., 1975, **Art and science of book preservation.** {BIS IIT MFL ZHL}

Agrawal, O.P., 1977, **Care and preservation of museum objects.** {NASSDOC}

Petrova, L.G., et al, eds., 1965, **Collection of materials on the preservation of library resources**. {INSA NASSDOC}

Singh A.P., 1987, **Conservation and museum techniques.** {NMML}

Kathpalia, Yash Pal, 1973, **Conservation and restoration of archive materials.** {NASSDOC}

Kuhn, Hermann, 1986, **Conservation and restoration of works of art and antiquities,** tr. by Alexandra Trone. {NMML}

Swartzburg, Susan Garretson, ed., 1983, **Conservation in the library** : A handbook of use and care of traditional and non-traditional materials. {JNU NMML}

Langwell, W.H., 1974, **Conservation of books and documents.** {NERC}

Chuna, George M. and Chuna, Dorothy G., 1972, **Conservation of library materials** : Manual of bibliography on the care, repair and restoration of library materials, 2 vols. {DUL IIT NMML USIS}

Agrawal, O.P., 1984, **Conservation of manuscripts and painting of South-East Asia**. {NMML}

Morrow, Carolyn Clark and Dual, Carole, 1986, **Conservation treatment procedure** : A manual of step by step procedures for the maintenance and repair of library materials. {NASSDOC}

Singer, Howard W. and Smith, Richard Daniel, eds., 1970, **Deterioration and preservation of library materials** : Conference of the Graduate Library School, 34th, August 4-6, 1969, Chicago. {AIU CRRI IIT INSA JNU NASSDOC NMML}

Elisworth, Ralph E., 1969, **Economics of book storage in college and university libraries**. {NASSDOC}

Weiss, Harry B. and Carruthers Ralph, H., 1945, **Insect** : Enemies of books. {JNU}

Barrow, W.J., 1972, **Manuscripts and documents** : Their deterioration and restoration. {NASSDOC NMML}

Mabbs, A.W., 1974, **Organisation of intermediate records storage**. [UNESCO]. {NIEPA NMML}

Morrow, Carolyn Clark and Walker, Gay, 1983, **Preservation challenge** : A guide to conserving library materials. {JNU NMML}

Plumbe, Wilfred J., 1964, **Preservation of books in tropical and subtropical countries**. {JNU}

Flyate, D.M., ed., 1968, **Preservation of documents and papers**. [Israel Programme for Scientific Transactions, Jerusalem]. {INSA}

Mukherjee, B.B., 1973, **Preservation of library materials, archives and documents**. {DUL ICHR NASSDOC NERC NIH NIPCCD NMML ZHL}

Gupta, R.D., 1970, **Preserving manuscripts and other research material in the Braj area of India**, (reprinted from the Bulletin of the British Association of Orientalists). [Vrindaban Research Institute]. {NMML}

Bhargava, K.D., 1967, **Repair and preservation of records.** [National Archives of

India]. {NASSDOC}

Cockerell, S.M., 1960, **Repairing of books**, 2nd edn. {NAI}

PRESS CLIPPINGS

See Newspapers/Periodicals/Press Clippings : Libraries

PRINTING

Hattery, Lowell H. and Bush, George P., 1973, **Technological change in printing and publishing.** {INSA}

PROBLEMS OF DAMAGE/LOSS/THEFT OF BOOKS

Bahr, Alic Harrison, n.d., **Book theft and library security systems**. {BIS JNU USIS}

Goswami, Badri Prasad, n.d., **Problems of misplacement, mutilation and theft of books in libraries.** {JNU}

PROCESSNG IN LIBRARIES

See Technical Processing

PROFESSIONAL ETHICS

Anon, 1984, **Papers** : IASLIC national seminar, 11th, November 26-29, 1984, Hyderabad, I : Toward a code of professional ethics; II : Document delivery, reproduction, translation. [Indian Association of Special Libraries and Information Centres]. {NASSDOC}

PROGRAMMED INSTRUCTION

Wilson, Vivian, 1970, **Strategies for problem solving** : Programmed instruction. {NASSDOC}

PROGRAMMES : COMPUTER

See Computer Programmes

PROGRAMMING : COMPUTERS

Dial, O. Eugene, 1968, **Computer programming and statistics for basic research**. {NASSDOC}

Emerick, Paul L. and Wilkinson, Joseph W., 1970, **Computer programming for business and social science.** {NASSDOC}

Leeds, Herbert D. and Winberg, Gerald M., 1966, **Computer programming fundamentals,** 2nd edn. {NASSDOC}

Rajaraman, V., 1971, **Computer programming in Fortran IV**. {NASSDOC}

Anon, 1973, **Computer programming problems** : Batch-I. [National Computer Centre, Manchester]. {NASSDOC}

Kapur, Gopal K., 1970, **IBM 360 assembler language programming**. {NASSDOC}

Davis, Charles H. and Lundeen, Gerald W., 1981, **Illustrative computer programming for libraries** : Selected examples for information specialists, 2nd edn. {NASSDOC USIS}

Tedd, L.A., 1977, **Introduction to computer based library systems**. {JNU NIH}

Wendel, Thomas M. and Williams, William H., 1969, **Introduction to data processing and COBOL**. {NASSDOC}

Mott, Thomas H. Jr., et al, 1972, **Introduction to PL-1 programming for library**

and information science. {BCL IIT JNU}

Lancaster, G.T., n.d., **Programming in COBOL**. {NASSDOC}

Weinberg, Gerald M., 1971, **Psychology of computer programming**. {NASSDOC}

Wyman, Forest Paul, 1970, **Simulation modelling** : A guide to using SIMSCRIPT. {NASSDOC}

Stabley, Don H., 1967, **System/360 Assembler language.** {NASSDOC}

PROOF READING

Anon, 1958, **Proof corrections for printers and authors**. (IS : 1250-1958). [Indian Standards Institution]. {NASSDOC}

PSEUDONYMS

See Anonyms and Pseudonyms

PSYCHOLOGY : DOCUMENTATION

Elliott, C.K., 1971, **Guide to the documentation of psychology**. {NIH}

PUBLIC ADMINISTRATION : ELECTRONIC DATA PROCESSING

See Electronic Data Processing : Public Administration

PUBLIC LIBRARIES

Sinclair, Dorothy, 1965, **Administration of the small public library**. [American Library Association]. {NASSDOC}

Thomas, Carl, et al, 1950, **Adult education activities for public libraries**. [UNESCO]. {IEG ZUL}

Anon, 1973, **Aspects of public library management** : The application of new management processes to the library services. [Library Advisory Council for England]. {NIPCCD ZHL}

Auduson, Herschel V., 1969, **Audio-visual services in the small public library**. {JNU}

Anon, 1980, **Buildings for small public libraries** : Remodelled and adapted including new designs for branches. [American Library Association]. {DUL}

Gross, Elizabeth Henry, 1983, **Children's service in public libraries** : Organisation and administration, with collaboration of Gene Inyart Namovicz. {NASSDOC}

Wilson, Pauline, 1977, **Community elite and the public library** : The use of information in leadership. {IIT NIPCCD}

Ellis, Lee Robert, 1966, **Continuing education for adults through the American Public Library, 1833-1964**. [American Library Association]. {USIS}

Myller, Rolf, 1966, **The design of the small public library**. {USIS}

Cambell, H.C., 1983, **Developing public library systems and services**. [UNESCO]. {NIEPA}

Newhouse, Joseph P. and Alexender, Arthur J., 1972, **Economic analysis of public library services**. {ISI}

Getz, Malcolm, 1979, **An economic view of public libraries** [U.S. National Bureau of Economic Research]. {USIS}

Seymour, Whitney North and Layne, Elizabeth N., 1979, **For the people** : Fightings for public libraries. {USIS}

Shera, Jesse H., 1949, **Foundations of the public library** : The origins of the public library movement in New England, 1629-1855. {USIS}

Anon, 1986, **Glossary of terms used in the Public Libraries Department** :

English-Telugu. [Government of Andhra Pradesh, Official Language Commission, Hyderabad]. {NASSDOC*}

Corbett, Edmund V., 1950, **Introduction to public librarianship for entrance examination students.** {ZHL}

Vishwanathan, C.G., 1955, **Introduction to public library organisation.** {NAI}

Vishwanathan, C.G., 1961, **An introduction to public library organisation,** 2nd edn. {SPA}

Vishwanathan, C.G., 1978, **Introduction to public library organisation with special reference to India**. {NERC}

Martin, Lowell A., et al, 1969, **Library response to urban change** : A study of the Chicago Public Library. [American Library Association]. {USIS}

Berelson, Bernard and Asheim, Lester, 1949, **Library's public** : Report of the public library inquiry. [Social Science Research Council]. {IEG}

Savage, E.A., 1949, **Manual of book classification and display for public libraries**. {BIS MMTC NAI NIH SPA ZHL}

Cambell, H.C., 1967, **Metropolitan public library planning throughout the work.** {DUL JNU NASSDOC SPA USIS}

Anon, 1967, **Minimum standards for public library systems, 1966**. [Standards committee and subcommittees of the Public Library Association; American Library Association]. {USIS}

Eastwood, C.R., 1967, **Mobile libraries and other public library transport.** [Association of Assistant librarians, London]. {BIS}

Ashburner, E.H., **Modern public libraries** : Their planning and design. {CRRI}

Trehan, G.L., 1982, **Modern public library movement and services in India.** {JNU}

Kalia, D.R., 1955, **National public library system**. {NASSDOC}

Heintze, Ingeborg, 1963, **The organisation of the small public library**. [UNESCO]. {ICA IEG NASSDOC NERC NIEPA}

Anon, 1978, **Papers** : All India public library convention, November, 16-18, 1978, New Delhi. [Delhi Library Association, Delhi]. {MMTC NMML}

Anon, 1968, **Planning the public library**. [American Society of Planning Officials]. {SPA}

Anon, 1959, **Plans for six public library buildings**. [American Library Association]. {USIS}

Schunk, Russell J., 1945, **Pointers for public library building planners.** {DUL}

Wheeler, Joseph L. and Goldhor, Herbert, 1962, **Practical administration of public libraries.** {IIT NMML USIS}

Reilly, Jane A., 1981, **The public librarian as adult learners' advisor** : An innovation in human services. {USIS}

Robbins-Carter, Jane, ed., 1982, **Public librarianship** : A reader. {USIS}

Anon, n.d., **Public libraries**, mimeo short bibliography. {NASSDOC*}

Kalia, D.R., n.d., **Public libraries** : Collection of papers on public libraries written at different times. {NASSDOC*}

Anon, 1975, **Public libraries and cultural activities.** [Department of Education and Science, Great Britain]. {NIPCCD}

Maurois, Andre, 1961, **Public libraries and their mission**. [UNESCO]. {ICA}

Anon, 1973, **Public libraries and their use.** [Department of Education and Science, Great Britain]. {NIPCCD}

Anon, 1956, **Public libraries for Asia** : The Delhi seminar. [UNESCO]. {NASSDOC NIEPA ZHL}

Daniel, Hawthorne, 1961, **Public libraries for every one.** {NASSDOC}

McColvin, Lionel R., 1947, **Public libraries in Australia** : Present conditions and future possibilities. {JNU}

Singh, R.S.P., 1988, **Public libraries in Bihar**. [Bihar Library Service Association, Patna].

Thorsen, Leif, 1972, **Public libraries in Denmark**, tr. by Megens Hay Larsen from Danish. {NASSDOC}

Anon, 1982, **Public libraries in developing society and planning for national information system** : Seminar papers : All India library conference, 28th, October 20-23, 1982, Lucknow. [Indian Library Association]. {ICA NASSDOC NIPCCD ZHL}

Sharma, Pandey S.K., 1985, **Public libraries in India**. {JNU}

Patil, P.K., n.d., **Pubic libraries in Karnataka** : Their scope and development. {AIU}

Cambell, H.C., 1973, **Public libraries in the urban metropolitan setting**. {DUL IIT}

Ekbole, Gopal Rao, 1987, **Public libraries system.** {NASSDOC*}

Harrison, K.C., 1963, **Public libraries today**. {DUL IIT NASSDOC}

Rayward, W. Boyd, ed., 1978, **The public library** : Circumstances and prospects : Papers presented at the 39th Annual Conference. {IIT USIS}

Viswandhan, C.G., 1985, **Public library** : Operations and services : A short manual, rev edn. {NASSDOC}

Brown, Royston, 1979, **Public library administration**. {IIT NIEPA}

Jefferson, George, 1965, **Public library administration** : An examination guide book. {MFL NERC SPA ZHL}

Conant, Ralph W., ed., 1965, **Public library and the city.** {JNU SPA}

Wellisch, J.B., et al, 1974, **Public library and federal policy.** {NIPCCD}

Davies, D.W., 1974, **Public library as culture and social centres** : The origin of the concept. {USIS}

Mevissen, W., 1958, **Public library building.** {IIT}

Mc Comb, Dana Quick, n.d., **Public library buildings** : Their financing, design, construction, equipment and operation. {DUL}

Wellard, James Howard, 1940, **The public library comes of age.** {CRRI}

Anon, 1985, **Public library development perspectives.** [Indian Library Association]. {NASSDOC*}

McColvin, Lionel R., 1950, **Public library extension**. [UNESCO]. {NASSDOC ZHL}

Guruswamy Naidu, N., 1990, **Public library finance**. {CRRI}

Adamson, Edith, 1962, **Public library finance** : A literature review. {JNU}

Rose, Ernstine, 1954, **Public library in American life.** {NAI USIS}

Brooks, Jean S. and Reich, David L., 1974, **The public library in non-traditional education.** {NASSDOC USIS}

Sykes, Paul, 1979, **Public library in perspective** : An examination of its origins and modern role. {IIT}

Leigh, Robert D., n.d., **Public library in the United States.** {IEG}

Carnovsky, Leon, 1968, **Public library in the urban setting** : The thirty second conference of the Graduate Library School, July 31-August 2, 1967. {NMML}

Jones, Clara Station, ed., 1978, **Public library information and referral service.** {USIS}

Mittal, R.L., 1971, **Public library law** : An international survey. {ICA NASSDOC NMML}

Gradiner, Frank M., 1971, **Public library legislation** : A comparative study. [UNESCO]. {JNU NASSDOC NIEPA}
Viswanathan, C.G., 1961, **Public library operations and services** : A short manual. {CRRI IIT MHA NERC SPA ZHL}
Anon, 1956, **Public library service**. [American Library Association]. {USIS}
Anon, 1943, **Public library service** : Its post-war reorganisation and development. [Library Association, London]. {NAI}
Anon, 1973, **Public library service** : Reorganisation and after. [Department of Education and Science, Great Britain]. {NIPCCD}
Anon, 1970, **Public library services** : Bahamas. [UNESCO]. {NASSDOC*}
McColvin, Lionel R., 1957, **Public library services for children,** [UNESCO]. {IEG JNU NASSDOC NERC NIPCCD}
Ranganathan, S.R. and Neelameghan, A., eds., 1972, **Public library system** : India, Sri Lanka, UK, USA. {BIS IEG IIC JNU NAI NMML ZHL}
Venkatappaiah, V., 1982, **Public library system in Andhra Pradesh**. [Andhra University]. {NASSDOC}
Augustine, C.A. and Devarajan, G., 1990, **Public library system in India**. {ZHL}
Anon, 1969, **Public library systems in the United States** : A survey of multi-jurisdictional systems. [American Library Association]. {USIS}
Rice, Betty, 1972, **Public relations for public libraries** : Creative problem solving. {USIS}
Anon, 1972, **Purchase of books by public libraries.** [Department of Education and Science, Great Britain]. {NIPCCD}
Ranganathan, S.R. and Neelameghan, A., eds., 1972, **A seminar on public library system**. [Sarada Ranganathan Endowment for Library Science, Bangalore]. {NASSDOC*}
Dennis, Donald D., 1965, **Simplifying work in small public libraries**. {Drexel Institute of Technology]. {NASSDOC}
Galvin, Hoyt R. and Van Buren, Martin, 1959, **The small public library building**, 2nd edn. [UNESCO]. {CRRI IEG IIMC IIT BIS NASSDOC NERC ZHL}
Eckard, Helen Mary, n.d., **Statistics of public libraries,** 1960-61. {JNU}
Mumford, W.A. comp., 1939, **Three thousand books for a public library** : Some significant and representative works for basic stock. {NAI}
Ramachandra Rao, T., 1974, **Torch-bearer of public library movement** : Andhra Pradesh library field workers conference, 1974, Gudiwada. {NASSDOC*}
Anon, n.d., **Use of television by public library**. [American Library Association]. {JNU}
Jennings, Jerdson T., 1930, **Voluntary education through the public library.** [American Library Association]. {NASSDOC*}

PUBLIC LIBRARIES : ADMINISTRATION
Shaffer, Kenneth, R., 1971, **Decision making** : A seminar in public library management. {USIS}
Anon, 1959, **Plans for six public library buildings**. [American Library Association]. {USIS}
Wheeler, Joseph L. and Goldhor, Herbert, 1962, **Practical administration of public libraries.** {IIT NMML USIS}
Brown, Royston, 1979, **Public library administration**. {IIT NIEPA}
Jefferson, George, 1965, **Public library administration** : An examination guide book. {MFL NERC SPA ZHL}

PUBLIC LIBRARIES : BIBLIOGRAPHY

Anon, n.d., **Public libraries**, mimeo short bibliography. {NASSDOC}

PUBLIC LIBRARIES : GEOGRAPHICAL AREA : AFRICA

Anon, 1954, **Development of public libraries in Africa** : Ibadan seminar. [UNESCO]. {IEG NASSDOC ZHL}

PUBLIC LIBRARIES : GEOGRAPHICAL AREA : ASIA

Anon, 1955, **Practical information for seminar members** : Working paper : International seminar on the development of public libraries in Asia, October 6-26, 1966, Delhi. [UNESCO]. {NASSDOC}

Anon, 1956, **Public libraries for Asia** : The Delhi seminar. [UNESCO]. {NASSDOC NIEPA ZHL}

PUBLIC LIBRARIES : GEOGRAPHICAL AREA : AUSTRALIA

McColvin, Lionel R., 1947, **Public libraries in Australia** : Present conditions and future possibilities. {JNU}

Anon, 1976, **Report** : Australia committee on inquiry on public libraries. {JNU}

PUBLIC LIBRARIES : GEOGRAPHICAL AREA : CANADA

Anon, 1964, **Working conditions in Canadian public libraries**. [Canadian Library Association]. {JNU}

PUBLIC LIBRARIES : GEOGRAPHICAL AREA : DENMARK

Thorsen, Leif, 1972, **Public libraries in Denmark**, tr. by Megens Hay Larsen from Danish. {NASSDOC}

PUBLIC LIBRARIES : GEOGRAPHICAL AREA : DEVELOPING COUNTRIES

Anon, n.d., **Dilemma of the urban public library in developing countries.** [International Federation of Library Associations and Institutions; International Council for Adult Education]. {IIMC}

PUBLIC LIBRARIES : GEOGRAPHICAL AREA : GREAT BRITAIN

Anon, 1973, **Public library service** : Reorganisation and after. [Department of Education and Science, Great Britain]. {NIPCCD}

Ranganathan, S.R. and Neelameghan, A., eds., 1972, **Public library system** : India, Sri Lanka, UK, USA. {BIS IEG IIC JNU NAI NMML ZHL}

Anon, 1962, **Standards of public library service in England and Wales** : Report of the working party appointed by the Minister of Education in March, 1961. {NASSDOC}

Hewitt, A.R., 1947, **Summary of public library law in England and Wales, Scotland, Northern Ireland and Eira**, 2nd edn. [Association of Assistant Librarians, London]. {NASSDOC}

PUBLIC LIBRARIES : GEOGRAPHICAL AREA : INDIA

Gangadhara Rao, P. and Raghavan, Q.S., eds., 1986, **Assessment of public library development in India** : Seminar papers. [University of Madras, Department of Library and Information Science]. {NASSDOC}

Barua, B.P., ed., 1986, **Directory of Indian public libraries** : A selected list of libraries. {NASSDOC}

Swaran Kumar, 1963, **East and West**. : Delhi Public Library, India, as seen against the background of the Rochester Public Library. {NASSDOC*}

O'Connor, V.C. Scott, 1977, **Eastern library** : An introduction to the Khuda Bakhsh Oriental Public Library, 2nd edn. {JNU NMML}

Corbett, Edmund V., 1950, **Introduction to public librarianship for entrance examination students**. {ZHL}

Vishwanathan, C.G., 1978, **Introduction to public library organisation with special reference to India**. {NERC}

Trehan, G.L., 1982, **Modern public library movement and services in India.** {JNU}

Anon, 1956, **Public libraries for Asia** : The Delhi seminar. [UNESCO]. {NASSDOC NIEPA ZHL}

Sharma, Pandey S.K., 1985, **Public libraries in India.** {JNU}

Ranganathan, S.R. and Neelameghan, A., eds., 1972, **Public library system** : India, Sri Lanka, UK, USA. {BIS IEG IIC JNU NAI NMML ZHL}

Augustine, C.A. and Devarajan, G., 1990, **Public library system in India**. {ZHL}

Narayana Rao, Kodati and Ramachandra Rao, T., 1981, **Rise and growth of public library movement in India**. [Iyyanki Library Awards Committee, Eluru]. {NASSDOC*}

Ranganathan, S.R. and Neelameghan, A., eds., 1972, **A seminar on public library system**. [Sarada Ranganathan Endowment for Library Science, Bangalore]. {NASSDOC*}

PUBLIC LIBRARIES : GEOGRAPHICAL AREA : INDIA : ANDHRA PRADDESH

Venkatappaiah, V., 1982, **Public library system in Andhra Pradesh**. [Andhra University]. {NASSDOC}

PUBLIC LIBRARIES : GEOGRAPHICAL AREA : INDIA : BIHAR

Athar, Shere, 1965, **Khuda Bakhsh Oriental Public Library, Patna**. [Khuda Bakhsh Oriental Public Library]. {ZHL}

Singh, R.S.P., 1988, **Public libraries in Bihar**. [Bihar Library Service Association, Patna].

PUBLIC LIBRARIES : GEOGRAPHICAL AREA : INDIA : DELHI

Anon, 1963, **Delhi Public Library** : Constitution, regulations of Delhi Library Board and rules of the library. [Delhi Library Board]. {NASSDOC}

Gardner, Frank M., 1957, **Delhi Public Library** : An evaluation report. {DSSW DUL}

Anon, 1976, **Delhi Public Library** : Silver jubilee souvenir, 27th October, 1976. {NASSDOC}

See also Delhi Public Library

PUBLIC LIBRARIES : GEOGRAPHICAL AREA : INDIA : KARNATAKA

Ijari, S.R., 1983, **A development plan for public library system in the Karnataka State**. Thesis. (Karnataka University). {NASSDOC}

Patil, P.K., n.d., **Pubic libraries in Karnataka** : Their scope and development. {AIU}

PUBLIC LIBRARIES : GEOGRAPHICAL AREA : MAHARASHTRA

Mahajan, S.G., 1984, **History of public library movement in Maharashtra**. {JNU

NASSDOC*}

Mahajan, S.G., 1979, **History of the public library movement in western Maharashtra, 1805-1921** : Thesis. (Poona University). {NASSDOC}

PUBLIC LIBRARIES : GEOGRAPHICAL AREA : LATIN AMERICA

Anon, 1952, **Development of public libraries in Latin America** : The Sao Paulo conference. [UNESCO]. {IEG NASSDOC ZHL}

PUBLIC LIBRARIES : GEOGRAPHICAL AREA : SRI LANKA

Ranganathan, S.R. and Neelameghan, A., eds., 1972, **Public library system** : India, Sri Lanka, UK, USA. {BIS IEG IIC JNU NAI NMML ZHL}

PUBLIC LIBRARIES : GEOGRAPHICAL AREA : SWEDEN

Hjelmquist, Bengt, comp., n.d., **Swedish public libraries in pictures** : Country and small town libraries. {IIT}

PUBLIC LIBRARIES : GEOGRAPHICAL AREA : USA

McDiarmid, W.W., et al, 1942, **Administration of the American public library.** [American Library Association]. {NAI}

Wheeler, Joseph L. and Githens, Alfred Morton, 1941, **The American public library building** : Its planning and design with special reference to its administration and service. [American Library Association]. {USIS}

Rose, Ernstine, 1954, **Public library in American life.** {NAI USIS}

Leigh, Robert D., n.d., **Public library in the United States**. {IEG}

Ranganathan, S.R. and Neelameghan, A., eds., 1972, **Public library system** : India, Sri Lanka, UK, USA. {BIS IEG IIC JNU NAI NMML ZHL}

Anon, 1969, **Public library systems in the United States** : A survey of multi-jurisdictional systems. [American Library Association]. {USIS}

PUBLIC LIBRARIES : GEOGRAPHICAL AREA : USA : NEW YORK

Lydenberg, H.M., 1932, **History of New York Public Library**. {NAI}

PUBLIC RELATIONS IN LIBRARIES

Mathews, Anne J., 1983, **Communicate** : A librarian's guide to interpersonal relations. [American Library Association]. {USIS}

Edsall, Marian S., 1980, **Library promotion handbook.** {IIT USIS}

McGarry, K.J., 1972, **Mass communications** : Selected readings for librarians. {NIPCCD}

Kies, Cosette, 1974, **Problems in library public relations**. {ISI}

Harrison, K.C., 1973, **Public relations for librarians.** {ICA MMTC ZHL}

Rice, Betty, 1972, **Public relations for public libraries** : Creative problem solving. {USIS}

See also Library Exhibits; Library Programmes; Library Publicity

PUBLISHERS AND PUBLISHING

See Book Industry and Trade

RAMESES, THE GREAT

Nicholas, Charles L., 1964, **Library of Rameses, the Great.** {DUL}

RAMPUR RAZA LIBRARY BILL

Anon, 1975, **Rampur Raza Library Bill**. [Lok Sabha, New Delhi]. {JNU}

RANGANATHAN, S.R.

Kaula, P.N., ed., 1965, **Library science today** : Ranganathan festschrift. {BIS CRRI ICHR IIT INSA MFL NIH SPA ZHL}

Satija, Mohinder Partap, 1978, **Ranganathan** : Method and style : A pastiche of opinions. {JNU}

Srivastava, A.P., 1977, **Ranganathan** : A pattern maker : A synthetic study of his contributions. {CRRI ISI JNU NIEPA NIPCCD ZHL}

Rajagopalan, T.S., ed., 1968, **Ranganathan's philosophy** : Assessment, impact and relevance. {JNU NMML}

Dudley, Edward, ed., 1974, **S.R. Ranganathan**, 1892-1972 : Papers : Memorial meeting, January 25, 1973. {JNU}

RANGOON

See Geographical Area subdivisions under main Descriptor, e.g., Library Resources : Geographical Area : Myanmar : Rangoon

RATTAN TATA LIBRARY, NEW DELHI

Sircar, Pankti, 1970, **Evaluation of the acquisition policy and procedure of periodicals in the Indian Institute of Foreign Trade Library and Rattan Tata Library**. {DUL}

RAZA LIBRARY, RAMPUR : BILL

See Rampur Raza Library Bill

READING

See Books and Reading

REFERENCE BOOKS

Shores, Louis, 1939, **Basic reference books** : An introduction to the evaluation study and use of reference materials with special emphasis on some 300 titles. {JNU}

Shores, Louis, 1954, **Basic reference sources**. [American Library Association]. {CRRI NAI USIS}

Shores, Louis, 1972, **Basic reference sources** : An introduction to materials and methods. {DUL USIS}

Taylor, Margaret T., 1973, **Basic reference sources** : A self study manual. {DUL USIS}

Taylor, Margaret T. and Powell, Ronald R., 1981, **Basic reference sources** : A self study manual, 2nd edn. {USIS}

Boyd, Jessie, et al, 1965, **Books, libraries and you** : A handbook on the use of reference books and the reference resources of the library, 3rd edn. {USIS}

Harrison, K.C., 1964, **Facts at your fingertips** : Everyman's guide to reference books. {MFL}

Winchell, C.M., 1967, **Guide to reference books**, 8th edn. [American Library Association]. {JNU NASSDOC}

Dority, G. Kim, 1984, **Guide to reference books for small and medium sized**

libraries, 1970-82. {NASSDOC}

Walford, A.J., ed., n.d., **Guide to reference material,** 3 vols. [Library Association, London]. {INSA NASSDOC NIPCCD ZHL}

Gidwani, N.N. and Navalani, K., 1974, **A guide to reference materials on India**, 2 vols. {INSA NAI NASSDOC NCAER NERC ZHL}

Murphey, R.W., 1958, **How and where to look it up**. {IIT}

Dunkin, Paul Shaner, 1973, **How to catalogue a rare book**, 2nd edn. {JNU}

Downs, Robert B., 1966, **How to do library research**. {ICA IIT JNU NIH USIS}

Chandler, G., 1967, **How to find out** : A guide to sources of information for all, arranged by the Dewey Decimal Classification, 2nd edn. {MHA}

Chandler, G., 1974, **How to find out** : A guide to sources of information for all, arranged by the Dewey Decimal Classification, 4th rev. edn. {NASSDOC}

Chandler, G., 1982, **How to find out** : Printed and on-line sources, 5th rev edn. {DUL NASSDOC}

Alexander, C. and Burke, A.J., 1958, **How to locate educational information and data,** 4th edn. {NIEPA}

Lynes, Alice, 1974, **How to organise a local collection.** {NASSDOC}

Adler, Mortimer J. and Van Doren, Charles, 1972, **How to read a book**, rev edn. {USIS}

Johnson, Herbert Weber, et al, 1972, **How to use the business library** : With sources of business information, 4th edn. {USIS}

Morton, Leslie T., 1979, **How to use a medical library**. {NIH}

Debons, Anthony, 1981, **Information professional** : Survey of an emerging field. {IIT JNU USIS}

Umapathy, K.S., 1978, **Information sources** : An international selective guide. {DUL ICA IIFT INSA}

Roberts A.D., 1948-1956, **Introduction to reference books,** 1948; 1952; 1956. {CRRI JNU SPA}

Ziskind, Sylvia, 1977, **Reference readiness** : A manual for librarians and students. {DUL NASSDOC}

Doyle, James M. and Grimes, George H., 1976, **Reference resources** : A systematic approach. {DUL NASSDOC}

Cowley, J.D., 1947, **Use of reference material.** {ZHL}

REFERENCE BOOKS : ACADEMIC LIBRARY

Bushnell, George H., 1951, **Reference librarian in university, municipal and specialised libraries**. {BIS CRRI DUL}

REFERENCE BOOKS : ARCHITECTURE

Smith, D.L., 1967, **How to find out in architecture and building.** {SPA}

REFERENCE BOOKS : BIBLIOGRAPHY

Anon, 1972, **Guide to selected computer based information services.** [Association of Special Libraries and Information Bureaux]. {CRRI}

REFERENCE BOOKS : ENGINEERING

Parsons, S.A.J., 1972, **How to find out about engineering.** {CRRI}

REFERENCE BOOKS : GEOGRAPHICAL AREA : ASIA : SOUTH

Anon, 1979, **Papers** : Seminar on reference sources on South Asia, 1979, Jaipur.

{JNU}

REFERENCE SERVICES : LIBRARIES

Weiner, Margery, 1974, **Answering any questions** : How to set up an information office. {BCL DUL}

Grogan, Denis, 1967, **Case studies in reference work.** {DUL IIT NIH}

Suseela Kumar, 1974, **Changing concepts of reference service**. {AIU DUL ICHR IIT MHA NERC NIPCCD NMML}

Methics, Lorraine M. and Watson, Peter G., 1976, **Computer based reference service.** {JNU}

Galvin, Thomas J., 1971, **Current problems in reference service.** {DUL JNU NERC USIS}

Ranganathan, S.R., 1953, **Depth classification and reference service and reference material**. [Indian Library Association]. {INSA ISI}

Samhel, Rothstein, 1955, **Development of reference services through academic traditions, public library practices and special librarianship.** {JNU}

Thomas, Diana M., 1981, **Effective reference librarian.** {IIT ISI NASSDOC}

Majumdar, S., 1980, **Evaluation of reference service in JNU library.** {JNU}

Cheney, Frances Neel, 1980, **Fundamental reference sources.** [American Library Association]. {DUL}

Sengupta, B., 1981, **Indian reference and information services.** {ICA NIH}

Long, Nicholas, 1975, **Information and referral services** : Research findings. [U.S. Department of Health, Education and Welfare]. {NASSDOC}

Hutchins, Margaret, 1944, **Introduction to reference work.** [American Library Association]. {BIS CRRI DUL ICHR IIFT NMML USIS}

Jahoda, Gerald and Braunagel, J.S., 1980, **Librarian and reference queries** : A systematic approach. {CRRI ISI USIS}

Collison, Robert L., 1869, **Library assistance to readers.** {DUL MHA}

Chirgwin, F. John and Oldfield, Phyllis, 1983, **Library assistant's manual.** 2nd rev. edn. {IIT}

Mukherjee, Ajit Kumar, 1957, **Manual of reference work.** {DUL SPA}

Grogan, Denis, 1972, **More case studies in reference work.** {DUL IIT}

McInnis, Raymond G., 1978, **New perspectives for reference service in academic libraries.** {CRRI IIT NIPCCD}

Anon, 1982, **Papers** : IASLIC seminar on information services in India, 1982, Kanpur. [Indian Association of Special Libraries and Information Centres]. {CRRI}

Katz, Bill and Fraley, Ruth A., eds., 1986, **Personnel issues in reference services**, {JNU NASSDOC}

Galvin, Thomas J., 1965, **Problems in reference service** : Case studies in method and policy. {DUL USIS}

Jones, Clara Station, ed., 1978, **Public library information and referral service.** {USIS}

Shastri, Dwarka Prasad, 1958, **Pustakalaya aur sandarbh seva.** {BIS DUL}

Shores, Hous, 1976, **Reference as the promotion of free enquiry**. {JNU}

Buter, Pierce, 1943, **Reference function of the library.** {DUL NAL}

Bushnell, George H., 1951, **Reference librarian in university, municipal and specialised libraries.** {BIS CRRI DUL}

Warner, J., 1928, **Reference library methods.** {NAI}

McColvin, Lionel R., 1952, **Reference library stack** : An informal guide. {CRRI}

Fenton, F.H., 1960, **Reference library stacks** : An enquiry into reference book provision in the rate-supported libraries of England and Wales. {JNU}

Dierickx, Harold and Hopkinson, Alan, eds., 1981, **Reference manual for machine-readable bibliographic descriptions**, 2nd rev edn. [UNESCO]. {NASSDOC}

Ziskind, Sylvia, 1977, **Reference readiness** : A manual for librarians and students. {DUL NASSDOC}

Anon, 1966, **Reference research and the regionalism** : Selected papers from 53rd conference of Texas Library Association. {JNU}

Doyle, James M. and Grimes, George H., 1976, **Reference resources** : A systematic approach. {DUL NASSDOC}

Davinson, Donald, 1980, **Reference service.** {DUL ICA}

Krishan Kumar, 1984, **Reference service.** {JNU NMML}

Ranganathan, S.R., 1961, **Reference service**, 2nd edn. {BIS CRRI DSSW DUL JNU MHA NASSDOC NIH NMML SPA ZHL}

Murfin, Marjorie E. and Wynar, Lubomyr R., 1984, **Reference service** : An annotated bibliographic guide supplement, 1976-1982. {JNU}

Ranganathan, S.R., 1940, **Reference service and bibliography**, Vol. 1, Pts. 1-4. {DSSW DUL}

Gleaves, Edwin S. and Tucker, John Mark, 1983, **Reference service and library education** : Essays in honour of Neel Chaney. {JNU}

Sharma, Jagdish Saran and Grover, D.R., 1987, **Reference service and sources of information.** {NMML}

Sewa Singh, 1986, **Reference service in academic libraries in India.** {JNU NASSDOC NMML}

Anon, 1970, **Reference service-in-action** : Processing and servicing of special material in libraries. [Indian Association of Special Libraries and Information Centres, Calcutta]. {IEG NAI}

Rowland, Arthur Ray, 1964, **Reference services.** {DUL USIS}

Kohl, David F., 1985, **Reference services and library instruction** : A handbook for library management. {NASSDOC}

Irving, Richard D. and Katz, Bill, 1988, **Reference services and public policy.** {NASSDOC}

Wyer, James I., 1930, **Reference work**. [American Library Association]. {ZHL}

Mukherjee, A.K., 1964, **Reference work and its tools.** {CRRI ICA NMML SPA}

Mukherjee, A.K., 1971, **Reference work and its tools,** 2nd edn. {DUL JNU NASSDOC NERC NIEPA NMML}

Mukherjee, A.K., 1975, **Reference work and its tools,** 3rd ed. {CRRI ICA IIT NIH NIPCCD}

Stevens, Rolland E. and Smith, Linda C., 1986, **Reference work in the university library**. {JNU}

Finer, Ruth, 1979, **Referral centres and services** : A review. [Association of Special Libraries and Information Bureaux]. {CRRI}

Simon, Herbert A. and Siklossy, Leurent, 1972, **Representation and meaning** : Experiments with information processing systems. {NASSDOC}

Anon, 1969, **Universal reference system**, 10 vols. {NMML}

Hillard, James M., 1975, **Where to find what** : A handbook to reference service. {JNU}

See also Information Services

REFERENCE SERVICES : LIBRARIES : GEOGRAPHICAL AREA : JAPAN

Anon, 1960, **American libraries** : Report : U.S. field seminar on library reference services for Japanese librarians, June 1960. [International House of Japan]. {DUL NASSDOC}

REGIONAL LIBRARIES

Scheuk, Gretchen Knief, 1954, **County and regional library development.** {NASSDOC}

REPRODUCTION OF CATALOGUE CARDS

See Catalogue Cards : Reproduction

REPROGRAPHY

Mason, Donald, 1968, **Document reproduction in libraries.** {DUL}

Duyvis, F. Donker and Schippers, M.E., n.d., **Document reproduction services** : Their efficient organisation and management. [UNESCO]. {IIMC NASSDOC}

Barrett, W.J., 1961, **Glossary of photocopying terms.** {DUL}

Corbett, Edmund V., 1957, **Photo charging** : Its operation and installation in British Public Library. {JNU}

Whitestone, Patricia, 1977, **Photocopying in libraries** : The librarians speak. {IIT}

Anon, 1950, **Photoduplication service**. [U.S. Library of Congress]. {DUL}

Cogoli, John E., 1960, **Photo-offset** : Fundamentals. {DUL}

Anon, 1961, **Reproductions reference guide**. 2nd edn. {NASSDOC}

Crix, F.C., 1975, **Reprographic management handbook**. {ISI}

Lahood, Charles G. and Sullivan, Robert C., 1975, **Reprographic services in libraries** : Organisation and administration. [American Library Association]. {BIS NMML}

New, Peter C., 1975, **Reprography for librarians.** {AIU JNU}

RESEARCH

Mann, Thomas, 1987, **Guide to library research methods**. {JNU}

Black, Dorothy M., 1975, **Guide to lists of Master's theses**. [American Library Association]. {NASSDOC}

Duckworth, Walter E., 1962, **Guide to operational research**. {NASSDOC}

Venderborght, G., 1979, **Guidelines for preparation of texts of dissertations for their presentation and publication**. {DUL}

Wolman, Perctz, 1975, **Guidelines on the conduct of a national inventory of current research and development projects**. {DUL}

Isaac, Stephen and Michael, William B, 1972, **Handbook in research and evaluation** : A collection of principles, methods and strategies useful in the planning, design and evaluation of studies in education and the behavioural sciences. {NASSDOC}

Struening, Elmer L. and Guttentag, Marcia, eds., 1975, **Handbook of evaluation research**, 2 vols. {NASSDOC}

Fowles, Jib, ed., 1978, **Handbook of futures research.** {NASSDOC}

Sears, Donald A., (1984), **Harbrace guide to the library and the research paper**, 4th ed. {IIMC}

Rolland, E. Stevens, ed., n.d., **Historical and bibliographical methods in library research**. {ICHR}

Downs, Robert B., 1966, **How to do library research**. {ICA IIT JNU NIH USIS}

Berry, Ralph, 1966, **How to write a research paper**. {DUL}

Stone, Sue, ed., 1980, **Humanities information research** : Proceedings of a seminar. {JNU}

Jahoda, Gerald, 1970, **Information storage and retrieval systems for individual researchers.** {ISI MHA USIS}

Martinson, Tom L., 1972, **Introduction to library research in geography**. {DUL}

Churchman, C. West, et al, 1969, **Introduction to operations research**. {NASSDOC}

Taverekere, Srikantaid and Hoffman, Herbert H., 1978, **Introduction to quantitative research methods for librarians**, 2nd rev edn. {DUL}

Hillian, Margret P., 1955, **Libraries for research and industry planning and equipment**. {DUL}

Daiute, Robert J. and Gorman, Kenneth A., 1974, **Library operations research** : Computer programming for circulation. {USIS}

Cohen, Nathan M., et al, 1963, **Library science dissertations, 1925-1960** : An annotated bibliography of doctoral studies. {USIS}

Magnoti, Shirley, 1982, **Library science research, 1974-79**. {DUL}

Turabian, Kate L., 1966, **Manual for writers of term papers, theses and dissertations**. {DUL}

Dugdale, Kathleen, 1962, **Manual of form for theses and term reports**, rev edn. {DUL}

Good, Carter V. and Scates, Dughlas E., 1954, **Methods of research** : Educational, psychological and sociological. {NASSDOC}

Barzun, Jacques and Graff, Henry F., 1977, **Modern researcher,** 3rd edn. {NASSDOC}

Katzan, Harry, 1973, **Operating systems** : A pragmatic approach. {NASSDOC}

White, Douglas, et al, 1969, **Operational research techniques,** Vol. 1 : Introduction. {NASSDOC}

Swanson, Don R. and Bookstein, Abraham, eds., 1972, **Operations research** : Implications for libraries. {NASSDOC}

Taha, Handy A., 1971, **Operations research** : An introduction. {NASSDOC}

House, William C., 1972, **Operations research** : An introduction to modern applications. {NASSDOC}

Rowley, J. E. and Rowley, Petter J., 1981, **Operations research** : A tool for library management. [American Library Association]. {USIS}

Anon, 1972, **Problems and prospects of fundamental research in multidisciplinary fields** : Computer science. [Organisation for Economic Co-operation and Development, Paris; Committee for Science Policy]. {NASSDOC}

Williams, Edwin E., ed., n.d., **Problems and prospects of the research library.** {IEG}

Karetzkey, Stephen, 1982, **Reading research and librarianship** : A history and analysis. {CRRI IIT JNU}

Anon, n.d., **Reading research in the Centre for Library Science and Methodology**, 1981-85. [Centre for Library Science and Methodology, Budapest]. {NASSDOC}

Ross, Robert, 1974, **Research** : An introduction. {NASSDOC}

Palmer, Archie M., 1972, **Research centres directory**, 4th edn. {NASSDOC}

Holmes, W. Robert and Raj Gopal, S., 1968, **Research facilities in Bangalore, Mysore, Ahmedabad.** {NMML}

Holmes, W. Robert and Raj Gopal, S., 1968, **Research facilities in Bombay,**

Calcutta and Madras. {NIPCCD NMML USIS}

Holmes, W. Robert and Raj Gopal, S., 1967, **Research facilities in Delhi.** {DSSW ICA NIEPA NIPCCD NMML USIS}

Holmes, W. Robert and Raj Gopal, S., 1967, **Research facilities in Hyderabad.** {NIPCCD NMML}

Jafar, S.M., 1971, **Research facilities in Uttar Pradesh**. {NMML}

Swisher, Robert and Mc Clure, Charles R., 1984, **Research for decision-making** : Methods for librarians. {DUL}

Brooks, Philip C., 1969, **Research in archives** : The use of unpublished primary sources. {NASSDOC USIS ZHL}

Kumar, P.S.G., comp., 1987, **Research in library in information science in India** : A bibliography of Ph.D, M.Phil. and MLIS dissertation. {NASSDOC NMML}

Anon, n.d., **Research in progress**, 4 vols. [Inter University Board of India and Ceylon]. {NASSDOC}

Harlow, Jacquis, 1963, **Research information retrieval.** {JNU}

Orne, Jerrold, ed., 1971, **Research librarianship** : Essays in honour of Robert B. Downs. {JNU NASSDOC USIS}

Williams, Cecil B. and Stevenson, Allan H., 1951, **Research manual for college studies and papers**, rev. edn. {ZHL}

Mumfort, Erid, et al, eds., 1985, **Research methods in information systems** : Proceedings of the IFIP WG 8.2 colloquium, Manchester Business School, September 1-3, 1984. {NASSDOC}

Stevens, Rolland E., ed., 1971, **Research methods in librarianship** : Historical and bibliographical methods in library research. {NASSDOC}

Busha, Charles H. and Herter, Stephen P., eds., 1980, **Research methods in librarianship** : Techniques and interpretation. {ISI}

Slater, M., ed., 1990, **Research methods in library and information studies.** [Library Association, London].{DUL}

Wynar, Bohdan S., 1974, **Research methods in library science** : A bibliographic guide with tropical outlines. {NASSDOC}

Anon, 1981, **Research services directory**. {USIS}

Ranganathan, S.R. and Girja Kumar, 1960, **Social science research and libraries** : Papers and summary proceedings of the library seminar on research in the social science, January 2-4, 1959. {NMML}

Anon, 1967, **Social science research and library development** : Summary proceedings. [Indian Council of World Affairs; Indian School of International Studies]. {NASSDOC*}

Anon; 1985, **The social sciences** : Information system. [USSR Academy of Sciences, Moscow]. {NASSDOC*}

Manhiemer, Martha L., 1973, **Style manual** : A guide for the preparation of reports and dissertations. {DUL}

Anon, 1966, **Style manual for authors and printers of Australian Government publications**. [Australia Style Manual Committee, 1964]. {DUL}

Arvinda Chandra and Saxena, T.P., 1979, **Style manual for writing theses, dissertations and papers in social sciences.** {DUL}

Anderson, Janathan, et al, 1970, **Thesis and assignment writing**. {DUL}

Saunders, W.L., ed., 1968, **University and research library studies.** {AIU DUL IIC IIT ISI JNU SPA}

RESEARCH : STATISTICAL METHODS

Fisher, Ronald A., 1970, **Statistical methods for research workers**, 14th edn.

{NASSDOC}

RESEARCH LIBRARIES

Clapp, Vener W., 1964, **Future of the research library.** {IEG JNU}

Anon, 1969, **On research libraries** : Statement and recommendations. [American Council of Learned Societies Devoted to Humanistic Studies, Committee on Research Libraries]. {IIT INSA USIS}

Fussler, Herman H. and Simon, Julian L., 1969, **Patterns in the use of books in large research libraries.** {NMML}

Metcalf, Keyes D., 1965, **Planning academic and research library buildings.** {BIS IIT NASSDOC NIH USIS}

Williams, Edwin E., ed., n.d., **Problems and prospects of the research library.** {IEG}

Fussler, Herman H., 1974, **Research libraries and technology** : A report. [Sloan Foundation]. {USIS}

Saunders, W.L., ed., 1968, **University and research library studies.** {AIU DUL IIC IIT ISI JNU SPA}

RESEARCH LIBRARIES : GEOGRAPHICAL AREA : DEVELOPING COUNTRIES

Krishan Kumar, 1973, **Research libraries in developing countries.** {AIU DUL IEG IIT JNU NASSDOC NIEPA NIPCCD NMML}

RESEARCH LIBRARIES : GEOGRAPHICAL AREA : GREAT BRITAIN

Roberts, Stephen, et al, eds., 1978, **Research libraries and collections in the United Kingdom** : A selective inventory and guide. {DUL ZHL}

RESTORATION OF MANUSCRIPTS

See Manuscripts : Conservation and Restoration

RIGHT TO READING PROGRAM

See also Books and Reading : Geographical Area : USA

ROCHESTER PUBLIC LIBRARY

Swaran Kumar, 1963, **East and West.** : Delhi Public Library, India, as seen against the background of the Rochester Public Library. {NASSDOC*}

RURAL LIBRARIES

Anon, 1978, **Library services in rural areas.** [Library Advisory Council, Wales]. {NIEPA}

Mittal, S.R., 1964, **Organising village library** : A guide book for social education workers and village librarians. [National Council for Educational Research and Training, New Delhi]. {ICA ISI NIPCCD}

SDI

=Selective Dissemination of Information

SMART (INFORMATION RETRIEVAL SYSTEM)

Salton, Gerald, ed., 1971, **The SMART retrieval system** : Experiments in automatic document processing. {MHA NASSDOC}

SPINES
=Science and Technology Policies Information Exchange Systems

SYNTOL (INFORMATION RETRIEVAL SYSTEM)
Gardin, J.C., 1965, **SYNTOL**, ed. by Susan Artandi, 2 vols. [New Jersey Graduate School of Library Science]. {IIT MFL}

SANSKRIT MANUSCRIPTS
See Manuscripts : Sanskrit

SAYERS, WILLIAM CHARLES BERWICK
Foskett, D.J. and Palmer, B.I., 1961, **Essays in librarianship** : In memory of William Charles Berwick Sayers. {MFL}

SCHOOL LIBRARIES
Fargo, Lucile F., 1964, **Activity book for school libraries.** {JNU}
Gardiner, Jewel, 1954, **Administering library service in the elementary school**, 2nd edn. [American Library Association]. {DUL NIEPA ZHL}
Trehan, G.L., 1965, **Administration and organisation of school libraries.** {NASSDOC}
Rice, Margaretta G., 1966, **Audio-visual aids for teaching the use of school library**. {JNU}
Rufsvold, Margaret I., 1949, **Audio-visual school library service** : A handbook for librarians. [American Library Association]. {ZHL}
Maheu, Mary Helen, 1958, **Certification of school librarians** : A compilation of State requirements, 1958. {NASSDOC}
Sharma, Satinder, 1982, **Contemporary approach to school library**. {DUL NASSDOC}
Anon, n.d., **Curriculum guide for the school libraries in the elementary school.** [Detroit Public School]. {JNU}
Lawrie, Jean Elizabeth, 1970, **Elementary school libraries.** {JNU}
Palouec, Lora and Goodman, Elezabeth B., 1969, **Elementary school library in action**. {JNU}
Gaver, Mary Virginia, 1962, **Every child needs a school library**. {JNU}
Anon, 1977, **Guide for the conversion of school libraries into media centres.** [UNESCO]. {DUL ICA JNU NIEPA}
Vishwanathan, C.G., 1957, **High school library** : Organisation and administration. {DUL NERC}
Magnanand and Vaish, J.D., n.d., **Higher secondary school libraries**. {DUL IEG}
Will Friedemann, 1972, **Libraries for schools and universities**. {CRRI}
Leyland, Eric, 1961, **Libraries in schools**. {JNU}
Taylor, James L., 1966, **Library facility for elementary and secondary schools.** {JNU}
Rossoft, Martin, 1955, **Library in the high school teaching.** {JNU}
Anon, n.d., **Library in the primary schools** : A report by sub-committee of School Library Association. {JNU}
Fargo, Lucile F., 1947, **Library in the school**, 4th edn. [American Library Association]. {DUL ZHL}
Anon, 1930, **Library instruction** : Junior and senior high schools. {ZHL}
Fenwick, Sara Innis, 1975, **Library services for children in New Zealand schools and public libraries** : A report. [New Zealand Library Association]. {JNU}
Ray, Sheila G., 1982, **Library service to schools**. {JNU}

Ray, Colin, 1979, **Library service to schools and children.** {JNU NIPCCD}

Saunders, Helen E., 1968, **Modern school library** : Its administration as a material centre. {JNU}

Delaney, Jalk J., 1968, **New school librarian**. {JNU}

Ireland, Norma Olin, 1952, **Picture file in school, college and public libraries**, rev edn. {ZHL}

Kennon, Mary Frances and Doyle, Leila Ann, 1962, **Planning school library development** : A report of the school library development project. {DUL NASSDOC}

Douglas, Mary Peacock, 1974, **Primary school library and its services.** [UNESCO]. {DUL IEG NERC NIPCCD}

Carroll, Frances Laverne, 1981, **Recent advances in school librarianship.** {NIEPA}

Dyer, C., 1970, **Role of school libraries in education**. {JNU}

Anon, 1967, **School library.** [Department of Education and Science, Great Britain]. {JNU}

Ellsworth, Ralph E. and Wagener, Hobart E., n.d., **School library**. {AIU DUL}

Davies, Ruth Ann, 1969, **The school library** : A force for educational excellence. {JNU USIS}

Mukherjee, A.K., 1965, **School library** : Some practical hints. {ISI MFL}

Wofford, Azile, 1959, **School library at work** : Acquisition, organisation and maintenance of materials in the school library. {JNU}

Vashishth, C.P., ed., 1986, **School library development**. [Indian Library Association]. {NASSDOC*}

Trehan, G.L. and Malhan, I.V., 1980, **School library management**. {NERC}

Allan, Margaret, 1974, **School library resource centre**. {JNU}

Cecil, Henry L. and Heap, Willard A., 1940, **School library service in the United States**. {ZHL}

Winstanley, Baroda, 1959, **School loan services.** {JNU}

Prostano, Emanuel T., 1974, **School media programmes** : Case studies in management, 2nd edn. {NIEPA}

See also Academic Libraries; Library Schools

SCHOOL LIBRARIES : GEOGRAPHICAL AREA : AFRICA : WEST

Crookall, R.E., 1961, **School libraries in West Africa**. {JNU NIEPA}

SCHOOL LIBRARIES : GEOGRAPHICAL AREA : AUSTRALIA

Fenwick, Sara Innis, 1966, **School and children's libraries in Australia**. {JNU}

SCHOOL LIBRARIES : GEOGRAPHICAL AREA : INDIA : UTTAR PRADESH

Anon, n.d., **Secondary school libraries in Uttar Pradesh**. [Department of Education, Allahabad University]. {IEG}

SCHOOL LIBRARIES : GEOGRAPHICAL AREA : NEW ZEALAND

Fenwick, Sara Innis, 1975, **Library services for children in New Zealand schools and public libraries** : A report. [New Zealand Library Association]. {JNU}

SCHOOL LIBRARIES : GEOGRAPHICAL AREA : PACIFIC : NORTH WEST

Kroll, Morton, 1960, **Elementary and secondary school libraries of the Pacific**

North West. {JNU}

SCHOOL LIBRARIES : GEOGRAPHICAL AREA : PUERTO RICO

Gaver, Mary Virginia and Velazquer, Gonzal, 1963, **School libraries in Puerto Rico** : A survey and plan for development. {NASSDOC}

SCHOOL LIBRARIES : GEOGRAPHICAL AREA : USA

Cecil, Henry L. and Heap, Willard A., 1940, **School library service in the United States**. {ZHL}

SCIENCE : ACRONYMS

See under Acronyms

SCIENCE : DOCUMENTATION

Carter, Launor F., et al, 1967, **National document handling systems for science and technology.** {BIS IIMC NIH USIS}

Loosjes, T.P., 1973, **On documentation of scientific literature**. {JNU}

Anon, n.d., **Scientific and technical documentation centres**. [UNESCO]. {AIU}

SCIENCE : INFORMATION SERVICES

Lynch, Michael Felix, 1974, **Computer based information services in science and technology** : Principles and techniques. {BCL}

See also Communication in Science; Scientific and Technical Information

SCIENCE : INFORMATION SERVICES : GEOGRAPHICAL AREA : INDIA

Anon, 1980, **Science information services in India**. [Indian National Scientific Documentation Centre, New Delhi]. {NASSDOC*}

SCIENCE : METHODOLOGY

Ackoff, Russell L., et al, 1962, **Scientific method** : Optimising applied research decision. {NASSDOC}

SCIENCE AND TECHNOLOGY POLICIES INFORMATION EXCHANGE SYSTEM

Coblans, H., et al, 1974, **Science and technology policies information exchange systems (SPINES) feasibility study**. {JNU}

SCIENCE INFORMATION SERVICES

See Science : Information Services

SCIENTIFIC AND TECHNICAL INFORMATION

Ackoff, Rusell L., et al, 1976, **Designing national scientific and technological communication system**. {USIS}

Coblans, H., et al, 1974, **Science and technology policies information exchange systems (SPINES) feasibility study**. {JNU}

Foskett, D.J., 1964, **Science, humanism and libraries**. {IIT JNU}

Anon, 1980, **Science information services in India**. [Indian National Scientific Documentation Centre, New Delhi]. {NASSDOC*}

Jenkins, Frances Briggs, 1965, **Science reference sources**, 4th edn. {DUL}

Anon, n.d., **Scientific and technical documentation centres**. [UNESCO]. {AIU}

Mikhailov, A.I., 1982, **Scientific and technical information** : Its impact on the development of science and technology. [UNESCO; UNIDO, Moscow]. {NASSDOC*}

Anon, 1969, **Scientific and technical information in Canada**. [Science Council of Canada]. {JNU}

Subramanyan, Krishna, 1981, **Scientific and technical information resources.** {DUL}

Chen, Ching-Chih, 1987, **Scientific and technical information sources**, 1977. {IIT INSA JNU NERC}

Pruett, Nancy Jones, 1986, **Scientific and technical libraries**, 2 vols. {JNU}

Strauss, Lucille J., et al, 1964, **Scientific and technical libraries** : Their organisation and administration. {BIS CRRI IIT INSA}

Strauss, Lucille J., et al., 1972, **Scientific and technical libraries** : Their organisation and administration, 2nd edn. {BIS ISI INSA JNU}

Anon, 1985, **Scientific and technological information for development**. [United Nations Information Systems]. {JNU}

Thornton, John L. and Tully, R.I.J., 1962, **Scientific books, libraries and collectors** : A study of bibliography and the book trade in relation to science, 2nd edn. {DUL}

Gray, John and Perry, Brian, 1975, **Scientific information**. {BCL INSA}

Rozsa, Gyorgy, 1973, **Scientific information and society**. {NASSDOC}

Dougherty, Richard M. and Heinritz, Fred J., 1966, **Scientific management of library operations**. {DUL USIS}

Ackoff, Russell L., et al, 1962, **Scientific method** : Optimising applied research decision. {NASSDOC}

Houghton, Bernard, 1975, **Scientific periodicals** : Their historical development, characteristics and control. {DUL}

Speterson, Martin, 1966, **Scientific thinking and scientific writing.** {DUL}

Voigt, Melvin J., n.d., **Scientist approaches to information**. [American Library Association]. {BIS}

Anon, 1978, **UNISIST** : A study on the application of scientific and technological information in development. [UNESCO]. {JNU}

SCIENTIFIC LIBRARIES

Pruett, Nancy Jones, 1986, **Scientific and technical libraries**, 2 vols. {JNU}

Strauss, Lucille J., et al, 1964, **Scientific and technical libraries** : Their organisation and administration. {BIS CRRI IIT INSA}

Strauss, Lucille J., et al., 1972, **Scientific and technical libraries** : Their organisation and administration, 2nd edn. {BIS ISI INSA JNU}

SCIENTIFIC METHODS

See Science : Methodology

SELECTIVE DISSEMINATION OF INFORMATION

Anon, 1980, **UNISIST guide for the establishment and evaluation of services for selective dissemination of information.** [UNESCO]. {CRRI}

Anon, 1968, **Working papers for the symposia** : IASLIC seminar, 5th, October 7-9, 1968, Durgapur, Pt. I : Selective dissemination of information for India; Pt. II : Functions and problems of library personnel in special libraries of India. [Indian Association of Special Libraries and Information Centres]. {NASSDOC}

SERIALS

Bhatnagar, Manjula, 1977, **Analysis of the current serial publications being subscribed to in the Delhi University Library System (DULS), Jawahar Lal Nehru University Library and Indian Institute of Technology Library.** (University of Delhi, Department of Library Science, Sessional Project, 1977). {DUL}

Anon, 1978, **Annotated bibliography of country serials.** [UNCTAD/GATT. International Trade Centre]. {MFL}

Anon, 1963-74, **Annual seminar.** No. 1: 1963; No. 2: 1964; No. 3: 1965; No. 4: 1966; No. 5: 1967; No. 6 : 1968, 2 pts; No. 7: 1969; No. 8: 1970; No. 9: 1971; No. 10: 1972, 2 pts; No. 11: 1974. [Documentation Research and Training Centre, Bangalore]. {IEG IIMC ISI JNU NASSDOC}.

Anon, n.d., **Automation in union catalogue of periodicals** : India and abroad, typed short bibliography. {NASSDOC}

Morpurgo, J.E., 1969, **Book and journal services for doctors and nurses** : An interim report on a National Book League investigation. {DUL}

Nicholas, David, 1975, **Characteristics of social science serials** : The construction and analysis of a file : Social science serial titles. [Bath University]. {BCL}

Anon, 1963, **Code of recommended practice for the form and presentation of periodicals of permanent value.** (CP 48 : 1963). [New Zealand Standards Institute, Wellington]. {NASSDOC}

Woodworth, David, comp., 1971, **Directory of publishers of British journals.** {NASSDOC}

Anon, 1970, **Guide for abbreviations of words in titles of periodicals using Roman alphabet**, rev edn. (IS : 18-1970). [Indian Standards Institution]. {NASSDOC}

Anon, 1976, **Guide for layout of learned periodicals**, rev edn. (IS : 795-1976). [Indian Standards Institution]. {NASSDOC}

Anon, 1968, **Guide for preparation of manuscript of an article in a learned periodical.** (IS : 4731-1968). [Indian Standards Institution]. {NASSDOC}

Maureen, J., 1966, **Guide to scientific periodicals** : Annotated bibliography. {DUL}

Anon, 1983, **Guidelines for presentation of abstract sheets in serial publications.** (IS : 10455-1983). [Indian Standards Institution]. {CRRI}

Kronick, David A., 1962, **History of scientific and technical periodicals** : The origins and development of the scientific and technical press. {DUL}

Mullis, A.A., ed., 1983, **ISDS manual**. (International Serial Data System). {NASSDOC}

Devsare, H.K., n.d., **Indexing of children's magazines in Hindi with particular reference to its impact on society and social sciences**. (typed copy). {NASSDOC}

Anon, 1954, **Layout of periodicals**. (ISO/R 8-1954) (E). [International Organisation for Standardisation, Geneva]. {NASSDOC}

Balwinder, Kaur comp., n.d., **Librarians' guide to Indian periodicals published for free distribution**. {NASSDOC}

Anon, 1961, **Library and documentation journals.** [International Federation for Documentation and Information]. {NASSDOC}

Anon, n.d., **Library and information science journals in India,** typed short bibliography. {NASSDOC}

Hernon, Peter, et al, 1973, **Library and library related publications** : A directory of publishing opportunities in journals, serials and annuals. {NASSDOC}

Martin, Laura Katherine, 1950, **Magazine for school libraries**, rev edn. {ZHL}

Katz, William Armstrong, 1971, **Magazine selection** : How to build a community-oriented collection. {USIS}

Taylor, David C., 1982, **Managing the serials explosion** : 1982 {JNU NMML}

Thomas, Nancy G. and O'Neil, Rosanna, comp., 1986, **Notes for serials cataloguing**. {NASSDOC*}

Anon, 1975, **Papers** : IASLIC conference, 10th, 1975, Lucknow, Pt. A. : Library documents aspects of utilisation; Pt. B. : Procurement of periodicals : Current problems in India [Indian Association of Special Libraries and Information Centres]. {IIMC}

Mayes, Paul, ed., 1978, **Periodicals administration in libraries** : A collection of essays. {IIT NASSDOC NCAER NIPCCD}

Davinson, D.E., 1969, **Periodicals collection** : Its purpose and uses in libraries. {NMML}

Anon, 1961, **Presentation of contributions to periodicals**. (ISO/R 215-1961) (E). [International Organisation for Standardisation, Geneval]. {NASSDOC}

Anon, 1967, **Recommendations for the abbreviation of titles of periodicals** (BS. 4148-1967). [British Standards Institution]. {CRRI}

Houghton, Bernard, 1975, **Scientific periodicals** : Their historical development, characteristics and control. {DUL}

Leong, C.L.H., 1989, **Serial cataloguing handbook** : An illustrative guide to the use of AACR2 and LC rule interpretation. [American Library Association]. {DUL}

Osborn, Andrew D., 1955, **Serial publications** : Their place and treatment in libraries. {MFL}

Osborn, Andrew D., 1973, **Serial publications** : Their place and treatment in libraries, 2nd edn. [American Library Association]. {NASSDOC}

Osborn, Andrew D., 1980, **Serial publications** : Their place and treatment in libraries, 3rd edn. [American Library Association]. {USIS}

Rodgers, Frank, comp., 1971, **Serial publications in the British Parliamentary papers, 1900-1968** : A bibliography. [American Library Association]. {NASSDOC}

Potter, William Gray and Sirkin, Arlne Farber, eds., 1981, **Serials automation for acquisition and inventory control.** [American Library Association]. {USIS}

Gellatly, P., ed., 1980, **Serials librarianship in transition** : Issues and development. {NASSDOC}

Walsh, Patricia M., 1979, **Serials management and microforms.** {IIT}

Anon, 1955, **Short contents list of periodicals or other documents**, (ISO/R 18-1955) (E). [International Organisation for Standardisation, Geneva]. {NASSDOC}

Anon, n.d., **Specification for the abbreviation of titles of periodicals**, 2 pts., Pt. 1 : Principles; Pt. 2 : World abbreviation. [British Standards Institution]. {CRRI NASSDOC}

Anon, 1979, **Technical and specialised periodicals published in Britain, 1972-73**. [Central Office of Information, London]. {NASSDOC}

Sarin, Ashok Kumar, 1987, **Use of journals in libraries** : A cost effectiveness analysis. {JNU}

See also Newspapers/Periodicals/Press Clippings : Libraries

SERIALS : BIBLIOGRAPHY

Anon, 1978, **Annotated bibliography of country serials**. [UNCTAD/GATT. International Trade Centre]. {MFL}

Anon, n.d., **National information** : Guide to Indian periodicals, 1953-1956. {DSSW}

Rodgers, Frank, comp., 1971, **Serial publications in the British Parliamentary papers, 1900-1968** : A bibliography. [American Library Association]. {NASSDOC}

SERIALS : GEOGRAPHICAL AREA : GREAT BRITAIN

Woodworth, David, ed., 1973, **Guide to current British journals**, vol. 1, 2nd edn. [Library Association, London]. {NASSDOC}

Rodgers, Frank, comp., 1971, **Serial publications in the British Parliamentary papers, 1900-1968** : A bibliography. [American Library Association]. {NASSDOC}

SERIALS : GEOGRAPHICAL AREA : INDIA

Balwinder, Kaur comp., n.d., **Librarians' guide to Indian periodicals published for free distribution**. {NASSDOC}

SHELVING

Gawrecki, Drahoslav, 1968, **Compact library shelving**. [American Library Association]. {DUL NASSDOC USIS}

Coplan, Kate, 1974, **Effective library exhibits** : How to prepare and promote good displays, 2nd edn. {CRRI USIS}

Murphey, R.W., 1958, **How and where to look it up**? {IIT}

Jesse, W.H., 1952, **Shelf work in library**. [American Library Association]. {DUL IIT}

Hyman, Richard Joseph, 1982, **Shelf access in libraries**. [American Library Association]. {DUL NASSDOC}

SHERA, JESSE H.

Rawski, Conrad H. and Towaid, A., eds., 1973, **Theory of librarianship** : Papers in honour of Jesse H. Shera. {NASSDOC*}

SIMULATION : COMPUTER

See also Computer Simulation

SIMULATION METHODS

See also Computer Simulation

SLAVIC CHARACTERS : TRANSLITERATION

Anon, 1968, **International system for the transliteration of Greek characters into Latin characters.** (ISO/R 843-1968) (E). [International Organisation for Standardisation, Geneva]. {NASSDOC}

SOCIAL SCIENCE LIBRARIES

Kister, Kenneth F., 1968, **Social issues and library problems** : Case studies in the social science. {NMML}

SOCIAL SCIENCES

Bulick, Stephen, 1982, **Structure and subject interaction** : Toward a sociology of knowledge in the social sciences. {BIS}

SOCIAL SCIENCES : ABSTRACTING AND INDEXING

Anon, 1976, **The planning of indexing and abstracting services in the social sciences** : Coverage overlap and content. [Bath University Library]. {BCL}

SOCIAL SCIENCES : BIBLIOGRAPHY

Anon, 1978, **BEPI** : Bibliography of English publications in India : An integrated author-title-subject index of scholarly and significant publications of the year, 1977-1978. {NASSDOC}

Kalia, D.R. and Jain, M.K., 1975, **A bibliography of bibliographies on India**. {ICA}

Needham, Christopher D. and Herman, Esther, eds., 1970, **Study of subject bibliography with special reference to the social sciences**. [School of Library and Information Services, Maryland]. {NASSDOC}

SOCIAL SCIENCES : DOCUMENTATION

Meyriat, Jean and Beauchet, Micheline, 1968, **Guide for the establishment of national social science documentation centres in developing countries.** [UNESCO] {IEG JNU NMML}

SOCIAL SCIENCES : INFORMATION SERVICES

Line, Maurice B., et al, 1971, **Experimental information service in the social sciences** : Report on work carried out in 1970, [University Library, Bath University of Technology]. {NASSDOC}

Anon, n.d., **National information system for social sciences**, typed short bibliography. {NASSDOC}

Anon, 1983, **Organisation of social science information and documentation**: Reports on 11 Asian countries. [UNESCO Regional Adviser for Social Science in Asia and the Pacific, Bangkok]. {NASSDOC}

Narula, Manju, 1973, **State of the art report on social science documentation in India**. {JNU}

SOCIAL SCIENCES : LIBRARIES

See Social Science Libraries

SOCIAL SCIENCES : SERIALS

Nicholas, David, 1975, **Characteristics of social science serials** : The construction and analysis of a file : Social science serial titles. [Bath University]. {BCL}

SOCIETIES : PROFESSIONAL

See Library Associations

SOCIOLOGY OF KNOWLEDGE

See Knowlege

SOFTWARE : COMPUTER

See Computer Programs; Programming : Computers

SOUTHEASTERN STATES COOPERATIVE LIBRARY SURVEY, 1972-74

Anders, Mary Edna, 1976, **Libraries and library services in the Southeast** : A report of the Southeastern states cooperative library survey, 1972-74. {BIS ISI}

SOUTH WEST MISSION LIBRARY SERVICE

Kenney, Brigitte L., 1959, **Cooperative centralised processing** : A report of the establishment and first year of operation of the South West Mission Library Service. {DUL}

SPECIAL COLLECTIONS IN LIBRARIES

Harleston, Robekah M. and Stoffle, Carla J., 1974, **Administration of government documents collections.** {USIS}

Benewick, Anne J., 1974, **Asian and African collections in British libraries** : Problems and prospects. {DUL NMML}

Anon, 1976, **Collection building in special purpose libraries.** {USIS}

Hammond, George P., 1972, **Guide to the manuscript collections of the Bancroft Library**, 2 Vols. {JNU}

Sayers, W.C. Berwick, 1939, **Library local collections.** {DUL NAI}

Meckler, Alan M. and Mc Mullin, Ruth, 1975, **Oral history collections.** {USIS}

Pearson, J.D., ed., 1971, **Papers on oriental library collections submitted to a library panel** : International congress of orientalists, 27th, August 17, 1967, Ann Arbor, Michigan. {NMML}

Ireland, Norma Olin, 1952, **Picture file in school, college and public libraries,** rev edn. {ZHL}

Gupta, R.D., 1970, **Preserving manuscripts and other research material in the Braj area of India**, (reprinted from the Bulletin of the British Association of Orientalists). [Vrindaban Research Institute]. {NMML}

Collison, Robert, n.d., **Scolma directory of libraries and special collections of Africa**, 2nd edn. {IIC IIT}

Burkett, J. and Morgan, T.S., 1963, **Special materials in the library**. [Library Association, London]. {IIT}

Ash, Lee, comp., 1978, **Subject collections** : A guide to special book collections and subject emphasis as reported by university, college, public and special libraries and museums in the United States and Canada, 5th edn. {USIS}

Anon, 1979, **Technical and specialised periodicals published in Britain, 1972-73**. [Central Office of Information, London]. {NASSDOC}

Collison, R.L., 1957, **Treatment of special material in libraries.** {MFL}

See also Map Collections

SPECIAL LIBRARIES

Anon, 1947, **ASLIB meeting on planning and equipment of special libraries, April 6, 1946, London.** {CRRI}

Anon, 1976, **Collection building in special purpose libraries.** {USIS}

Collison, Robert, comp., 1970, **Directory of libraries and special collections on Asia and North Africa**. {NASSDOC NCERT NMML}

Anon, 1962, **Directory of special and research libraries in India**. [Indian Association of Special Libraries and Information Centres]. {IIT ISI MFL NMML ZHL}

Anon, 1985, **Directory of special and research libraries in India**. 2nd edn. [Indian Association of Special Libraries and Information Centres]. {ICCR ICWA IDSA IIPA NASSDOC NMML UGC}

Kruzas, Authony T., ed., 1963, **Directory of special libraries and information**

centres. {ICCR ICWA IIPA}

Young, M.L. and Young, H.C., eds., 1974-79, **Directory of special libraries and information centres : 1974; 1979**. {IIFT}

Young, M.L. and Young, H.C., eds., 1981-83, **Directory of special libraries and information centres : 1981 to 1983**. {USIS}

Anon, n.d., **Economic analysis of special libraries with special reference to CSIR libraries**, memeo short bibliography. {NASSDOC}

Mukherjee, A.K., 1969, **Fundamentals of special librarianship and documentation**. [Indian Association of Special Libraries and Information Centres]. {AIU DUL IIT}

Hobson, Anthony, 1970, **Great libraries**. {NMML USIS}

Ashworth, W., ed., 1955, **Handbook of special librarianship and information work**. [Association of Special Libraries and Information Bureaux]. {BIS IEG}

Ashworth, W., ed., 1962, **Handbook of special librarianship and information work**. 2nd edn. [Association of Special Libraries and Information Bureaux]. {IIT SPA}

Ashworth, W., ed., 1967, **Handbook of special librarianship and information work**, 3rd edn. [Association of Special Libraries and Information Bureaux]. {MHA MMTC NASSDOC NIH}

Batten, W.E., ed., 1975, **Handbook of special librarianship and information work,** 4th edn. [Association of Special Libraries and Information Bureaux]. {CRRI IIT}

Anon, 1966, **INSDOC seminar on work-flow in libraries**, November 21-24, 1966, New Delhi, 3 pts. Pt-1 : Special libraries; Pt-2 : University libraries; Pt-3 : Government libraries. {BIS}

Bakewell, K.G.B., 1969, **Industrial libraries throughout the world.** {IIFT IIT ISI NASSDOC}

Anon, n.d., **Industrial technical libraries of paperback books** : Little Libraries. [U.S. State Department]. {BIS}

Houghton, Bernard, 1972, **Out of the dinosaurs** : The evolution of the National Lending Library for Science and Technology. {NASSDOC}

Campbell, D.J., 1973, **Small technical libraries.** [UNESCO]. {DUL ICA NERC NIEPA}

Ada, Winifred John, 1968, **Special libraries** : Development of the concept, their organization and their service. {JNU}

Strable, Edward G., ed., 1966, **Special libraries** : Guide for management. [Special Libraries Association, New York]. {IIC IIT}

Astall, Raland, 1966, **Special libraries and information bureau** : An examination guidebook. {BIS ICA IIC IIFT IIT MFL NMML SPA}

Thornton, J.L., 1940, **Special library methods** : An introduction to special librarianship. {IEG NAI}

Slater, M., 1964, **Technical libraries.** {IIT}

Jackson, Lucille, ed., 1951, **Technical libraries** : Their organisation and management. [Special Libraries Association, New York]. {CRRI ISI}

Maltha, D.J., 1976, **Technical literature search and the written report.** {BCL}

See also Map Collections

SPECIAL LIBRARIES : ADMINISTRATION

White, Herbert S., 1984, **Managing the special library** : Strategies for success within the larger organisation. {NASSDOC}

Strable, Edward G., ed., 1966, **Special libraries** : Guide for management. [Special Libraries Association, New York]. {IIC IIT}

Ahrensfelf, Janet L., et al, 1981, **Special libraries** : Guide for management, 2nd edn. {MMTC}

Lewis, Chester M., n.d., **Special libraries** : How to plan and equip them. [Special Libraries Association, New York]. {BIS NMML}

SPECIAL LIBRARIES : DIRECTORIES

Young, M.L., et al, eds., 1975, **Subject directory of special libraries and information centres.** {IIFT}

SPECIAL LIBRARIES : GEOGRAPHICAL AREA : GREAT BRITAIN

Burkett, J., ed., 1965, **Special library and information services in the United Kingdom**, 2nd edn. [Library Association, London]. {NIEPA}

SPECIAL LIBRARIES : GEOGRAPHICAL AREA : INDIA

Bhatia, Brajesh, and Goyal, M.M.L., 1971, **Directory of family planning and population libraries in India**. [National Institute of Family Planning]. {NIH}

Krishnamurty, P.G., 1980, **Directory of health science libraries and documentation centres in India**. [National Institute of Health and Family Welfare, New Delhi]. {NIH}

Chatterjee, Nihar Kanti, 1980, **Directory of research and special libraries in India and Sri Lanka**, 2 vols. {MMTC ZHL}

Kalia, D.R. and Surender Kumar, 1988, **Directory of scientific and technical libraries in India.** {DUL}

Anon, 1962, **Directory of special and research libraries in India.** [Indian Association of Special Libraries and Information Centres]. {IIT ISI MFL NMML ZHL}

Anon, 1985, **Directory of special and research libraries in India**. 2nd edn. [Indian Association of Special Libraries and Information Centres]. {ICCR ICWA IDSA IIPA NASSDOC NMML UGC}

Anon, n.d., **Economic analysis of special libraries with special reference to CSIR libraries**, memeo short bibliography. {NASSDOC}

Rajagopalan, T.S. and Ramaswami, K., n.d., **Libraries serving the CSIR complex.** [Indian National Scientific Documentation Centre]. {IIT NASSDOC}

Anon, n.d., **Papers** : IASLIC symposium on the development of libraries in India under the Third Five Year Plan with particular reference to special libraries, January 23-25, 1960, Calcutta. [Indian Association of Special Libraries and Information Centres]. {BIS}

Saha, J., 1969, **Special libraries and information services in India and in the U.S.A.** {IEG IIT NASSDOC}

SPECIAL LIBRARIES : GEOGRAPHICAL AREA : NETHERLANDS

Burkett, Jack, 1963, **Special libraries and documentation centres in the Netherlands** {IIT JNU NASSDOC SPA}

SPECIAL LIBRARIES : GEOGRAPHICAL AREA : SRI LANKA

Chatterjee, Nihar Kanti, 1980, **Directory of research and special libraries in India**

and Sri Lanka, 2 vols. {MMTC ZHL}

SPECIAL LIBRARIES : GEOGRAPHICAL AREA : USA

Buckner, B.C., comp., 1973, **Directory of population libraries and information centres in the United States**. [Carolina Population Centre, University of North Carolina]. {NIH RTL}

Saha, J., 1969, **Special libraries and information services in India and in the U.S.A.** {IEG IIT NASSDOC}

Anon, 1968, **Survey of special libraries serving the Federal Government.** [U.S. Department of Health Education and Welfare]. {BIS}

SRI LANKA

See Geographical Area subdivision under main Descriptor, e.g., Special Libraries : Geographical Area : Sri Lanka

STANDARDS

Anon, 1961, **Abstracts and synopses**. [International Organisation for Standardisation, Geneva]. (ISO/R 214-1961) (E). {NASSDOC}

Anon, 1969, **American national standards for the abbreviation of titles of periodicals.** (ANSI Z39.5-1969). [American National Standards Institute]. {NASSDOC}

Anon, 1971, **American national standards for directories of libraries and information centres**. (ANSI Z39.5.-1971). [American National Standards Institute]. {NASSDOC}

Anon, 1971, **American national standards for identification number for serial publications**. (ANSI Z39.5-1971). [American National Standards Institute].{NASSDOC}

Anon, 1968, **American national standards for library statistics**. (ANSI Z39.5-1968). [American National Standards Institute]. {NASSDOC}

Anon, 1967, **American national standards for periodicals** : Format and arrangement. (ANSI Z39.5-1967). [American National Standards Institute]. {NASSDOC}

Anon, 1971, **American national standards for title leaves of a book.** (ANSI Z39.5-1971). [American National Standards Institute]. {NASSDOC}

Anon, 1971, **American national standards for writing abstracts**. (ANSI Z39.5-1971). [American National Standards Institute]. {NASSDOC}

Anon, 1970, **American national standards practice for storage of processed silver-gelatin micro-film**. (ANSI PH5.4-1970). [American National Standards Institute]. {NASSDOC}

Anon, 1972, **American national standards system for the romanisation of Arabic**, 12th rev edn. (ANSI Z39.12-1972). [American National Standards Institute]. {NASSDOC}

Anon, 1972, **American national standards system for the romanisation of Japanese**, rev edn. (ANSI Z39.11-1972). [American National Standards Institute]. {NASSDOC}

Schuchmann, M., 1958, **Bibliography of standards on documentation**. {BIS ISI}

Anon, 1966, **Code of practice for the processing of microfilms**, Silver halide. (IS : 3083-1966). [Indian Standards Institution]. {NASSDOC}

Anon, 1964, **Code of practice relating to primary elements in the design of buildings for archives**. (IS : 2663-1964). [Indian Standards Institution]. {NASSDOC}

Anon, 1960, **Code of practice relating to primary elements in the design of library buildings**. (IS : 1553-1960). [Indian Standards Institution]. {NASSDOC}

Anon, 1971, **College libraries** : Recommended standards of library provision in colleges of technology and other establishment of further education. [Library Association, London]. {DUL ICA}

Anon, 1966, **Development of performance standards for library binding**, Phase 1: Report of the survey, April, 1961; Phase 2: Report on a study conducted by library technology project. [American Library Association]. {BIS IIT}

Gray, Max, 1969, **Documentation standards**. {BIS DUL NIEPA}

Rubin, Martin L., ed., 1979, **Documentation standards and procedures for on-line systems**. {CRRI}

Anon, 1979, **Formation of necessary standards for different types of libraries in India** : Working paper : ILA seminar, 1979, Trivandrum. [Indian Library Association]. {NASSDOC}

Anon, 1984, **Guide for drafting Indian standards**, 2nd edn. (IS : 12-1984). [Indian Standards Institution]. {NASSDOC}

Anon, 1977, **Guide for standard book numbering**. {IS : 8310-1977). [Indian Standards Institution]. {NAI NASSDOC}

Anon, 1988, **Guidelines for drafting and presentation of Indian standards.** [Bureau of Indian Standards]. {BIS NASSDOC}

Anon, n.d., **ISBD (B)** : International standard bibliographic description for books. [International Federation of Library Associations and Institutions]. {JNU}

Anon, 1977, **ISBD (CH)** : International standard bibliographic description for cartographic material. [International Federation of Library Association and Institutions]. {NASSDOC}

Anon, 1977, **ISBD (G)** : General international standard bibliographic description : Annotated text. [International Federation of Library Associations and Institution, Working Group on the General International Standard Bibliographic Description]. {NASSDOC}

Anon, 1978, **ISBD (M)** : International standard bibliographic description for monographic publications, rev edn. [International Federation of Library Associations and Institutions]. {NASSDOC}

Anon, 1977, **ISBD (NBM)** : International standard bibliographic description for non-book materials. [International Federation of Library Associations and Institutions, Working Group on the International Standard Bibliographic Description for Non-Book Materials]. {NASSDOC}

Anon, 1974, **ISBD (S)** : International standard bibliographic description for serials. [International Federation of Library Associations and Institutions, Joint Working Group on the International Standard Bibliographic Description for Serials]. {NASSDOC}

Anon, 1972, **ISBN** : International standard book numbering (incorporating the recommendations for implementing the Standard Book Numbering Scheme). [Standard Book Numbering Agency, London]. {NASSDOC}

Anon, 1982, **ISO standards handbook, 1982** : Information transfer. [UNESCO]. {NASSDOC}

Surinder Kumari, 1975-76, **Indian Standards Institution and its role in the development of library and documentation standards**. (University of Delhi, Department of Library and Information Science, Sessional project 1975-76). {BIS}

Sharma, M.S., 1987, **International standard book numbering system in India.** {NASSDOC}

Anon, 1972, **International standard classification of education** (ISCED) : Three stage classification system, 2pts. [UNESCO]. {AIU}

Anon, 1972, **International standardisation of library and documentation techniques**. [UNESCO]. {ICA}

Anon, n.d., **International standards for computers and information processing.** [International Organisation for Standardisation]. {BIS}

Anon, n.d., **International standards for documentation and terminology**, 3rd edn. [International Organisation for Standardisation]. {BIS}

Anon, 1961, **International system for the transliteration of Arabic characters.** (ISO/R 233-1961) (E). [International Organisation for Standardisation]. {NASSDOC}

Anon, 1968, **International system for the transliteration of Greek characters into Latin characters.** (ISO/R 843-1968) (E). [International Organisation for Standardisation, Geneva]. {NASSDOC}

Anon, 1968, **International system for the transliteration of Slavic Cyrillic characters**, 2nd edn. (ISO/R 9-1968) (E). [International Organisation for Standardisation, Geneva]. {NASSDOC}

Anon, 1967, **Minimum standards for public library systems, 1966**. [Standards committee and subcommittees of the Public Library Association; American Library Association]. {USIS}

Anon, n.d., **National agency for International Standard Book Numbering System** : A manual. [Raja Rammohan Roy National Educational Resources Centres, New Delhi]. {NASSDOC}

Choudhary, Anil Roy, 1959, **National standards for cataloguing and indexing art museum objects and documents**. {ZHL}

Jenssen, Gudbrand, n.d., **A small country in the world of standards** : ANSINBS symposium on international standards information and ISONET. {BIS}

Anon, n.d., **Specification for the abbreviation of titles of periodicals**, 2 pts., Pt. 1 : Principles; Pt. 2 : World abbreviation. [British Standards Institution]. {CRRI NASSDOC}

Anon, n.d., **Specification for alphabetical arrangement and the filing order of numerals and symbols**. (BS 1749 : 1969). [British Standards Institution]. {CRRI NASSDOC}

Anon, n.d., **Specification for bibliographic information interchange format for magnet tape**. (BS 4748 : 1971). [British Standards Institution]. {CRRI}

Anon, n.d., **Specification for book binding leather**. (IS : 2960-1964). [Indian Standards Institution]. {CRRI}

Anon, n.d., **Specification for book numbering.** (BS 4762 : 1971). [British Standards Institution]. {NASSDOC}

Anon, n.d., **Specification for data elements for the generation and exchange of serials records**. (BS 3532 : 1982). [British Standards Institution]. {CRRI}

Anon, n.d., **Specification for drawing filling equipment,** rev. edn. (IS : 2695-1974). [Indian Standards Institution]. {NASSDOC}

Anon, n.d., **Specification for general structure of preliminary pages of a book (tentative)**. (IS : 790-1956). [Indian Standards Institution]. {NASSDOC}

Anon, n.d., **Specification for librachine (mobile library)**. (IS : 2661-1964). [Indian Standards Institution]. {NASSDOC}

Anon, n.d., **Specification for library catalogue and abstract card**. (IS : 7150-1974) [Indian Standards Institution]. {NASSDOC}

Anon, n.d., **Specification for library furniture and fittings**. (IS : 785-1829 (Pt 1) :

1961). 2 pts. Pt. 1 : Timber; Pt. 2 : Steel. [Indian Standards Institution]. {CRRI NASSDOC}

Anon, n.d., **Specification for packages for use of libraries.** (IS : 2662-1964). [Indian Standards Institution]. {CRRI}

Anon, n.d., **Specification for page sizes for books.** (BS 1413 : 1970). [British Standards Institution]. {NASSDOC}

Anon, n.d., **Specification for the presentation of library directories.** (BS 4605 : 1970) [British Standards Institution]. {CRRI NASSDOC}

Anon, n.d., **Specification for the presentation of serial of publications, including periodicals**. (BS 2509 : 1970). [British Standards Institution]. {NASSDOC}

Anon, n.d., **Specification for sizes of folders and files.** (IS : 5457-1969). [Indian Standards Institution]. {NASSDOC}

Anon, n.d., **Specification for steel filing cabinets for general office purposes,** rev. edn. (IS : 3313-1974). [Indian Standards Institution]. {NASSDOC}

Anon, n.d., **Specification for steel shelving cabinets**, rev. edn. (IS : 3312-1974). [Indian Standards Institution]. {NASSDOC}

Anon, n.d., **Specification for the title leaves of a book.** (BS 4719 : 1971). [British Standards Institution]. {NASSDOC}

Anon, n.d., **Specification for title-page and back of title-page of a book,** rev. edn. (IS : 792-1964). [Indian Standards Institution]. {NASSDOC}

Anon, n.d., **Specification for wooden shelving cabinets (adjustable type).** (IS : 4116-1967). [Indian Standards Institution]. {NASSDOC}

Winger, Peter Van and Davis, Stephen Paul, 1982, **Standard citation forms for published bibliographies and catalog used in rare book cataloguing**. [U.S. Library of Congress]. {NASSDOC}

Thillainayagam, V., 1968, **Standard for a book** : The Tamils view. {NASSDOC*}

Anon, 1972, **Standard industrial classification manual.** {TDA}

Anon, 1975, **Standard international trade classification**, 2nd edn. [United Nations Department of Economic and Special Affairs]. {TDA}

Houghton, Bernard, 1969, **Standardization for documentation.** {JNU}

Anon, 1975, **Standardisation in computerised information system** : Papers for technical session. [Indian Standards Institution]. {JNU}

Anon, n.d., **Standardization in the domain of documentation.** [International Organization for Standardization, Hague]. {BIS}

Vashishth, C.P., ed., 1989, **Standardisation in library and information work and services.** [Indian Library Association]. {NASSDOC}

Deshmukh, P.P., 1990, **Standardisation of library and information services** : With special reference to scientific and agricultural libraries. {JNU}

Anon, 1968, **Standards and objectives for school libraries.** [Library Association of Australia]. {JNU}

Anon, 1970, **Standards for library functions at the state level,** rev edn., [American Association of State Libraries, Standards Revision Committee. {USIS}

Withers, E.N., 1976, **Standards for library services** : An international survey. [UNESCO]. {BIS IEG JNU NASSDOC NIEPA NMML}

Anon, 1967, **Standards for library services for the blind and visually handicapped.** [American Library Association]. {DUL}

Anon, 1977, **Standards for public libraries.** (CIFLA publications). {NASSDOC*}

Anon, 1960, **Standards for school library programmes**. [American Association of School Librarians]. {JNU}

Anon, 1967, **Standards for teachers college libraries.** [New Zealand Library Association]. {JNU}

Buhler, Curt F., et al, 1949, **Standards of bibliographical description.** {DUL}

Anon, 1962, **Standards of public library service in England and Wales** : Report of the working party appointed by the Minister of Education in March, 1961. {NASSDOC}

Anon, 1980, **UNISIST guide to standards for information handling.** [UNESCO]. {BIS DUL MMTC}

Anon, n.d., **USA standard** : Basic criteria for indexes, rev edn., (USAS Z 39. 4-1968). [American National Standards Institute]. {NASSDOC}

Anon, 1968, **USA standard for compiling book publishing statistics.** (USAS Z 39.8-1968). [American National Standards Institute]. {NASSDOC}

Anon, 1969, **USA standard for permanent and durable library catalogue cards.** (USAS Z 35.1-1969). [American National Standards Institute]. {NASSDOC}

STATISTICAL DESIGN

See Experimental Design

STATISTICAL METHODS

Carpenter, Ray L. and Vasu, Ellan Storey, 1979, **Statistical methods for librarians.** {ISI}

Sardana, J.L. and Sehgal, R.L., 1982, **Statistical methods for librarians.** {ICHR ISI JNU NASSDOC}

Fisher, Ronald A., 1970, **Statistical methods for research workers,** 14th edn. {NASSDOC}

STATISTICS

Simpson, I.S., 1975, **Basic statistics for librarians.** {ISI JNU}

John, Peter W., 1971, **Statistical design and analysis of experiments.** {NASSDOC}

See also Experimental Design

STOCK VERIFICATION IN LIBRARIES

Urquhart, J.A., 1976, **Relegation and stock control in libraries.** {DUL IIT ZHL}

Gupta, S.R., 1990, **Stock verification in libraries** : Problems and solutions. {DUL}

STORAGE

See Preservation, Restoration and Storage

SUBJECT ANALYSIS

See under Content Analysis : Communication

SUBJECT CATALOGUES

See Catalogues : Subject

SUBJECT CATALOGUING

Metcalfe, J., 1957, **Information indexing and subject cataloguing** : Alphabetical classified, coordinate, mechanical. {DUL IEG IIT}

Stavley, Ronald, et al, 1967, **Introduction to subject study.** {AIU IIT NASSDOC}

Anon, 1981, **Subject authorities** : A guide to subject cataloguing. {USIS}

SUBJECT HEADINGS

Anon, 1969, **Aligned list of descriptors** : Alphabetical order. [Organisation for Economic Co-operation and Development, Paris]. {NASSDOC}

Metcalfe, John, ed., 1965, **Alphabetical subject indication of information**. {IIT USIS}

Williams, James G., et al, eds., 1972, **Classified Library of Congress subject headings**, 2 vols., V. 1: Classified list; V. 2: Alphabetical list. {IIT JNU NASSDOC NIH}

Williams, James G., et al, eds., 1982, **Classified Library of Congress subject headings**, 2nd edn., Part A : Classified list; Part B : Alphabetical list. {IIT JNU NASSDOC}

Atkins, Thomas V., et al, eds., 1974, **Cross reference index** : A subject heading guide. {NASSDOC USIS}

Corrigan, Phillip, 1967, **Introduction to Sears list of subject headings**. {IIMC IIT}

Anon, 1980, **Library of Congress subject headings**, 9th edn. [U.S. Library of Congress, Subject Cataloguing Division]. {USIS}

Chan, Lois Mai, 1986, **Library of Congress subject headings** : Principles and application, 2nd edn. (Research studies in library science, No. 19). {NASSDOC}

Anon, 1975, **Library of Congress subject headings** : Quarterly cumulative supplement to the 8th edn. [U.S. Library of Congress]. {NASSDOC}

Anon, 1982, **Library of Congress subject headings** : Quarterly cumulative supplements to the 9th edn., 1979-80. [Library of Congress]. {NASSDOC}

Sears, Minnie Earl, 1959, **List of subject headings**, 8th edn., ed by Bertha Margret Frick. {DUL}

Sears, Minnie Earl, 1944, **List of subject headings for small libraries including practical suggestings for the beginner in subject heading work**, 5th edn. {MHA}

Anon, 1911, **List of subject headings for use in dictionary catalogue**, 3rd rev. edn. [American Library Association]. {NAI}

Fox, Gertrude, 1964, **List of subject headings in home building and allied fields**. [National Housing Centre Library, Washington]. {SPA}

Rue, Eloise and Laplanie, Effie, 1952, **Subject heading for children's materials**. [American Library Association]. {ZHL}

Pettee, Julla, 1947, **Subject headings** : The history and theory of the alphabetical subject approach to books. {NAI}

Saifuddin, comp., 1962, **Subject headings** : A list with CC and DDC numbers. {NASSDOC}

Anon, 1951, **Subject headings** : A practical guide. [U.S. Library of Congress]. {CRRI USIS}

Anon, 1954, **Subject headings for financial libraries**. [Special Libraries Association, New York]. {ISI}

Martin, Nella Jane, 1948, **Subject headings used in the dictionary catalogues**, 5th edn. [U.S. Library of Congress]. {ZHL}

Quattlebaum, Marguerite V., ed., n.d., **Subject headings used in the dictionary catalogs of the Library of Congress from 1897 through December 1955**, 6th edn. [U.S. Library of Congress]. {BIS IEG USIS}

Quattlebaum, Marguerite V., ed., n.d., **Subject headings used in the dictionary catalogs of the Library of Congress from 1897 through December 1955** : Supplement to the 6th edn., January 1956-December 1959. [U.S. Library of

Congress]. {IEG}

SURVEYS

Chandler, George, ed., 1972, **International librarianship** : Surveys of recent developments in developing countries and in advanced librarianship submitted to the 1971 IFLA pre-session seminar for developing countries, August 24—September 1, 1971. [Library Association, London]. {NASSDOC}

Line, Maurice, B., 1969, **Library surveys** : An introduction to their use, planning, procedure and presentation. {CRRI IIT NASSDOC USIS}

Anon, 1986, **Opinion poll survey among visitors to the New Delhi World Book Fair** : A report. [National Book Trust, New Delhi]. {NASSDOC*}

Polak, Fred L., 1971, **Prognostics** : A science in the making surveys and creates the future. {NASSDOC}

Mittal, R.L., 1971, **Public library law** : An international survey. {ICA NASSDOC NMML}

Sudman, Seymour, 1967, **Reducing the cost of surveys.** {NASSDOC}

Anon, 1967, **A survey of the contents of existing national bibliographies.** [UNESCO]. {NASSDOC*}

Ravilious, C.P., 1975, **Survey of existing systems and current proposals for the cataloguing and description of non-book materials collected by libraries with preliminary suggestions for their international co-ordination.** [UNESCO]. {BIS}

Arora, Meena, 1980, **Survey of government documents in Central Secretariat Library : 1979-80.** (University of Delhi, Department of Library Science, sessional project). {DUL}

Taylor, James C. and Bowers, David G., 1967, **Survey of organisations : A machine standardised questionnaire instruments.** [Institute of Social Research, Michigan]. {NASSDOC}

Bracken, Marlyn C. and Shilling, Charles W., 1967, **Survey of practice training in information science.** {JNU}

Kalia, D.R., 1965, **Survey of public library services in India** : Tabulated and analysed : Working group on libraries. [Planning Commission, New Delhi]. {NASSDOC*}

Anon, 1957, **Survey of secondary school libraries in U.P.** : Report. [Ministry of Education, New Delhi]. {MHA}

Anon, 1968, **Survey of special libraries serving the Federal Government.** [U.S. Department of Health Education and Welfare]. {BIS}

White, Carl M., 1965, **Survey of the University of Delhi library.** {AIU DSSW DUL IEG IIC NASSDOC NERC SPA}

Ashoor, Mohammed Salem, 1978, **Survey of user attitude towards resource and services of three university libraries in Saudi Arabia.** {JNU}

Tull, Donald S. and Albaum, Gerald S., 1973, **Survey research** : A decisional approach. {NASSDOC}

Srivastava, S.S., 1971, **Survey research technique.** {NASSDOC}

Anon, 1981, **User surveys and evaluation of library services** [Association of Research Libraries, Washington]. {NASSDOC}

SURVEYS : BIBLIOGRAPHY

Almasy, Elina, et al, 1976, **Comparative survey analysis** : An annotated bibliography, 1967-1978. {NASSDOC}

SWEDEN

See Geographical Area subdivision under main Descriptor, e.g., Public Libraries : Geographical Area : Sweden

SYSTEMS ANALYSIS

Morse, Philip M., 1968, **Library effectiveness** : A systems approach. {AIU DUL JNU NASSDOC NMML SPA USIS}

Chapman, Edward A., et al, 1970, **Library systems analysis guidelines**. {DUL ICA IIT JNU NASSDOC NIH NMML USIS}

Foskett, D.J., 1970, **Library systems and information services**. {IIMC NASSDOC}

Leimkuhler, F.F., 1967, **Mathematical models for library systems analysis.** {JNU}

Srinath, Laxmipuram Srinivasascher, 1975, **PERT and CPM** : Principles and applications. {JNU}

Parkin, Andrew, 1980, **System analysis.** {JNU}

Youssef, Leon A., 1975, **System analysis and design**. {JNU}

Thieravht, Robert J. and Reynolds, George W., 1966, **Systems analysis and design** : A Case study approach. {JNU}

Townley, Helen M., 1978, **System analysis for information retrieval**. {BCL}

Anon, n.d., **System analysis for information sciences**. [Department of Science and Technology, New Delhi]. {BIS CRRI JNU}

Robinson, F., 1969, **System analysis in libraries**. {JNU}

Katzan, Harry, 1976, **System design and documentation.** {JNU}

Raffel, J.A. and Shiskho, Robert, 1969, **Systematic analysis of university libraries** : Application of cost benefit analysis to the M.I.T. libraries. {AIU DUL IIT JNU NIPCCD SPA}

Optner, Stanford L., ed., 1973, **Systems analysis**. {NASSDOC}

Semprevivo, Philip C., 1976, **Systems analysis** : Definition, process and design. {NASSDOC}

Gough, Chet and Taverekere, Srikantaiah, 1978, **Systems analysis in libraries** : A question and answer approach. {BCL DUL}

Goldberg, Robert L., 1976, **A systems approach to library program development.** {JNU USIS}

Johnson, Richard A., et al, 1973, **Theory and management of systems**. {JNU}

SYSTEMS THEORY

Von Bertalanffy, Ludwig, 1968, **General system theory** : Foundations, development, applications. {NASSDOC*}

Sutherland, John W., 1973, **General systems philosophy for the social and behavioural sciences**, ed. by Erwinlaszlo. {NASSDOC}

Johnson, Richard A., et al, 1973, **Theory and management of systems**. {JNU}

See also Operation Research

TECHNICAL INFORMATION : COMMUNICATION

See Communication of Technical Information

TECHNICAL LIBRARIES

Sarkar, P.K., 1977, **Administration of technical libraries**. {BIS CRRI ICHR

NCAER ZHL}

Lamp, J.P., 1955, **Commercial and technical libraries.** {BIS}

Rees, Alan, ed., 1974, **Contemporary problems in technical library and information centre management** : A state-of-the-art. [American Society for Information Science]. {USIS}

Campbell, D.J., 1973, **Small technical libraries.** [UNESCO]. {DUL ICA NERC NIEPA}

Neal, K.W., 1965, **Technical college libraries** : Finchfield. {DUL IIT}

Thompson, G.A., 1969, **Technical college library** : A primer for its development. {AIU DUL IIT}

Slater, M., 1964, **Technical libraries.** {IIT}

Jackson, Lucille, ed., 1951, **Technical libraries** : Their organisation and management. [Special Libraries Association, New York]. {CRRI ISI}

See also Information Storage and Retrieval Systems : Technology

TECHNICAL LIBRARIES : GEOGRAPHICAL AREA : INDIA

Rajagopalan, T.S. and Ramaswami, K., n.d., **Libraries serving the CSIR complex.** [Indian National Scientific Documentation Centre]. {IIT NASSDOC}

TECHNICAL LITERATURE SEARCH

See Information Storage and Retrieval Systems : Technology

TECHNICAL PROCESSING

Leonard, Lawrence E., et al, 1969, **Centralised book processing** : A feasibility study based on Colorado academic libraries. {USIS}

Hendricks, Donald D., 1966, **Comparative costs of book processing in a processing centre and in five individual libraries.** {DUL}

Kenney, Brigitte L., 1959, **Cooperative centralised processing** : A report of the establishment and first year of operation of the South West Mission Library Service. {DUL}

Salton, Gerard, 1975, **Dynamic information and library processing.** {CRRI DUL ICHR INSA ISI NASSDOC USIS}

Herald, Alther Canley, 1963, **Processing manual** : A pictorial work book of catalogue cards, rev. edn. {DUL}

Frarey, Carlyle J., 1959, **Processing services of the Dallas Public Library** : A report on their organisation, operation and administration. {DUL}

TECHNOLOGY : INFORMATION SERVICES

Carey, R.J.P., 1966, **Finding and using technical information.** {MHA}

Radhakrishnan, S., and Iyengar, T.K.S., eds., 1977, **Proceedings** : International conference on technical information services for developing countries, March, 1977, Madras. [International Council of Scientific Unions, Committee of Science and Technology in Developing Countries]. {BCL BIS CRRI IIT JNU}

Anon, 1975, **World guide to technical information and documentation services,** 2nd edn. [UNESCO]. {JNU NASSDOC}

See also Communication of Technical Information; Science : Information Services

THAILAND

See Geographical Area subdivision under main Descriptor, e.g., Libraries : Geographical Area : Thailand

THESAURI

Anon, 1982, **EUDISED multilingual thesaurus** : Alphabetical list of deseriptors. {NASSDOC}

Viet, Jean, 1973, **EUDISEO multilingual thesaurus for information processing in the field of education.** {NASSDOC}

Anon, 1985, **ILO thesaurus**. [International Labour Office, Geneva]. {NASSDOC}

Soergel, Dagobert, 1974, **Indexing languages and thesauri** : Construction and maintenance. {CRRI IIT NASSDOC}

Viet, Jean, 1978, **Macrothesaurus for information processing in the field of economic and social development**. {JNU}

Anon, 1974, **NCC thesaurus of computing terms**, 7th edn. {NASSDOC}

Anon, 1981, **Root thesaurus**. 2 pts., Pt.-1 : Subject display; Pt.-2 : Alphabetical list. [British Standards Institution]. {NASSDOC}

Mac Cafferty, Maxine, 1977, **Thesauri and thesauri construction**. [Association of Special Libraries and Information Bureaux]. {CRRI NASSDOC}

Agrawal, S.P., ch ed., 1987, **Thesauri, glossaries, terminologies and dictionaries**. {NASSDOC}

Gilchrist, Alan, 1971, **Thesauri in retrieval.** [Association of Special Libraries and Information Bureaux]. {BCL CRRF DUL IIT NASSDOC}

Anon, 1969, **Thesaurus and faceted classification for engineering and related subjects.** {IIT}

Aitchison, Jean and Gilchrist, Alan, 1972, **Thesaurus construction** : A practical manual. {CRRI}

Lancaster, F.W., 1985, **Thesaurus construction and use** : A condensed course. [UNESCO]. {NASSDOC}

Townley, Helen M. and Goe, Ralph C., 1980, **Thesaurus-making** : Grow your own word-stock. {NASSDOC}

Weiss, Irving and Weiss, Anne De Lavergne, eds., and comps., 1981, **Thesaurus of book digests, 1950-1980.** {USIS}

Anon, 1976, **Thesaurus of descriptors used for information processing in the ILO library**. [ILO]. {NASSDOC}

Goodman, Frederick, 1970, **Thesaurus of ERIC descriptors, with a special chapter on the role and function of thesaurus in education.** [U.S. Educational Resources Information Centre]. {USIS}

Anon, 1981, **UNBIS thesaurus** : List of terms used in indexing and cataloguing of documents and other materials relevant to United Nations programmes and activities. [Dag Hammerskjold Library]. {JNU}

Aitchison, Jean, comp., 1977, **UNESCO thesaurus**, Vol. 1 : Introduction, classified thesaurus permitted index hierarchical display; Vol. 2 : Alphabetical thesaurus. [UNESCO]. {NASSDOC}

Anon, 1981, **UNISIST guidelines for the establishment and development of monolingual thesauri**, 2nd edn. [UNESCO]. {BIS}

See also Indexes and Indexing

TRANSLATION

Garvin, Paul L., 1972, **On machine translation** : Selected papers. {USIS}

Kaiser, Frances E., 1959, **Translators and translations** : Services and sources. {JNU}

TRANSLITERATION

See under Arabic Character Transliteration; Cyrillic Character Transliteration; Greak Character Transliteration; Hebrew Character Transliteration; Slavic Character Transliteration

TRINIDAD AND TOBAGO

See Geographical Area subdivision under main Descriptor, e.g, Libraries : Geographical Area : Trinidad and Tobago

UN

=United Nations

UNESCO

=United Nations Educational, Scientific and Cultural Organisation

US LIBRARY OF CONGRESS

Anon, 1963, **Automation and the Library of Congress.** [U.S. Library of Congress]. {BIS}

Cole, John Y., 1979, **For Congress and the nation** : A chronological history of the Library of Congress. [U.S. Library of Congress]. {USIS}

Goodrum, Charles A. and Darlsymple, Helan W., 1982, **The Library of Congress**, 2nd ed. {IIC JNU NASSDOC NMML USIS}

Small, Herbert, 1982, **The Library of Congress** : Its architecture and decoration ed. by Henry Hope Reed. {USIS}

Gurney, Gene and Apple, Nick, 1981, **The Library of Congress** : A picture story of the world's largest library, rev. edn. {JNU}

Anon, 1979, **The Library of Congress** : A portrait of an institution. {USIS}

Cole, John, Y., ed., 1978, **The Library of Congress in perspective** {NASSDOC}

Melville, Annette, comp., 1980, **Special collection in the Library of Congress** : A selective guide. [U.S. Library of Congress]. {USIS}

Goodrum, Charles A., 1980, **Treasures of the Library of Congress.** {USIS}

See also Library of Congress Subject Headings

US NATIONAL ARCHIVES

Anon, 1974, **Guide to the National Archives of the United States**. [U.S. National Archives and Records Service]. {USIS}

Mc Coy, Donald R., comp., 1978, **The National Archives** : America's Ministry of Documents, 1934-1968. {USIS}

USA

See Geographical Area subdivision under main Descriptor, e.g., Archives : Geographical Area : USA

USA : GOVERNMENT PUBLICATIONS

See Government Publications : Geographical Area : USA

USSR

See Russia

UNION CATALOGUES

Anon; n.d., **Automation in union catalogue of periodicals** : India and abroad, typed short bibliography. {NASSDOC}

Willemin, Silvere, 1966, **Technique of union catalogue** : A practical guide. [UNESCO]. {IIMC NASSDOC NERC}

Hall, David E., 1971, **Union catalogue of Asian publications, 1965-1970.** {NASSDOC}

Das, A.R., n.d., **Union catalogue of the books in the libraries of the Botanical Survey of India**, 3 vols. [Botanical Survey of India]. {INSA}

Dutta, Rajeshwari, 1970, **Union catalogue of the Central Government of India publications held by libraries in London, Oxford and Cambridge.** [Centre of South Asian Studies, University of Cambridge, Mansell]. {NASSDOC}

MacDonald, Teresa, 1970, **Union catalogue of the Government of Ceylon publications held by libraries in London, Oxford and Cambridge.** [Centre of South Asian Studies, University of Cambridge, Mansell]. {NASSDOC}

Agrawal, S.P., ch. ed., 1986, **Union catalogue of library and information science publications** : Delhi libraries. {NASSDOC}

Chopra, R.N., 1979, **Union catalogue of library science periodical holdings in Delhi University Library system, Jawahar Lal Nehru University Library and National Science Library.** [Indian National Scientific Documentation Centre]. {DUL}

Agrawal, S.P., ch. ed., 1983, **Union catalogue of newspapers** : Delhi libraries. {NASSDOC}

Agrawal, S.P., ch. ed., 1973-76, **Union catalogue of social science periodicals/serials**, 32 vols. {NASSDOC}

Brummel, L., 1956, **Union catalogues** : Their problems and organisation. [UNESCO]. {CRRI}

Agrawal, S.P., ch. ed., 1983, **Union list of current social science periodicals** : Delhi libraries. {NASSDOC}

Agrawal, S.P., ch. ed., 1986, **Union list of social science periodicals** : Lucknow. {NASSDOC}

Agrawal, S.P., ch. ed., 1982, **Union list of social science periodicals received in Delhi libraries.** {NASSDOC}

UNITED KINGDOM

See Great Britain

UNITED NATIONS

Anon, 1979, **Directory of libraries and documentation centres in the United Nations system.** {JNU}

Anon, 1985, **Directory of United Nations databases and information systems** [United Nations Advisory Committee for Coordination of Information Systems]. {NASSDOC}

Anon, 1980, **Directory of United Nations information systems**, 2 vols. [United Nations Inter-Organisation Board of Information Systems, Geneva]. {MMTC RTL}

Brimmer, Brenda, et al, 1962, **A guide to the use of United Nations documents, including reference to the specialised agencies and special U.N. bodies.** {MFL USIS}

Anon, 1966, **Libraries of the United Nations** : A descriptive guide. [United Nations]. {ICWA IIC IIT JNU NIH}

Anon, 1978, **United Nations document series symbols, 1946-1977** : Cumulative list with index. [United Nations]. {IIFT}

Garde, P.K., 1970, **The United Nations family of libraries**. {ICA ICHR INSA NASSDOC NMML}

Dale, Doris Cruger, 1970, **United Nations library** : Its origin and development. {JNU NASSDOC USIS}

UNITED NATIONS EDUCATIONAL, SCIENTIFIC AND CULTURAL ORGANISATION

Anon, 1973, **Bibliography of publications issued by UNESCO or under its auspices, 1946-1971**. [UNESCO]. {NASSDOC}

Anon, 1946-67, **General catalogue of UNESCO publications and UNESCO sponsored publications**. supplements : 1946/59-1964/67. [UNESCO]. {NASSDOC}

Anon, 1979, **Selective list of activities in the field of information** : UNESCO Intergovernmental conference on scientific and technical information for development, 1979, Paris. {JNU}

Parker, J. Stephen, 1985, **UNESCO and library development planning**. {DUL}

Anon, n.d., **UNESCO list of documents and publications** : 1972/76, 1980-81. [UNESCO]. {NASSDOC}

Aitchison, Jean, comp., 1977, **UNESCO thesaurus**, Vol. 1 : Introduction, classified thesaurus permitted index hierarchical display; Vol. 2 : Alphabetical thesaurus. [UNESCO]. {NASSDOC}

UNITED STATES OF AMERICA
See USA

UNIVERSAL DECIMAL CLASSIFICATION
See Classification Schemes : Universal Decimal

UNIVERSITY OF DELHI, DELHI

Kipp, Laurence and Kipp, Re Cedlia, 1968, **Prediction of the future** : The development programme of the University of Delhi. {JNU}

UNIVERSITY OF DELHI LIBRARY
See Delhi University Library, Delhi

UTTAR PRADESH
See Geographical Area subdivision under main Descriptor, e.g., School Libraries : Geographical Area : India : Uttar Pradesh

UTTAR PRADESH : GOVERNMENT PUBLICATIONS
See Government Publications : Geographical Area : India : Uttar Pradesh

WEEDING : LIBRARY COLLECTIONS

Slote, Stanley J., 1982, **Weeding library collections**, 2nd rev edn. {DUL USIS}

WEST GERMANY
See Germany

3

LIBRARY INDEX

{AIU}
Association of Indian Universities
[*formerly* Inter-University Board of India and Ceylon]
AIU House, 16, Kotla Road
New Delhi-110002

{BCL}
British Council Library
British High Commission
AIFACS Building, Rafi Marg
New Delhi-110001

{BIS}
Bureau of Indian Standards
[*formerly* Indian Standards Institution]
9 Bahadur Shah Zafar Marg
New Delhi-110002

{CPR}
Centre for Policy Research
Dharma Marg, Chanakayapuri
New Delhi-110021

{CRRI}
Central Road Research Institute
Delhi-Mathura Road
New Delhi-110020

{DEPT}
Department of Library and Information Science
University of Delhi
Delhi-110007

{DSSW}
Delhi School of Social Work
University of Delhi
3, University Road
Delhi-110007

{DUL}
Delhi University Library System
Central Library
University of Delhi
Delhi-110007

{GPF}
Gandhi Peace Foundation
221/223 Deendayal Upadhyaya Marg
New Delhi-110002

{ICA}
International Cooperative Alliance
Regional Office and Education Centre for South East Asia,
Post Box No. 7011
New Delhi-110065

{IAMR}
Institute of Applied Manpower Research
Indraprastha Estate
New Delhi-110002

{ICCR}
Indian Council for Cultural Relations
Azad Bhavan
Indraprastha Estate
New Delhi-110002

{ICHR}
Indian Council of Historical Research
35, Ferozeshah Road
New Delhi-110001

{ICWA}
Indian Council of World Affairs
Sapru House
Barakhamba Road
New Delhi-110001

{IDSA}

Institute of Defence Studies and Analysis
Sapru House
Barakhamba Road
New Delhi-110001

{IEG}
Institute of Economic Growth
University Enclave
Delhi-110007

{IIC}
India International Centre
40, Max Mueller Marg
New Delhi-110003

{IIFT}
Indian Institute of Foreign Trade
B-21, Institutional Area, South of IIT
New Delhi-110016

{IIMC}
Indian Institute of Mass Communication
Sector XIII, Institutional Area
Shaheed Jit Singh Marg
New Delhi-110067

{IIPA}
Indian Institute of Public Administration
Indraprastha Estate
New Delhi-110002

{IIT}
Indian Institute of Technology
Central Library
Hauz Khas
New Delhi-110016

{ILI}
Indian Law Institute
Bhagwan Das Road
New Delhi-110001

{INSA}
Indian National Science Academy
Bahadur Shah Zafar Marg
New Delhi-110002

{ISI}
Indian Statistical Institute
Delhi Centre
7 S.J.S. Sansanwal Marg
New Delhi-110016

{JNU}
Jawaharlal Nehru University
New Mehrauli Road
New Delhi-110067

{MFL}
Ministry of Finance Library
North Block
New Delhi-110001

{MHA}
Ministry of Home Affairs Library
North Block
New Delhi-110001

{MMTC}
Minerals and Metals Trading Corporation of India
Express Building, Post Box 7051
Bahadur Shah Zafar Marg
New Delhi-110002

{NAI}
National Archives of India
Janpath
New Delhi-110001

{NASSDOC} {NASSDOC}*
National Social Science Documentation Centre
ICSSR, 35 Ferozeshah Road
New Delhi-110001

* Indicates D.R. Kalia collection and S.P. Agrawal collection donated to the library. These collections were not fully processed by the time this survey was conducted.

{NCAER}
National Council of Applied Economic Research
Parisila Bhawan
Indraprastha Estate
New Delhi-110002

{NCDC}
National Cooperative Development Corporation
4, Siri Institutional Area
New Delhi-110016

{NCERT}
National Council of Educational Research and Training
NIE Campus
Sri Aurobindo Marg
New Delhi-110016

{NERC}
Raja Rammohan Roy National Educational Resources Centre
1-W-3 Curzon Road Barracks
Kasturba Gandhi Marg
New Delhi-110001

{NIEPA}
National Institute of Educational Planning and Administration
17-B, Aurobindo Marg
New Delhi-110016

{NIH}
National Institute of Health and Family Welfare
National Documentation Centre
New Mehrauli Road
New Delhi-110067

{NIPCCD}
National Institute of Public Cooperation and Child Development
5, Siri Institutional Area
New Delhi-110016

{NMML}
Nehru Memorial Museum and Library
Teen Murti House
New Delhi-110011

{RTL}
Rattan Tata Library
Delhi School of Economics
Univeristy of Delhi
Delhi-110007

{SPA}
School of Planning and Architecture
4, Block B,
Indraprastha Estate
New Delhi-110002

{TDA}
Trade Development Authority
16, Sansad Marg
Bank of Baroda Bldg.
P.O. Box 767
New Delhi-110001

{UGC}
University Grants Commission
Bahadur Shah Zafar Marg
New Delhi-110002

{USIS}
United States Information Service
American Centre Library
24, Kasturba Gandhi Marg
New Delhi-110001

{ZHL}
Dr. Zakir Husain Library
Jamia Millia Islamia,
Jamia Nagar
New Delhi-110025

CICIL LIST

CONCEPTS IN COMMUNICATION, INFORMATICS & LIBRARIANSHIP

(CICIL)

General Editor: **S.P. AGRAWAL**

CICIL-1 Development of Library Services in India: Social Science Information
S.P. Agrawal Rs. 150

CICIL-2 Development of Documentation in India: Social Science Information
S.P. Agrawal Rs. 250

CICIL-3 UNESCO and Social Sciences: Retrospect and Prospect
S.P. Agrawal and **J.C. Aggarwal** Rs. 250

CICIL-4 INDIANA : A Bibliography of Bibliographical Sources
M.K. Jain Rs. 200

CICIL-5 Dimensions of Library and Information Science: Kaula Festschrift
V. Venkatappaiah (Eds.) Rs. 600

CICIL-6 Book Numbers: Some Indian Methods
M.P. Satija and **S.P. Agrawal** Rs. 100

CICIL-7 National Policy for University Libraries in India: Problems and Perspectives
N.B. Inamdar and **L.S. Ramaiah** (Ed.) Rs. 250

CICIL-8 Media Utilisation for the Development of Women and Children
B.S. Thakur and **Binod C. Agrawal** Rs. 150

CICIL-9 Terrorism: An Annotated Bibliography
Susheela Bhan (Ed.) Rs. 275

CICIL-10 Transnational Library Relations: The Indo-American Experience
M.B. Konnur Rs. 175

CICIL-11 Geography of Marketing and Commercial Activities in India (Documentation on Research Information)
R.S. Dixit Rs. 130

CICIL-12 Information India 1988: Global View
S.P. Agrawal and **J.C. Aggarwal** Rs. 200

CICIL-13 Women's Education in India: Historical Review, Present Status and Perspective Plan
S.P. Agrawal and **J.C. Aggarwal** Rs. 360

CICIL-14 Cultural Communication in India: Role and Impact of Phonograms
J.M. Ojha Rs. 220

CICIL-15 Second Historical Survey of Educational Development in India: Select Documents 1985-1989
S.P. Agrawal and **J.C. Aggarwal** Rs. 490

CICIL-16 Documentation Encyclopaedia of UNESCO and Education
J.C. Aggarwal and **S.P. Agrawal** Rs. 800 (set of 2 parts)

CICIL-17 Attitude Towards Information: A Study of Post-Graduate Teachers and Researchers in Social Sciences
N.G. Satish (in press)

CICIL-18 Librarianship and Bureaucratic Organisation: A Study in the Sociology of Library Profession in India
P.K. Jayaswal Rs. 175

CICIL-19 Literature Search
K.A. Isaac Rs. 150

CICIL-20 Child Education in India: Index to Scholarly Writings in Indian Educational Journals and Newspapers since independence
S.P. Agrawal and **Naresh Kanta** Rs. 100

CICIL-21 Lok Sabha and Vidhan Sabha Elections in India 1989 & 1990: Process and Results with Comparative Study of Manifestos
S.P. Agrawal and **J.C. Aggarwal** Rs. 250

CICIL-22 Islamic Studies in India: A Survey of Human, Institutional and Documentary Sources
Mohamed Taher Rs. 180

CICIL-23 Panchayati Raj: An Annotated Bibliography
N.B. Inamdar, N.G. Satish and **Anil Takalkar** 290

CICIL-24 Information India 1989-90: Global View
S.P. Agrawal and **J.C. Aggarwal** Rs. 500

CICIL-25 First Handbook of Psychological and Social Instruments
Udai Pareek and **T. Venkateswara Rao** Rs. 500

CICIL-26 Educational and Social Uplift of Backward Classes: At What Cost and How? Mandal Commission and After
S.P. Agrawal and **J.C. Aggarwal** Rs. 275

CICIL-27 Mass Media and New Horizons: Impact of TV & Video an Urban Milieu
H.R. Trivedi Rs. 180

CICIL-28 Indian Writings on Education : An Indicator to Indian Educational Journals Grouped by Subject Deseriptors 1979 to 1986 (in two parts)
S.P. Agarwal Rs. 900 (per set)

CICIL-29 Nation in Crisis
S.P. Agrawal and **J.C. Aggarwal** Rs. 200

CICIL-30 Information India 1990-91: Global View
S.P. Agrawal and **J.C. Aggarwal** Rs. 500

CICIL-31 Development of University Libraries in India after Independence
O.P. Gupta Rs. 270

CICIL-32 Handbook on Child : With Historical Background
Pramila Pandit Barooah Rs. 320

CICIL-33 Weaker Section in Indian Society : Undiscovered Past, Uncertain Present and Unpredictable Future : Index to Writings in Indian Scholarly Journals and 10 National Newspapers Classified under 1500 Descriptors 1886-1990
S.P. Agrawal and **Rajeev Kumar Sharma** Rs. 600

CICIL-34 Communication Informatics and Librarianship in India : An Introductory Guide to Publications Based on a Survey of Libraries in Capital City of India
S.P. Agrawal and **Pushpa Rani Sharma** Rs. 720

CICIL-35 Problems of Collection Development in Special Libraries
M.S. Sridhar Rs. 225

CICIL-36 National Information Resources for Social Sciences in India : Mobilisation, Dispersal and International Enhancement
S.P. Agrawal Rs. 225

CICIL-37 Modern History of Punjab : A Look Back into Ancient Peaceful Punjab Focusing Confrontation and Failures Leading to Present Punjab Problem, and a Peep Ahead : Relevant Select Documents
J.C. Aggarwal and **S.P. Agrawal** Rs. 400

CICIL-38 India Information Sources : Economics and Business
Kyllikki Ruokonen and **Manohar Lal** Rs.

CICIL-39 Educational Planning in India : With a Slant to Educational Financing and Administration, Vol. 1, Reports of Committees and Commissions, Five Year Plans, Statistical Tables
J.C. Aggarwal and **S.P. Agrawal** Rs. 650

CICIL-40 Integrated Library System : Two Case Studies : Latin America and India
Maria Luiza Rigo Pasquarelli, Rosaly Favero Krzyanowski, Ines Maria M. Imperatriz and S.P. Agrawal Rs. 160

CICIL-41 Social Science Information in India: Effort towards Bibliographical Control
S.D. Vyas Rs. 300

CICIL-42 Higher Education in India Since Independence: U.G.C. and Its Approach
O.P. Gupta Rs. 360

CICIL-43 Government and Politics in India: A Bibliographical Study of Contemporary Scenario Chronicling Rajiv Gandhi Era
S.P. Agrawal and **Rajeev Kumar Sharma** Rs. 500

CICIL-44 Second Handbook of Psychological and Social Instruments
D.M. Pestonjee Rs. 300

CICIL-45 Development/Digression Diary of India; 3D Companion Volume to Information India: 1990-91
S.P. Agrawal Rs. 200

CICIL-46 Development/Digression Diary of India; 3D Companion Volume to Information India: 1991-92
S.P. Agrawal Rs. 300

CICIL-47 Information India 1991-92: Global View
S.P. Agrawal and **J.C. Aggarwal** Rs. 500

CICIL-48 Committees and Commissions in India 1974, A Concept's Project, Compiled by a team of professionals guided by **Virender Kumar** (Vol. 12) Rs. 450

CICIL-49 Committees and Commissions in India 1975, A Concept's Project, Compiled by a team of professionals guided by **Virender Kumar** (Vol. 13) Rs. 450

CICIL-50 Committees and Commissions in India 1976, A Concept's Project, Compiled by a team of professionals guided **Virender Kumar** (Vol. 14) Rs. 450

CICIL-51 Committees and Commissions in India 1977, A Concept's Project, Compiled by a team of professionals guided by **Virender Kumar** (Vol. 15) (in four parts) Rs. 450 each

CICIL-52 Committees and Commissions in India 1978, A Concept's Project, Compiled by a team of professionals guided by **Virender Kumar** (Vol. 16) (in two parts) Rs. 450 each

CICIL-53 Subject Guide to Communication, Informatics and Librarianship in India (Based on a Survey of Library Holdings in Capital City of India)
S.P. Agrawal and **Pushpa Rani Sharma** Rs. 400